CSS Instant Results

CSS Instant Results

Richard York

Wiley Publishing, Inc.

CSS Instant Results

Published by
Wiley Publishing, Inc.
10475 Crosspoint Boulevard
Indianapolis, IN 46256
www.wiley.com

Copyright © 2006 by Wiley Publishing, Inc., Indianapolis, Indiana

Published simultaneously in Canada

ISBN-13: 978-0-471-75126-7
ISBN-10: 0-471-75126-X

Manufactured in the United States of America

10 9 8 7 6 5 4 3 2 1

1MA/SY/QT/QW/IN

Library of Congress Cataloging-in-Publication Data:

York, Richard, 1978-
  CSS instant results / Richard York.
    p. cm.
  Includes bibliographical references and index.
  ISBN-13: 978-0-471-75126-7 (paper/cd-rom : alk. paper)
  ISBN-10: 0-471-75126-X (paper/cd-rom : alk. paper)
  1. Web sites--Design. 2. Cascading style sheets. I. Title: Cascading style sheets instant results. II. Title.
  TK5105.888.Y68 2006
  006.7--dc22
                          2006003348

No part of this publication may be reproduced, stored in a retrieval system or transmitted in any form or by any means, electronic, mechanical, photocopying, recording, scanning or otherwise, except as permitted under Sections 107 or 108 of the 1976 United States Copyright Act, without either the prior written permission of the Publisher, or authorization through payment of the appropriate per-copy fee to the Copyright Clearance Center, 222 Rosewood Drive, Danvers, MA 01923, (978) 750-8400, fax (978) 646-8600. Requests to the Publisher for permission should be addressed to the Legal Department, Wiley Publishing, Inc., 10475 Crosspoint Blvd., Indianapolis, IN 46256, (317) 572-3447, fax (317) 572-4355, or online at http://www.wiley.com/go/permissions.

For general information on our other products and services please contact our Customer Care Department within the United States at (800) 762-2974, outside the United States at (317) 572-3993 or fax (317) 572-4002.

Trademarks: Wiley, the Wiley logo, Wrox, the Wrox logo, Programmer to Programmer, and related trade dress are trademarks or registered trademarks of John Wiley & Sons, Inc. and/or its affiliates, in the United States and other countries, and may not be used without written permission. All other trademarks are the property of their respective owners. Wiley Publishing, Inc., is not associated with any product or vendor mentioned in this book.

Wiley also publishes its books in a variety of electronic formats. Some content that appears in print may not be available in electronic books.

About the Author

Richard York

Richard York is a web application developer for Trilithic, Inc., a company specializing in test equipment for the telecommunications industry. He wrote his first book, *Beginning CSS: Cascading Style Sheets for Web Design* (Wrox Press) in 2004.

Richard began his web development career taking courses at Indiana University-Purdue University, Indianapolis. Since college, he has continued a self-imposed curriculum, mastering various technologies used in web development including HTML/XHTML, CSS, JavaScript, PHP, and MySQL. An avid supporter of open source software, he has written an open source webmail application for PHP PEAR, and is currently working on an open source PHP library and framework called Hierophant, which he hopes to release in 2006.

Richard maintains a personal web site at `http://www.richard-york.com` where you can learn more about his professional and personal interests.

Credits

Senior Acquisitions Editor
Jim Minatel

Development Editor
Tom Dinse

Technical Editors
Marshal Antony
Alexei Gorkov

Production Editor
Angela Smith

Copy Editor
Kim Cofer

Editorial Manager
Mary Beth Wakefield

Production Manager
Tim Tate

Vice President and Executive Group Publisher
Richard Swadley

Vice President and Executive Publisher
Joseph B. Wikert

Project Coordinator
Ryan Steffen

Graphics and Production Specialists
Joyce Haughey
Barbara Moore
Barry Offringa
Alicia B. South

Quality Control Technicians
John Greenough
Jessica Kramer

Proofreading and Indexing
Techbooks

Acknowledgments

I would like to thank my boss at Trilithic, Karalee Slayton for believing in me, giving me the tools to get the job done, and for being wonderfully supportive and encouraging every step of the way.

I would like to thank my very best friend Richelle Brown. We have learned so much from each other through life's joys and hardships. I couldn't have done this without you. Vive le Paul!

I'd like to thank my editors at Wiley: Jim Minatel for giving me the opportunity to write for Wrox again, and my development editor, Tom Dinse, for putting up with my procrastination with seemingly endless patience.

Finally, I'd like to thank my parents, Tammy and John, who have always been there for me through good times and bad. I'd also like to thank my sister Laura and her husband Steven. I love you all very much!

Contents

Acknowledgments   ix
Introduction   xv

Chapter 1: Tabs   1

Design   2
Code and Code Explanation   3
Testing and Caveats   13
What the IE7 JavaScript Provides for This Project   14
Using and Modifying the Project   16
Tabs with Background Images   16
Background Images That Include Text   19
Liquid Tabs   23

Chapter 2: Multi-column Layouts   31

Design   32
Code and Code Explanation   33
Testing and Caveats   39
Using and Modifying this Project   41
Two-Column Layout   42
Liquid Secondary Columns   44
The Float Method   49
Good, Old-Fashioned Internet Explorer Hacking   55

Chapter 3: Dynamic Drop-Down Menus   63

Design   64
Code and Code Explanation   64
Testing and Caveats   71
Other Caveats   77
Using and Modifying the Project   78
Implementing JavaScript-enabled Drop-Down Menus   79
Custom Backgrounds and Borders   85
Drop Down, Not Sideways!   94

Contents

Chapter 4: More Dynamic Drop-down Menus and the Incredible, Versatile :target   **99**

Design   **100**
Code and Code Explanation   **101**
Testing and Caveats   **109**

Chapter 5: Slide Show   **111**

Design   **111**
Code and Code Explanation   **112**
Testing and Caveats   **123**

Chapter 6: Custom Borders and Rounded Corners   **137**

Design   **138**
Code and Code Explanation   **138**
Testing and Caveats   **145**
Using and Modifying the Project   **147**

Chapter 7: Applying CSS to a Webmail Application   **157**

Design   **158**
Code and Code Explanation   **161**
Testing and Caveats   **175**
Using and Modifying the Project   **180**
    Adding a Message Preview Pane   180
    Three-Column Layout a la Microsoft Outlook 2003   185

Chapter 8: Styling Input Forms   **199**

Design   **200**
Code and Code Explanation   **202**
Testing and Caveats   **236**

Chapter 9: User-Interface for a Web-based File Viewer   **243**

Design   **245**
Code and Code Explanation   **246**
    Laying the Foundation   266
    Applying Menus   269
    Styling a Directory Tree   274
    Styling Multiple Methods of Viewing a Directory's Contents   279
    CSS Popup Windows   293

Testing and Caveats   **299**

Using and Modifying the Project   **308**

Windows Details View   308

Save As Dialog   313

Choose a Directory Dialog   328

Chapter 10: Calendar   335

Design   **335**

Code and Code Explanation   **336**

Testing and Caveats   **351**

Using and Modifying the Project   **358**

Index   **371**

Introduction

Cascading Style Sheets have an increasingly diverse place in a web designer's arsenal, and more and more, CSS can do what previously could be done only with JavaScript. In *CSS Instant Results*, I present some of CSS's most common applications, from simple navigational tabs to drop-down menus, to a browser-based slide show. CSS is capable of much more today than it was at its inception in 1996. Browsers are not only expanding their CSS capability, but are also getting much better at the features they already support. With the latest generation of modern browsers expanding support for CSS 3 and Microsoft finally updating CSS support in its Internet Explorer 7 browser, it is an exciting time in the world of Cascading Style Sheets.

In this book, I present ten already complete CSS projects. All the hacks and tricks required to achieve a specific end (and associated caveats) are explained with each project, in addition to how to modify a particular project to accommodate alternative approaches in design.

The projects in *CSS Instant Results*, as the title implies, are designed to be easy to implement in your own projects, and come ready to implement out-of-the-box, with the only necessary adjustments being to modify the project to suit your own particular aesthetic taste.

Who This Book Is For

In *CSS Instant Results* I present complete CSS projects that are ready to implement in real-world web sites. I present all the necessary source code and instructions for how to use the projects within this book in a real-world project.

Because I present complete projects, I assume a fundamental knowledge of web programming languages such as CSS, XHTML, and JavaScript (all three are discussed in this book). I don't spend as much time explaining why a feature does what it does as I do in discussing what features are suited for a particular project and how they work together to achieve the desired end result. I avoid discussion of JavaScript in detail, because the topic of this book is CSS and not JavaScript. However, for some advanced applications of CSS it is impossible to achieve a professional, cross-browser design without some JavaScript. For some projects JavaScript may also be better suited than CSS. If a project may have a purely CSS approach and an alternative approach involving JavaScript, I present both. Several projects have a purely CSS approach in some browsers, but are prevented from functioning in other browsers for reasons that can be remedied with the application of JavaScript. In those cases I present how to hack the incompatible browsers using JavaScript to achieve the same design as possible in other browsers that support the required CSS natively.

For a beginner's guide to CSS I recommend my book *Beginning CSS: Cascading Style Sheets for Web Design* (Wiley Publishing, Inc., ISBN: 0764576429). Likewise for JavaScript I recommend Paul Wilton's *Beginning JavaScript, 2nd Edition* (Wiley Publishing, Inc., ISBN: 0764555871). If you are entirely new to web programming, with no previous knowledge of any web programming language, you should start with Jon Duckett's *Beginning Web Programming with HTML, XHTML, and CSS* (Wiley Publishing, Inc., ISBN: 0764570781), and then progress to the two titles I mentioned previously.

What This Book Covers

This book presents ten ready for the real-world CSS projects. Within each chapter, I begin with an overview of the project—why the project is useful and why I chose to present that particular project. I move on to discuss what components will come together in the design of the project to achieve the desired result. Then I present the complete source code, and an explanation of the source code. After presenting the source code, I discuss testing the project and any associated caveats, and what, if anything, must be done to address things such as browser incompatibilities. Finally, I wrap up each project with a discussion about how you might change a project to accommodate alternative approaches in its design. When presenting alternative approaches, the complete modified source code is presented, followed by a detailed explanation of each change made.

How This Book Is Structured

In ten projects, I present a variety of ways to approach the implementation of one feature. The various projects are outlined in detail in the following list:

❑   **Chapter 1, "Tabs":** In the first chapter I describe a variety of methods used to create tab-based navigation. The main project focuses on how to create a no-frills tab navigation using simple HTML lists and CSS. In the alternative approaches I present how to evolve the same design to include background images, background images that include text, and liquid tabs that stretch and contract to fill the area available to them. I also introduce Dean Edwards' IE7 JavaScript and explain how this JavaScript is bridging the CSS compatibility gap between more CSS-capable browsers like Mozilla Firefox, and Microsoft's Internet Explorer 5, 5.5 and 6 browsers.

❑   **Chapter 2, "Multi-column Layouts":** In the second chapter I present how to create a multi-column design vis-a-vis CSS and XHTML. The main project describes how to create a multi-column design using CSS positioning. I also describe how to correct rendering in Internet Explorer 6 with either with or without the IE7 JavaScript. In the alternative approaches, I describe how to modify the design to get a two-column layout instead of three, how to use floating instead of positioning to lay out the columns, and how to make the secondary columns liquid.

❑   **Chapter 3, "Dynamic Drop-down Menus":** In the third chapter I elaborate on a variety of methods available to create dynamic drop-down menus. In the main project I present how to create drop-down menus using the CSS `:hover` dynamic pseudo-class. In the alternative approaches I discuss why the `:hover` dynamic pseudo-class alone is not the best approach, and present how the project can be modified to use a JavaScript-driven menu system that falls back on the CSS approach if CSS is not available. I also present how to modify the drop-down menus so that they have custom borders and backgrounds, in addition to presenting how to create menus that drop sideways instead of down. Chapter 3 also introduces how a CSS 3 pseudo-class, `:target`, can play a role in anything from drop-down menus to popup dialogs to slide shows.

❑   **Chapter 4, "More Dynamic Drop-down Menus and the Incredible, Versatile :target":** In the fourth chapter I discuss yet another approach to the dynamic drop-down menu system that I presented in Chapter 3.

❑ **Chapter 5, "Slide Show":** In the fifth chapter I present a web-based slide show that largely relies upon the use of the :target pseudo-class to function. Because the :target pseudo-class works only in Safari and Mozilla Firefox, I also present the steps you need to take to get a functioning slide show in Internet Explorer and Opera.

❑ **Chapter 6, "Custom Borders and Rounded Corners":** The sixth chapter elaborates on a common desire among web designers: how to customize borders and corners. I present two popular techniques for making custom borders and rounded corners.

❑ **Chapter 7, "Applying CSS to a Webmail Application":** In the seventh chapter I present a more complex application of CSS, styling a web-based mail application. Although you do not create a fully functional webmail application, you see the steps and challenges associated with setting up the user-interface for one. I also present a few alternative approaches in the design, including an optional message preview pane, and how to modify the webmail application so it mimics Microsoft Outlook 2003's three-column view.

❑ **Chapter 8, "Styling Input Forms":** In the eighth chapter I discuss how to style the Wrox P2P web site registration form, updating the original from legacy presentational HTML to more modern CSS and XHTML. I also present a technique that you can use to customize the look and feel of text input fields.

❑ **Chapter 9, "User-Interface for a Web-based File Viewer":** In the ninth chapter I present a complex project called "hFinder," an open source web-based file management application that I originally developed for my company's corporate intranet as part of a content management system (CMS). As was the case for project 7, you won't have a fully functioning file management system when you complete the project, but you will learn more about the challenges associated with the aesthetic aspects of making a web-based file viewer. I discuss techniques that help the web-based file viewer look and function like its desktop counterparts, Windows Explorer and Mac OS X Finder. You learn how to implement different methods of viewing files and directories, like details, icons, list, and tiles views. I also discuss techniques for creating pseudo-popup windows and dialogs, using only markup and CSS.

❑ **Chapter 10, "Calendar":** In the last chapter I elaborate on how to style a web-based calendar. I discuss techniques that enable you to create either a static calendar, where you enter in events manually, or how to prepare the application for a more sophisticated application, where the calendar and events are generated by JavaScript or a server-side programming language.

Throughout *CSS Instant Results* I discuss techniques and challenges that you'll face with the world's most popular browser, Microsoft Internet Explorer, which consequently also has the worst support for CSS among the most popular browsers. Included within each chapter are the hacks and workarounds that you'll need to make all ten projects function in Internet Explorer.

What You Need to Use This Book

You'll need a few browsers available for testing. In this book I test in the following browsers.

❑ Mozilla Firefox 1.0 (or later), available from http://www.mozilla.org

❑ Opera 8, available from http://www.opera.com

❑   Microsoft Internet Explorer 6 for Windows, available from `http://www.microsoft.com/ie`

❑   Safari 1.3 for Mac OS X, available from `http://www.apple.com/safari`

If you have a Windows PC but no Mac, or vise versa, you should be able to follow along with what's going on. The majority of testing takes place on the cross-platform capable Mozilla Firefox web browser, which works on either Windows or Mac OS X.

Internet Explorer 6, at the time of this writing, has the largest chunk of browser market share. The Mozilla Firefox browser follows in second with a market share approaching 10% on mainstream web sites, and 30% on tech-oriented web sites.

You may have noticed that I left out one big browser name: Netscape. The latest Netscape browser (available only for Windows) is based on both Internet Explorer 6 and Mozilla Firefox 1.0. It features the ability to view a web page using either IE's rendering engine or Firefox's. For that reason, there is no need to add the Netscape browser to the testing pool.

All of the projects of this book are focused on interoperable designs that work in as many browsers as possible—on Windows, Macintosh, or Linux. Some caveats still remain, however. As is true of most things CSS, not every approach will be cross-browser friendly.

Conventions

To help you get the most from the text and keep track of what's happening, we've used a number of conventions throughout the book.

> **Boxes like this one hold important, not-to-be-forgotten information that is directly relevant to the surrounding text.**

Tips, hints, tricks, and asides to the current discussion are offset and placed in italics like this.

As for styles in the text:

❑   We *highlight* important words when we introduce them

❑   We show keyboard strokes like this: Ctrl+A

❑   We show file names, URLs, and code within the text like so: `persistence.properties`

❑   We present code in two different ways:

```
In code examples we highlight new and important code with a gray background.
```

```
The gray highlighting is not used for code that's less important in the present
context, or has been shown before.
```

Source Code

As you work through the examples in this book, you may choose either to type in all the code manually or to use the source code files that accompany the book. All of the source code used in this book is available on the CD-ROM accompanying the book and it's available for download at http://www.wrox.com. Once at the site, simply locate the book's title (either by using the Search box or by using one of the title lists) and click the Download Code link on the book's detail page to obtain all the source code for the book.

> Because many books have similar titles, you may find it easiest to search by ISBN; for this book the ISBN is 0-471-75126-X.

Once you download the code, just decompress it with your favorite compression tool. Alternatively, you can go to the main Wrox code download page at http://www.wrox.com/dynamic/books/download.aspx to see the code available for this book and all other Wrox books.

Errata

We make every effort to ensure that there are no errors in the text or in the code. However, no one is perfect, and mistakes do occur. If you find an error in one of our books, like a spelling mistake or faulty piece of code, we would be very grateful for your feedback. By sending in errata you may save another reader hours of frustration and at the same time you will be helping us provide even higher quality information.

To find the errata page for this book, go to http://www.wrox.com and locate the title using the Search box or one of the title lists. Then, on the book details page, click the Book Errata link. On this page you can view all errata that has been submitted for this book and posted by Wrox editors. A complete book list including links to each's book's errata is also available at www.wrox.com/misc-pages/booklist.shtml.

If you don't spot "your" error on the Book Errata page, go to www.wrox.com/contact/techsupport.shtml and complete the form there to send us the error you have found. We'll check the information and, if appropriate, post a message to the book's errata page and fix the problem in subsequent editions of the book.

p2p.wrox.com

For author and peer discussion, join the P2P forums at p2p.wrox.com. The forums are a web-based system for you to post messages relating to Wrox books and related technologies and interact with other readers and technology users. The forums offer a subscription feature to email you topics of interest of your choosing when new posts are made to the forums. Wrox authors, editors, other industry experts, and your fellow readers are present on these forums.

At http://p2p.wrox.com you will find a number of different forums that will help you not only as you read this book, but also as you develop your own applications. To join the forums, just follow these steps:

1. Go to p2p.wrox.com and click the Register link.
2. Read the terms of use and click Agree.

3. Complete the required information to join as well as any optional information you wish to provide and click Submit.

4. You will receive an email with information describing how to verify your account and complete the joining process.

You can read messages in the forums without joining P2P but in order to post your own messages, you must join.

Once you join, you can post new messages and respond to messages other users post. You can read messages at any time on the Web. If you would like to have new messages from a particular forum emailed to you, click the Subscribe to this Forum icon by the forum name in the forum listing.

For more information about how to use the Wrox P2P, be sure to read the P2P FAQs for answers to questions about how the forum software works as well as many common questions specific to P2P and Wrox books. To read the FAQs, click the FAQ link on any P2P page.

Tabs

Tabs have become fairly ubiquitous in web design — you can find them nearly anywhere you look these days. (Apple.com is a great example of a mainstream site that implements tabs.) Earlier web design relied more heavily on image maps or on simple linked images and tables to create tabs. This chapter discusses several techniques that employ CSS for tab implementations, which naturally lead to more meaningful, accessible markup.

Each of the major browsers is capable of stable, simple, friendly tab designs. Some caveats still remain, however. As with most things CSS, not every approach will be cross-browser friendly, but this chapter covers all the necessary workarounds and outright hacks required to make a tab implementation shine in as many browsers as possible. Later in this chapter you see how an open source JavaScript named "IE7" helps bring compatibility to Internet Explorer 5.5 and 6 for some of the more advanced approaches, and how sometimes a little JavaScript goes a long way to bridge compatibility gaps between browsers, not only with the open source IE7 JavaScript, but also using other JavaScript-centered tools, such as Internet Explorer's proprietary CSS feature, `expression()`, which also plays a large role in many of the projects presented in this book.

Before presenting the tabs project, some planning is required. You should ask, "What do I expect of the tab implementation?" The following list outlines the design goals of the tabs project:

❑   The tabs must be contained in simple, meaningful markup.

❑   The text of each tab must not be images.

❑   A mouseover effect must be supplied for each tab so that the tab changes color when the user's mouse is hovering over it.

❑   The tab of the currently loaded page must be highlighted.

The next section discusses the CSS, XHTML, and JavaScript components that play a role in meeting these goals.

Design

The design presented in this chapter isn't particularly aesthetically appealing — it is a simple, down-to-the-wires presentation of how to create CSS tabs without images or tables. Later in this chapter you learn how to alter this design, both for liquid, stretchable tabs, and for custom borders and backgrounds. But the initial design is very simple and basic. The following list expands on the goals of the CSS tabs project covered in the preceding section and discusses the CSS and markup that will play a role in meeting those goals:

❑ **The tabs must be contained in simple, meaningful markup.** The first design goal is relatively trivial to meet. In simple terms, it means the right markup must be used for the data it encloses. In the tabs project, that means that the tabs are going to be structured in the document as an unordered HTML list. Because what is being presented is really a sequence of hyperlinks (not necessarily appearing in a particular order), the <ul> and <li> elements make the most sense. CSS provides the ability to transform the presentation of an unordered list to that of tabs. This is done by removing the default list styling provided via the margin, padding, and list-style properties. Then each list item (<li>) is styled with borders, some margin, and in order to place the <li> elements next to each other — as you expect to see with tabs — either the float property or absolute positioning via the position: absolute; declaration. For this project, you use the float property, because it is just a smidge simpler than positioning.

❑ **The text of each tab must not be images.** The second design goal involves accessibility and search engine visibility. If the text of the tab is contained in an image, it cannot be read to a blind user who is accessing the site with a voice browser like JAWS. Placing the text in images also impedes search visibility, because the text in the image is likely valuable keywords that you'd want the search engines to pick up on. Later in this chapter you see a method of using background images for each tab while preserving the text and maintaining search visibility and accessibility.

❑ **A mouseover effect must be supplied for each tab so that the tab changes colors when the user's mouse is hovering over it.** The next design goal is trivial to implement. You merely want there to be some visual cue to the user that the tab is for navigation. Changing the background colors or other aspects of it is one way to provide this visual cue. You achieve this in the project by applying the CSS :hover pseudo-class to some rules in the style sheet.

❑ **The tab of the currently loaded page must be highlighted.** The fourth design goal is a common one. Put simply, there must be some visual cue that the currently loaded page is the same page that is linked via a tab. To achieve this, a slightly more verbose approach is available, and this is demonstrated in the tabs project by marking up five separate XHTML documents. Each document's <body> element is provided with a different unique ID name, and then each <li> element that contains a single tab is also given a unique name. This approach provides some hooks that allow you to provide a different style for the tab of the currently loaded page.

Without further ado, the code and code explanation for the tabs project are presented in the next section. Keep in mind that this project's source code is provided on the CD-ROM accompanying this book, or you can download it from www.wrox.com.

Code and Code Explanation

To create tabs using CSS and XHTML, follow these steps:

1. Create the following markup documents; the differences between each document are highlighted:

```
<!DOCTYPE html PUBLIC "-//W3C//DTD XHTML 1.0 Transitional//EN"
"http://www.w3.org/TR/xhtml1/DTD/xhtml1-transitional.dtd">
<html xmlns='http://www.w3.org/1999/xhtml' xml:lang='en'>
    <head>
        <meta http-equiv='Content-Type' content='text/html; charset=UTF-8' />
        <title></title>
        <link rel='stylesheet' type='text/css' href='tabs.css' />
        <!-- compliance patch for microsoft browsers -->
        <!--[if lt IE 7]>
            <script src='/ie7/ie7-standard-p.js' type='text/javascript'></script>
        <![endif]-->
    </head>
    <body id='wrox'>
        <ul id='tabs'>
            <li id='tab1'><a href='wrox.html'><span>Wrox P2P</span></a></li>
            <li id='tab2'><a href='amazon.html'><span>Amazon</span></a></li>
            <li id='tab3'><a href='google.html'><span>Google</span></a></li>
            <li id='tab4'><a href='slashdot.html'><span>Slashdot</span></a></li>
            <li id='tab5'>
                <a href='twit.html'><span>This Week in Tech</span></a>
            </li>
        </ul>
        <div id='iframe'>
            <iframe src='http://p2p.wrox.com'
                    frameborder='0' marginheight='0' marginwidth='0'></iframe>
        </div>
    </body>
</html>
```

2. Save the first document as `wrox.html`.

```
<!DOCTYPE html PUBLIC "-//W3C//DTD XHTML 1.0 Transitional//EN"
"http://www.w3.org/TR/xhtml1/DTD/xhtml1-transitional.dtd">
<html xmlns='http://www.w3.org/1999/xhtml' xml:lang='en'>
    <head>
        <meta http-equiv="Content-Type" content="text/html; charset=UTF-8" />
        <title></title>
        <link rel='stylesheet' type='text/css' href='tabs.css' />
        <!-- compliance patch for microsoft browsers -->
        <!--[if lt IE 7]>
            <script src="/ie7/ie7-standard-p.js" type="text/javascript"></script>
        <![endif]-->
    </head>
    <body id='amazon'>
        <ul id='tabs'>
```

```
            <li id='tab1'><a href='wrox.html'><span>Wrox P2P</span></a></li>
            <li id='tab2'><a href='amazon.html'><span>Amazon</span></a></li>
            <li id='tab3'><a href='google.html'><span>Google</span></a></li>
            <li id='tab4'><a href='slashdot.html'><span>Slashdot</span></a></li>
            <li id='tab5'>
                <a href='twit.html'><span>This Week in Tech</span></a>
            </li>
        </ul>
        <div id='iframe'>
            <iframe src='http://www.amazon.com'
                    frameborder='0' marginheight='0' marginwidth='0'></iframe>
        </div>
    </body>
</html>
```

3. Save the second document as `amazon.html`.

```
<!DOCTYPE html PUBLIC "-//W3C//DTD XHTML 1.0 Transitional//EN"
"http://www.w3.org/TR/xhtml1/DTD/xhtml1-transitional.dtd">
<html xmlns='http://www.w3.org/1999/xhtml' xml:lang='en'>
    <head>
        <meta http-equiv='Content-Type' content='text/html; charset=UTF-8' />
        <title></title>
        <link rel='stylesheet' type='text/css' href='tabs.css' />
        <!-- compliance patch for microsoft browsers -->
        <!--[if lt IE 7]>
            <script src='/ie7/ie7-standard-p.js' type='text/javascript'></script>
        <![endif]-->
    </head>
    <body id='google'>
        <ul id='tabs'>
            <li id='tab1'><a href='wrox.html'><span>Wrox P2P</span></a></li>
            <li id='tab2'><a href='amazon.html'><span>Amazon</span></a></li>
            <li id='tab3'><a href='google.html'><span>Google</span></a></li>
            <li id='tab4'><a href='slashdot.html'><span>Slashdot</span></a></li>
            <li id='tab5'>
                <a href='twit.html'><span>This Week in Tech</span></a>
            </li>
        </ul>
        <div id='iframe'>
            <iframe src='http://www.google.com'
                    frameborder='0' marginheight='0' marginwidth='0'></iframe>
        </div>
    </body>
</html>
```

4. Save the third document as `google.html`.

```
<!DOCTYPE html PUBLIC "-//W3C//DTD XHTML 1.0 Transitional//EN"
"http://www.w3.org/TR/xhtml1/DTD/xhtml1-transitional.dtd">
<html xmlns='http://www.w3.org/1999/xhtml' xml:lang='en'>
    <head>
        <meta http-equiv='Content-Type' content='text/html; charset=UTF-8' />
        <title></title>
        <link rel='stylesheet' type='text/css' href='tabs.css' />
```

```
            <!-- compliance patch for microsoft browsers -->
            <!--[if lt IE 7]>
                <script src='/ie7/ie7-standard-p.js' type='text/javascript'></script>
            <![endif]-->
    </head>
    <body id='slashdot'>
        <ul id='tabs'>
            <li id='tab1'><a href='wrox.html'><span>Wrox P2P</span></a></li>
            <li id='tab2'><a href='amazon.html'><span>Amazon</span></a></li>
            <li id='tab3'><a href='google.html'><span>Google</span></a></li>
            <li id='tab4'><a href='slashdot.html'><span>Slashdot</span></a></li>
            <li id='tab5'>
                <a href='twit.html'><span>This Week in Tech</span></a>
            </li>
        </ul>
        <div id='iframe'>
            <iframe src='http://www.slashdot.org'
                    frameborder='0' marginheight='0' marginwidth='0'></iframe>
        </div>
    </body>
</html>
```

5. Save the fourth document as `slashdot.html`.

```
<!DOCTYPE html PUBLIC "-//W3C//DTD XHTML 1.0 Transitional//EN"
"http://www.w3.org/TR/xhtml1/DTD/xhtml1-transitional.dtd">
<html xmlns='http://www.w3.org/1999/xhtml' xml:lang='en'>
    <head>
            <meta http-equiv='Content-Type' content='text/html; charset=UTF-8' />
            <title></title>
            <link rel='stylesheet' type='text/css' href='tabs.css' />
            <!-- compliance patch for microsoft browsers -->
            <!--[if lt IE 7]>
                <script src='/ie7/ie7-standard-p.js' type='text/javascript'></script>
            <![endif]-->
    </head>
    <body id='twit'>
        <ul id='tabs'>
            <li id='tab1'><a href='wrox.html'><span>Wrox P2P</span></a></li>
            <li id='tab2'><a href='amazon.html'><span>Amazon</span></a></li>
            <li id='tab3'><a href='google.html'><span>Google</span></a></li>
            <li id='tab4'><a href='slashdot.html'><span>Slashdot</span></a></li>
            <li id='tab5'>
                <a href='twit.html'><span>This Week in Tech</span></a>
            </li>
        </ul>
        <div id='iframe'>
            <iframe src='http://www.twit.tv'
                    frameborder='0' marginheight='0' marginwidth='0'></iframe>
        </div>
    </body>
</html>
```

6. Save the fifth document as `twit.html`.

7. Next, key in the following style sheet:

```css
body, html {
    margin: 0;
    padding: 0;
}
ul#tabs {
    list-style: none;
    margin: 0;
    padding: 10px 0 0 0;
    height: 25px;
    border-bottom: 1px solid black;
    background: rgb(222, 222, 222);
}
ul#tabs li {
    float: left;
    margin: 0 5px;
    height: 23px;
    text-align: center;
    position: relative;
    width: 150px;
    border: 1px solid black;
    top: 1px;
    background: rgb(128, 128, 128);
}
ul#tabs li:hover {
    border-bottom: 1px solid white;
    background: white;
}
ul#tabs a {
    display: block;
    height: 100%;
    text-decoration: none;
    color: white;
    font: 14px Arial, sans-serif;
}
body#wrox li#tab1,
body#amazon li#tab2,
body#google li#tab3,
body#slashdot li#tab4,
body#twit li#tab5 {
    background: white;
    border-bottom: 1px solid white;
}
ul#tabs a:hover,
body#wrox li#tab1 a,
body#amazon li#tab2 a,
body#google li#tab3 a,
body#slashdot li#tab4 a,
body#twit li#tab5 a {
    color: black;
}
ul#tabs span {
    display: block;
    padding: 4px 10px 0 10px;
}
```

```
div#iframe {
    position: absolute;
    top: 0;
    bottom: 0;
    right: 0;
    left: 0;
    margin-top: 50px;
    border-top: 1px solid black;
}
iframe {
    position: absolute;
    top: 0;
    bottom: 0;
    right: 0;
    left: 0;
    width: 100%;
    height: 100%;
}
```

8. Save the style sheet as `tabs.css`.

The result of this in Mozilla Firefox is depicted in Figure 1-1.

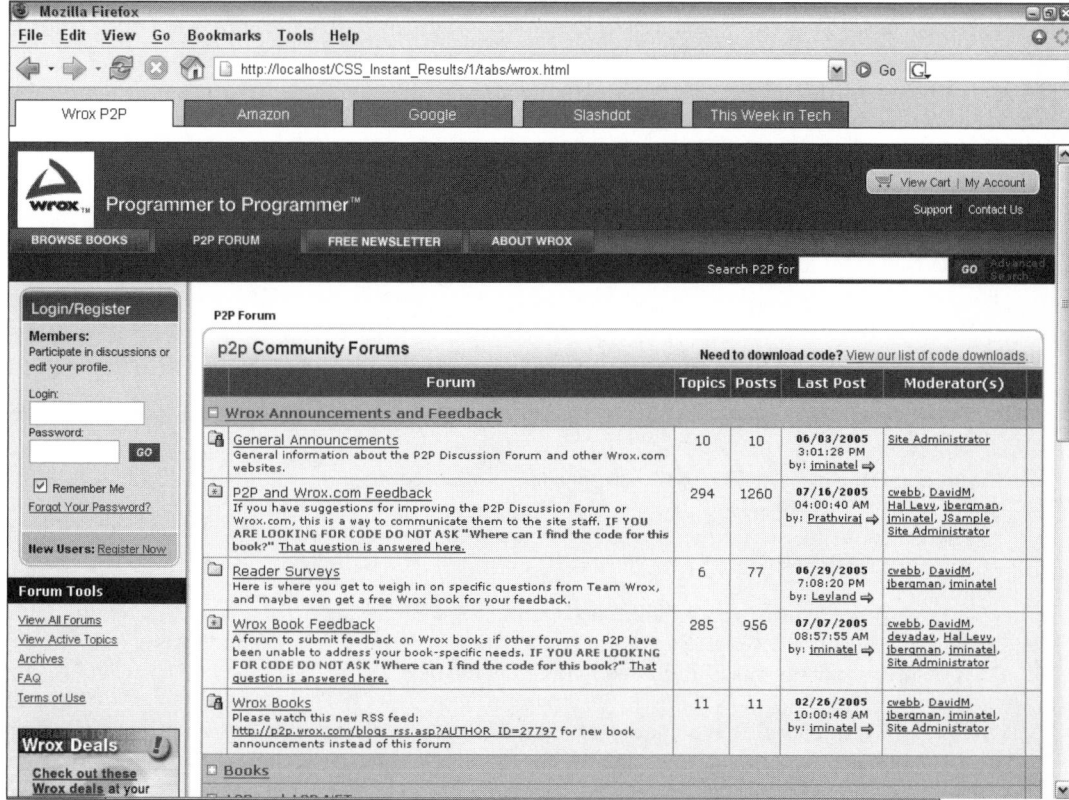

Figure 1-1

In Figure 1-1, you see that the tab for Wrox P2P is highlighted when the `wrox.html` page is loaded. If another tab is clicked, the tab for that page is highlighted, as is depicted in Figure 1-2.

Figure 1-2

Figure 1-2 shows that the tab for Google is highlighted when the `google.html` page is loaded.

Before getting into the explanation, take a look at this markup, which may seem a little curious:

```
<!-- compliance patch for microsoft browsers -->
<!--[if lt IE 7]>
    <script src="/ie7/ie7-standard-p.js" type="text/javascript"></script>
<![endif]-->
```

This markup is used to bring compatibility to Internet Explorer 5.5 and 6 for a few CSS features appearing in the style sheet that Internet Explorer doesn't natively support. Set this (and testing in Internet Explorer) aside for now — this is discussed in detail in the next section, "Testing and Caveats."

The following is a rule-by-rule explanation of each declaration appearing in the `tabs.css` style sheet, which is provided as an aid to customizing the tabs project for your own use.

The first rule appearing in the `tabs.css` style sheet removes default margin and padding from the `<body>` element:

```
body, html {
    margin: 0;
    padding: 0;
}
```

This rule isn't necessary for a tabs implementation, but was added merely for the sake of presenting the example here. Some browsers (IE and Firefox) apply some margin by default to the `<body>` element and others (Opera) apply default padding to the `<body>` element; this rule covers both.

The next rule styles the `<ul>` element that contains the list items that eventually become tabs:

```
ul#tabs {
    list-style: none;
    margin: 0;
    padding: 10px 0 0 0;
    height: 25px;
    border-bottom: 1px solid black;
    background: rgb(222, 222, 222);
}
```

The first declaration in this rule, `list-style: none;`, removes the default bullet styling of each `<li>` item. Subsequently, `margin: 0;` removes the default spacing each browser applies to the `<ul>` element, though as was the case with the `<body>` element, some browsers apply padding instead of margin to the `<ul>` element; `padding: 10px 0 0 0;` takes care of this, and you add 10 pixels of space to the top padding, which appears between the top border of the browser's viewport and the top border of each tab. Like the modification for the `<body>` element, this space isn't really necessary to create a tab implementation and can be customized to suit your own needs.

The next declaration sets a fixed height for the `<ul>` element. Without a fixed height, the background and bottom border specified for the `<ul>` element would appear above the tabs instead of flush with the bottom border of each `<li>` element. This happens because each `<li>` element is floated, and because they are floated, they no longer affect the height of the `<ul>` element since floated elements leave the normal flow and affect only content, but not box model–related properties such as height, padding, margin, and so on. The last two declarations are also not necessary for a tab implementation and can be customized. `border-bottom: 1px solid black;` and `background: rgb(222, 222, 222);` are applied — the former goes along the bottom of all of the tabs, and the latter provides some color contrast from the `<li>` elements and the `<ul>` containing them. The bottom border is only necessary to create the tab effect where the tab of the current page has no bottom border. As shown in Figure 1-1, the Wrox P2P tab is highlighted with no bottom border, and in Figure 1-2 the tab for the Google page is highlighted with no bottom border. If this effect is desired, the bottom border for the `<ul>` element plays a role in creating it.

To make the tab design truly portable, it can also be positioned absolutely and set to any place in a document desired via the offset properties of CSS (`top`, `right`, `bottom`, or `left`).

The next rule sets styles for each `<li>` element:

```
ul#tabs li {
    float: left;
    margin: 0 5px;
```

```
        height: 23px;
        text-align: center;
        position: relative;
        width: 150px;
        border: 1px solid black;
        top: 1px;
        background: rgb(128, 128, 128);
    }
```

This project uses the CSS float model for laying out the tabs. This places each <li> element side by side instead of how they would appear in a normal list (each on a new line). This is done with the float: left; declaration. To overlap the bottom border of each tab with the bottom border of the containing <ul> element, you apply a position: relative; declaration, and then subsequently a top: 1px; declaration, which moves the position of each tab down a single pixel to overlap with the bottom border of the <ul> element. Next, to put some space between each tab, you apply margin. margin: 0 5px; sets the top and bottom margins to zero and the left and right margins to 5 pixels. This puts 10 pixels of space between each tab, and 5 pixels of space between the left border of the containing <ul> element and the left border of the first tab. The next declaration sets a fixed height for each tab. This provides consistency between <li> height and <ul> height, though it isn't absolutely necessary. The height could be removed and the top: 1px; declaration could be changed to top: 4px; to maintain synchronicity between the bottom border of each <li> element and the bottom border of the <ul> element. The height is applied to vertically center the text, though this can also be achieved by applying a vertical-align property to each <li> element. To center the text, naturally, a text-align: center; declaration is applied. Next, a fixed width is added with the width: 150px; declaration. This property is also optional; it is applied here so that each tab is of the same width.

> If the <ul> element containing each tab is absolutely positioned, a fixed width larger than the <li> elements' cumulative widths will need to be applied to maintain compatibility with Opera. This is required because each <li> element is floated and the containing <ul> is not expanded horizontally to accommodate the nested <li> elements in Opera. This behavior is the result of an ambiguity in the CSS 2 specification, the wording of which actually leads to both Firefox and Opera being correct through a mutually exclusive interpretation of the specification. The conflict revolves around absolutely positioned elements using the shrink-to-fit width sizing algorithm, and at which point that width is determined. Opera calculates the absolutely positioned element's width before taking its floating descendants into account; Firefox floats those elements first and then gives the absolutely positioned element its width.

Finally, a background and borders are applied to each <li> element to set them apart from the containing <ul> element.

In the next rule, a hovering effect is added to each <li> element:

```
ul#tabs li:hover {
    border-bottom: 1px solid white;
    background: white;
}
```

This rule is very straightforward: if the user's mouse hovers over one of the <li> elements, the <li> element's background becomes white instead of the gray color applied in the previous rule with background: rgb(128, 128, 128);. The bottom border also changes color to white, instead of black as it was specified in the previous rule. This provides the effect of the tab appearing "on top," as you saw in Figures 1-1 and 1-2; although those figures show that the current page's tab is highlighted, this hover effect does the same thing for the tabs of the other pages, but only when the user's mouse is hovering over a tab.

The next rule styles the links within each `<li>` element:

```
ul#tabs a {
    display: block;
    height: 100%;
    text-decoration: none;
    color: white;
    font: 14px Arial, sans-serif;
}
```

The first declaration switches the display of the `<a>` element from inline, its default display state, to block, which is the default for elements like `<div>` and `<p>`. This makes the `<a>` element take up all the horizontal space available to it (up to the left and right borders of the `<li>` element that contains it). Next, a `height: 100%;` declaration is applied; this makes the whole inner space of each `<li>` element (within the borders) a hyperlink. Then the default underline of links is removed with the `text-decoration: none;` declaration. The `color: white;` declaration sets the color of the link to white (usually blue, by default, and purple if visited). Like other stylistic aspects of this project, `color: white;` is unnecessary, but provided here for the sake of presenting a CSS tabs implementation. Finally, `font: 14px Arial, sans-serif;` is applied to change the font.

In the five documents that you created, you applied a different id name to the `<body>` element of each document. The next rule takes advantage of that naming convention to style the tab for the currently loaded page differently than the other tabs:

```
body#wrox li#tab1,
body#amazon li#tab2,
body#google li#tab3,
body#slashdot li#tab4,
body#twit li#tab5 {
    background: white;
    border-bottom: 1px solid white;
}
```

The concept is simple enough. By taking advantage of the cascade and uniquely naming each page, you are able to style the tab for the currently loaded page differently than the other tabs. This also requires each tab to be uniquely named as well. Combined with the `<body>` element's id name, the rule can override the previous rule, `ul#tabs li`, because the `body#wrox li#tab1` selector's cascading specificity is greater than that of the former rule. In the latter selector, when the `<body>` has a "wrox" id name, and a `<li>` element has an id name of `tab1`, it overrides the `ul#tabs li` selector, and applies a white background and a solid white bottom border giving the current page's tab a different style than the tabs for the other pages.

The previous rule can, in fact, be grouped with the `ul#tabs li:hover` rule that you saw previously — they are presented separately here for the sake of segregating the two different concepts, but in fact they specify the same declarations, which makes it an ideal situation for selector grouping. This can be observed in the next rule:

```
ul#tabs a:hover,
body#wrox li#tab1 a,
body#amazon li#tab2 a,
body#google li#tab3 a,
body#slashdot li#tab4 a,
body#twit li#tab5 a {
    color: black;
}
```

This rule begins with six separate selectors, which have been grouped together to avoid repetition in the style sheet. The first selector selects <a> elements that are descendants of <ul> elements with a tabs id name, but only when the user's mouse is hovering over the <a> element. The subsequent selectors, as you saw in the last rule, select the link of the current page that is loaded based on the id name of the <body> element and the id name of the <li> element. Because the links within each <li> element are white, and the background of each <li> element is made white when either the user's mouse is hovering over a tab or the tab is the tab of the currently loaded page. The link color must be changed in those circumstances to contrast with the white background, so a declaration of color: black; is applied when that criteria is met.

The next rule applies styling to the <span> element nested inside of each <a> element:

```
ul#tabs span {
    display: block;
    padding: 4px 10px 0 10px;
}
```

The first declaration in this rule changes the display state of the <span> element from its default, inline, to block. This enables you to apply padding via the block box model instead of the inline box model. This is done to control the spacing around the text of each tab, which may or may not be desired, depending on the stylistic requirements of your particular project.

You might be wondering, why not use a <div> instead of a <span> element? Semantically speaking, enclosing block elements like <div> with inline elements like <a> is technically illegal (even though you change its display state to block), and could foster mixed results with browsers. From the standpoint of standards, it is both technically correct and more appropriate to use <span>, because it can legally be nested inside another inline element, like <a>. This approach takes care of validation errors using the W3C validator, at http://validator.w3.org, which is used by markup authors to find markup errors and to ensure that their markup adheres to the standards.

Again, the extra <span> may or may not be desired, as mentioned previously, you may or may not desire fixed height tabs, and may or may not want to use a <span> element to control the vertical spacing of text (as opposed to the vertical-align property).

The final two rules have nothing to do with implementing a tabs design and are included merely to fill the void of the rest of the document with supplemental content, via the inclusion of external documents from popular web sites by inline frame.

Testing and Caveats

This section describes some of the challenges that come as a result of expanding the test bed of browsers. Typically when I begin a project, I ignore all browsers but Firefox until the project matures to something resembling the final product. When that point in development comes, I begin testing in other browsers such as Internet Explorer, Opera, Safari, and so on. In a typical project only minor adjustments may need to be made for more standards-aware browsers such as Opera and Safari, which is why you see in this section that the focus is only on Internet Explorer and the challenges you face when introducing standards to Internet Explorer that it may not already understand, or understands only poorly or incorrectly.

The previous section mentioned a snippet of markup that helps bring compatibility to Internet Explorer 5.5 and 6 for a few CSS features that Internet Explorer 5.5 and 6 do not natively support. To refresh your memory, this was the markup in question:

```
<!-- compliance patch for microsoft browsers -->
<!--[if lt IE 7]>
    <script src='/ie7/ie7-standard-p.js' type='text/javascript'></script>
<![endif]-->
```

If you've read my book, *Beginning CSS: Cascading Style Sheets for Web Design* (also published by Wiley Publishing, Inc.), you might remember that I introduced the IE7 JavaScript in Chapter 18 and described how to download and install it in that chapter. Because this book is intended for readers with more advanced knowledge of web site design, I won't reiterate every step involved here but will provide a general overview of the installation process and the background of the IE7 JavaScript.

The IE7 JavaScript was written by London, UK native Dean Edwards to help designers cope with the fact that Microsoft's Internet Explorer browser hasn't received significant CSS updates in five years. Edwards uses JavaScript to implement CSS features in Internet Explorer that it previously did not support to bring IE 5.5 and IE 6 onto a more level playing field with other browsers, such as Safari and Mozilla Firefox, which both have (at the time of this writing) far better CSS support. The IE7 library is written in a transparent way, so that it appears that Explorer supports these CSS features natively, and the person making use of IE7 need not have any more JavaScript knowledge than that required to link to the IE7 library. Some of the top CSS features that IE7 provides are as follows:

- ❑   `min-width`, `max-width`, and `min-height` properties
- ❑   `:hover`, `:active`, and `:focus` pseudo-classes (on any element, not just the `<a>` element)
- ❑   Various advanced selectors such as the direct child selector (`>`), attribute selectors (`input[type]`), adjacent sibling selector (`+`), and indirect adjacent sibling selector (`~`)
- ❑   Structural pseudo-classes, such as `:root`, `:first-child`, and `:last-child`
- ❑   `::before` and `::after` pseudo-elements and the `content` property

Of course, Edwards doesn't stop there; those are only some of the top features. The truly amazing part is IE7's size and speed. The IE7 JavaScript library is modularized; this helps keep down the download size and lets designers include only the features that they need. The main library is only about 24KB in size. It provides all of the preceding functionality and then some (with the exception of `:last-child`, which he includes in a special CSS3 selector library).

The IE7 JavaScript is hosted on SourceForge, an organization that hosts thousands of open source projects, and can be downloaded at the following URL: `https://sourceforge.net/project/showfiles.php?group_id=109983`.

After downloading IE7, it must be unzipped and placed in the root directory of your web server. For example, if your web site is `http://www.example.com/`, the IE7 JavaScript must appear at `http://www.example.com/ie7/`. You can also install IE7 to a different directory, but the source examples provided in this book must be updated to reflect the path you install IE7 to.

The IE7 JavaScript is open source and is available under a Creative Commons LGPL license (Lesser General Public License). You can obtain the full text (legalese-free) at `http://creativecommons.org/licenses/LGPL/2.1`.

You can find more information about IE7 from the IE7 homepage at `http://dean.edwards.name/ie7`.

The next section discusses what specific functionality Edwards' IE 7 JavaScript provides for this project.

What the IE7 JavaScript Provides for This Project

The functionality the IE7 JavaScript provides for this project is best observed by simply opening up the tabs project in Internet Explorer without installing the IE7 JavaScript. The output of `wrox.html` without IE7 functionality in Internet Explorer 6 is shown in Figure 1-3.

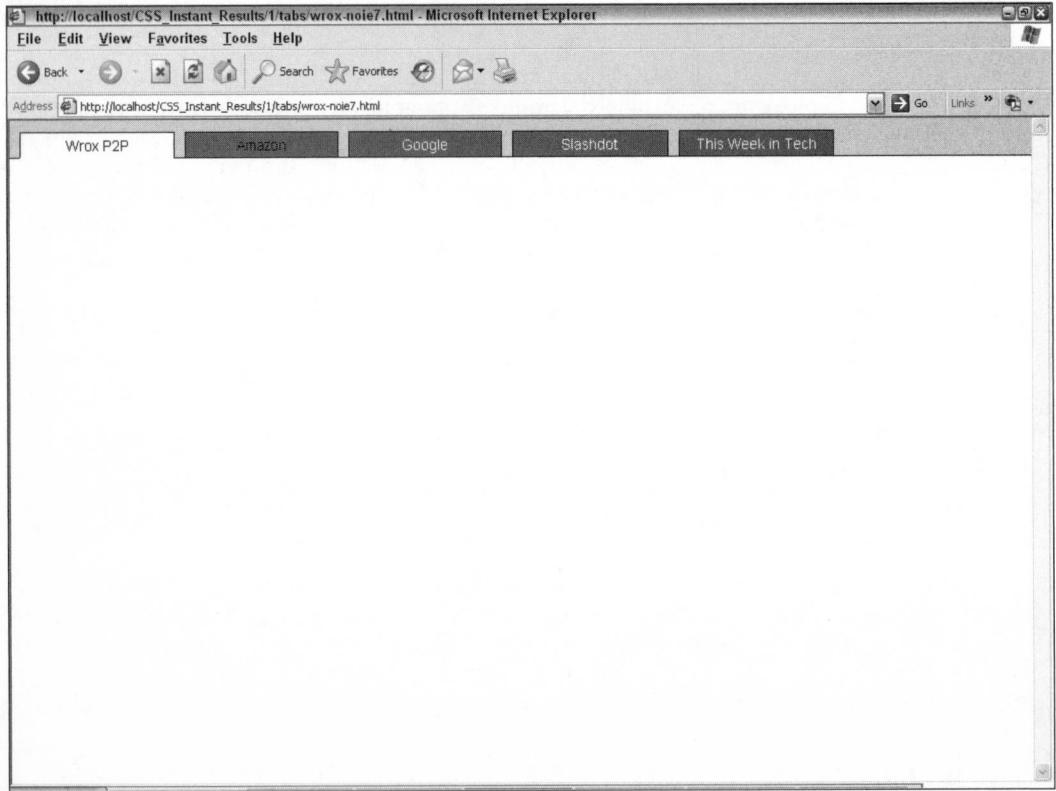

Figure 1-3

It doesn't look much different in Explorer, with a few minor exceptions:

❑ The tabs do not have a white background when the mouse is hovering over one.

❑ The `<iframe>` isn't visible at all.

The situation described in the first bullet point happens because Internet Explorer 6 only supports the `:hover` dynamic pseudo-class on `<a>` elements instead of all elements, as does Firefox, Opera, and Safari. The latter bullet point is because Explorer 6 does not support the combination of the `top`, `right`, `bottom`, and `left` properties to imply dimensions on absolutely positioned or fixed positioned elements. Edwards' IE7 JavaScript provides both of those features and brings Internet Explorer 6 to the same level of functionality as is provided by Firefox, Opera, and Safari. Figure 1-4 shows output from Internet Explorer 6 with Edwards' IE7 JavaScript applied.

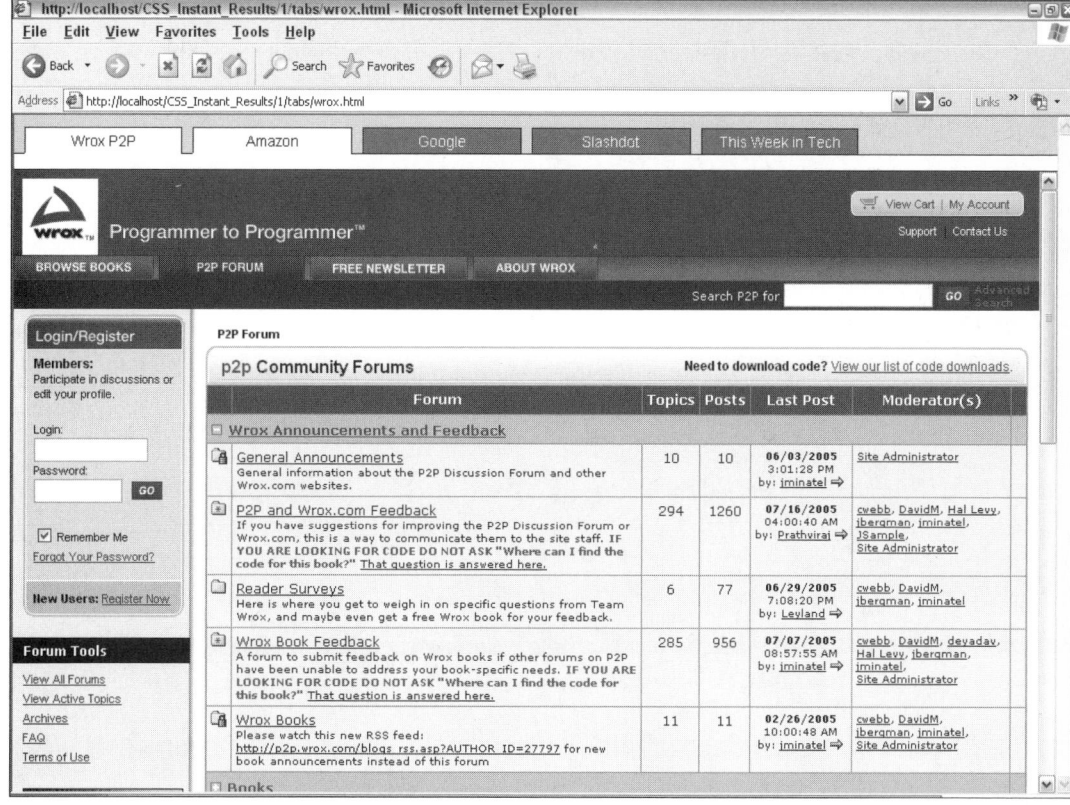

Figure 1-4

Figure 1-4 demonstrates that the other tabs now change colors when the user's mouse is hovering over them, and the `<iframe>` is now visible.

The next section discusses how to modify the tabs project for a variety of alternative approaches in design.

Using and Modifying the Project

This section presents a few alternative approaches to the tabs project design because not everyone will want the tabs project as it has been presented. The alternative approaches discussed in this section are as follows:

❑   Using background images instead of solid colors and square borders

❑   Using background images that include text without compromising accessibility

❑   Using background images in such a way that the tabs are liquid and can be fluid between a minimum and maximum constraint

Naturally, these alternative approaches increase the complexity and difficulty of the project, but they are included to provide maximum flexibility and to cover as many scenarios of tab implementation as possible.

The first alternative approach shows you how to use background images instead of the default solid colors and square borders.

Tabs with Background Images

To create tabs with background images, follow these steps. The source code of the following approach, as well as the accompanying images, is available on the book's web site and on the source CD-ROM accompanying this book in the folder "with-background" in the "Project 1" folder.

1.   Enter the following style sheet. Changes from `tabs.css` in the original project are highlighted:

```
body, html {
    margin: 0;
    padding: 0;
}
ul#tabs {
    list-style: none;
    margin: 0;
    padding: 10px 0 0 0;
    height: 23px;
    border-bottom: 1px solid black;
    background: rgb(218, 218, 218);
}
ul#tabs li {
    float: left;
    margin: 0;
    height: 23px;
    text-align: center;
    width: 160px;
    background: transparent url('images/tab.png') no-repeat scroll top;
}
ul#tabs a {
    display: block;
```

```
        height: 100%;
        text-decoration: none;
        color: white;
        font: 14px Arial, sans-serif;
    }
ul#tabs li:hover,
body#wrox li#tab1,
body#amazon li#tab2,
body#google li#tab3,
body#slashdot li#tab4,
body#twit li#tab5 {
        background: transparent url('images/tab_hover.png') no-repeat scroll top;
    }
ul#tabs a:hover,
body#wrox li#tab1 a,
body#amazon li#tab2 a,
body#google li#tab3 a,
body#slashdot li#tab4 a,
body#twit li#tab5 a {
        color: black;
    }
ul#tabs span {
        display: block;
        padding: 4px 10px 0 10px;
    }
div#iframe {
        position: absolute;
        top: 0;
        bottom: 0;
        right: 0;
        left: 0;
        margin-top: 50px;
        border-top: 1px solid black;
    }
iframe {
        position: absolute;
        top: 0;
        bottom: 0;
        right: 0;
        left: 0;
        width: 100%;
        height: 100%;
    }
```

2. Save the resulting style sheet as `tabs.css`.

You can see the result of these modifications in Figure 1-5.

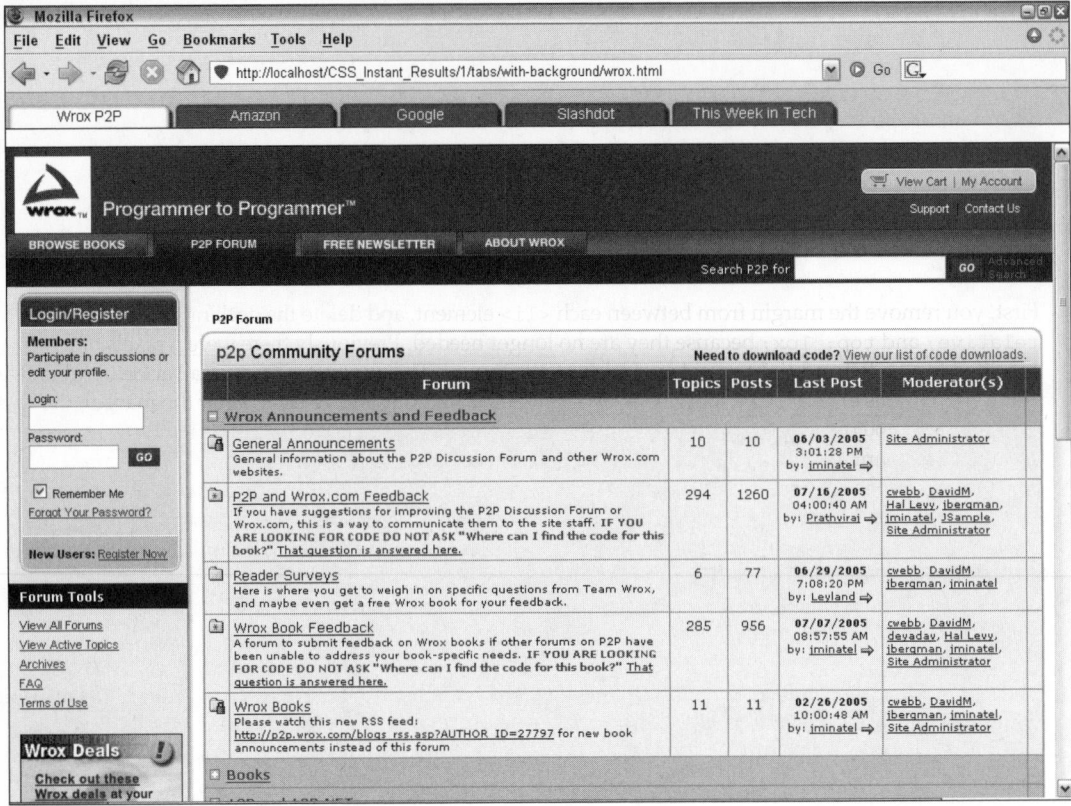

Figure 1-5

The required modifications to use background images instead of borders and solid colors are surprisingly few. The following explains in detail each modification made.

The first modification is to the height of the `<ul>` element, which corresponds directly to the height of the background image to be used for each `<li>` element:

```
ul#tabs {
    list-style: none;
    margin: 0;
    padding: 10px 0 0 0;
    height: 23px;
    border-bottom: 1px solid black;
    background: rgb(218, 218, 218);
}
```

The second modification is to the solid background of the `<ul>` element containing the five tabs. The background is made slightly lighter to match the background of the Adobe Photoshop–generated tab background images. Although an RGB value of 222, 222, 222 was used originally, and an identical RGB value was used in Adobe Photoshop for the background of the tab, the two did not match in any of the browsers. To bring these closer, you simply darken the gray background of the `<ul>` element slightly.

The next modification is to the rule for the `<li>` elements:

```
ul#tabs li {
    float: left;
    margin: 0;
    height: 23px;
    text-align: center;
    width: 160px;
    background: transparent url('images/tab.png') no-repeat scroll top;
}
```

First, you remove the margin from between each `<li>` element, and delete the declarations `position: relative;` and `top: 1px;` because they are no longer needed. Previously there were 5 pixels of margin specified for the left and right margins of each `<li>` element. This was done because a background image is being used in this example; the margin can exist in the background image itself. After the margin, the width is modified to 160 pixels. This is set to include the margin that was removed from the left and right sides of each `<li>` element. Finally, in the last declaration of the previous rule, a background image is applied. The background image is generated at 160 × 23 pixels, which matches exactly the width and height specified for the `<li>` element. To modify the example for tabs of different dimensions, keep in mind the `width` and `height` properties appearing in the previous rule, and the `height` property of the ul#tabs rule, which will be the starting point for modifying the dimensions of each tab to accommodate a larger or smaller background tab. Other things to consider when modifying the dimensions are the padding values of the `<span>` element that wraps the text of each tab, which is used to control vertical alignment.

The last modifications modify the tab of the page that is loaded, or the background image that appears when a user hovers over a tab:

```
ul#tabs li:hover,
body#wrox li#tab1,
body#amazon li#tab2,
body#google li#tab3,
body#slashdot li#tab4,
body#twit li#tab5 {
    background: transparent url('images/tab_hover.png') no-repeat scroll top;
}
```

In the original tabs example you defined `ul#tabs li:hover` as a separate rule. Here you have simply grouped them with the rule that defines the tab of the currently loaded document and modified the background declaration to reference `tab_hover.png`.

That's it. The next section discusses how to use background images that include text without compromising accessibility.

Background Images That Include Text

To create tabs with background images that include text, follow these steps. The source code and accompanying images of the following approach are available on the book's web site and on the source CD-ROM in the folder "with-text" in the "Project 1" folder.

1. Enter the following modifications to `tabs.css`. Changes from the previous background image approach are highlighted, though some declarations have also been removed:

```css
body, html {
    margin: 0;
    padding: 0;
}
ul#tabs {
    list-style: none;
    margin: 0;
    padding: 10px 0 0 0;
    height: 23px;
    border-bottom: 1px solid black;
    background: rgb(218, 218, 218);
}
ul#tabs li {
    float: left;
    margin: 0;
    height: 23px;
    text-align: center;
    width: 160px;
}
ul#tabs a {
    display: block;
    height: 100%;
    text-decoration: none;
    color: white;
    font: 14px Arial, sans-serif;
}
ul#tabs li#tab1 {
    background: transparent url('images/wrox-tab.png') no-repeat scroll top;
}
ul#tabs li#tab1:hover,
body#wrox li#tab1 {
    background: transparent url('images/wrox-tab-hover.png') no-repeat scroll top;
}
ul#tabs li#tab2 {
    background: transparent url('images/amazon-tab.png') no-repeat scroll top;
}
ul#tabs li#tab2:hover,
body#amazon li#tab2 {
    background: transparent url('images/amazon-tab-hover.png') no-repeat scroll
top;
}
ul#tabs li#tab3 {
    background: transparent url('images/google-tab.png') no-repeat scroll top;
}
ul#tabs li#tab3:hover,
body#google li#tab3 {
    background: transparent url('images/google-tab-hover.png') no-repeat scroll
top;
}
ul#tabs li#tab4 {
    background: transparent url('images/slashdot-tab.png') no-repeat scroll top;
}
ul#tabs li#tab4:hover,
```

```
body#slashdot li#tab4 {
    background: transparent url('images/slashdot-tab-hover.png') no-repeat scroll
top;
}
ul#tabs li#tab5 {
    background: transparent url('images/twit-tab.png') no-repeat scroll top;
}
ul#tabs li#tab5:hover,
body#twit li#tab5 {
    background: transparent url('images/twit-tab-hover.png') no-repeat scroll top;
}
ul#tabs a:hover,
body#wrox li#tab1 a,
body#amazon li#tab2 a,
body#google li#tab3 a,
body#slashdot li#tab4 a,
body#twit li#tab5 a {
    color: black;
}
ul#tabs span {
    display: block;
    padding: 4px 10px 0 10px;
    visibility: hidden;
}
div#iframe {
    position: absolute;
    top: 0;
    bottom: 0;
    right: 0;
    left: 0;
    margin-top: 50px;
    border-top: 1px solid black;
}
iframe {
    position: absolute;
    top: 0;
    bottom: 0;
    right: 0;
    left: 0;
    width: 100%;
    height: 100%;
}
```

2. Save as `tabs.css`.

These modifications result in the output depicted in Figure 1-6.

Although the modifications to this approach are more extensive than the last approach that used only background images with no text, much of the revision is redundant because a different background image must be used for each tab.

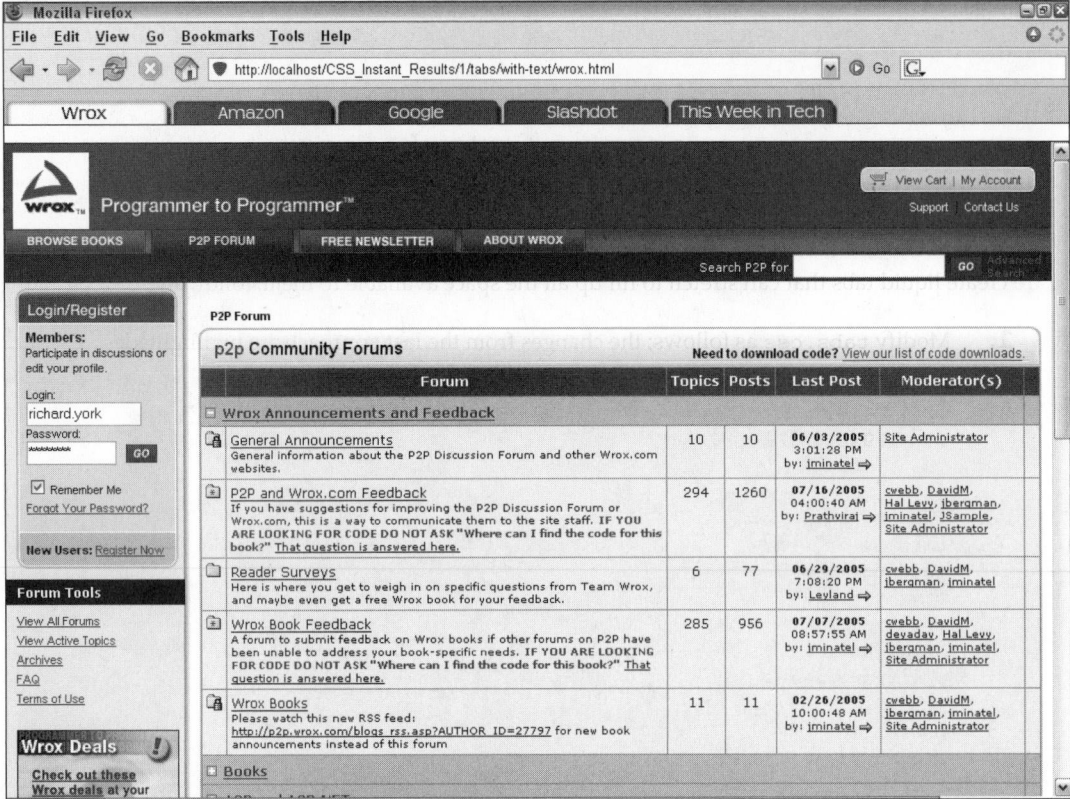

Figure 1-6

```
ul#tabs li#tab1 {
    background: transparent url('images/wrox-tab.png') no-repeat scroll top;
}
ul#tabs li#tab1:hover,
body#wrox li#tab1 {
    background: transparent url('images/wrox-tab-hover.png') no-repeat scroll top;
}
```

The former snippet from the style sheet is the background images of the first tab, which links to the Wrox P2P web site. First you remove the `background` declaration from the `ul#tabs li` rule, then beginning with the former snippet separate rules are defined for all five tabs, because all five tabs now have the text of the tab in the background image itself.

Later in the style sheet, in order to preserve accessibility, the text of each tab that appears in the `<span>` elements nested within each tab is made invisible:

```
ul#tabs span {
    display: block;
    padding: 4px 10px 0 10px;
    visibility: hidden;
}
```

Making the text invisible hides it from the end user, but because search robots like Googlebot and screen readers like JAWS do not yet support CSS, the text is still "visible" to search engines and screen readers, which preserves accessibility.

The final approach demonstrates how to make the tabs liquid, so that they stretch and contract in response to minimum and maximum constraints.

Liquid Tabs

To create liquid tabs that can stretch to fill up all the space available to them, follow these steps:

1. Modify `tabs.css` as follows; the changes from the last approach are highlighted:

```
body, html {
    margin: 0;
    padding: 0;
}
ul#tabs {
    list-style: none;
    margin: 0;
    padding: 10px 0 0 0;
    height: 23px;
    border-bottom: 1px solid black;
    background: rgb(218, 218, 218);
    position: relative;
}
ul#tabs li {
    position: absolute;
    bottom: 0;
    margin: 0;
    height: 23px;
    text-align: center;
    width: 20%;
    background: transparent url('images/tab/tab_01.png') no-repeat scroll left;
}
ul#tabs li > div {
    height: 23px;
    background: transparent url('images/tab/tab_03.png') no-repeat scroll right;
}
ul#tabs li > div > div {
    height: 23px;
    background: transparent url('images/tab/tab_02.png') repeat-x scroll center;
    margin: 0 8px 0 7px;
}
ul#tabs a {
    display: block;
    height: 100%;
    text-decoration: none;
    color: white;
    font: 14px Arial, sans-serif;
}
ul#tabs li#tab1 {
    left: 0;
```

```
}
ul#tabs li#tab2 {
    left: 20%;
}
ul#tabs li#tab3 {
    left: 40%;
}
ul#tabs li#tab4 {
    left: 60%;
}
ul#tabs li#tab5 {
    left: 80%;
}
ul#tabs li:hover,
body#wrox li#tab1,
body#amazon li#tab2,
body#google li#tab3,
body#slashdot li#tab4,
body#twit li#tab5 {
    background: transparent url('images/tab-hover/tab-hover_01.png') no-repeat
scroll left;
}
ul#tabs li:hover > div,
body#wrox li#tab1 > div,
body#amazon li#tab2 > div,
body#google li#tab3 > div,
body#slashdot li#tab4 > div,
body#twit li#tab5 > div {
    background: transparent url('images/tab-hover/tab-hover_03.png') no-repeat
scroll right;
}
ul#tabs li:hover > div > div,
body#wrox li#tab1 > div > div,
body#amazon li#tab2 > div > div,
body#google li#tab3 > div > div,
body#slashdot li#tab4 > div > div,
body#twit li#tab5 > div > div {
    background: transparent url('images/tab-hover/tab-hover_02.png') repeat-x
scroll center;
}
ul#tabs a:hover,
body#wrox li#tab1 a,
body#amazon li#tab2 a,
body#google li#tab3 a,
body#slashdot li#tab4 a,
body#twit li#tab5 a {
    color: black;
}
ul#tabs span {
    display: block;
    padding: 4px 10px 0 10px;
}
div#iframe {
```

```
    position: absolute;
    top: 0;
    bottom: 0;
    right: 0;
    left: 0;
    margin-top: 50px;
    border-top: 1px solid black;
}
iframe {
    position: absolute;
    top: 0;
    bottom: 0;
    right: 0;
    left: 0;
    width: 100%;
    height: 100%;
}
```

2. Save `tabs.css`.

3. Modify `wrox.html`, `amazon.html`, `google.html`, `slashdot.html`, and `twit.html` with the following changes:

```
<!DOCTYPE html PUBLIC "-//W3C//DTD XHTML 1.0 Transitional//EN"
"http://www.w3.org/TR/xhtml1/DTD/xhtml1-transitional.dtd">
<html xmlns='http://www.w3.org/1999/xhtml' xml:lang='en'>
    <head>
        <meta http-equiv='Content-Type' content='text/html; charset=UTF-8' />
        <title></title>
        <link rel='stylesheet' type='text/css' href='tabs.css' />
        <!-- compliance patch for microsoft browsers -->
        <!--[if lt IE 7]>
            <link rel='stylesheet' type='text/css' href='tabs-ie.css' />
            <script src="/ie7/ie7-standard-p.js" type="text/javascript"></script>
        <![endif]-->
    </head>
    <body id='wrox'>
        <ul id='tabs'>
            <li id='tab1'>
                <div><div>
                    <a href='wrox.html'><span>Wrox P2P</span></a>
                </div></div>
            </li>
            <li id='tab2'>
                <div><div>
                    <a href='amazon.html'><span>Amazon</span></a>
                </div></div>
            </li>
            <li id='tab3'>
                <div><div>
                    <a href='google.html'><span>Google</span></a>
                </div></div>
            </li>
```

```
            <li id='tab4'>
                <div><div>
                    <a href='slashdot.html'><span>Slashdot</span></a>
                </div></div>
            </li>
            <li id='tab5'>
                <div><div>
                    <a href='twit.html'><span>This Week in Tech</span></a>
                </div></div>
            </li>
        </ul>
        <div id='iframe'>
            <iframe src='http://p2p.wrox.com'
                    frameborder='0' marginheight='0' marginwidth='0'></iframe>
        </div>
    </body>
</html>
```

4. Save `wrox.html`, `amazon.html`, `google.html`, `slashdot.html`, and `twit.html`.

5. Create a new style sheet and enter the following CSS:

```
ul#tabs {
    height: 22px
}
```

6. Save the new style sheet as `tabs-ie.css`.

This approach results in the output depicted in Figure 1-7.

The last variation of the tabs project is the most complex, but it creates some flexibility because this design can easily be adapted into a project that requires minimum or maximum constraints on the element in which the tabs reside. In this example there are no minimum or maximum constraints as there would be if you had used the `min-width` or `max-width` property on the `ul#tabs` element.

The first modification made to `tabs.css` is to add a `position: relative;` declaration to the tabs `<ul>` element:

```
ul#tabs {
    list-style: none;
    margin: 0;
    padding: 10px 0 0 0;
    height: 23px;
    border-bottom: 1px solid black;
    background: rgb(218, 218, 218);
    position: relative;
}
```

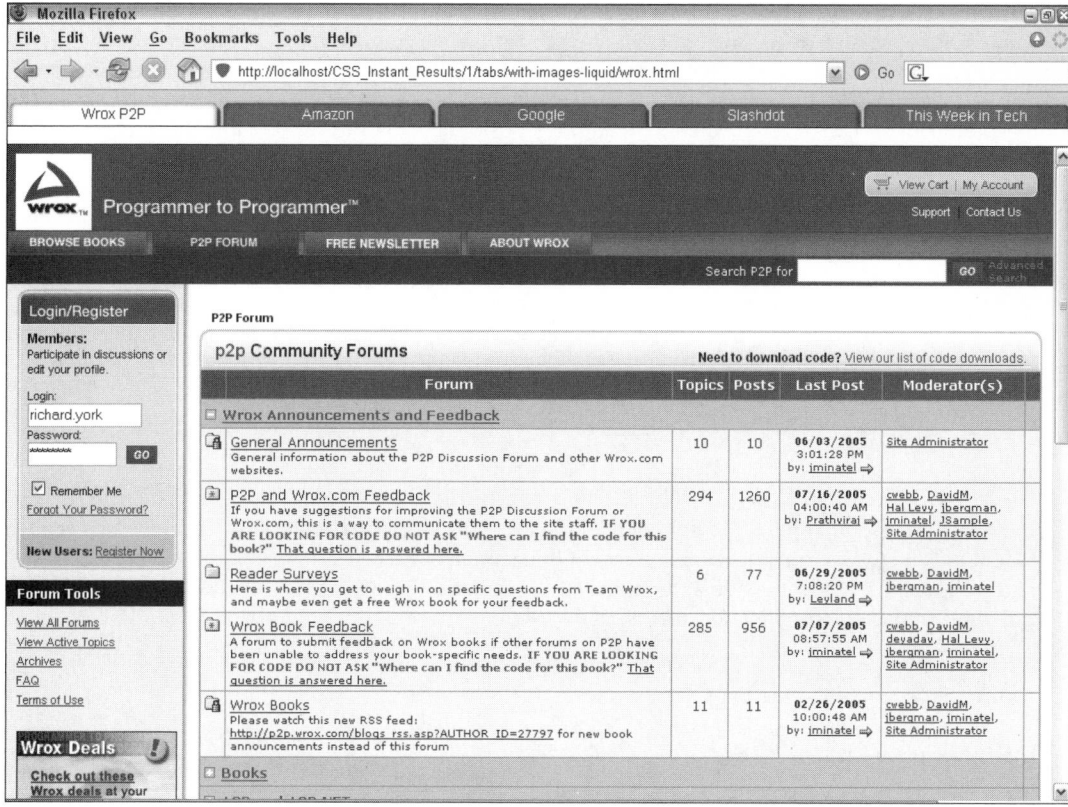

Figure 1-7

The addition of `position: relative;` causes the `<li>` elements that it contains, which are absolutely positioned, to be positioned relative to the tabs `<ul>` element. I use positioning in this approach because Explorer has some bugs with percentage width measurements. Simply applying a 20% width to each `<li>` element results in the last `<li>` element appearing on a new line in Explorer, even though 20% * 5 = 100%!

```
ul#tabs li {
    position: absolute;
    bottom: 0;
    margin: 0;
    height: 23px;
    text-align: center;
    width: 20%;
    background: transparent url('images/tab/tab_01.png') no-repeat scroll left;
}
```

The first declaration, naturally, causes the `<li>` elements to be positioned absolutely, relative to the `<ul>` element that contains them. The `bottom: 0;` declaration positions each `<li>` element relative to the bottom of the `<ul>` element that contains them. The next declaration, `width: 20%;`, makes each `<li>` element take up 20% of the width of the `<ul>` element that contains them. The bug in Explorer is defeated because each `<li>` element is absolutely positioned, and it is impossible for the fifth `<li>` element to appear on the next line.

The last declaration applies the first background image. I used the slice tool of Photoshop to cut the image into three parts. The first part is the left corner and side. The second part is the middle of the tab, and the third part is the right corner and side. The first image is applied and positioned non-repeating on the left side of each `<li>` element. Then, in order to make stretching tabs, you added some extra `<div>` elements into each of the XHTML documents, which provide hooks to place the sliced up tab:

```
ul#tabs li > div {
    height: 23px;
    background: transparent url('images/tab/tab_03.png') no-repeat scroll right;
}
```

In the next rule, you applied the right side of the tab. This is applied in the first `<div>`, which is given a height of 23 pixels to mirror the `<li>` element that contains it. The right side of the tab is then applied and positioned on the right side of the first `<div>` element. The next `<div>` element is nested inside of the last one; this one contains the middle of the tab:

```
ul#tabs li > div > div {
    height: 23px;
    background: transparent url('images/tab/tab_02.png') repeat-x scroll center;
    margin: 0 8px 0 7px;
}
```

It is also given a height of 23 pixels, to mirror the dimensions of the `<div>` and `<li>` elements that contain it. The background is applied to the center of the `<div>` element and set to repeat on the x axis, or horizontally. Finally, in the last declaration, to control overlapping, you apply left and right margins to the `<div>` equal to the width of the left and right tab slices, respectively.

The next five rules set the horizontal position of each `<li>` element:

```
ul#tabs li#tab1 {
    left: 0;
}
ul#tabs li#tab2 {
    left: 20%;
}
ul#tabs li#tab3 {
    left: 40%;
}
ul#tabs li#tab4 {
    left: 60%;
}
ul#tabs li#tab5 {
    left: 80%;
}
```

Each tab is positioned to the left relative to the containing `<ul>` element in increasing increments of 20% (20% being relative to the width of the containing `<ul>` element).

Finally, the layering technique for each tab slice is repeated for the tab of the currently loaded page and when the user hovers over a tab:

```
ul#tabs li:hover,
body#wrox li#tab1,
body#amazon li#tab2,
body#google li#tab3,
body#slashdot li#tab4,
body#twit li#tab5 {
    background: transparent url('images/tab-hover/tab-hover_01.png') no-repeat
scroll left;
}
ul#tabs li:hover > div,
body#wrox li#tab1 > div,
body#amazon li#tab2 > div,
body#google li#tab3 > div,
body#slashdot li#tab4 > div,
body#twit li#tab5 > div {
    background: transparent url('images/tab-hover/tab-hover_03.png') no-repeat
scroll right;
}
ul#tabs li:hover > div > div,
body#wrox li#tab1 > div > div,
body#amazon li#tab2 > div > div,
body#google li#tab3 > div > div,
body#slashdot li#tab4 > div > div,
body#twit li#tab5 > div > div {
    background: transparent url('images/tab-hover/tab-hover_02.png') repeat-x
scroll center;
}
```

This time only the background image needs to be changed, of course, because this technique takes advantage of the cascade to replace the background of the tab for the currently loaded page, and when the user hovers over a tab.

You also modified the markup of each document to reference a conditional comment style sheet that only Internet Explorer can see:

```
<!--[if lt IE 7]>
    <link rel='stylesheet' type='text/css' href='tabs-ie.css' />
    <script src='/ie7/ie7-standard-p.js' type='text/javascript'></script>
<![endif]-->
```

The style sheet is referenced within Internet Explorer–proprietary conditional comments, which provides a way to serve up style sheet fixes for Internet Explorer exclusively.

Within this style sheet you entered a single rule:

```
ul#tabs {
    height: 22px
}
```

The preceding rule corrects a space 1 pixel in height that appears below the tabs.

Having discussed four different approaches to designing tabs with XHTML and CSS, the next chapter shows you how to create multi-column designs with XHTML and CSS.

Multi-column Layouts

This chapter presents all the necessary code to create functioning, cross-browser compatible multi-column layouts with XHTML and CSS. In the world of web development, the single most compelling argument for CSS, as opposed to presentational HTML that's dependent on table-based layout, is that browser support for multi-column layouts using simple XHTML and CSS is reasonably good, especially the fifth-generation browsers of the Microsoft and Netscape families onward. Mozilla, being born of Netscape, has always been a robust standards-compliant browser, because it was designed that way from its inception (early versions of Mozilla were quite buggy, but standards-oriented nonetheless). Opera, Konqueror, and Safari (which is based on Konqueror) boast excellent support in this arena as well.

There are some quirks, however, with Microsoft Internet Explorer in particular, and if you aren't familiar with those quirks, creating a functioning multi-column layout with XHTML and CSS can be a daunting undertaking. In this chapter you see how to work around those quirks using all the tools available at the time of this writing, and in addition you learn how to create a multi-column design that will reach the largest audience possible.

Before presenting the tools necessary, you need to understand what it is you want to achieve. In general, you need a multi-column layout that works across the board in Internet Explorer 5.5, 6, and 7, Mozilla 1.7, Firefox 1.0, Firefox 1.1, Safari 1.2, and Opera 8. In addition to the former, overall design goal, the following specific goals must be met:

❑ The layout must stretch to accommodate the longest column on the page, and each column must be the same length.

❑ The footer cannot be overlapped by any column.

❑ The main content must be fluid, stretching to a larger width for larger screen resolutions and shrinking to fit smaller screen resolutions.

Initially, the task seems simple enough. I choose the latest versions of less-popular browsers because users of these browsers tend to update to the latest version as soon as it's available, although the design may work just as well in earlier versions of those browsers. All of the goals outlined here are achievable with the current capabilities of CSS.

The next section discusses what to consider for the design of the markup and what CSS is most suited for accomplishing the tasks at hand.

Design

The design of a multi-column layout, in terms of markup, is relatively straightforward. The design is much more flexible than any table-based design and allows far more style sheet possibilities. For example, the design allows you to move columns, if necessary, without modifying the markup. The design also allows you to offer alternative style sheets (for instance, different skins and even variations in the physical placement of each column), if the browser provides alternative style sheet functionality. This project uses simple, generic <div> elements to enclose each column, and a container <div> that wraps around all of the content (you see what this looks like in the next section). I am avoiding the use of tables for layout, because they don't offer the same flexibility that <div> elements do, even though I could use tables and face far fewer quirks in Internet Explorer's CSS support.

In terms of CSS, a few properties are essential for this design to succeed. Where the columns are concerned two approaches exist to create multi-column layouts: positioning and floating. This chapter focuses on the positioning method, because it offers fewer caveats than floating — and because you are essentially creating layers, absolute positioning is the right tool for the job. Later in the chapter, you learn how to modify the style sheet to use the floating method, and what caveats to consider when taking that approach.

Corresponding CSS properties will enable you to meet the design goals:

❑ **The layout must stretch to accommodate the longest column on the page, and each column must be the same length.** You must decide which columns are going to be the longest. Typically, this will be the column containing the web page's content. The other columns are more likely to be associated with navigation or information, and by design these won't grow as long as the content column is likely to grow. Therefore, the focus is on how to stretch the secondary columns to the length of the content column. Because each column is positioned absolutely (and relative to the <div> element that encloses all of the columns), with the exception of the content column, which is positioned statically (more on this in the next paragraph), CSS offers two methods of making those columns as long as the content column: percentage height and implying height via the presence of both the top and bottom offset properties. Which of these methods is better suited depends on whether or not the secondary columns must have padding, margin, or borders. Because percentage height is based on the height of the parent element of the element it is applied to, margin, borders, and padding are added in addition to the parent element's height. With the latter method — using both the top and bottom offset properties — the height of the element will be whatever space is left over after margin, borders, and padding are applied. As far as browser support is concerned, Internet Explorer supports neither method on absolutely positioned elements, so regardless of the method chosen, a hack must be supplied to Internet Explorer. For the utmost compatibility with future changes in the design, I opt for the top and bottom method of defining secondary column heights.

The previous paragraph mentioned that the secondary columns are positioned absolutely, relative to the containing <div>, and the content column is positioned statically; that is, it remains in the normal flow of the document with no positioning applied. This approach forces the containing <div> element to grow with the content of the document, and because the containing <div> grows, this also allows a point of reference for the secondary columns to retrieve their height from the methods mentioned in the preceding paragraph, thus allowing the second goal to be achieved. Overlapping between the secondary columns and the content column is prevented by applying left or right margins (or both) to the content column that are equal to the widths of the secondary columns.

❏ **The footer cannot be overlapped by any column.** In this project the footer is placed after the containing `<div>` element, which prevents overlapping in most situations. In the event that the secondary columns are longer than the content column, the secondary columns will overlap the footer. To prevent this, you must determine the longest possible length of the secondary columns, and define a minimum height on the containing `<div>` element equal to that length. Essentially, the containing `<div>` will always be as long as the longest secondary column to prevent footer overlapping.

❏ **The main content must be fluid and stretch to a larger width for larger screen resolutions and shrink to fit smaller screen resolutions.** This goal will be achieved via the `minimum` and `maximum` width properties that CSS provides. An upper constraint and a lower constraint will be provided to the style sheet so that the content gracefully accommodates larger or smaller screen resolutions.

The single biggest challenge for the project at this point is that Internet Explorer 5.5 and 6 support almost none of the strategic CSS required to meet the design goals just outlined in the preceding paragraphs — at least not in standard form. Two options are available to accommodate Internet Explorer 5.5 and 6. The first is Dean Edwards' IE7 JavaScript, which implements the required CSS in IE 5.5 and 6. This is done by including a small JavaScript file wrapped in Explorer-proprietary conditional comments. The second option is to use a few Explorer-proprietary CSS features. You see both methods in this project.

Now that you've seen some of the most important aspects of the project's design, you're ready for the source code for the project.

Code and Code Explanation

This section presents the underlying code that is required to create a multi-column layout in the manner described in the previous section. Later you see how to modify the project to accommodate alternative approaches in design and how the design can be altered to accommodate more or fewer columns.

First you see the XHTML markup, although XHTML is not a requirement — the same result can be achieved with HTML 4.01–compliant markup. Follow these steps to create a bare-bones multi-column layout design:

1. Enter the following markup. Alternatively, you can find this example on the book's web site and in the source CD-ROM accompanying this book in the Chapter 2 folder, named `multi-column .html`.

```
<!DOCTYPE html PUBLIC "-//W3C//DTD XHTML 1.0 Strict//EN"
"http://www.w3.org/TR/xhtml1/DTD/xhtml1-strict.dtd">
<html xmlns='http://www.w3.org/1999/xhtml' xml:lang='en'>
    <head>
        <meta http-equiv="Content-Type" content="text/html; charset=UTF-8" />
        <title></title>
        <link rel='stylesheet' type='text/css' href='multi-column.css' />
        <!-- compliance patch for microsoft browsers -->
        <!--[if lt IE 7]>
            <link rel='stylesheet' type='text/css' href='multi-column-ie.css' />
            <script src="/ie7/ie7-standard-p.js" type="text/javascript"></script>
```

```
            <![endif]-->
    </head>
    <body>
        <div id='header'>
            <h1>Header</h1>
        </div>
        <div id='container'>
            <div id='first-column'>
                Text in the first column.
            </div>
            <div id='content'>
                Text in the content column.
            </div>
            <div id='third-column'>
                Text in the third column.
            </div>
        </div>
        <div id='footer'>
            <h6>Footer</h6>
        </div>
    </body>
</html>
```

2.   Save the file as `multi-column.html`.

There is nothing extraordinary or particularly exciting in the markup, just standard XHTML 1.0. The headers reference two style sheets and Dean Edwards' IE7 JavaScript. The first style sheet is for all browsers to read. The second style sheet appears in Microsoft-proprietary conditional comments; a feature that only works in Internet Explorer and can be used to segregate Internet Explorer–specific bug-fixes from the normal styles.

3.   The first style sheet contains the following rules. In the source CD-ROM, this file is called `multi-column.css`:

```
body {
    background: white;
    font-family: sans-serif;
    margin: 0;
    padding: 0;
}
h1, h6 {
    margin: 0;
    font-weight: normal;
}
div#container {
    position: relative;
    min-height: 400px;
    border: 1px solid gray;
    background: lightgrey;
    max-width: 1000px;
    min-width: 750px;
    margin: auto;
}
div#first-column,
div#third-column {
```

```
        position: absolute;
        top: 0;
        bottom: 0;
        border: 1px solid gray;
        background: rgb(240, 240, 240);
        width: 200px;
        margin: 3px;
}
div#first-column {
        left: 0;
}
div#third-column {
        right: 0;
}
div#content {
        margin: 3px 208px 3px 208px;
        background: rgb(240, 240, 240);
        border: 1px solid gray;
        min-height: 392px;
}
div#header,
div#footer {
        background: rgb(240, 240, 240);
        padding: 3px;
        border: 1px solid gray;
        max-width: 994px;
        min-width: 744px;
        margin: auto;
}
div#header {
        border-bottom: none;
}
div#footer {
        border-top: none;
}
```

4. Save this file as `multi-column.css`.

5. For the conditional comment style sheet, add the following:

```
div#content {
        position: relative;
        top: 3px
}
```

6. Save this file as `multi-column-ie.css`.

The resulting output should appear as it does in Figure 2-1 in Mozilla Firefox.

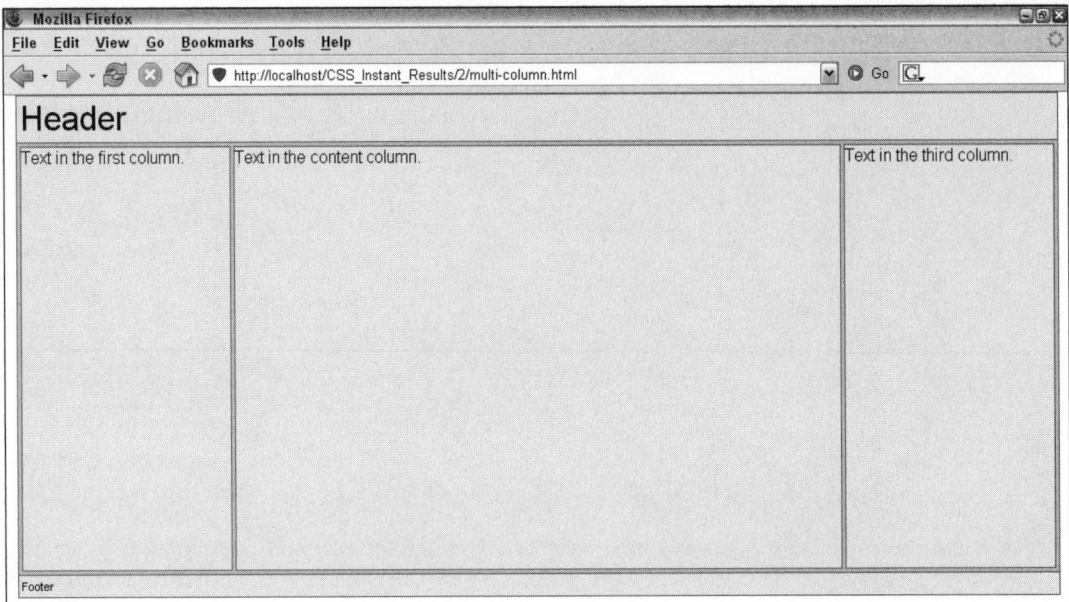

Figure 2-1

Although the first rule has no real impact on the project, it is necessary for several reasons:

```
body {
    background: white;
    font-family: sans-serif;
    margin: 0;
    padding: 0;
}
```

First, a background color is specified for the document. This is important because users may customize their operating system or browser and specify a background color that may clash with the design. By applying a background to the entire body, this is avoided. In the second declaration a font is specified. Here again the user may have a completely different font specified than the font used by the developer's browser. By specifying a specific font, in this case generic sans-serif, you avoid the possibility of the user having a different font specified. Finally, you remove any default margin or padding from the `<body>` element, which improves cross-browser consistency because different browsers may have different default values for margin or padding on the `<body>` element.

In the next rule you remove the default margin and make the font normal instead of bold for the `<h1>` and `<h6>` elements, which contain the page heading and footer text, respectively:

```
h1, h6 {
    margin: 0;
    font-weight: normal;
}
```

Here again, you do the preceding to avoid the default browser margin and font to make the design more consistent from browser to browser, and for this project, you don't happen to want any margin or bold-faced font on these elements.

The next rule defines styles for the containing <div> element that houses the three columns:

```
div#container {
    position: relative;
    min-height: 400px;
    border: 1px solid gray;
    background: lightgrey;
    max-width: 1000px;
    min-width: 750px;
    margin: auto;
}
```

First you give the containing <div> element a relative position, so the absolutely positioned columns within the containing <div> will position relative to the containing <div>, rather than relative to the browser's viewport. You give the containing <div> element a min-height property next; the measurement provided — 400px — is just a guess because you have no way of knowing how long the longest absolutely positioned column is likely to be. As the project progresses, you can adjust the minimum height defined here to accommodate longer secondary columns and avoid them overlapping with the footer. Next, a border and background are specified to clarify the dimensions of the container, though this is not necessary and can be changed should the aesthetic design take a different direction. After the border and background have been specified, minimum and maximum widths are specified, which prevent the content from getting stretched too thin when viewed on high-resolution monitors, and also prevents the design from contracting too much when viewed on low-resolution monitors. Finally, the last declaration centers the block in the viewport. This is not a necessary addition because the content can be left or right aligned if necessary.

The next rule defines the styles of the secondary columns, which are given id names of first-column and third-column. In a real-world project I recommend giving your columns more meaningful names, such as "navigation" or "adverts," something that describes the purpose of the element more transparently:

```
div#first-column,
div#third-column {
    position: absolute;
    top: 0;
    bottom: 0;
    border: 1px solid gray;
    background: rgb(240, 240, 240);
    width: 200px;
    margin: 3px;
}
```

The two columns are given absolute positions, which means they leave the normal flow of the document and occupy space along the z-axis, instead of purely the x- and y-axis, as is the case with static positioning. This rule contains styles that are shared by both columns. The top: 0; and bottom: 0; declarations cause each column to stretch to the height of the containing <div> element. That height is the space left over after margin, borders, and padding have been applied. Next, here again a border and background are specified to clarify the dimensions of the two columns. Then both columns are given a fixed width of 200 pixels. This is done because in designs such as this one it is not possible to create columns that can shrink and grow with increases in screen real estate. The crux of this concerns how the content column is styled. The content column is given left and right margins equal to the width of the two secondary columns, and in order for the secondary columns to grow and shrink with minimum and maximum constraints, there would also need to be minimum and maximum margins on the content <div>, which is something that CSS does not currently offer. Alternatively, percentage width can be applied to the columns, and percentage margins applied to the content <div>, which will achieve a similar effect, but still without the possibility of defining minimum and maximum constraints, which are often desired on liquid designs to prevent the design from breaking. Percentage width also makes it more difficult to apply borders, padding, and margin directly to the columns. If this is desired, another <div> can be placed within each column, and the borders, padding, and margin can be applied to those. You see an example of this in the section "Using and Modifying This Project" later in this chapter.

The next rule positions each column to the left and right of the content, respectively:

```css
div#first-column {
    left: 0;
}
div#third-column {
    right: 0;
}
```

The rule after these defines styles for the content column:

```css
div#content {
    margin: 3px 208px 3px 208px;
    background: rgb(240, 240, 240);
    border: 1px solid gray;
    min-height: 392px;
}
```

The first declaration specifies margin, which is the most important declaration in this rule, because it prevents the content from begin overlapped by the left and right columns. Here, 3 pixels of margin are applied to the top and bottom, as was applied to the left and column, and 208 pixels of margin are applied to the left and right sides of the columns, which is equal to the width, borders, padding, and margins of the left and right columns. Additionally, a background and a border are specified to clarify the dimensions of the content column. Finally, a minimum height is specified, so that the height of the content column is always equal to the height of the left and right columns, even when there isn't enough content to fill it.

The subsequent rule defines styles for the heading and footer <div> elements:

```css
div#header,
div#footer {
    background: rgb(240, 240, 240);
    padding: 3px;
    border: 1px solid gray;
    max-width: 994px;
    min-width: 744px;
    margin: auto;
}
```

A background, padding, and border are specified for aesthetic consistency. Then as was done for the container <div>, a minimum and maximum width is specified for the header and footer <div> elements, but because padding is specified the measurement is 6 pixels less than it was for the containing <div> element. Lastly, the blocks are centered with the margin: auto; declaration.

Finally, the last rule adjusts the borders on the heading and footer elements, removing the bottom border of the header <div> and the top border of the footer <div>:

```
div#header {
    border-bottom: none;
}
div#footer {
    border-top: none;
}
```

The next section describes the caveats associated with this design.

Testing and Caveats

In this section you take the completed project as it now fully functions in Firefox and test it in Internet Explorer 5.5 and 6 and see what caveats, if any, exist for the project.

As with any web development project, I always approach a project from the standpoint of standards first, and then work in hacks for specific browsers only when necessary, and only using the least invasive approach possible. This allows me to create a standard web document that is likely to work well or degrade gracefully in the majority of browsers. However, I cannot ignore the browser with the largest market share, Internet Explorer. Out of the box, IE 5.5 and 6 fail to meet my design goals, although it is still functional and viewable even despite Explorer's CSS limitations. But, not content with shoddy rendering in Explorer, I decided to apply Dean Edwards' IE7 JavaScript. For this project, Edwards' JavaScript implements several important CSS features that otherwise wouldn't work in Internet Explorer. Those features are as follows:

❑   The min-width, max-width, and min-height properties

❑   Using the top and bottom offset properties to imply height on the secondary columns

Other methods of working around non-support of these properties exist (and they are discussed in the next section), but Edwards' IE7 JavaScript is very small in file size (about 24KB!) and very fast. By applying the IE7 JavaScript, you come very close to what Firefox and Opera give you in the output in Internet Explorer. In the markup you reference Edwards' IE7 JavaScript and a style sheet:

```
<!-- compliance patch for microsoft browsers -->
<!--[if lt IE 7]>
    <link rel='stylesheet' type='text/css' href='multi-column-ie.css' />
    <script src='/ie7/ie7-standard-p.js' type='text/javascript'></script>
<![endif]-->
```

These are enclosed in Microsoft-proprietary conditional comments, which prevents browsers other than the versions of Internet Explorer specified from seeing the content enclosed. The condition is if the version of Internet Explorer is less than version 7, include the markup appearing in the comments. Conditional comments let you target Internet Explorer specifically, but other browsers ignore the conditional comments, and see the content within them as HTML comments.

The only inconsistency that remains after applying the IE7 JavaScript is that there is not 3 pixels of margin between the top border of the content <div> and the top border of the containing <div>. This is fixed with a conditional comment style sheet. The contents of the conditional comment style sheet are as follows:

```
div#content {
    position: relative;
    top: 3px
}
div#first-column {
    top: 3px;
}
div#third-column {
    bottom: 3px;
}
div#container {
    margin-top: -3px;
    margin-bottom: -3px;
}
```

Only three rules appear in the style sheet, which is named multi-column-ie.css. The content <div> is given a relative position, and then is offset from the top 3 pixels to correct the spacing problem in Internet Explorer. Then two rules are applied to correct the position of the first and third columns, the first column is offset from the top 3 pixels, and the third column is offset from the bottom 3 pixels. Finally, the margins of the container <div> element are adjusted minus 3 pixels on the top and bottom. The result of these modifications is output that is consistent with that seen in Mozilla Firefox.

As the style sheet becomes more complex, it may be necessary to add other rules to correct minor inconsistencies in Internet Explorer, but for the most part the IE7 JavaScript is spot on.

Figure 2-2 shows the output of the project in Internet Explorer 6 before applying Edwards' IE7 JavaScript and conditional comment style sheet.

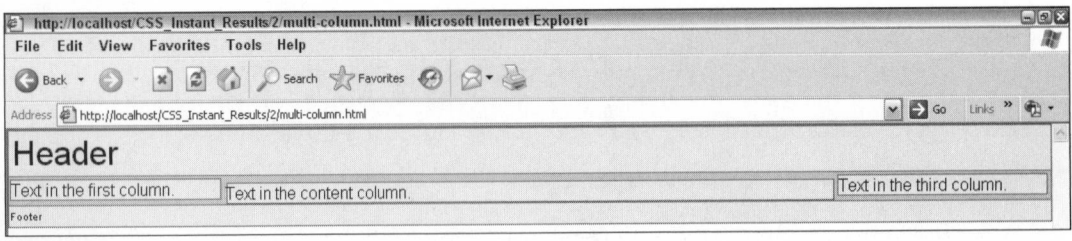

Figure 2-2

Figure 2-3 shows the output of the project in Internet Explorer 6 after applying the IE7 JavaScript and conditional comment style sheet.

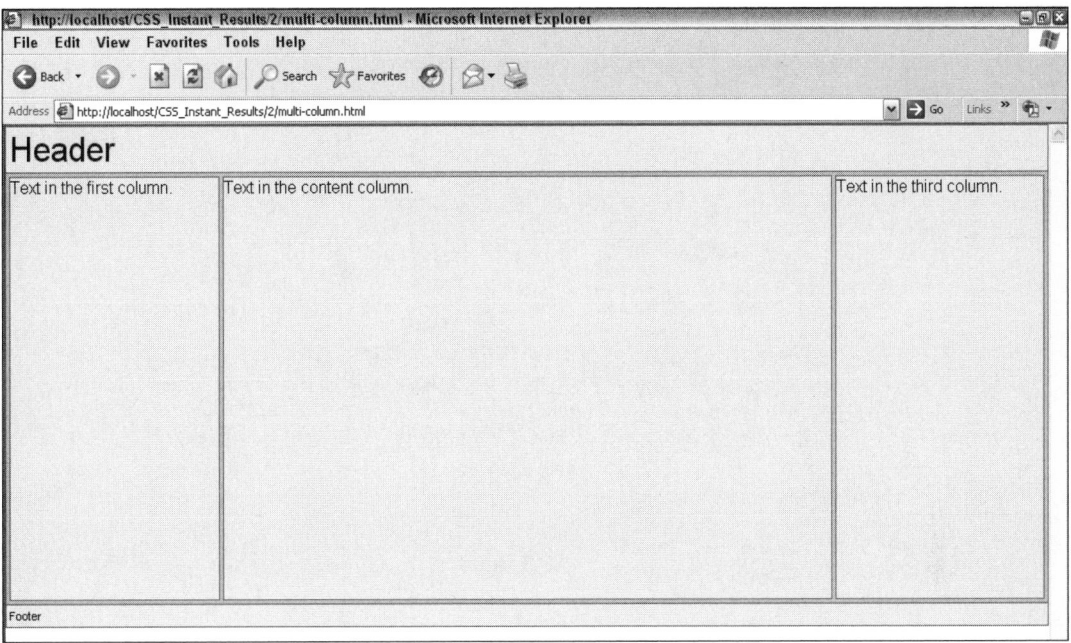

Figure 2-3

The next section describes how to modify the project.

Using and Modifying this Project

The concept design presented in the previous sections is ready to be implemented as it stands. Various aspects of the layout can be altered to suit your project's needs. This section covers how to modify the project in the following ways:

❑ A two column layout

❑ Liquid secondary columns, as opposed to fixed-width columns

❑ The float method, as opposed to the positioning method already presented

❑ Internet Explorer 5.5 and 6 compatibility without Edwards' IE7 JavaScript

Covering every conceivable variation that a designer might envision would be impossible. I have chosen the top four most likely variants in the design. The first is the easiest to implement, a simple two-column layout. Most designers would see how this is done immediately, but for the sake of completeness, the next section reiterates the steps to take to create a two-column layout from the original design.

Two-Column Layout

For a two-column layout there are only a few subtractions to make from the original design. The steps required to create a two-column layout are as follows:

1. Eliminate the third column from the markup, so that it appears as it does here:

```
<!DOCTYPE html PUBLIC "-//W3C//DTD XHTML 1.0 Strict//EN"
"http://www.w3.org/TR/xhtml1/DTD/xhtml1-strict.dtd">
<html xmlns='http://www.w3.org/1999/xhtml' xml:lang='en'>
    <head>
        <meta http-equiv="Content-Type" content="text/html; charset=UTF-8" />
        <title></title>
        <link rel='stylesheet' type='text/css' href='two-column.css' />
        <!-- compliance patch for microsoft browsers -->
        <!--[if lt IE 7]>
            <link rel='stylesheet' type='text/css' href='two-column-ie.css' />
            <script src="/ie7/ie7-standard-p.js" type="text/javascript"></script>
        <![endif]-->
    </head>
    <body>
        <div id='header'>
            <h1>Header</h1>
        </div>
        <div id='container'>
            <div id='first-column'>
                Text in the first column.
            </div>
            <div id='content'>
                Text in the content column.
            </div>
        </div>
        <div id='footer'>
            <h6>Footer</h6>
        </div>
    </body>
</html>
```

2. Save the file as `two-column.html`.

3. Remove the references to the third column from the style sheet, and set the right margin of the content `<div>` element to 3 pixels instead of 208 pixels. The resulting style sheet should look like this:

```
body {
    background: white;
    font-family: sans-serif;
    margin: 0;
    padding: 0;
}
h1, h6 {
    margin: 0;
    font-weight: normal;
}
div#container {
    position: relative;
```

```
        min-height: 400px;
        border: 1px solid gray;
        background: lightgrey;
        max-width: 1000px;
        min-width: 750px;
        margin: auto;
    }
    div#first-column {
        position: absolute;
        top: 0;
        bottom: 0;
        border: 1px solid gray;
        background: rgb(240, 240, 240);
        width: 200px;
        margin: 3px;
    }
    div#first-column {
        left: 0;
    }
    div#content {
        margin: 3px 3px 3px 208px;
        background: rgb(240, 240, 240);
        border: 1px solid gray;
        min-height: 392px;
    }
    div#header,
    div#footer {
        background: rgb(240, 240, 240);
        padding: 3px;
        border: 1px solid gray;
        max-width: 994px;
        min-width: 744px;
        margin: auto;
    }
    div#header {
        border-bottom: none;
    }
    div#footer {
        border-top: none;
    }
```

4. Save the style sheet as `two-column.css`.

5. Create a copy of the conditional comment style sheet, from the original `multi-column-ie.css` file and name it `two-column-ie.css`. It should contain the following rules:

```
    div#content {
        position: relative;
        top: 3px
    }
    div#first-column {
        top: 3px;
    }
    div#container {
        margin-top: -3px;
        margin-bottom: -3px;
    }
```

This variation of the design is depicted in Figure 2-4.

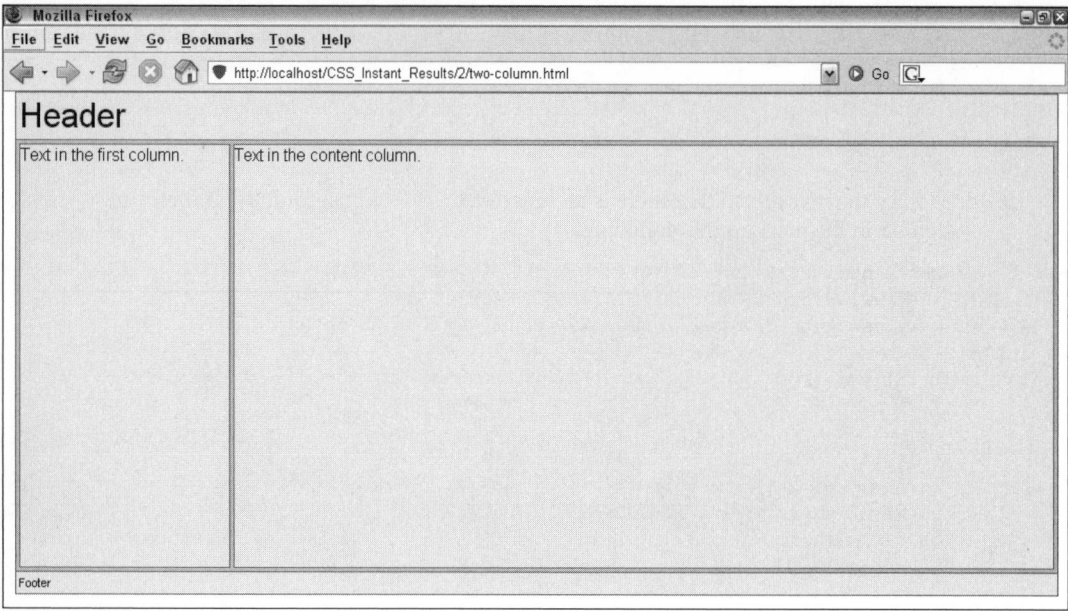

Figure 2-4

Figure 2-4 shows that the two-column design has been achieved. That's it! The two-column variation of this project appears in the accompanying source code as `two-column.html`, `two-column.css`, and `two-column-ie.css`, respectively.

Liquid Secondary Columns

Next you learn how to create liquid secondary columns. This feat is not immediately easy to pull off, and it's one that may not meet the design goals of all projects wishing to incorporate liquid secondary columns. First, here are the caveats of this approach:

❑ It is not possible to set upper and lower constraints on the width of the secondary columns while using a liquid approach, because CSS does not allow upper and lower constraints on the margin of the content `<div>`, which must be equal to the width of the secondary columns.

❑ In order to use borders, padding, and margin on the columns themselves, more markup must be inserted into the columns. This is because the width used for the secondary columns will be a percentage width, and the margins of the content `<div>` must have the same width. Unfortunately CSS does not allow expressions in the style sheet — at least not as part of the official standard. That is, you cannot write 25% + 2px as a value for the margin property. (This is covered in more depth later in this section.) This would be desired if you needed to specify a border on the secondary columns themselves. To get around this, you insert more markup into the document.

*Immediately the limitations of this approach are glaring and apparent. In this particular design it may
be more appropriate to revisit table-based designs, or the table values of the* display *property of CSS,
because this type of design is much easier to pull off with tables.*

On the positive side, the secondary columns will be resizable to a given percentage, which allows these
to expand and contract with the available space.

To create liquid secondary columns, take the following steps:

1. Modify the markup so that there is an inner <div> for each secondary column (these are highlighted in the markup that follows):

```
<!DOCTYPE html PUBLIC "-//W3C//DTD XHTML 1.0 Strict//EN"
"http://www.w3.org/TR/xhtml1/DTD/xhtml1-strict.dtd">
<html xmlns='http://www.w3.org/1999/xhtml' xml:lang='en'>
    <head>
        <meta http-equiv="Content-Type" content="text/html; charset=UTF-8" />
        <title></title>
        <link rel='stylesheet' type='text/css' href='liquid-columns.css' />
        <!-- compliance patch for microsoft browsers -->
        <!--[if lt IE 7]>
            <link rel='stylesheet' type='text/css' href='liquid-columns-ie.css' />
            <script src="/ie7/ie7-standard-p.js" type="text/javascript"></script>
        <![endif]-->
    </head>
    <body>
        <div id='header'>
            <h1>Header</h1>
        </div>
        <div id='container'>
            <div id='first-column'>
                <div id='first-column-inner'>
                    Text in the first column.
                </div>
            </div>
            <div id='content'>
                Text in the content column.
            </div>
            <div id='third-column'>
                <div id='third-column-inner'>
                    Text in the third column.
                </div>
            </div>
        </div>
        <div id='footer'>
            <h6>Footer</h6>
        </div>
    </body>
</html>
```

2. Save the markup as liquid-columns.html.

3. Modify the style sheet. The necessary CSS is as follows:

```
body {
    background: white;
    font-family: sans-serif;
    margin: 0;
    padding: 0;
}
h1, h6 {
    margin: 0;
    font-weight: normal;
}
div#container {
    position: relative;
    min-height: 400px;
    border: 1px solid gray;
    background: lightgrey;
    max-width: 1000px;
    min-width: 750px;
    margin: auto;
}
div#first-column,
div#third-column {
    position: absolute;
    top: 0;
    bottom: 0;
    width: 20%;
}
div#first-column-inner,
div#third-column-inner {
    position: absolute;
    top: 0;
    bottom: 0;
    left: 0;
    right: 0;
    border: 1px solid gray;
    background: rgb(240, 240, 240);
    margin: 3px;
}
div#first-column {
    left: 0;
}
div#third-column {
    right: 0;
}
div#content {
    margin: 3px 20% 3px 20%;
    background: rgb(240, 240, 240);
    border: 1px solid gray;
    min-height: 392px;
}
div#header,
div#footer {
    background: rgb(240, 240, 240);
    padding: 3px;
    border: 1px solid gray;
```

```
        max-width: 994px;
        min-width: 744px;
        margin: auto;
}
div#header {
        border-bottom: none;
}
div#footer {
        border-top: none;
}
```

4. Save the style sheet as `liquid-columns.css`.

5. Create a copy of the original `multi-column-ie.css` conditional comment style sheet, and name it `liquid-columns-ie.css`.

This results in the output in Figure 2-5.

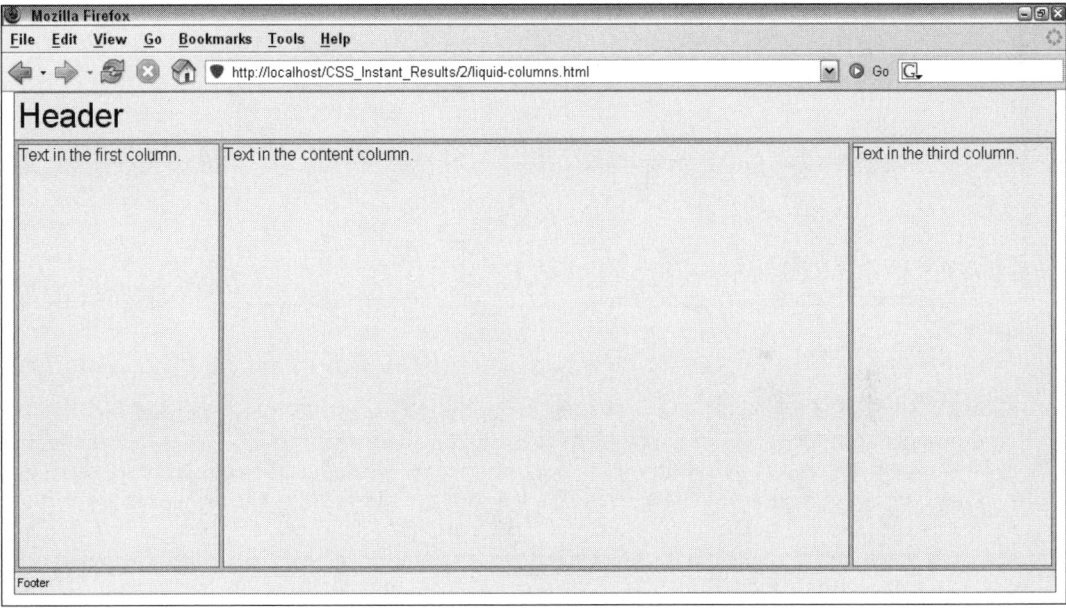

Figure 2-5

Figure 2-5 shows that the design doesn't look much different from the original multi-column design shown in Figure 2-1. The difference is that now, when the browser window is resized, the secondary columns adjust in width as the containing `<div>` is made smaller. This can be seen in Figure 2-6.

You can find this variation of the project in the accompanying source code as `liquid-columns.html`, `liquid-columns.css`, and `liquid-columns-ie.css`.

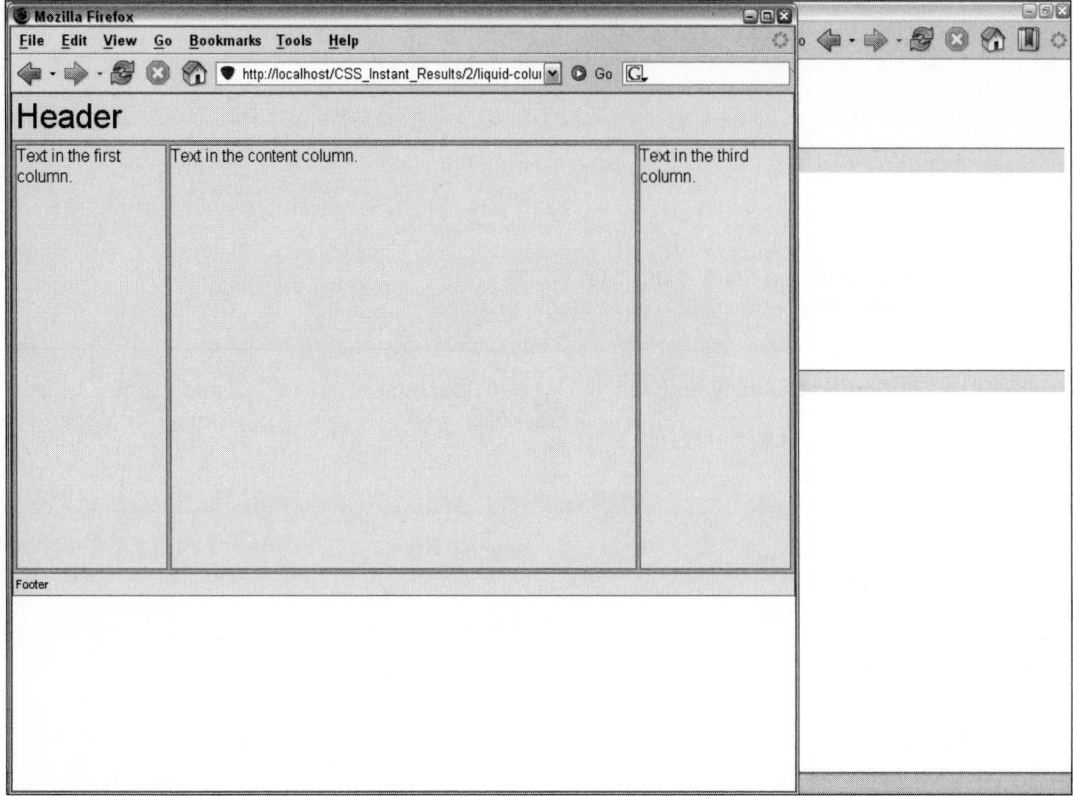

Figure 2-6

The first modification you made was to the markup of the document. To specify borders, padding, and margins on the secondary columns, a new `<div>` element was created, named first-column-inner and third-column-inner, respectively. Without the two inner `<div>` elements, the amount of space occupied by the secondary columns would have been 20% + 6 pixels of margin (left and right) and 2 pixels of border (also left and right). Because the left and right margins of the content `<div>` must equal that amount of space, and because it is impossible to specify a margin value as 20% + 8px, the inner `<div>` exists as a work-around. Now the width of the secondary columns is all that matters, and the left and right margins of the content `<div>` can simply be 20%. This becomes clearer in each of the style sheet modifications. The first is setting the width of the first-column and third-column `<div>` elements to 20%:

```
div#first-column,
div#third-column {
    position: absolute;
    top: 0;
    bottom: 0;
    width: 20%;
}
```

The next modification styles the inner-first-column and inner-third-column <div> elements:

```
div#first-column-inner,
div#third-column-inner {
    position: absolute;
    top: 0;
    bottom: 0;
    left: 0;
    right: 0;
    border: 1px solid gray;
    background: rgb(240, 240, 240);
    margin: 3px;
}
```

These are positioned absolutely, and with the top: 0; bottom: 0; left: 0; and right: 0; declarations, the width and height of the two inner <div> elements are wholly dependent on the dimensions of the first-column and third-column <div> elements, and margin, padding, borders, and background are applied to these elements rather than their parent elements, because the parent elements have percentage widths. This allows you to specify percentage margins on the content <div> element that are equal to the width of the first and third columns. The last modification ties it all together:

```
div#content {
    margin: 3px 20% 3px 20%;
    background: rgb(240, 240, 240);
    border: 1px solid gray;
    min-height: 392px;
}
```

A left and right margin of 20% is applied to the content <div> element, which is equal to the 20% width of the first-column and third-column <div> elements.

The next section covers the float method.

The Float Method

The next alternative to the multi-column design is the float method. The float method is riddled with bugs that are not easily identified without some prior experience of them. These bugs come out in a number of different scenarios; for instance, the peek-a-boo bug of Internet Explorer.

> *Most of Internet Explorer's float bugs are discussed in detail in my book* Beginning CSS: Cascading Style Sheets for Web Design *(also published by Wiley Publishing, Inc.), as well as on various web sites like* positioniseverything.net, *so I won't go into detail about bugs that don't affect the float variation of the bare-bones three-column layout presented in this chapter.*
>
> *Because the float method is susceptible to more bugs than the positioning method, I strongly recommend the positioning method over the floating method. Now that you have been warned, proceed with the float method at your own risk!*

Follow these steps to create a multi-column layout using the float method:

1. Because floating requires the elements in the document to appear in a specific order, the markup of the document must be altered. Modify the markup so that it appears as follows. The deviations from the original design are highlighted:

```
<!DOCTYPE html PUBLIC "-//W3C//DTD XHTML 1.0 Strict//EN"
"http://www.w3.org/TR/xhtml1/DTD/xhtml1-strict.dtd">
<html xmlns='http://www.w3.org/1999/xhtml' xml:lang='en'>
    <head>
        <meta http-equiv="Content-Type" content="text/html; charset=UTF-8" />
        <title></title>
        <link rel='stylesheet' type='text/css' href='float-columns.css' />
        <!-- compliance patch for microsoft browsers -->
        <!--[if lt IE 7]>
            <link rel='stylesheet' type='text/css' href='float-columns-ie.css' />
            <script src="/ie7/ie7-standard-p.js" type="text/javascript"></script>
        <![endif]-->
    </head>
    <body>
        <div id='header'>
            <h1>Header</h1>
        </div>
        <div id='container'>
            <div id='content'>
                <div id='first-column'>
                    Text in the first column.
                </div>
                <div id='third-column'>
                    Text in the third column.
                </div>
                <div id='content-inner'>
                    Text in the content column.
                </div>
            </div>
        </div>
        <div id='footer'>
            <h6>Footer</h6>
        </div>
    </body>
</html>
```

2. Save the XHTML as `float-columns.html`.

3. Modify the style sheet. Again, the deviations from the original design are highlighted, but some styles have also been subtracted. The style sheet should appear as follows:

```
body {
    background: white;
    font-family: sans-serif;
    margin: 0;
    padding: 0;
}
h1, h6 {
    margin: 0;
    font-weight: normal;
}
div#container {
```

```
    min-height: 400px;
    border: 1px solid gray;
    background: lightgrey;
    max-width: 1002px;
    min-width: 750px;
    margin: auto;
    overflow: hidden;
}
div#first-column,
div#third-column {
    width: 200px;
    border: 1px solid gray;
    background: rgb(240, 240, 240);
    min-height: 392px;
}
div#first-column {
    float: left;
    margin-left: -205px;
}
div#third-column {
    float: right;
    margin-right: -205px;
}
div#content {
    margin: 3px 208px 3px 208px;
}
div#content-inner {
    background: rgb(240, 240, 240);
    border: 1px solid gray;
    min-height: 392px;
}
div#header,
div#footer {
    background: rgb(240, 240, 240);
    padding: 3px;
    border: 1px solid gray;
    max-width: 994px;
    min-width: 744px;
    margin: auto;
}
div#header {
    border-bottom: none;
}
div#footer {
    border-top: none;
}
```

4.   Save the style sheet as `float-columns.css`.

5.   Modify the Internet Explorer conditional comment style sheet:

```
div#container {
    max-width: 1000px;
}
div#first-column,
```

```
div#third-column {
    /* Correct double-margin bug */
    display: inline;
}
div#content {
    margin: 3px 205px 3px 205px;
}
div#first-column {
    margin-left: -202px;
}
```

6. Save the conditional comment style sheet as `float-columns-ie.css`.

The preceding changes result in the screenshot shown in Figure 2-7.

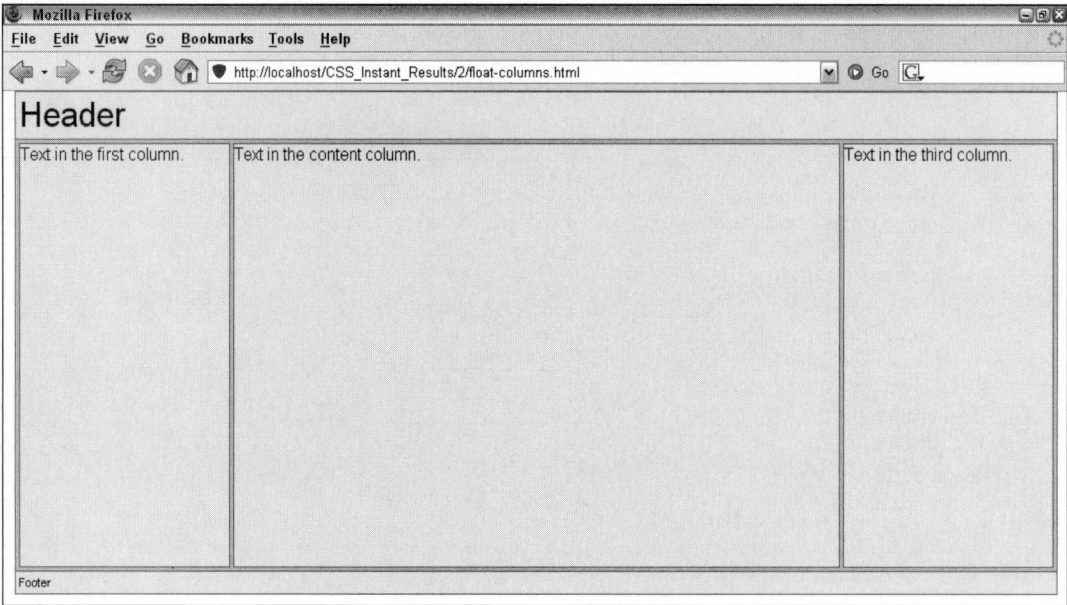

Figure 2-7

Figure 2-7 shows that the design achieved in Figure 2-1 with positioning can also be achieved with floating. This design reveals some odd bugs in Internet Explorer, which aren't easy to pinpoint. The design ensures that Internet Explorer outputs pixel for pixel the same output observed in Firefox. (You can find the source of the preceding documents on the source CD-ROM accompanying this book and on the book's web site. The documents are named `float-columns.html`, `float-columns.css`, and `float-columns-ie.css`.)

Now that you've successfully implemented the float method, the remainder of this section explains how the CSS works to achieve the results in Figure 2-7.

First the markup is altered, because a floated element must appear before the content that it is to be floated beside of. To work around several odd spacing bugs in Internet Explorer, place both elements in the content `<div>` itself:

```
<div id='content'>
    <div id='first-column'>
        Text in the first column.
    </div>
    <div id='third-column'>
        Text in the third column.
    </div>
    <div id='content-inner'>
        Text in the content column.
    </div>
</div>
```

Another <div> element is added around the content itself, which has been named content-inner. The reason for this will become obvious as each modification to the style sheet is presented.

The first modifications are made to the container <div>. A look in Firefox reveals that the width of the container element is off when compared to the header and footer <div> elements. An adjustment of 2 pixels is made:

```
div#container {
    min-height: 400px;
    border: 1px solid gray;
    background: lightgrey;
    max-width: 1002px;
    min-width: 750px;
    margin: auto;
    overflow: hidden;
}
```

The second modification in the container <div> rule is to apply an overflow: hidden; declaration. This prevents overlapping between the floated secondary columns and the footer <div>, though this may not always be desired, because this could affect other aspects of the design. If that is the case, alternatively, a clear: both; declaration can be applied to the footer <div>, and the overflow: hidden; declaration removed.

The next modification sees a min-height property applied to both secondary columns:

```
div#first-column,
div#third-column {
    width: 200px;
    border: 1px solid gray;
    background: rgb(240, 240, 240);
    min-height: 392px;
}
```

A minimum height is applied to both secondary columns to keep these the same height as the content <div>. Depending on the height of the longest possible secondary column, this, along with the minimum height for the content <div>, may need to be adjusted to prevent overlapping with the footer (if clear: both; is used), or clipped content (if overflow: hidden; is used).

The next two rules position both secondary columns into place:

```
div#first-column {
    float: left;
    margin-left: -205px;
}
div#third-column {
    float: right;
    margin-right: -205px;
}
```

The first-column <div> element is floated to the left, which of course places it to the left of the content. Likewise, the third-column <div> element is floated to the right. Then the left margin of the first-column is offset negative, which causes the element to be pulled outside of the content <div> element. The third-column <div> element is also given a negative margin, but this time on the right side. With this rule you're much closer to exactly the same output seen in Figure 2-1 with the positioning method.

The modification of the previous two rules leads directly to the next rule:

```
div#content {
    margin: 3px 208px 3px 208px;
}
```

The content <div> still must have left and right margins equal to the amount of offset provided in the previous two rules. This provides exactly 3 pixels of space between the content column, the secondary columns, and the border around the containing <div> element.

The next rule styles the content-inner <div>, which was added to separate the content from the columns, and to work around several spacing bugs in Internet Explorer. The declarations provided in this rule make the content-inner <div> element match the two columns in borders, background, and height:

```
div#content-inner {
    background: rgb(240, 240, 240);
    border: 1px solid gray;
    min-height: 392px;
}
```

Explorer's float bugs do not always have a tangible rhyme or reason to them; sometimes the only way to defeat them is to begin experimenting and tweaking. In this case I was experiencing a difference in spacing between Firefox's output and Explorer's. Explorer didn't provide exactly 3 pixels of space between the content and the columns. Tweaking the margins of the content <div> in the conditional comment style sheet for Explorer was fruitless, because it wouldn't allow the left and right margins of the content <div> to be altered via the cascade, which would have allowed me to close the gap. After a few hours of experimenting I went with a different approach to floating the columns, choosing to place both floated columns in the content <div> itself where I controlled their placement with negative margins, thus allowing me to work around the spacing bug. After doing this I realized that I was still having problems with spacing, at which point I added another <div> element to wrap the content, the inner-content <div> element, which brought me much closer to the desired result, though there were other problems — which brings me to the modifications made to the conditional comment style sheet for Explorer.

In the first rule of the conditional comment style sheet I tweak the `max-width` property again, and bring it back down to 1000 pixels. At this point this looks like a bug in Firefox, because Opera wants a 1000-pixel width on the container as well to bring the container straight and level with the header and footer `<div>` elements:

```
div#container {
    max-width: 1000px;
}
```

Another inconsistency with the float method, it seems.

The next rule I applied because as I first began shifting the positioning design to the float method, I saw that the Explorer double-margin bug was making a cameo appearance in my design:

```
div#first-column,
div#third-column {
    /* Correct double-margin bug */
    display: inline;
}
```

Later, after flip-flopping the columns into the content `<div>` and experimenting with alternative approaches to the spacing bug, I took out this declaration and the columns disappeared completely. Then I discovered the double-margin bug doubles negative margins as well! Because Explorer doubled the negative margin, and combined with the fact that I used `overflow: hidden;` on the container element, both secondary columns appear to have disappeared in Explorer. The `display: inline;` declaration corrects the deformity and brings the columns closer to their rightful homes.

The design is much closer to what Firefox is showing, but it isn't quite there. The extra space that I mentioned previously is still there. The next two rules correct the spacing issue once and for all:

```
div#content {
    margin: 3px 205px 3px 205px;
}
div#first-column {
    margin-left: -202px;
}
```

The next section covers implementing the positioning method in Internet Explorer without Dean Edwards' IE7 JavaScript.

Good, Old-Fashioned Internet Explorer Hacking

Before Dean Edwards' IE7 JavaScript came along, Internet Explorer CSS hacks were spread out and relied exclusively on a few proprietary features to do their deeds. Because of the robustness of Edwards' IE7 for CSS support, its centralization of these hacks, and its very quick speed, I strongly recommend against forsaking it in lieu of other hacks that provide the same functionality. Edwards' IE7 lets those conditional comment style sheets become much smaller and provides loads of standard CSS support that Microsoft didn't provide in its IE 5, IE 5.5, and IE 6 browsers. Edwards' IE7 is also continually evolving and getting much better at what it does, and did I mention it's really small in size? However, for the sake of presenting complete information for hacking Explorer, this section demonstrates how to implement the positioning method using raw, good, old-fashioned Explorer hacks that don't need the IE7 JavaScript to function properly.

All of the Explorer hacking presented in this section revolves around a proprietary Explorer feature called `expression()`. `expression()` can be used as a length value for any CSS property accepting a length value. It allows JScript, the Microsoft variant of ECMAScript (the standardized name for the language formerly known as JavaScript) to be called upon and executed directly from within a style sheet. To alleviate any confusion, I'll always refer to this language as JavaScript, because all of the variants are commonly called JavaScript in the real world. `expression()` makes it possible to implement maximum widths in Explorer. For minimum dimensions like `min-width` and `min-height`, there is no need for `expression()` — Explorer's implementation of the `width` and `height` CSS properties already behave like the standard `min-width` and `min-height` properties, and it's easy to exploit this behavior with a conditional comment style sheet. `expression()` is also used here to re-create in Explorer the combination of the `top` and `bottom` offset properties to imply height. There is but one drawback to this method: because it relies on JavaScript, it is not available if scripting is disabled in Explorer.

If you don't know JavaScript, don't panic. The required JavaScript is very tiny and quite straightforward to understand.

Follow these steps to create a multi-column design that functions as expected in Internet Explorer without the IE7 JavaScript:

1. Remove the reference to the IE7 JavaScript from the markup, and modify the file references to the style sheet and the conditional comment style sheet:

```
<!DOCTYPE html PUBLIC "-//W3C//DTD XHTML 1.0 Strict//EN"
"http://www.w3.org/TR/xhtml1/DTD/xhtml1-strict.dtd">
<html xmlns='http://www.w3.org/1999/xhtml' xml:lang='en'>
    <head>
        <meta http-equiv="Content-Type" content="text/html; charset=UTF-8" />
        <title></title>
        <link rel='stylesheet' type='text/css' href='hack-columns.css' />
        <!-- compliance patch for microsoft browsers -->
        <!--[if lt IE 7]>
            <link rel='stylesheet' type='text/css' href='hack-columns-ie.css' />
        <![endif]-->
    </head>
    <body id='body'>
        <div id='header'>
            <h1>Header</h1>
        </div>
        <div id='container'>
            <div id='first-column'>
                Text in the first column.
            </div>
            <div id='content'>
                Text in the content column.
            </div>
            <div id='third-column'>
                Text in the third column.
            </div>
        </div>
        <div id='footer'>
            <h6>Footer</h6>
```

```
        </div>
      </body>
   </html>
```

2. Save the resulting XHTML document as `hack-columns.html`.

3. The main style sheet remains unchanged from the original example. Create a copy of it and name it `hack-columns.css`.

4. Make the following modifications to the conditional comment style sheet:

```
div#container {
    width: expression(
        document.getElementById('body').offsetWidth > 1000?

            // If the width of the body is greater than 1000 pixels
            // set the max-width to 1000

            1000

        :
            // If the width of the body is less than 1000, perform
            // another check.

            document.getElementById('body').offsetWidth > 750?

                // If the width of the body is greater that 750 pixels,
                // but less than 1000 make it auto.

                'auto'

            :
                // If the width of the body is 750 pixels or less,
                // make the min-width of the container 750 pixels.

                750
    );
    /* In IE, height behaves like min-height */
    height: 400px;
}
div#first-column,
div#third-column {
    height: expression(
        document.getElementById('container').offsetHeight - 10
    );
}
div#content {
    position: relative;
    top: 3px;
    height: 392px;
}
div#header,
div#footer {
    width: expression(
        document.getElementById('body').offsetWidth > 994?
            994
        :
            document.getElementById('body').offsetWidth > 744?
```

```
            'auto'
       :
          744
   );
 }
```

5. Save the conditional comment style sheet as `hack-columns-ie.css`.

In the source code CD-ROM accompanying this book, the files are named `hack-columns.html`, `hack-columns.css`, and `hack-columns-ie.css`.

Loading this in Internet Explorer results in the output shown in Figure 2-8.

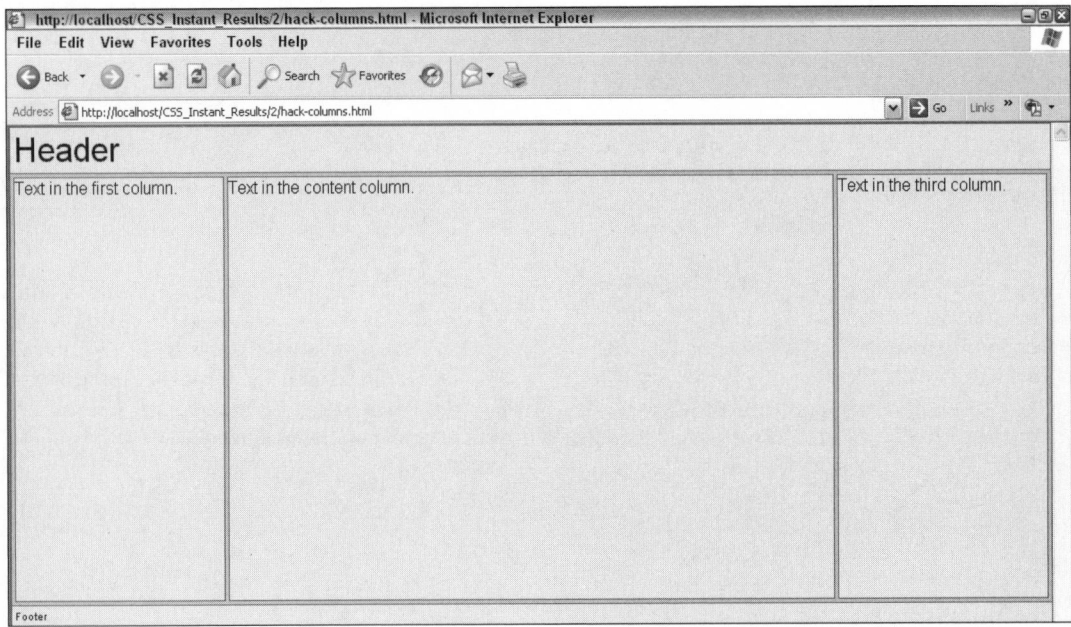

Figure 2-8

The output in Figure 2-8 is identical to the output in Figure 2-3, which shows the original positioning methods after applying Dean Edwards' IE7 JavaScript.

This approach circumvents the IE7 JavaScript and applies several well-known CSS hacks directly to Internet Explorer to compensate for its lack of support for the `min-width`, `max-width`, and `min-height` properties, as well as its non-support of using the `top` and `bottom` offset properties to imply height on absolutely positioned elements.

The first rule in the style sheet references the container `<div>` element. The first declaration is the `width` property calling on the proprietary Microsoft `expression()` feature:

```
width: expression(
    document.getElementById('body').offsetWidth > 1000?

        // If the width of the body is greater than 1000 pixels
        // set the max-width to 1000

        1000
    :
        // If the width of the body is less than or equal to 1000, perform
        // another check.

        document.getElementById('body').offsetWidth > 750?

            // If the width of the body is greater that 750 pixels,
            // but less than 1000 make it auto.

            'auto'
        :
            // If the width of the body is 750 pixels or less,
            // make the min-width of the container 750 pixels.

            750
);
```

Within the `expression()`, some JavaScript code is included to re-create (roughly) the effects of applying the standard `max-width` and `min-width` CSS properties. I say roughly, because the design won't honor the `max-width` like more standards-compliant browsers do, where if there is more content than available space the content overflows the edges of the element (this isn't really a broken sizing model in Explorer, but rather a broken implementation of `overflow: visible;`), but the element does not resize. In Explorer, the element will resize when there is more content than available space.

The following is a breakdown of the JavaScript, piece by piece.

First you call on `document.getElementById('body').offsetWidth > 1000`. `document.get ElementById('body')` refers to the element on the page that is uniquely named `'body'`. In this example, this happens to be the `<body>` element (you applied an id name of `'body'` to it, making this possible). `offsetWidth` is a Microsoft-proprietary JavaScript property that references the real width of an element. I say real width because this isn't the value of the `width` property, but rather the actual width of the element. Because width in Explorer is dynamic, the value of the `width` property may not be the real width. This property lets you reference the real width. The right angle bracket is a test for "greater than," so in whole this part of the statement is saying "if the real width of the element with an id name of `'body'` is greater than 1000 pixels. . . ." After this you see a question mark, called the *ternary operator*. Essentially, it works like this:

```
(condition)? true : false;
```

The condition combines with the question mark and colon to create a *ternary expression*. If the condition is true, the code before the colon applies. If the condition is false, the code after the colon applies. To put this in the context of the `expression()`, if the real width of the element with a `'body'` id name is greater than 1000 pixels, make its width 1000 pixels, but if it isn't greater than 1000 pixels, begin a second, nested ternary expression. In the second ternary expression you check to see if the real width of the 'body' element is greater than 750 pixels, your lower width constraint:

```
document.getElementById('body').offsetWidth > 750
```

If that width is in fact greater than 750 pixels, make the width 'auto', its default behavior. If that width is 750 pixels or less, set the width to be 750 pixels, the minimum width.

The next declaration in this rule sets a minimum height constraint:

```
/* In IE, height behaves like min-height */
height: 400px;
```

Internet Explorer's implementation of height is more like the standard min-height property. This behavior is exploited here as a minimum height of 400 pixels is applied to the container <div> element.

The next rule also makes use of the expression() feature of Explorer to re-create the combination of the top and bottom offset properties to imply height:

```
div#first-column,
div#third-column {
    height: expression(
        document.getElementById('container').offsetHeight - 10
    );
}
```

Here, like you did for the element named 'body', you are referencing the real height of the element named 'container'. This height is retrieved via the Explorer-proprietary offsetHeight property of JavaScript, and then 10 pixels are subtracted from its value. This is done to compensate for borders and margin on the secondary columns; though the real value of borders plus margins actually equals 8 pixels, 10 pixels makes the output in Explorer match that of Firefox.

The next rule you've already seen from the original conditional comment style sheet. This time it appears with one more declaration:

```
div#content {
    position: relative;
    top: 3px;
    height: 392px;
}
```

A height: 392px; declaration is added to supply a minimum height to the content <div> element.

Last, minimum and maximum dimensions are set on the header and footer <div> elements in the same manner as they were for the container <div> element:

```
div#header,
div#footer {
    width: expression(
        document.getElementById('body').offsetWidth > 994?
```

```
            994
       :

       document.getElementById('body').offsetWidth > 744?
           'auto'
       :
           744
   );
}
```

The extra spacing is applied for visual clarity — Explorer doesn't care whether the whole expression() appears on one line or on several.

Explorer's bugs are legendary, and today its hacks are becoming just as well known. In this section you've seen how Explorer's proprietary features and behaviors can be used to create a design that is in synch with its more standards-oriented brethren.

The multi-column design presented in this chapter is intended to be a feature-complete starting point for any design requiring a multi-column layout. Its aesthetic aspects are easily customized with CSS.

In the next chapter you learn how to create cross-browser, pure-CSS drop-down menus.

Dynamic Drop-Down Menus

Drop-down menus using CSS have become commonplace on today's Internet. Drop-down menus provide a quick, intuitive method of navigation, though CSS menus aren't always the most ideal or accessible solution. Later, this chapter presents some alternative approaches that make use of JavaScript to extend both the functionality and the flexibility of a drop-down navigation system while providing the capability to fall back on a CSS-only approach if JavaScript is disabled.

Drop-down menus enable a web designer to systematically categorize relevant links in a method any computer user can identify with, because such menus are implemented in virtually all computer applications.

Some hurdles exist, however, in Internet Explorer 6, which does not natively support some of the required functionality that enables a pure-CSS drop-down menu system, but as in previous chapters you get around this lack of support by putting to use Dean Edwards' IE7 JavaScript.

The CSS-based drop-down navigation system presented in this chapter was first popularized by Eric Meyer, a well-known CSS guru and author of several popular CSS books, in his famous "Pure CSS Menus" demo. The concept presented initially isn't much different from his, though later in this chapter you see some added functionality that is only possible with the application of some JavaScript.

In addition to our usual goals of cross-browser compatibility, the goals of the dynamic drop-down menu project are as follows:

- ❏ Menus must be accessible by keyboard
- ❏ Menus must open and close with a click, rather than mousing over
- ❏ Links or topics must be highlighted when mousing over

These goals and how you achieve them are discussed in the next section.

Design

In the pure-CSS version of my dynamic drop-down menu project, I rely on two specific CSS features to create interactivity: the :hover dynamic pseudo-class and the direct child ">" selector. Using these two in tandem, it becomes possible to display and hide elements when a user's mouse hovers over a specific element in a web document. For the mark-up of the document (as you did in Chapter 1 with the tabs project), you'll be using unordered lists to structure the navigation system and CSS properties like list-style to control styling of the lists.

You might be thinking to yourself that what I've just mentioned as the tools for accomplishing the project do not meet the first two goals. You're right. It is impossible to create accessible drop-down menus with CSS alone! The project you're about to see cannot meet the first two goals of the project. However, later in the chapter, in the section titled "Using and Modifying the Code," you see how the drop-down menu project can be coupled with JavaScript to meet the first two design goals, and fall back on the CSS-driven approach only when JavaScript is disabled in the user's browser.

The next section discusses the CSS-driven approach for drop-down menus.

Code and Code Explanation

To create pure-CSS drop-down menus, follow these steps. The source code for this example is available on the accompanying CD-ROM in the Project 3 folder, as drop_down_menus.html and drop_down_menus.css, respectively.

1. Enter the following markup in your text editor:

```
<!DOCTYPE html PUBLIC "-//W3C//DTD XHTML 1.0 Strict//EN"
"http://www.w3.org/TR/xhtml1/DTD/xhtml1-strict.dtd">
<html xmlns='http://www.w3.org/1999/xhtml' xml:lang='en'>
    <head>
        <meta http-equiv="Content-Type" content="text/html; charset=UTF-8" />
        <title>Top sites all CSS developers should know about</title>
        <link rel='stylesheet' type='text/css' href='drop_down_menus.css' />
    </head>
    <body>
        <ul class='menu'>
            <li class='menu'>
                <a href='http://p2p.wrox.com'>Wrox P2P</a>
                <ul>
                    <li>
                        <a href='http://p2p.wrox.com/forum.asp?FORUM_ID=151'>
                            Beginning CSS: Cascading Style Sheets for Web Design
                        </a>
                    </li>
                    <li>
                        <a href='http://p2p.wrox.com/forum.asp?FORUM_ID=143'>
                            CSS
                        </a>
                    </li>
                    <li>
                        <a href='http://p2p.wrox.com/forum.asp?FORUM_ID=84'>
                            HTML Code Clinic
```

```
                        </a>
                    </li>
                </ul>
            </li>
            <li><a href='http://www.google.com'>Google</a></li>
            <li class='menu'>
                <a href='http://www.mozilla.org'>Mozilla</a>
                <ul>
                    <li>
                        <a href='http://www.mozilla.org/products/firefox'>
                            Firefox
                        </a>
                    </li>
                    <li>
                        <a href='http://www.mozilla.org/products/thunderbird'>
                            Thunderbird
                        </a>
                    </li>
                    <li>
                        <a href='http://bugzilla.mozilla.org'>
                            Bugzilla
                        </a>
                    </li>
                </ul>
            </li>
            <li class='menu'>
                <a href='http://www.apple.com'>Apple</a>
                <ul>
                    <li class='menu'>
                        <a href='http://www.apple.com/safari'>Safari</a>
                        <ul>
                            <li>
                                <a href='http://webkit.opendarwin.org'>
                                    Webkit Open Source Project
                                </a>
                            </li>
                            <li>
                                <a href='http://webkit.opendarwin.org/blog/'>
                                    Surfin Safari
                                </a>
                            </li>
                        </ul>
                    </li>
                    <li>
                        <a href='http://www.apple.com/macosx'>
                            Mac OS X
                        </a>
                    </li>
                    <li>
                        <a href='http://www.apple.com/itunes'>
                            iTunes
                        </a>
                    </li>
                </ul>
            </li>
```

```
            <li class='menu'>
                <a href='http://www.microsoft.com'>Microsoft</a>
                <ul>
                    <li>
                        <a href='http://blogs.msdn.com/ie'>
                            Internet Explorer Blog
                        </a>
                    </li>
                    <li>
                        <a
href='http://channel9.msdn.com/wiki/default.aspx/Channel9.InternetExplorerFeedback'>
                            Internet Explorer Wiki
                        </a>
                    </li>
                </ul>
            </li>
            <li class='menu'>
                <a href='http://www.w3.org'>W3c</a>
                <ul>
                    <li>
                        <a href='http://validator.w3.org'>
                            W3C Markup Validation Service
                        </a>
                    </li>
                    <li>
                        <a href='http://jigsaw.w3.org/css-validator/'>
                            W3C CSS Validation Service
                        </a>
                    </li>
                    <li>
                        <a href='http://www.w3.org/TR/CSS21/'>
                            CSS 2.1 Specification
                        </a>
                    </li>
                    <li>
                        <a href='http://www.w3.org/Style/CSS/current-work'>
                            CSS 3
                        </a>
                    </li>
                </ul>
            </li>
            <li class='menu'>
                <a href='#'>Other</a>
                <ul>
                    <li>
                        <a href='http://www.quirksmode.org'>
                            Peter-Paul Koch's Quirksmode.org
                        </a>
                    </li>
                    <li>
                        <a href='http://www.meyerweb.com'>
                            Eric A. Meyer
                        </a>
                    </li>
                    <li>
                        <a href='http://www.alistapart.com'>
```

```
                                A List Apart
                            </a>
                        </li>
                        <li>
                            <a href='http://www.positioniseverything.net'>
                                Position is Everything
                            </a>
                        </li>
                        <li>
                            <a href='http://annevankesteren.nl'>
                                Anne's Weblog About Markup and Style
                            </a>
                        </li>
                        <li>
                            <a href='http://dean.edwards.name'>
                                Dean Edwards
                            </a>
                        </li>
                        <li>
                            <a href='http://www.csszengarden.com'>
                                CSS Zen Garden
                            </a>
                        </li>
                    </ul>
                </li>
            </ul>
        </body>
    </html>
```

2. Save the markup as `drop_down_menus.html`.

3. Enter the following style sheet:

```
body {
    font: 14px sans-serif;
    margin: 0;
    padding: 0;
}
ul.menu a {
    color: white;
    text-decoration: none;
    display: block;
    width: 100%;
}
ul.menu,
ul.menu ul {
    background: rgb(128, 128, 128);
    list-style: none;
    padding: 0;
    margin: 0;
    width: 222px;
}
ul.menu ul {
    position: absolute;
    top: 0;
    left: 222px;
```

```
        visibility: hidden;
    }
    ul.menu li {
        position: relative;
        padding: 2px;
    }
    ul.menu li:hover {
        background: rgb(142, 142, 142);
    }
    ul.menu li:hover > ul {
        visibility: visible;
    }
    li.menu > a {
        background: url('arrow.png') no-repeat right;
    }
```

4. Save the style sheet as `drop_down_menus.css`.

The output from the preceding code appears in Figure 3-1 when rendered in Safari or Mozilla Firefox.

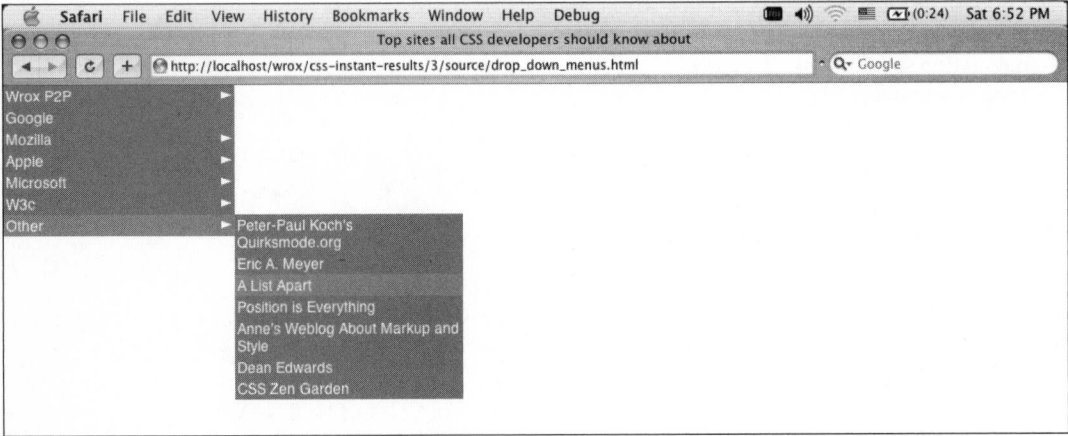

Figure 3-1

The markup and CSS required to create the pure-CSS solution is fairly simple and straightforward. First, you begin by marking up the structure of the drop-down menus in a series of unordered lists.

I have not introduced any complicated hacks for Internet Explorer for Windows yet. I do this in the next section, "Testing and Caveats."

```
    <ul class='menu'>
        <li class='menu'>
            <a href='http://p2p.wrox.com'>Wrox P2P</a>
            <ul>
                <li>
                    <a href='http://p2p.wrox.com/forum.asp?FORUM_ID=151'>
                        Beginning CSS: Cascading Style Sheets for Web Design
```

```
                              </a>
                        </li>
                        <li>
                           <a href='http://p2p.wrox.com/forum.asp?FORUM_ID=143'>
                              CSS
                           </a>
                        </li>
                        <li>
                           <a href='http://p2p.wrox.com/forum.asp?FORUM_ID=84'>
                              HTML Code Clinic
                           </a>
                        </li>
                     </ul>
                  </li>
```

The `<ul>` element that contains all of the drop-down menus is given a `menu` class name. Then, each subsequent `<li>` element that contains a nested `<ul>` element also receives a `menu` class name. This is done so that you have some way of identifying which `<li>` elements contain menus, and an arrow or some other identifier can be added to visually signify the presence of a submenu. This schema is repeated for the whole structure of the drop-down navigation system.

Now, with some well-structured markup in place you can begin the task of styling the drop-down navigation system. The first rule merely creates some cross-browser consistency and isn't necessary for a drop-down menu implementation:

```
body {
    font: 14px sans-serif;
    margin: 0;
    padding: 0;
}
```

It sets the font for the whole document in 14-pixel sans-serif, then removes the default padding or margin of the `<body>` element.

The next rule styles each link:

```
ul.menu a {
    color: white;
    text-decoration: none;
    display: block;
    width: 100%;
}
```

The first two declarations are a matter of personal taste. The first sets the color to white, and the second removes the default underline from the links. The next two, on the other hand, make the drop-down navigation system more usable. You set the display to block so that the whole `<li>` element containing the link is clickable, instead of only the link text, because links are displayed inline by default. The last declaration is a little preparation for addressing bugs in Internet Explorer for Windows. IE has a well-known bug with links. Even if you format links as block elements, only the text portion of the link is clickable. Setting the width to 100% defeats this bug, though it makes it more difficult to apply box model properties like margin, padding, and borders to `<a>` elements.

Next comes styling of the `<ul>` elements themselves:

```
ul.menu,
ul.menu ul {
    background: rgb(128, 128, 128);
    list-style: none;
    padding: 0;
    margin: 0;
    width: 222px;
}
```

Here again, some of these declarations are a matter of personal taste. In the section "Using and Modifying the Project" later in this chapter, you see some alternative approaches to the styling of the `<ul>` elements, including how to make menus that drop below each `<li>` element instead of to the right. The declarations that matter most are the list-style declaration, which removes the default, bullet formatting of the `<li>` elements, and the `padding: 0;` and `margin: 0;` declarations that help to create cross-browser consistency. You do this because some browsers apply padding to `<ul>` elements by default, and some browsers apply margin to `<ul>` elements by default. Identical styles are provided to the containing `<ul>` elements that house the drop-down navigation system and the drop-down menus themselves. These styles can be separated by writing two different rules for `ul.menu` and `ul.menu ul`.

The next rule further styles the drop-down menus by positioning those absolutely:

```
ul.menu ul {
    position: absolute;
    top: 0;
    left: 222px;
    visibility: hidden;
}
```

At this point each drop-down menu is positioned absolutely — you see in the next rule that they are positioned absolutely relative in position to the `<li>` element that contains them. Relative to the parent `<li>` element, each drop-down is offset zero pixels from the top of the parent `<li>` element, and then left by 222 pixels (the width of the parent `<li>` element). Finally, visibility is set to `hidden`. You could also use `display: none;` instead of `visibility: hidden;`. I chose the `visibility` property because occasionally there are bugs with Internet Explorer and the `display` property. This bug has to do with the differences between the `display` and `visibility` properties. With the `display: none;` declaration, an element is not rendered, so it occupies no space. With the `visibility: hidden;` declaration, an element is rendered, and it does occupy space — it simply isn't visible. In some circumstances setting an element to `display: block;` from `display: none;` causes some twitchy rendering in Explorer, particularly in quirks mode. This doesn't happen with the `visibility` property.

The next rule sets the position of each `<li>` element to relative, which causes each nested `<ul>` drop-down menu to position relative to the `<li>` element that contains it:

```
ul.menu li {
    position: relative;
    padding: 2px;
}
```

The next rule applies a visual cue when users move their mouse cursor over each element contained in the menu:

```
ul.menu li:hover {
    background: rgb(142, 142, 142);
}
```

This causes the background of each <li> element to shift to a lighter shade of gray when the user's mouse hovers over a menu item.

The next rule is the meat of the project, and is what enables you to create dynamic drop-down menus using only CSS:

```
ul.menu li:hover > ul {
    visibility: visible;
}
```

When the user mouses over a <li> element that contains a <ul> element as its direct child, the visibility of that <ul> element is set to visible.

In the final rule, the arrow.png image is set as the background image for each <a> element, where a drop-down menu exists. The arrow.png image is set non-repeating to the right of each <a> element that is the direct child of a <li> element with a menu class name:

```
li.menu > a {
    background: url('arrow.png') no-repeat right;
}
```

If it seems that I've left out an important browser in this discussion, the next section remedies that by discussing how to mangle the drop-down menu project for compatibility with Microsoft Internet Explorer.

Testing and Caveats

In the previous section I noted that the drop-down menu project does not yet function in Internet Explorer. This section discusses what to do to get the drop-down menu example functioning in Internet Explorer, and the caveats associated with CSS-driven drop-down menus.

In Internet Explorer 6, you see that there are no arrows signifying where a submenu exists, no lighter shade of gray when hovering over a <li> item, and no drop-down menus appear. As with previous projects, this project will be enabled in Internet Explorer using Dean Edwards' IE7 JavaScript.

To make the drop-down menus function in Internet Explorer 6, follow these steps:

1. In drop_down_menus.html, apply the following highlighted changes to the markup:

```
<!DOCTYPE html PUBLIC "-//W3C//DTD XHTML 1.0 Strict//EN"
"http://www.w3.org/TR/xhtml1/DTD/xhtml1-strict.dtd">
<html xmlns='http://www.w3.org/1999/xhtml' xml:lang='en'>
```

```html
<head>
    <meta http-equiv="Content-Type" content="text/html; charset=UTF-8" />
    <title>Top sites all CSS developers should know about</title>
    <link rel='stylesheet' type='text/css' href='drop_down_menus.css' />
    <!-- compliance patch for microsoft browsers -->
    <!--[if lt IE 7]>
        <style type='text/css'>
            ul.menu ul {
                left: 220px;
            }
        </style>
        <script src="/ie7/ie7-standard-p.js" type="text/javascript">
            IE7_PNG_SUFFIX = ".png";
        </script>
    <![endif]-->
</head>
<body>
    <ul class='menu'>
        <li class='menu'>
            <a href='http://p2p.wrox.com'>Wrox P2P<span></span></a>
            <ul>
                <li>
                    <a href='http://p2p.wrox.com/forum.asp?FORUM_ID=151'>
                        Beginning CSS: Cascading Style Sheets for Web Design
                    </a>
                </li>
                <li>
                    <a href='http://p2p.wrox.com/forum.asp?FORUM_ID=143'>
                        CSS
                    </a>
                </li>
                <li>
                    <a href='http://p2p.wrox.com/forum.asp?FORUM_ID=84'>
                        HTML Code Clinic
                    </a>
                </li>
            </ul>
        </li>
        <li><a href='http://www.google.com'>Google</a></li>
        <li class='menu'>
            <a href='http://www.mozilla.org'>Mozilla<span></span></a>
            <ul>
                <li>
                    <a href='http://www.mozilla.org/products/firefox'>
                        Firefox
                    </a>
                </li>
                <li>
                    <a href='http://www.mozilla.org/products/thunderbird'>
                        Thunderbird
                    </a>
                </li>
                <li>
                    <a href='http://bugzilla.mozilla.org'>
```

```
                            Bugzilla
                        </a>
                    </li>
                </ul>
            </li>
            <li class='menu'>
                <a href='http://www.apple.com'>Apple<span></span></a>
                <ul>
                    <li class='menu'>
                        <a href='http://www.apple.com/safari'>
                            Safari<span></span>
                        </a>
                        <ul>
                            <li>
                                <a href='http://webkit.opendarwin.org'>
                                    Webkit Open Source Project
                                </a>
                            </li>
                            <li>
                                <a href='http://webkit.opendarwin.org/blog/'>
                                    Surfin Safari
                                </a>
                            </li>
                        </ul>
                    </li>
                    <li>
                        <a href='http://www.apple.com/macosx'>
                            Mac OS X
                        </a>
                    </li>
                    <li>
                        <a href='http://www.apple.com/itunes'>
                            iTunes
                        </a>
                    </li>
                </ul>
            </li>
            <li class='menu'>
                <a href='http://www.microsoft.com'>Microsoft<span></span></a>
                <ul>
                    <li>
                        <a href='http://blogs.msdn.com/ie'>
                            Internet Explorer Blog
                        </a>
                    </li>
                    <li>
                        <a
href='http://channel9.msdn.com/wiki/default.aspx/Channel9.InternetExplorerFeedback'>
                            Internet Explorer Wiki
                        </a>
                    </li>
                </ul>
            </li>
            <li class='menu'>
```

```
                    <a href='http://www.w3.org'>W3C<span></span></a>
        <ul>
            <li>
                <a href='http://validator.w3.org'>
                    W3C Markup Validation Service
                </a>
            </li>
            <li>
                <a href='http://jigsaw.w3.org/css-validator/'>
                    W3C CSS Validation Service
                </a>
            </li>
            <li>
                <a href='http://www.w3.org/TR/CSS21/'>
                    CSS 2.1 Specification
                </a>
            </li>
            <li>
                <a href='http://www.w3.org/Style/CSS/current-work'>
                    CSS 3
                </a>
            </li>
        </ul>
    </li>
    <li class='menu'>
            <a href='#'>Other<span></span></a>
        <ul>
            <li>
                <a href='http://www.quirksmode.org'>
                    Peter-Paul Koch's Quirksmode.org
                </a>
            </li>
            <li>
                <a href='http://www.meyerweb.com'>
                    Eric A. Meyer
                </a>
            </li>
            <li>
                <a href='http://www.alistapart.com'>
                    A List Apart
                </a>
            </li>
            <li>
                <a href='http://www.positioniseverything.net'>
                    Position is Everything
                </a>
            </li>
            <li>
                <a href='http://annevankesteren.nl'>
                    Anne's Weblog About Markup and Style
                </a>
            </li>
```

```
            <li>
                <a href='http://dean.edwards.name'>
                    Dean Edwards
                </a>
            </li>
            <li>
                <a href='http://www.csszengarden.com'>
                    CSS Zen Garden
                </a>
            </li>
        </ul>
    </li>
</ul>
</body>
</html>
```

2. Save the modified document in a new folder called "ie" as drop_down_menus.html.

3. Make the following edit to drop_down_menus.css:

```
ul.menu li {
    position: relative;
    padding: 2px;
}
ul.menu li:hover {
    background: rgb(142, 142, 142);
}
ul.menu li:hover > ul {
    visibility: visible;
}
li.menu > a {
    position: relative;
}
li.menu > a > span {
    position: absolute;
    width: 15px;
    height: 15px;
    top: 0;
    right: 0;
    background: url('arrow.png') no-repeat right;
}
```

Now you have output in Internet Explorer 6 for Windows that matches that of Safari 1.3, Mozilla Firefox, and Opera 8. This can be observed in the output in Figure 3-2.

The hacks required for this project are few because Dean Edwards' IE7 JavaScript does most of the work for you. It enables the direct child selector, the :hover dynamic pseudo-class on any element, and corrects Explorer's lack of out-of-the-box support for alpha transparency. The following explains why each hack is necessary, and what's going on behind the scenes in the IE7 JavaScript.

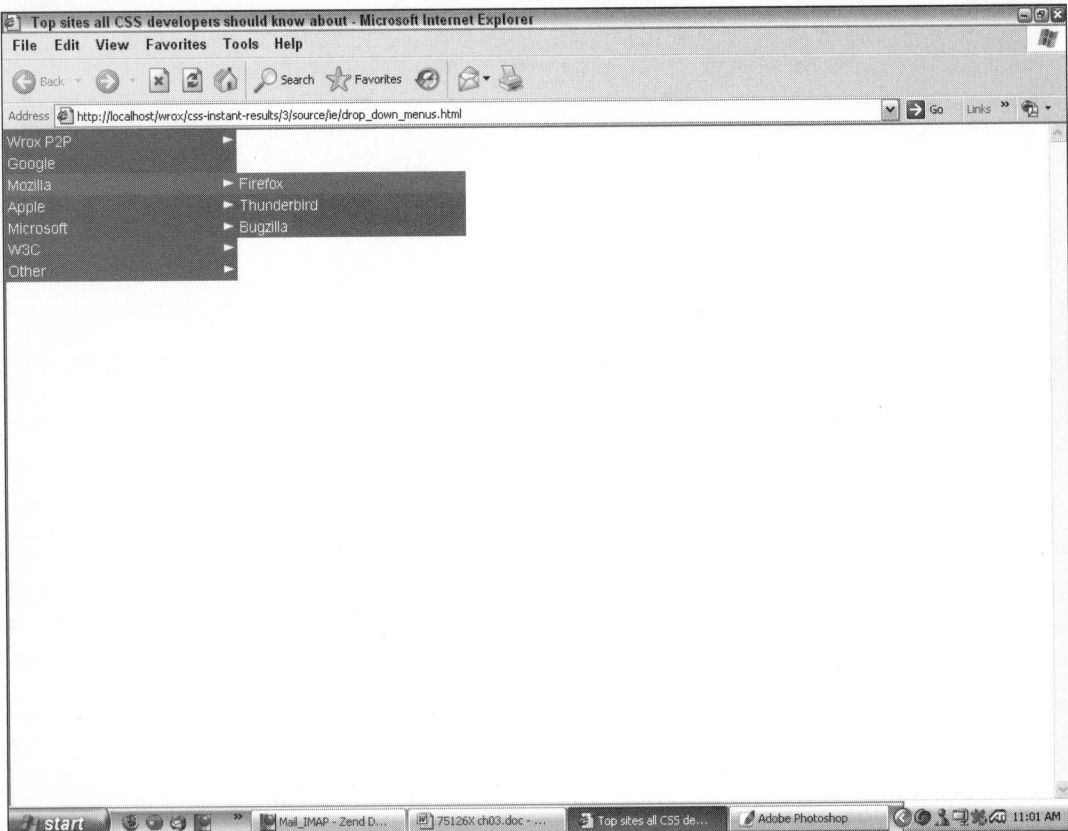

Figure 3-2

Alpha transparency is an optional feature of the PNG image format. Essentially, it enables portions of a PNG image to become see-through either partially or completely. In web design this is useful for creating effects where the background area behind a PNG image with transparent parts can be seen through the image. Internet Explorer 6 and earlier versions do not support the alpha transparency portion of the PNG image format, but can be made to support it using the Internet Explorer–proprietary CSS filter property, which is how Dean Edwards' IE7 enables alpha transparency for PNG images in Internet Explorer. Internet Explorer 7 has full support for alpha transparency in PNG images.

First you applied a conditional comment to the markup that selects all Internet Explorer browsers earlier than version 7:

```
<!--[if lt IE 7]>
    <style type='text/css'>
        ul.menu ul {
            left: 220px;
        }
    </style>
    <script src="/ie7/ie7-standard-p.js" type="text/javascript">
        IE7_PNG_SUFFIX = ".png";
    </script>
<![endif]-->
```

The first edit is the inclusion of an inline style sheet, which can just as well be an external style sheet. Within the inline style sheet a correction is made to the left offset positioning of the drop-down menus. Changing the left offset to 220 pixels (from 222 pixels) causes Explorer to match the output of Mozilla Firefox, Safari, and Opera 8. Next, you reference Dean Edwards' IE7 JavaScript. Between the script tags, you set a global JavaScript variable that tells Edwards' PNG correct script which PNG images need alpha transparency correction. By default, it looks for PNG images that are suffixed '-trans.png'. Setting this global variable allows you to tell it to look for all PNG images (even PNG images that don't need alpha transparency correction). This is a matter of personal preference and can be changed depending on the needs of your particular project.

In the body of the markup you also applied empty `<span>` tags to each `<li>` element containing a nested `<ul>` element. These are necessary because of the hack that allows PNG transparency to be possible in Explorer. This hack utilizes a CSS-proprietary feature of Explorer known as filters — specifically, Microsoft's `AlphaImageLoader` filter. Edwards' IE7 JavaScript looks for PNGs that need correction in the CSS background or background-image properties, and swaps those with a Microsoft-proprietary `filter` property that looks like this:

```
filter: progid:DXImageTransform.Microsoft.AlphaImageLoader(src='arrow.png',
sizingMethod='scale');
```

The problem with the `filter` property, besides being overly verbose, is that it provides no way to position the image, and setting the `background-position` property has no effect on the position of the image loaded using the `filter` property. This is where the empty `<span>` element comes in. It is provided as a container for the image that can be positioned relative to the `<a>` element that contains it.

Other Caveats

In addition to the issues with Internet Explorer just covered, quite a few caveats exist with this approach to drop-down menus that apply to other browsers as well:

- ❏ The navigation is not accessible by keyboard only, and adding such accessibility is impossible using only markup and CSS.

- ❏ The submenus are very touchy and are quick to disappear when the mouse leaves the outer edge of a drop-down menu.

- ❏ The drop-down system cannot be converted to a click-based navigation instead of mouseover navigation. CSS provides no "onclick" functionality. For that you need JavaScript.

- ❏ Explorer doesn't natively support the `:hover` and direct child selectors, so any benefit to using pure-CSS drop-down navigation instead of JavaScript is lost, because JavaScript is required to make pure-CSS menus work in Internet Explorer.

Those are some serious limitations to the pure-CSS approach, and they all center on the most important component of a well-designed navigation system: accessibility. The pure-CSS approach to navigation is inherently flawed and counter-intuitive to what CSS usually stands for. Moreover, interaction between the user and document should not be handled with CSS in the first place — interaction lives with JavaScript. The next section discusses how to modify the project to make use of a JavaScript that I have written that can provide these important accessibility features. I take the best of both worlds and combine the two: CSS drop-down menus (only if scripting is disabled) and JavaScript (when scripting isn't disabled) to provide the most accessible menu system possible. If you aren't familiar with JavaScript, don't worry, I'll explain anything that you'd want to be able to modify in detail.

If you'd like to learn how the JavaScript that I have written for this project works, I recommend you pick up Paul Wilton's Beginning JavaScript, 2nd Edition *(Wiley Publishing, Inc., ISBN: 0764555871).*

Using and Modifying the Project

It isn't possible to get very far in the world of web site development without learning JavaScript. Although JavaScript has earned a reputation as a pop-up spawning, marquee scrolling, riddled-with-annoyances language, it has a good side as well. In fact, JavaScript can enhance a document's accessibility and interactivity in ways not possible with XHTML and CSS alone. In the following modification to the original drop-down menu example, you leverage the power of JavaScript and CSS in tandem to create a more-accessible, dynamic drop-down menu system that isn't possible using CSS alone. Before you begin, you'll need another of Dean Edwards' fantastic JavaScripts — this one is called cssQuery. It allows a developer to use CSS selectors to grab elements in JavaScript. Moreover, it's cross-browser compatible, and works with IE 5, 5.5, 6, and 7 for Windows, Safari 1.3, Mozilla Firefox 1.0, and Opera 8. Leveraging Dean's pioneering work in web development will allow you to use something you're already comfortable with, CSS, from within JavaScript, in a way not natively supported by the JavaScript available in browsers at the time of this writing.

You can get Dean's cssQuery JavaScript from his web site at `http://dean.edwards.name/my/cssQuery`. Like IE7, cssQuery is made available under the open source LGPL license. You can obtain the full text of the license at `http://creativecommons.org/licenses/LGPL/2.1`. The cssQuery JavaScript also appears on the source CD-ROM accompanying this book, in the Project 3 folder.

I combine Dean's cssQuery with a JavaScript that I have prepared for this project. Because the title of this book is *CSS Instant Results*, and not JavaScript Instant Results, I won't be going into the inner workings of the dynamic drop-down JavaScript that I have prepared, but rather I will impart only the portions that you might desire to edit to customize for your particular project. The JavaScript I have prepared works almost out of the box using the markup and CSS presented earlier in this chapter, but a few modifications must be made, and there are a few caveats to point out as well.

You can use this JavaScript to create dynamic drop-down menus that meet the following criteria:

❏ Fall back on pure-CSS drop-down menus, if JavaScript is disabled

❏ Accessible from the keyboard without interfering with keyboard shortcuts already in use by the browser

❏ Drop-down menus that are activated by clicking on a menu topic, rather than by hovering the mouse cursor over a menu topic

The source files of this approach are available on the source CD-ROM, in the "js" folder within the Project 3 folder. If the source CD-ROM is not available, you can also obtain the source from `http://www.wrox.com`. Dean Edwards' cssQuery also appears in this folder, though you should check his web site at `http://dean.edwards.name/my/cssQuery` for newer versions containing bug fixes made since the book was released.

This section also presents some other possible modifications to the look and feel of the drop-down menus, including custom backgrounds, borders, and menus that drop down instead of to the right.

Implementing JavaScript-enabled Drop-Down Menus

To create JavaScript-enabled drop-down menus, follow these steps:

1. Make the following modifications to `drop_down_menus.html` (using the version you created in the "Testing and Caveats" section that contains Internet Explorer hacks):

```html
<!DOCTYPE html PUBLIC "-//W3C//DTD XHTML 1.0 Strict//EN"
"http://www.w3.org/TR/xhtml1/DTD/xhtml1-strict.dtd">
<html xmlns='http://www.w3.org/1999/xhtml' xml:lang='en'>
    <head>
        <meta http-equiv="Content-Type" content="text/html; charset=UTF-8" />
        <title>Top sites all CSS developers should know about</title>
        <link rel='stylesheet' type='text/css' href='drop_down_menus.css' />
        <!-- compliance patch for microsoft browsers -->
        <!--[if lt IE 7]>
            <style type='text/css'>
                ul.menu ul {
                    left: 220px;
                }
            </style>
            <script src='/ie7/ie7-standard-p.js' type='text/javascript'>
                IE7_PNG_SUFFIX = ".png";
            </script>
        <![endif]-->
        <script src='cssQuery/cssQuery-p.js' type='text/javascript'></script>
        <script src='drop_down_menus.js' type='text/javascript'></script>
        <noscript>
            <style type='text/css'>
                ul.menu li:hover > ul {
                    visibility: visible;
                }
            </style>
        </noscript>
    </head>
    <body>
        <ul class='menu'>
            <li class='menu' id='menu-0'>
            Wrox P2P<span></span>
                <ul>
                    <li>
                        <a href='http://p2p.wrox.com/forum.asp?FORUM_ID=151'>
                            Beginning CSS: Cascading Style Sheets for Web Design
                        </a>
                    </li>
                    <li>
                        <a href='http://p2p.wrox.com/forum.asp?FORUM_ID=143'>
                            CSS
                        </a>
                    </li>
                    <li>
                        <a href='http://p2p.wrox.com/forum.asp?FORUM_ID=84'>
                            HTML Code Clinic
                        </a>
                    </li>
                </ul>
```

```
        </li>
        <li><a href='http://www.google.com'>Google</a></li>
        <li class='menu' id='menu-1'>
            Mozilla<span></span>
            <ul>
                <li>
                    <a href='http://www.mozilla.org/products/firefox'>
                        Firefox
                    </a>
                </li>
                <li>
                    <a href='http://www.mozilla.org/products/thunderbird'>
                        Thunderbird
                    </a>
                </li>
                <li>
                    <a href='http://bugzilla.mozilla.org'>
                        Bugzilla
                    </a>
                </li>
            </ul>
        </li>
        <li class='menu' id='menu-2'>
            Apple<span></span>
            <ul>
                <li class='menu' id='menu-3'>
                    Safari<span></span>
                    <ul>
                        <li>
                            <a href='http://webkit.opendarwin.org'>
                                Webkit Open Source Project
                            </a>
                        </li>
                        <li>
                            <a href='http://webkit.opendarwin.org/blog/'>
                                Surfin Safari
                            </a>
                        </li>
                    </ul>
                </li>
                <li>
                    <a href='http://www.apple.com/macosx'>
                        Mac OS X
                    </a>
                </li>
                <li>
                    <a href='http://www.apple.com/itunes'>
                        iTunes
                    </a>
                </li>
            </ul>
        </li>
        <li class='menu' id='menu-4'>
            Microsoft<span></span>
            <ul>
                <li>
```

```
                    <a href='http://blogs.msdn.com/ie'>
                        Internet Explorer Blog
                    </a>
                </li>
                <li>
                    <a
href='http://channel9.msdn.com/wiki/default.aspx/Channel9.InternetExplorerFeedback'>
                        Internet Explorer Wiki
                    </a>
                </li>
            </ul>
        </li>
        <li class='menu' id='menu-6'>
            W3C<span></span>
            <ul>
                <li>
                    <a href='http://validator.w3.org'>
                        W3C Markup Validation Service
                    </a>
                </li>
                <li>
                    <a href='http://jigsaw.w3.org/css-validator/'>
                        W3C CSS Validation Service
                    </a>
                </li>
                <li>
                    <a href='http://www.w3.org/TR/CSS21/'>
                        CSS 2.1 Specification
                    </a>
                </li>
                <li>
                    <a href='http://www.w3.org/Style/CSS/current-work'>
                        CSS 3
                    </a>
                </li>
            </ul>
        </li>
        <li class='menu' id='menu-7'>
            Other<span></span>
            <ul>
                <li>
                    <a href='http://www.quirksmode.org'>
                        Peter-Paul Koch's Quirksmode.org
                    </a>
                </li>
                <li>
                    <a href='http://www.meyerweb.com'>
                        Eric A. Meyer
                    </a>
                </li>
                <li>
                    <a href='http://www.alistapart.com'>
                        A List Apart
                    </a>
                </li>
                <li>
                    <a href='http://www.positioniseverything.net'>
```

```
                            Position is Everything
                    </a>
            </li>
            <li>
                <a href='http://annevankesteren.nl'>
                    Anne's Weblog About Markup and Style
                </a>
            </li>
            <li>
                <a href='http://dean.edwards.name'>
                    Dean Edwards
                </a>
            </li>
            <li>
                <a href='http://www.csszengarden.com'>
                    CSS Zen Garden
                </a>
            </li>
        </ul>
      </li>
    </ul>
  </body>
</html>
```

2. Save drop_down_menus.html.

3. Make the following modifications to drop_down_menus.css:

```css
body {
    font: 14px sans-serif;
    margin: 0;
    padding: 0;
}
ul.menu a {
    color: white;
    text-decoration: none;
    display: block;
    width: 100%;
}
ul.menu,
ul.menu ul {
    background: rgb(128, 128, 128);
    list-style: none;
    padding: 0;
    margin: 0;
    width: 222px;
}
ul.menu ul {
    position: absolute;
    top: 0;
    left: 222px;
    visibility: hidden;
}
ul.menu li {
    position: relative;
    padding: 2px;
    color: white;
```

```
}
ul.menu li:hover,
li.menu-highlight,
li.menu-link-highlight {
    background: rgb(142, 142, 142);
}
li.menu > a {
    position: relative;
}
li.menu > span,
li.menu > a > span {
    position: absolute;
    width: 15px;
    height: 15px;
    top: 0;
    right: 0;
    background: url('arrow.png') no-repeat right;
    border: none;
}
```

4. Save `drop_down_menus.css`.

Remember that these two files must appear in the same folder as `drop_down_menus.js`, the unzipped directory containing `cssQuery-p.js`, which should be called `cssQuery`, and the `arrow.png` image. Once all linked up, you should see output like that in Figure 3-3.

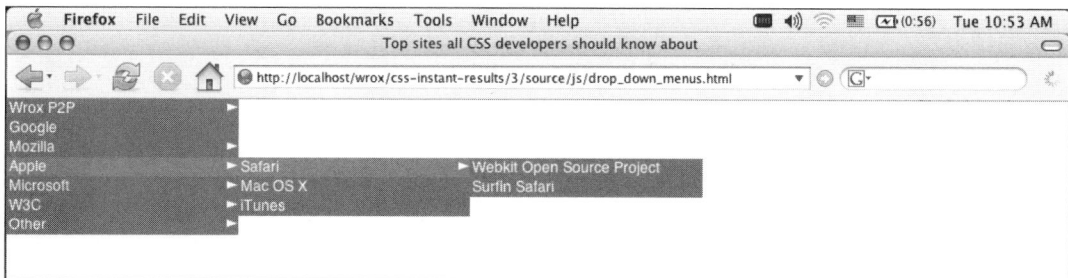

Figure 3-3

Figure 3-3 shows the output from this incarnation of `drop_down_menus.html`. You should be able to use the up or down arrows of the keyboard to select links, the return key to navigate to the selected link, and the left or right arrows of the keyboard to navigate submenus. Using the mouse, you should be able to click to open a submenu, and when the mouse cursor is not over a menu a click should close all menus. Finally, disabling JavaScript in your browser should invoke the pure-CSS menu system, if your browser supports the `:hover` dynamic pseudo-class on any element, and the direct child selector.

The JavaScript-driven drop-down menu system is the best approach, because it brings together the best of both worlds to make the document as accessible as possible. The following explains the edits you made and why you made them.

First, you link up `drop_down_menus.js` and `cssQuery-p.js`; these provide the engine that drives the JavaScript-enabled drop-down menu system. Of the two, `cssQuery-p.js` must appear first. The next modification that you made was to enable the pure-CSS menu system if JavaScript is disabled:

```
<noscript>
    <style type='text/css'>
        ul.menu li:hover > ul {
            visibility: visible;
        }
    </style>
</noscript>
```

The contents of the `<noscript>` tag are included only in the event that JavaScript has been disabled.

Next, you modify each of the top menu items. Each menu item must have a unique id, and the links must be removed:

```
<li class='menu' id='menu-0'>
    Wrox P2P<span></span>
```

A unique id provides a way of keeping track of user-initiated events from the `drop_down_menus.js` file. Links had to be removed because it is not possible to have a drop-down menu system where the submenus only appear by clicking, and to have a link on that item as well, because that would naturally be a conflict.

To further customize the project for your own needs, you may want to change the class names. Because the class names are utilized by the `drop_down_menus.js` file, you'll need to edit the class names in that file as well. At the top of the file, you'll see four variables containing four different class names:

```
var $CSSIR_liClassName = 'menu';
var $CSSIR_ulClassName = 'menu';
var $CSSIR_liHighlight = 'menu-highlight';
var $CSSIR_aHighlight  = 'menu-link-highlight';
```

The first variable refers to each `<li>` element that contains a drop-down menu; these have a `menu` class name by default. The second variable refers to the `<ul>` element that contains the entire drop-down menu system. This also has a `menu` class name by default. The next two I've not yet discussed. These are the `menu-highlight` and `menu-link-highlight` class names. These are dynamically applied in the JavaScript. `menu-highlight` is applied to the `<li>` elements that contain submenus that are currently selected by users, whether by using the arrows of their keyboard or via the mouse. `menu-link-highlight` only applies when users are using the up or down arrows of their keyboard to select links within a menu. Because these are class names, you can set the styles for these in a normal style sheet. In fact, you applied these class names here:

```
ul.menu li:hover,
li.menu-highlight,
li.menu-link-highlight {
    background: rgb(142, 142, 142);
}
```

`<li>` elements with a `menu-highlight` or `menu-link-highlight` class name receive the same styling as do `<li>` elements that the user's mouse is currently hovering over.

In the next section you take this approach one step further by applying custom backgrounds and borders to it.

Custom Backgrounds and Borders

In the next example, you make use of some advanced CSS to apply custom borders and background to the drop-down menus project. This example builds on the last approach, which implemented JavaScript in the drop-down menu project.

To apply custom backgrounds and borders to the drop-down menus, follow these steps:

1. Make the following modifications to `drop_down_menus.html`:

```
<!DOCTYPE html PUBLIC "-//W3C//DTD XHTML 1.0 Strict//EN"
"http://www.w3.org/TR/xhtml1/DTD/xhtml1-strict.dtd">
<html xmlns='http://www.w3.org/1999/xhtml' xml:lang='en'>
    <head>
        <meta http-equiv="Content-Type" content="text/html; charset=UTF-8" />
        <title>Top sites all CSS developers should know about</title>
        <link rel='stylesheet' type='text/css' href='drop_down_menus.css' />
        <!-- compliance patch for microsoft browsers -->
        <!--[if lt IE 7]>
            <style type='text/css'>
                ul.menu ul {
                    left: 220px;
                }
            </style>
            <script src='/ie7/ie7-standard-p.js' type='text/javascript'>
                IE7_PNG_SUFFIX = "arrow.png";
            </script>
            <script src='/ie7/ie7-recalc.js' type='text/javascript'></script>
        <![endif]-->
        <!--[if lt IE 6]>
            <style type='text/css'>
                ul.menu span {
                    margin-left: -15px;
                    padding-left: 15px;
                }
            </style>
        <![endif]-->
        <script src='cssQuery/cssQuery-p.js' type='text/javascript'></script>
        <script src='drop_down_menus.js' type='text/javascript'></script>
        <noscript>
            <style type='text/css'>
                ul.menu li:hover > ul {
                    visibility: visible;
                }
            </style>
        </noscript>
    </head>
    <body>
        <div class='menu'><div>
        <ul class='menu'>
            <li class='menu' id='menu-0'>
                <span>Wrox P2P</span><span class='arrow'></span>
                <div class='menu'><div>
                <ul>
                    <li>
                        <a href='http://p2p.wrox.com/forum.asp?FORUM_ID=151'>
```

```
                        <span>Beginning CSS:
                        Cascading Style Sheets for Web Design</span>
                    </a>
                </li>
                <li>
                    <a href='http://p2p.wrox.com/forum.asp?FORUM_ID=143'>
                        <span>CSS</span>
                    </a>
                </li>
                <li>
                    <a href='http://p2p.wrox.com/forum.asp?FORUM_ID=84'>
                        <span>HTML Code Clinic</span>
                    </a>
                </li>
            </ul>
            </div></div>
        </li>
        <li><a href='http://www.google.com'><span>Google</span></a></li>
        <li class='menu' id='menu-1'>
            <span>Mozilla</span><span class='arrow'></span>
            <div class='menu'><div>
            <ul>
                <li>
                    <a href='http://www.mozilla.org/products/firefox'>
                        <span>Firefox</span>
                    </a>
                </li>
                <li>
                    <a href='http://www.mozilla.org/products/thunderbird'>
                        <span>Thunderbird</span>
                    </a>
                </li>
                <li>
                    <a href='http://bugzilla.mozilla.org'>
                        <span>Bugzilla</span>
                    </a>
                </li>
            </ul>
            </div></div>
        </li>
        <li class='menu' id='menu-2'>
            <span>Apple</span><span class='arrow'></span>
            <div class='menu'><div>
            <ul>
                <li class='menu' id='menu-3'>
                    <span>Safari</span><span class='arrow'></span>
                    <div class='menu'><div>
                    <ul>
                        <li>
                            <a href='http://webkit.opendarwin.org'>
                                <span>Webkit Open Source Project</span>
                            </a>
                        </li>
                        <li>
                            <a href='http://webkit.opendarwin.org/blog/'>
                                <span>Surfin Safari</span>
                            </a>
```

```
                            </li>
                        </ul>
                    </div></div>
                </li>
                <li>
                    <a href='http://www.apple.com/macosx'>
                        <span>Mac OS X</span>
                    </a>
                </li>
                <li>
                    <a href='http://www.apple.com/itunes'>
                        <span>iTunes</span>
                    </a>
                </li>
            </ul>
        </div></div>
    </li>
    <li class='menu' id='menu-4'>
        <span>Microsoft</span><span class='arrow'></span>
        <div class='menu'><div>
            <ul>
                <li>
                    <a href='http://blogs.msdn.com/ie'>
                        <span>Internet Explorer Blog</span>
                    </a>
                </li>
                <li>
                    <a
href='http://channel9.msdn.com/wiki/default.aspx/Channel9.InternetExplorerFeedback'>
                        <span>Internet Explorer Wiki</span>
                    </a>
                </li>
            </ul>
        </div></div>
    </li>
    <li class='menu' id='menu-6'>
        <span>W3C</span><span class='arrow'></span>
        <div class='menu'><div>
            <ul>
                <li>
                    <a href='http://validator.w3.org'>
                        <span>W3C Markup Validation Service</span>
                    </a>
                </li>
                <li>
                    <a href='http://jigsaw.w3.org/css-validator/'>
                        <span>W3C CSS Validation Service</span>
                    </a>
                </li>
                <li>
                    <a href='http://www.w3.org/TR/CSS21/'>
                        <span>CSS 2.1 Specification</span>
                    </a>
                </li>
                <li>
                    <a href='http://www.w3.org/Style/CSS/current-work'>
```

```
                          <span>CSS 3</span>
                        </a>
                      </li>
                    </ul>
                  </div></div>
              </li>
              <li class='menu' id='menu-7'>
                  <span>Other</span><span class='arrow'></span>
                  <div class='menu'><div>
                  <ul>
                      <li>
                          <a href='http://www.quirksmode.org'>
                              <span>Peter-Paul Koch's Quirksmode.org</span>
                          </a>
                      </li>
                      <li>
                          <a href='http://www.meyerweb.com'>
                              <span>Eric A. Meyer</span>
                          </a>
                      </li>
                      <li>
                          <a href='http://www.alistapart.com'>
                              <span>A List Apart</span>
                          </a>
                      </li>
                      <li>
                          <a href='http://www.positioniseverything.net'>
                              <span>Position is Everything</span>
                          </a>
                      </li>
                      <li>
                          <a href='http://annevankesteren.nl'>
                              <span>Anne's Weblog About Markup and Style</span>
                          </a>
                      </li>
                      <li>
                          <a href='http://dean.edwards.name'>
                              <span>Dean Edwards</span>
                          </a>
                      </li>
                      <li>
                          <a href='http://www.csszengarden.com'>
                              <span>CSS Zen Garden</span>
                          </a>
                      </li>
                  </ul>
                  </div></div>
              </li>
          </ul>
        </div></div>
    </body>
  </html>
```

2. Save drop_down_menus.html.

3. Make the following modifications to `drop_down_menus.css`:

```css
body {
    font: 16px sans-serif;
    margin: 20px;
    padding: 0;
    color: white;
    background: url('shell_mound.jpg') no-repeat center;
}
div.menu,
li.menu div {
    width: 222px;
    background: transparent url('images/transparent_01.png') no-repeat top;
}
div.menu > div,
li.menu > div > div {
    width: 222px;
    background: transparent url('images/transparent_03.png') no-repeat bottom;
    padding: 20px 0 20px 0;
}
ul.menu a {
    color: white;
    text-decoration: none;
    width: 100%;
    display: inline-block;
    height: 100%;
    position: relative;
}
ul.menu,
ul.menu ul {
    background: transparent url('images/transparent_02.png') repeat-y center;
    list-style: none;
    padding: 0;
    margin: 0;
    width: 222px;
}
li.menu > div {
    position: absolute;
    top: -20px;
    left: 222px;
    visibility: hidden;
    z-index: 4;
    width: 222px;
}
ul.menu li {
    position: relative;
    padding: 2px;
}
ul.menu li:hover,
li.menu-highlight,
li.menu-link-highlight {
    background: transparent url('images/highlight_02.png') repeat-y center;
}
ul.menu span {
    display: block;
    padding: 2px 10px;
}
```

```
li.menu > span.arrow {
    position: absolute;
    width: 15px;
    height: 15px;
    top: 5px;
    right: 15px;
    background: url('arrow.png') no-repeat right;
    border: none;
    padding: 0;
    margin: 0;
}
```

4. Save `drop_down_menus.css`.

The `drop_down_menus.js` file for this approach was also modified to account for the additional `<div>` elements included. Use the file provided in the Project 3 folder on the source CD-ROM, in the "custom-bg" folder.

The result of the modifications is shown in Figure 3-4.

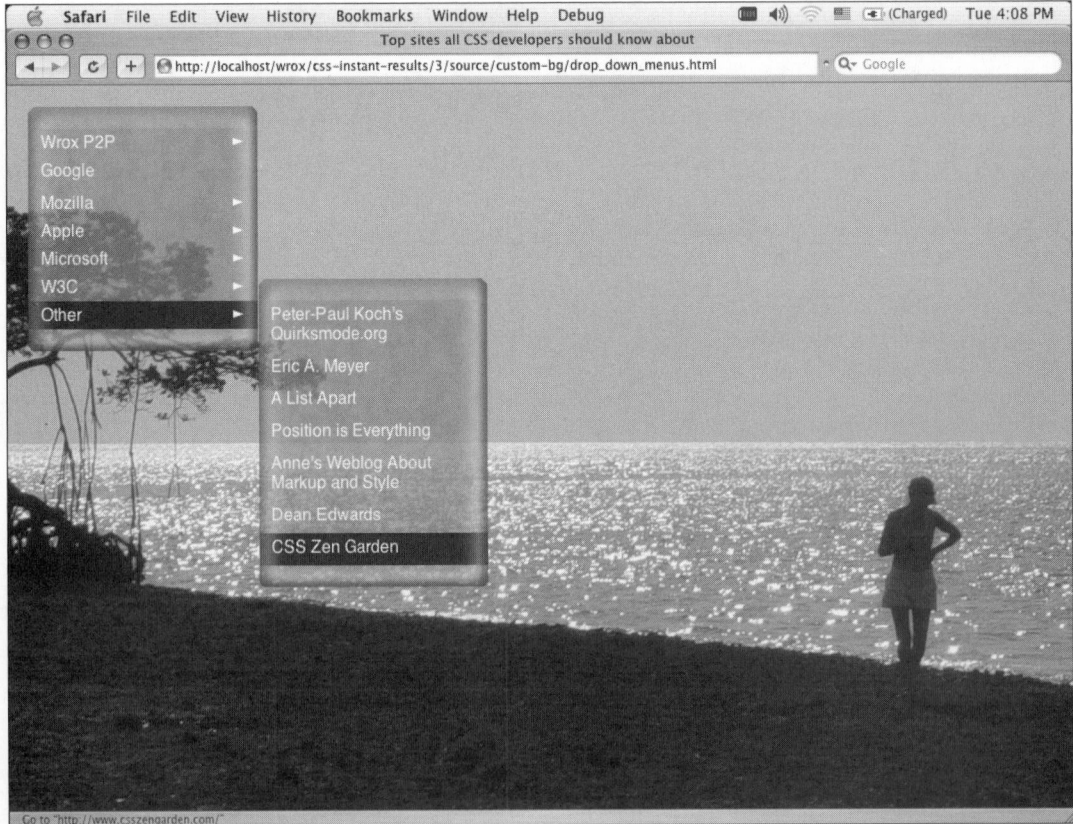

Figure 3-4

The resulting document works as expected in Internet Explorer 5.5 and 6, Firefox 1.0, Opera 8, and Safari 1.3.

Internet Explorer 6, as mentioned in the section "Testing and Caveats," does not support PNG transparency natively, and where this project is concerned, it is impossible to apply transparent PNG images to the backgrounds of the drop-down menus. You can work around this by using gifs or other web-supported image formats. The gif format unfortunately does not support partial transparency, as observed in Figure 3-4, where you can see the shell_mound.jpg image showing through the background PNG images used for the menu system. Therefore, transparent PNGs cannot be utilized here in Internet Explorer 5.5 and 6. This approach will fail even with the filter hack, because the filter hack disables links and causes other aesthetic problems that cannot be overcome. Internet Explorer 7, on the other hand, does support transparent PNG images natively.

You also applied a few new hacks to Internet Explorer 6, so that it can render the drop-down menus using the advanced CSS pseudo-classes :first-child and :last-child, which are not supported natively.

```
<!--[if lt IE 7]>
    <style type='text/css'>
        ul.menu ul {
            left: 220px;
        }
    </style>
    <script src='/ie7/ie7-standard-p.js' type='text/javascript'>
        IE7_PNG_SUFFIX = "arrow.png";
    </script>
    <script src='/ie7/ie7-recalc.js' type='text/javascript'></script>
<![endif]-->
```

The IE7_PNG_SUFFIX variable is altered so that it will only target the arrow.png images appearing in <li> elements that contain drop-down menus. Without this, the hack would also be applied to the other background PNG images, which would cause all sorts of chaos in Internet Explorer. The best way to remedy this, without complicated layering, is to simply choose an opaque image format, or the less-sophisticated transparency available with the GIF format. Finally, because some aspects of the drop-down menus are altered dynamically via JavaScript, Dean's ie7-recalc.js module is required; this functionality is used exclusively by drop_down_menus.js.

You only need a few modifications to make the project compatible with IE 5.5. The following does a back-flip over an IE5.5 bug:

```
<!--[if lt IE 6]>
    <style type='text/css'>
        ul.menu span {
            margin-left: -15px;
            padding-left: 15px;
        }
    </style>
<![endif]-->
```

Oddly enough, this corrects the offset positioning of the submenus. It doesn't mirror pixel-for-pixel what IE 6 outputs, but the differences are subtle and unnoticeable to the casual observer.

As you noticed from the example, applying custom backgrounds or borders requires additional markup to be added to the document. Until browsers support CSS 3 multiple backgrounds and borders, we're likely to be stuck with techniques like this for years to come. The first modification you made to `drop_down_menus.html` was to wrap each `<ul>` element in two `<div>` blocks:

```
<div class='menu'><div>
<ul class='menu'>
    <li class='menu' id='menu-0'>
        <span>Wrox P2P</span><span class='arrow'></span>
        <div class='menu'><div>
        <ul>
```

The two `<div>` blocks will serve as elements you can latch onto to apply background images. The outer `<div>` element, with a menu class name, contains the top image of the background:

```
div.menu,
li.menu div {
    width: 222px;
    background: transparent url('images/transparent_01.png') no-repeat top;
}
```

The image `transparent_01.png` is part of the same image. It has been sliced in PhotoShop using the slice tool, then the "Save for Web" feature saves each individual slice as a separate image. This allows each submenu to have customized corners.

The inner `<div>` element receives the bottom slice of the image:

```
div.menu > div,
li.menu > div > div {
    width: 222px;
    background: transparent url('images/transparent_03.png') no-repeat bottom;
    padding: 20px 0 20px 0;
}
```

After applying the image, the height of the top and bottom slice is applied to the padding of the inner `<div>`. This prevents the top and bottom slice from overlapping with the middle slice of the image. In this case the height of the top and bottom slice is 20 pixels.

The middle slice is applied to the `<ul>` elements themselves:

```
ul.menu,
ul.menu ul {
    background: transparent url('images/transparent_02.png') repeat-y center;
    list-style: none;
    padding: 0;
    margin: 0;
    width: 222px;
}
```

The middle slice is repeated along the y-axis only and positioned in the center of the `<ul>` element. This gives the background an appearance of seamlessness and allows the submenus to accommodate menus long and short alike.

A hack is applied for Internet Explorer, which has some rendering issues with one of the drop-down menus:

```
ul.menu a {
    color: white;
    text-decoration: none;
    width: 100%;
    display: inline-block;
    height: 100%;
    position: relative;
}
```

A bug known to creep up in Explorer when applying `display: block;` to links within `<li>` elements reared its ugly head. So instead of setting `display` to `block`, you set it to `inline-block`, and then apply width and height of 100%, in addition to `position: relative;`.

For the other browsers, the `display: block;` is no longer necessary; you apply this to the `<span>` elements that you added:

```
ul.menu span {
    display: block;
    padding: 2px 10px;
}
li.menu > span.arrow {
    position: absolute;
    width: 15px;
    height: 15px;
    top: 5px;
    right: 15px;
    background: url('arrow.png') no-repeat right;
    border: none;
    padding: 0;
    margin: 0;
}
```

The `<span>` elements you added previously for the menu arrows are all given an `arrow` class name:

```
<li class='menu' id='menu-7'>
    <span>Other</span><span class='arrow'></span>
    <div class='menu'><div>
    <ul>
        <li>
            <a href='http://www.quirksmode.org'>
                <span>Peter-Paul Koch's Quirksmode.org</span>
            </a>
        </li>
```

Then an extra `<span>` is added to the inner text of each link and menu item. The extra `<span>` allows another element to latch onto to control spacing, as well as providing a way to side-step that Explorer white-space bug.

Drop Down, Not Sideways!

To create a dynamic menu system that drops down and not sideways, follow these steps:

1. Add a menu id name to the following `<div>` element appearing in `drop_down_menus.html`:

```
<noscript>
    <style type='text/css'>
        ul.menu li:hover > ul {
            visibility: visible;
        }
    </style>
</noscript>
</head>
<body>
    <div class='menu' id='menu'><div>
    <ul class='menu'>
        <li class='menu' id='menu-0'>
            <span>Wrox P2P</span><span class='arrow'></span>
```

2. Save `drop_down_menus.html`.

3. Make the following modifications to `drop_down_menus.css`:

```
body {
    font: 16px sans-serif;
    margin: 20px;
    color: white;
    background: white url('shell_mound.jpg') no-repeat scroll center;
}
div#menu {
    background: black;
    height: 27px;
    width: 1000px;
    margin: auto;
}
div.menu > div > ul.menu > li {
    width: 125px;
    float: left;
}
li.menu div {
    background: transparent url('images/highlight_01.png') no-repeat top;
}
li.menu div {
    width: 222px;
}
li.menu > div > div {
    width: auto;
    background: transparent url('images/highlight_03.png') no-repeat bottom;
    padding: 20px 0 20px 0;
}
ul.menu a {
    color: white;
    text-decoration: none;
    width: 100%;
```

```
       display: inline-block;
       height: 100%;
       position: relative;
   }
   ul.menu,
   ul.menu ul {
       background: transparent url('images/highlight_02.png') repeat-y center;
       list-style: none;
       padding: 0;
       margin: 0;
   }
   ul.menu ul {
       width: 222px;
   }
   li.menu > div {
       position: absolute;
       top: -20px;
       left: 222px;
       visibility: hidden;
       z-index: 4;
       width: 222px;
   }
   div.menu > div > ul.menu > li.menu > div {
       top: 29px;
       left: 0;
   }
   ul.menu li {
       position: relative;
       padding: 2px;
   }
   ul.menu li:hover,
   li.menu-highlight,
   li.menu-link-highlight {
       background: transparent url('images/transparent_02.png') repeat-y center;
   }
   ul.menu span {
       display: block;
       padding: 2px 10px;
   }
   li.menu > span.arrow {
       position: absolute;
       width: 15px;
       height: 15px;
       top: 5px;
       right: 15px;
       background: url('arrow.png') no-repeat right;
       border: none;
       padding: 0;
       margin: 0;
   }
```

4. Save drop_down_menus.css.

The resulting output is shown in Figure 3-5.

Figure 3-5

Figure 3-5 shows the top-level menu items are side-by-side now, and the drop-down menus drop down, not sideways.

The first modification you made was to give the top-level `<div>` that contains the whole menu system a unique identifier:

```
<div class='menu' id='menu'><div>
```

Having applied a `menu` id name to the top-level `<div>`, you can now add styles that are unique to it:

```
div#menu {
    background: black;
    height: 27px;
    width: 1000px;
    margin: auto;
}
```

In the preceding rule you apply a solid, black background to the top-level <div> element, a fixed height of 27 pixels and a fixed width of 1000 pixels, and then the <div> is centered with the margin: auto; declaration. A fixed width and height are necessary because the <li> elements containing the submenus are floated to the left to make them side-by-side:

```
div.menu > div > ul.menu > li {
    width: 125px;
    float: left;
}
```

The top-level <li> elements are also given a fixed width, which keeps the arrow from overlapping the text.

The remaining background styles flip around the backgrounds a bit from the last approach:

```
background: transparent url('images/highlight_01.png') no-repeat top;
```

Finally, the positioning of the drop-down menus is adjusted slightly:

```
li.menu > div {
    position: absolute;
    top: -20px;
    left: 222px;
    visibility: hidden;
    z-index: 4;
    width: 222px;
}
div.menu > div > ul.menu > li.menu > div {
    top: 29px;
    left: 0;
}
```

The new rule overrides positioning for the submenus of the top-level <li> elements to position the submenus below instead of to the right.

In the next project, you see how to create drop-down menus similar to these without JavaScript.

More Dynamic Drop-Down Menus and the Incredible, Versatile :target

Chapter 3 might have made it sound impossible to create dynamic drop-down menus using only CSS and XHTML, at least if you want to use only a click to open a menu. Although the points made were true, there is an approach using only CSS that allows a user to click to open a menu. That approach, which I focus on in this chapter, is useful for a number of things, from creating drop-down menus to custom pop-up dialogs.

I decided not to go into this approach in Chapter 3 because it does have some limitations, albeit limitations that are not impossible to work around. I also decided to focus on this approach in a chapter all its own, because it is possible to do more than merely create drop-down menus. The technique presented here can also be used to create other stylistic changes when a user clicks on something within a web document. For instance, it can be used to show a custom pop-up dialog, or to create tab-based navigation where the content of every tab exists within the same document instead of in separate documents, as demonstrated in Chapter 1.

The great benefit of this approach is that it conforms to the accessibility requirements presented in Chapter 3; that is, the document remains accessible from the keyboard, and all with very little or no JavaScript required. You also get an idea of how this technique works for the project in Chapter 5, which further explores the possibilities of using :target in a web project.

The most compelling benefit of this approach is that it removes the need for complex JavaScript. I do not feel that using JavaScript is a bad thing, or that JavaScript should be avoided — in fact quite the contrary, JavaScript makes rich, interactive applications possible. However, I believe that a web designer should take the easiest, most intuitive, most efficient route possible, while preserving accessibility. This approach, when compared to the JavaScript I prepared for Chapter 3, wins hands down for simplicity and superior accessibility. The next section elaborates on the components used in the design of this project and discusses this in more detail.

Design

The approach I focus on in this chapter centers on a little-supported CSS 3 dynamic pseudo-class called `:target`. `:target`, like `:hover` and `:active`, enables a web designer to make some stylistic modifications based on a user-initiated event. `:target` applies style based on *URL fragments*, or as they were known in the yesteryear of web design, HTML anchors. URL fragments are the portion of the URL after the hash symbol (#, or pound sign), which not coincidentally also happens to be the id selector in CSS. For example, if you want to create URLs that link to specific points in a lengthy document, you can create id names for elements within the document, and not only can you style those elements using the id selector, you can also use URL fragments to jump to those positions in the document. This is best demonstrated with the following HTML code. If you have the following link

```
<a href='#some-fragment'>Jump to the paragraph</a>
```

which, for instance, is followed by perhaps hundreds of paragraphs of content, and at some point in the markup is this paragraph

```
<p id='some-fragment'>A paragraph</p>
```

you have a URL fragment link and anchor. The `:target` dynamic pseudo-class allows you to capture this event within CSS and make a stylistic change in the target of the fragment link.

This technique can be utilized in a number of different ways. For example, you can also use `:target` to dynamically reveal and hide content in the same way that the `:hover` dynamic pseudo-class was used in Chapter 3 to create drop-down menus. `:target` can be used to create not only a drop-down menu system (albeit one limited in its flexibility), it can also be used to create custom pop-up dialogs, tooltips, and a plethora of features that previously required JavaScript.

`:target` also lends itself naturally to good accessibility. The following lists detail the pros and cons of this approach.

First, the pros:

❑ Providing a hard-coded id for an element makes it possible to link to that element from any other document, not just from within the same document. You could, for example, link to a menu from deep within a document or from another document, and when users click the link, they'll be taken to the already open menu or dialog.

❑ In browsers that allow the `<a>` element to receive focus, the user can navigate the page entirely from the keyboard using the Tab key, which consequently also supercedes my own JavaScript keyboard navigation included in Chapter 3. This is because the Tab key is already used to navigate links and other elements within a document, so the user already understands how to navigate the menu system from the keyboard.

❑ There is no complex JavaScript to maintain or debug, and stylistic or structural changes are easier to implement.

❑ `:target` can be used if JavaScript is not available, so long as the browser supports `:target` natively.

And now, the cons:

❏ It is only possible to create a drop-down navigation system one menu deep, because only one element can be the :target at any given time, and CSS does not provide a selector to access an element's parent or ancestors. Though this is a limitation, it can also be worked around with a little JavaScript.

❏ Using :target will cause the document to jump to the target, which may or may not be desired, depending on where in the document you are attempting to use the :target pseudo-class.

❏ Support is spotty. Internet Explorer does not support :target natively at the time of this writing, but it can with the help of Dean Edwards' IE7 JavaScript. Opera 8 also does not support :target. On the other hand, Mozilla Firefox and Safari do support :target.

The next section presents and describes the necessary code to create drop-down menus and pop-up dialogs using CSS.

Code and Code Explanation

You'll find the following code is identical to the last approach discussed in Chapter 3. (The modifications are highlighted.) The following code is also available on the source CD-ROM, in the Project 4 folder, and the subfolder titled "drop-down."

To implement a drop-down navigation system using :target, follow these steps:

1. Using the source code in Project 3 from the "Drop down, not Sideways!" approach, make the following modifications to drop_down_menus.html:

```
<!DOCTYPE html PUBLIC "-//W3C//DTD XHTML 1.0 Strict//EN"
"http://www.w3.org/TR/xhtml1/DTD/xhtml1-strict.dtd">
<html xmlns='http://www.w3.org/1999/xhtml' xml:lang='en'>
    <head>
        <meta http-equiv="Content-Type" content="text/html; charset=UTF-8" />
        <title>Top sites all CSS developers should know about</title>
        <link rel='stylesheet' type='text/css' href='drop_down_menus.css' />
        <!-- compliance patch for microsoft browsers -->
        <!--[if lt IE 7]>
            <style type='text/css'>
                ul.menu ul {
                    left: 220px;
                }
            </style>
            <script src='/ie7/ie7-standard-p.js' type='text/javascript'>
                IE7_PNG_SUFFIX = "arrow.png";
            </script>
        <![endif]-->
        <!--[if lt IE 6]>
            <style type='text/css'>
                ul.menu span {
                    margin-left: -15px;
```

```
                        padding-left: 15px;
                }
            </style>
        <![endif]-->
        <script type='text/javascript'>
            document.onmousedown = function($e)
            {
                ($e || ($e = window.event));

                if (
                    $e.target &&
                    $e.target.nodeName != 'A' &&
                    $e.target.parentNode.nodeName != 'A'

                    ||

                    $e.srcElement &&
                    $e.srcElement.nodeName != 'A' &&
                    $e.srcElement.parentNode.nodeName != 'A'
                ) {
                    location.href = '#';
                }
            }       </script>
    </head>
    <body>
        <div class='menu' id='menu'><div>
        <ul class='menu'>
            <li class='menu' id='menu-0'>
                <a href='#menu-0'>
                    <span>Wrox P2P</span>
                </a>
                <span class='arrow'></span>
                <div class='menu'><div>
                <ul>
                    <li>
                        <a href='http://p2p.wrox.com/forum.asp?FORUM_ID=151'>
                            <span>Beginning CSS: Cascading Style
                                Sheets for Web Design</span>
                        </a>
                    </li>
                    <li>
                        <a href='http://p2p.wrox.com/forum.asp?FORUM_ID=143'>
                            <span>CSS</span>
                        </a>
                    </li>
                    <li>
                        <a href='http://p2p.wrox.com/forum.asp?FORUM_ID=84'>
                            <span>HTML Code Clinic</span>
                        </a>
                    </li>
                </ul>
                </div></div>
            </li>
```

```
<li><a href='http://www.google.com'><span>Google</span></a></li>
<li class='menu' id='menu-1'>
    <a href='#menu-1'>
        <span>Mozilla</span>
    </a>
    <span class='arrow'></span>
    <div class='menu'><div>
    <ul>
        <li>
            <a href='http://www.mozilla.org/products/firefox'>
                <span>Firefox</span>
            </a>
        </li>
        <li>
            <a href='http://www.mozilla.org/products/thunderbird'>
                <span>Thunderbird</span>
            </a>
        </li>
        <li>
            <a href='http://bugzilla.mozilla.org'>
                <span>Bugzilla</span>
            </a>
        </li>
    </ul>
    </div></div>
</li>
<li class='menu' id='menu-2'>
    <a href='#menu-2'>
        <span>Apple</span>
    </a>
    <span class='arrow'></span>
    <div class='menu'><div>
    <ul>
        <li>
            <a href='http://www.apple.com/safari'>
                <span>Safari</span>
            </a>
        </li>
        <li>
            <a href='http://webkit.opendarwin.org'>
                <span>Webkit Open Source Project</span>
            </a>
        </li>
        <li>
            <a href='http://webkit.opendarwin.org/blog/'>
                <span>Surfin Safari</span>
            </a>
        </li>
        <li>
            <a href='http://www.apple.com/macosx'>
                <span>Mac OS X</span>
            </a>
        </li>
```

```
        <li>
            <a href='http://www.apple.com/itunes'>
                <span>iTunes</span>
            </a>
        </li>
    </ul>
        </div></div>
</li>
<li class='menu' id='menu-4'>
        <a href='#menu-4'>
            <span>Microsoft</span>
        </a>
        <span class='arrow'></span>
        <div class='menu'><div>
        <ul>
            <li>
                <a href='http://blogs.msdn.com/ie'>
                    <span>Internet Explorer Blog</span>
                </a>
            </li>
            <li>
                <a
href='http://channel9.msdn.com/wiki/default.aspx/Channel9.InternetExplorerFeedback'>
                    <span>Internet Explorer Wiki</span>
                </a>
            </li>
        </ul>
        </div></div>
</li>
<li class='menu' id='menu-6'>
        <a href='#menu-6'>
            <span>W3C</span>
        </a>
        <span class='arrow'></span>
        <div class='menu'><div>
        <ul>
            <li>
                <a href='http://validator.w3.org'>
                    <span>W3C Markup Validation Service</span>
                </a>
            </li>
            <li>
                <a href='http://jigsaw.w3.org/css-validator/'>
                    <span>W3C CSS Validation Service</span>
                </a>
            </li>
            <li>
                <a href='http://www.w3.org/TR/CSS21/'>
                    <span>CSS 2.1 Specification</span>
                </a>
            </li>
```

```
            <li>
                <a href='http://www.w3.org/Style/CSS/current-work'>
                    <span>CSS 3</span>
                </a>
            </li>
        </ul>
        </div></div>
    </li>
    <li class='menu' id='menu-7'>
        <a href='#menu-7'>
            <span>Other</span>
        </a>
        <span class='arrow'></span>
        <div class='menu'><div>
        <ul>
            <li>
                <a href='http://www.quirksmode.org'>
                    <span>Peter-Paul Koch's Quirksmode.org</span>
                </a>
            </li>
            <li>
                <a href='http://www.meyerweb.com'>
                    <span>Eric A. Meyer</span>
                </a>
            </li>
            <li>
                <a href='http://www.alistapart.com'>
                    <span>A List Apart</span>
                </a>
            </li>
            <li>
                <a href='http://www.positioniseverything.net'>
                    <span>Position is Everything</span>
                </a>
            </li>
            <li>
                <a href='http://annevankesteren.nl'>
                    <span>Anne's Weblog About Markup and Style</span>
                </a>
            </li>
            <li>
                <a href='http://dean.edwards.name'>
                    <span>Dean Edwards</span>
                </a>
            </li>
            <li>
                <a href='http://www.csszengarden.com'>
                    <span>CSS Zen Garden</span>
                </a>
            </li>
        </ul>
        </div></div>
    </li>
```

```
            </ul>
          </div></div>
      </body>
  </html>
```

2. Save `drop_down_menus.html`.

3. Next, make the following changes to `drop_down_menus.css`:

```css
body {
    font: 16px sans-serif;
    margin: 20px;
    color: white;
    background: white url('shell_mound.jpg') no-repeat scroll center;
}
div#menu {
    background: black;
    height: 27px;
    width: 1000px;
    margin: auto;
}
div.menu > div > ul.menu > li {
    width: 125px;
    float: left;
}
li.menu div {
    background: transparent url('images/highlight_01.png') no-repeat top;
}
li.menu div {
    width: 222px;
}
li.menu > div > div {
    width: auto;
    background: transparent url('images/highlight_03.png') no-repeat bottom;
    padding: 20px 0 20px 0;
}
ul.menu a {
    color: white;
    text-decoration: none;
    width: 100%;
    display: inline-block;
    height: 100%;
    position: relative;
}
ul.menu a:focus {
    color: yellow;
}
ul.menu,
ul.menu ul {
    background: transparent url('images/highlight_02.png') repeat-y center;
    list-style: none;
    padding: 0;
    margin: 0;
}
```

```
    }
div.menu li:target > div {
    visibility: visible;
}
ul.menu ul {
    width: 222px;
}
li.menu > div {
    position: absolute;
    top: -20px;
    left: 222px;
    visibility: hidden;
    z-index: 4;
    width: 222px;
}
div.menu > div > ul.menu > li.menu > div {
    top: 29px;
    left: 0;
}
ul.menu li {
    position: relative;
    padding: 2px;
}
ul.menu li:hover,
li.menu-highlight,
li.menu-link-highlight {
    background: transparent url('images/transparent_02.png') repeat-y center;
}
ul.menu span {
    display: block;
    padding: 2px 10px;
}
li.menu > span.arrow {
    position: absolute;
    width: 15px;
    height: 15px;
    top: 5px;
    right: 15px;
    background: url('arrow.png') no-repeat right;
    border: none;
    padding: 0;
    margin: 0;
}
```

4. Save `drop_down_menus.css`.

Figure 4-1 shows the resulting output in Mozilla Firefox.

From the output in Figure 4-1 and the code, you can see that not many modifications were required to enable a :target-driven dynamic drop-down menu system.

Figure 4-1

The first modification you made was to `drop_down_menus.html`. Here you added a few lines of JavaScript:

```
<script type='text/javascript'>
    document.onmousedown = function($e)
    {
        ($e || ($e = window.event));

        if (
            $e.target &&
            $e.target.nodeName != 'A' &&
            $e.target.parentNode.nodeName != 'A'

            ||

            $e.srcElement &&
            $e.srcElement.nodeName != 'A' &&
            $e.srcElement.parentNode.nodeName != 'A'
        ) {
            location.href = '#';
```

```
        }
    }          </script>
```

This JavaScript is the mechanism that closes open menus when the user clicks the document. It sets the URL fragment target to blank (this action is not associated with any style sheet rule) and closes the menu. You can also add links within the document itself without JavaScript to close menus. For example

```
<a href='#'>Close</a>
```

provides the same functionality as what the preceding JavaScript provides, but the JavaScript approach seems the most intuitive. The menu remains open until the user clicks somewhere on the document that isn't a link.

Next, you applied several links within the body of the document itself that link to their parent <li> elements:

```
<li class='menu' id='menu-7'>
    <a href='#menu-7'>
        <span>Other</span>
    </a>
```

The link links to the parent <li> element with the same id name that appears in the URL fragment. Then, via the style sheet, you can initiate styles based on that target:

```
div.menu li:target > div {
    visibility: visible;
}
```

Because the element that is a target is an <li> element, the preceding style sheet rule applies. It says that when any <li> element that is a descendant of a <div> element with a menu class name contains an id which is the same as found in the URL fragment, and it has a direct child <div> element, make that element visible.

Finally, to provide a visual cue for users who are navigating the menu system with their keyboard, a :focus dynamic pseudo-class is applied:

```
ul.menu a:focus {
    color: yellow;
}
```

This causes links to become yellow when they receive focus.

Testing and Caveats

You haven't yet achieved compatibility with Internet Explorer because even though Dean Edwards' IE7 JavaScript has support for the :target pseudo-class, it isn't included in the default IE7 library. This is because Dean Edwards modularized the IE7 JavaScript, separating different functionality, so that you could include only the fixes that you need, rather than wasting bandwidth and browser loading speed on features you don't need.

To enable this project in Internet Explorer, add the following line to `drop_down_menus.html`:

```
<!-- compliance patch for microsoft browsers -->
<!--[if lt IE 7]>
    <style type='text/css'>
        ul.menu ul {
            left: 220px;
        }
    </style>
    <script src='/ie7/ie7-standard-p.js' type='text/javascript'>
        IE7_PNG_SUFFIX = "arrow.png";
    </script>
    <script src='/ie7/ie7-css3-selectors.js' type='text/javascript'>
    </script>
<![endif]-->
```

Save `drop_down_menus.html`. That's it! Now the `:target` pseudo-class works in Internet Explorer 5, 5.5, and 6.

In the next chapter you continue using the `:target` pseudo-class with a project called "all-in-one tabs." That project uses a tab-based navigation system where the content of each tab is contained in the same document.

Slide Show

In Chapter 4 you saw how the :target pseudo-class might be useful for click-driven events. However, it's not always useful because the functionality of the :target pseudo-class is driven by HTML anchors; because of this, sometimes :target-driven drop-down menus are not ideal when a document has scrolling content, because clicking an anchor causes the document to jump to the position of the anchor. This chapter presents a slightly more useful application of the :target pseudo-class: creating a standards-driven slide show.

Slide shows are typical features of desktop applications like Microsoft Office's Power Point, but the idea of a web-based slide show isn't new. Eric Meyer, CSS guru and author of several popular CSS books, such as *Eric Meyer on CSS* (New Riders) and *CSS the Definitive Guide* (O'Reilly), first popularized the idea of web-based slide shows with his S5. S5 stands for Simple Standards-based Slide Show System. Originally inspired by a slide show developed by Tantek Çelik (former lead developer of Internet Explorer for the Macintosh) and another CSS guru, S5 is driven by XHTML, CSS, and JavaScript. The difference between Eric Meyer's S5 and the slide show application presented in this chapter is that Eric Meyer's S5 uses JavaScript to reduce the setup time required to make a standards-driven slide show. He uses JavaScript to automatically generate the slide show navigation, and some semantically oriented naming conventions that facilitate the easy creation of a web-based slide show. Because S5 makes use of JavaScript to automate certain aspects of a web-based slide show, it is inherently superior to the project presented in this chapter. S5 also automatically generates alternative style sheets for other mediums such a print or projector, whereas all aspects of navigation and alternative style sheets presented in this chapter must be created manually.

The next section covers some of the design requirements for a web-based slide show.

Design

In Chapter 3 you learned that some people don't believe CSS should have any event-driven functionality. I tend to digress from rigid adherence to the idea that CSS is for presentation and presentation only—rather, I advocate the simplest path possible. In some cases event-driven functionality fits well with CSS; at other times event-driven functionality belongs with JavaScript. In Chapter 4 you saw how the :target pseudo-class can enable a much greater degree of accessibility and usability than simple mouseover pure-CSS menus, because using the :target pseudo-class allows you to link to a document in a particular state—for instance, linking to a document in which a particular menu is open. The :target pseudo-class also allows a web document to continue to be accessible by keyboard without any extra intervention via JavaScript.

The slide show presented in this chapter is contained in a single document. Different slides are contained in different <div> elements. Each <div> element is uniquely named with an id name, which enables a particular <div> to be anchored using HTML anchors—which subsequently lets the :target pseudo-class enable different styles based on which <div> element is the current target in the anchor.

The next section presents the source code for a web-based slide show.

Code and Code Explanation

To create a standards-driven slide show using CSS and XHTML, follow these steps:

1. Enter the following markup:

```
<!DOCTYPE html PUBLIC "-//W3C//DTD XHTML 1.0 Strict//EN"
"http://www.w3.org/TR/xhtml1/DTD/xhtml1-strict.dtd">
<html xmlns='http://www.w3.org/1999/xhtml' xml:lang='en'>
    <head>
        <meta http-equiv="Content-Type" content="text/html; charset=UTF-8" />
        <title>:target Slideshow</title>
        <link rel='stylesheet' type='text/css' href='styles/slideshow.css' />
    </head>
    <body>
        <div id='slide-new-features' class='slide'>
            <h1>New Features in Microsoft Internet Explorer 7</h1>
            <p>
                The latest version of Microsoft's flagship Internet Explorer
                7 browser contains many key enhancements that promise
                to make a web developer's job easier.
            </p>
        </div>
        <div id='slide-bug-fixes' class='slide'>
            <h1>IE7 Bug Fixes</h1>
            <p>
                Internet Explorer 7 has bug fixes for several, infamous bugs that
                plagued Internet Explorer 6, and made the IE platform a thorn in
                the sides of developers everywhere.
            </p>
            <p>
                Some of the most well-known rendering bugs have been fixed.
            </p>
            <ul>
                <li>
                    Layering of the
                    <span class='code'>&lt;select&gt;</span> element
                </li>
                <li>Peek-a-boo</li>
                <li>Guillotine</li>
                <li>Duplicate character</li>
                <li>Border chaos</li>
```

```
        <li>No Scroll</li>
        <li>Three-pixel text jog</li>
        <li>Magic creeping text</li>
        <li>Bottom margin bug on hover</li>
        <li>Losing the ability to highlight text under the top border</li>
    </ul>
</div>
<div id='slide-bug-fixes-2' class='slide'>
    <h1>More IE7 Bug Fixes</h1>
    <p>Also fixed in IE7</p>
    <ul>
        <li>IE/Win line height bug</li>
        <li>Double-margin float bug</li>
        <li>Quirky percentages</li>
        <li>Duplicate indent</li>
        <li>Moving viewport scrollbar outside HTML borders</li>
        <li>1px border style</li>
        <li>Disappearing list background</li>
        <li>Auto width</li>
    </ul>
</div>
<div id='slide-css-support' class='slide'>
    <h1>New CSS Support in IE7</h1>
    <p>
        In addition to CSS bug fixes, Microsoft has added some support
        for other CSS features.
    </p>
    <ul>
        <li>Fixed positioning</li>
        <li>
            Fixed backgrounds on all elements, not just the
            <span class='code'>&lt;body&gt;</span> element
        </li>
        <li>CSS 2 selectors
            <ul>
                <li>Direct Child</li>
                <li>Adjacent Sibling</li>
                <li>Attribute</li>
            </ul>
        </li>
        <li>CSS 2 pseudo-classes
            <ul>
                <li class='code'>:first-child</li>
                <li>
                    <span class='code'>:hover</span> on all elements,
                    not just the <span class='code'>&lt;a&gt;</span>
                    element
                </li>
            </ul>
        </li>
    </ul>
</div>
<div id='slide-markup' class='slide'>
    <h1>Markup Improvements</h1>
```

```
            <p>
                Some markup improvements have also been made in IE7.
            </p>
            <ul>
                <li>
                    Including an <span class='code'>&lt;?xml</span> prolog
                    in IE7 no longer triggers quirks mode in XHTML
                    documents.
                </li>
                <li>
                    IE7 includes native support for the
                    <span class='code'>&lt;abbr&gt;</span> element.
                </li>
                <li>
                    IE7 boasts improved support for
                    <span class='code'>&lt;object&gt;</span> element fallback.
                </li>
            </ul>
        </div>
        <div id='slide-ie7-release' class='slide'>
            <h1>IE7 Release Date</h1>
            <p>
                Microsoft has not commited to a definitive release date
                for IE7 at the time of this writing. As of now, only a public
                beta of IE7 has been announced, and is expected for the first
                quarter of 2006.
            </p>
        </div>
        <div id='slide-navigation'>
            <ul>
                <li><a href='#slide-new-features'>New Features in IE7</a></li>
                <li><a href='#slide-bug-fixes'>IE7 Bug Fixes</a></li>
                <li><a href='#slide-bug-fixes-2'>More IE7 Bug Fixes</a></li>
                <li><a href='#slide-css-support'>New CSS Support in IE7</a></li>
                <li><a href='#slide-markup'>IE7 Markup Improvements</a></li>
                <li><a href='#slide-ie7-release'>IE7 Release Date</a></li>
            </ul>
        </div>
    </body>
</html>
```

2. Save the preceding markup document as `slideshow.html`.

3. Enter the following style sheet:

```
body {
    font: 12px sans-serif;
}
.code {
    font-family: monospace;
```

```
}
div.slide {
    display: none;
    position: absolute;
    top: 0;
    bottom: 0;
    left: 0;
    right: 0;
    font-size: 15px;
    border: 50px solid #369;
    margin: 50px;
    padding: 50px;
}
div.slide:target {
    display: block;
}
div#slide-navigation {
    position: absolute;
    bottom: 0;
    right: 0;
    opacity: 0.0;
    width: 200px;
    background: white;
    border: 1px solid black;
    padding: 10px;
    margin: 10px;
}
div#slide-navigation ul {
    margin: 0;
    padding: 0;
    list-style: none;
}
div#slide-navigation li {
    margin-top: 5px;
}
div#slide-navigation a {
    text-decoration: none;
    color: black;
}
div#slide-navigation:hover {
    opacity: 1;
}
```

4. Save the preceding style sheet as `slideshow.css`.

The preceding code results in the output shown in Figure 5-1. When rendered in a browser, hovering the mouse cursor in the lower right-hand corner of the browser window reveals the slide navigation.

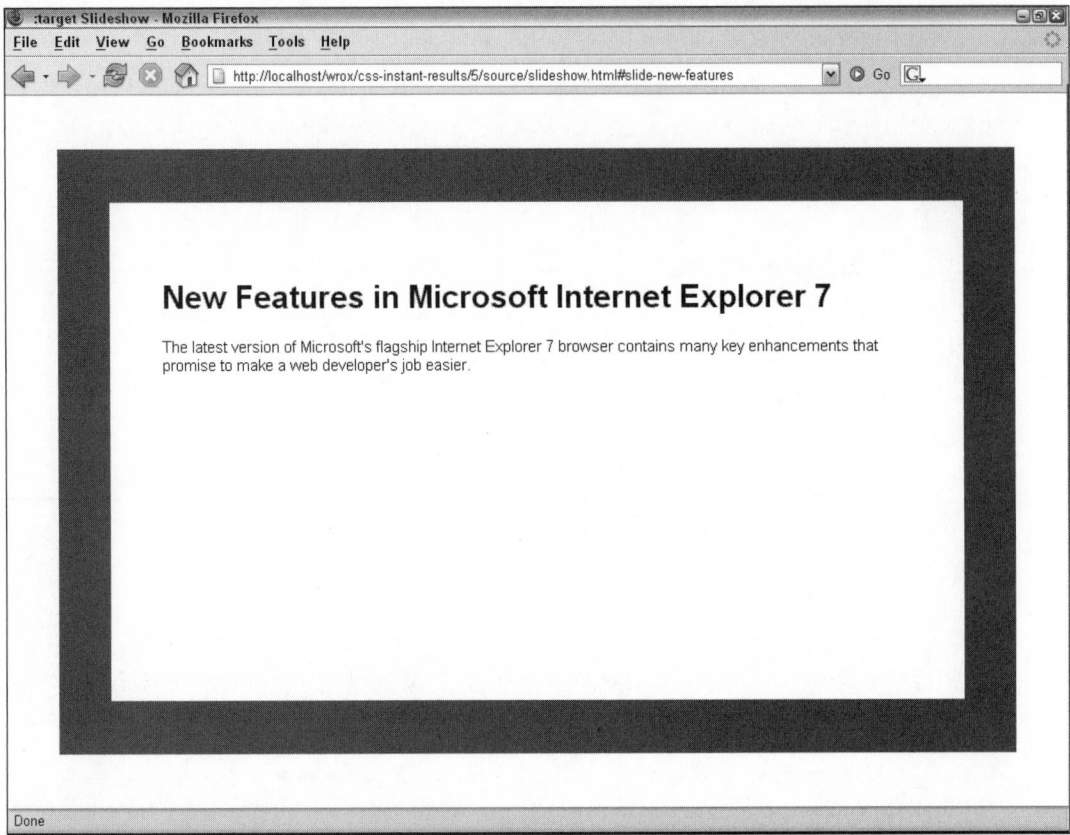

Figure 5-1

Figure 5-2 shows the contents of slide 2, "IE7 Bug Fixes."

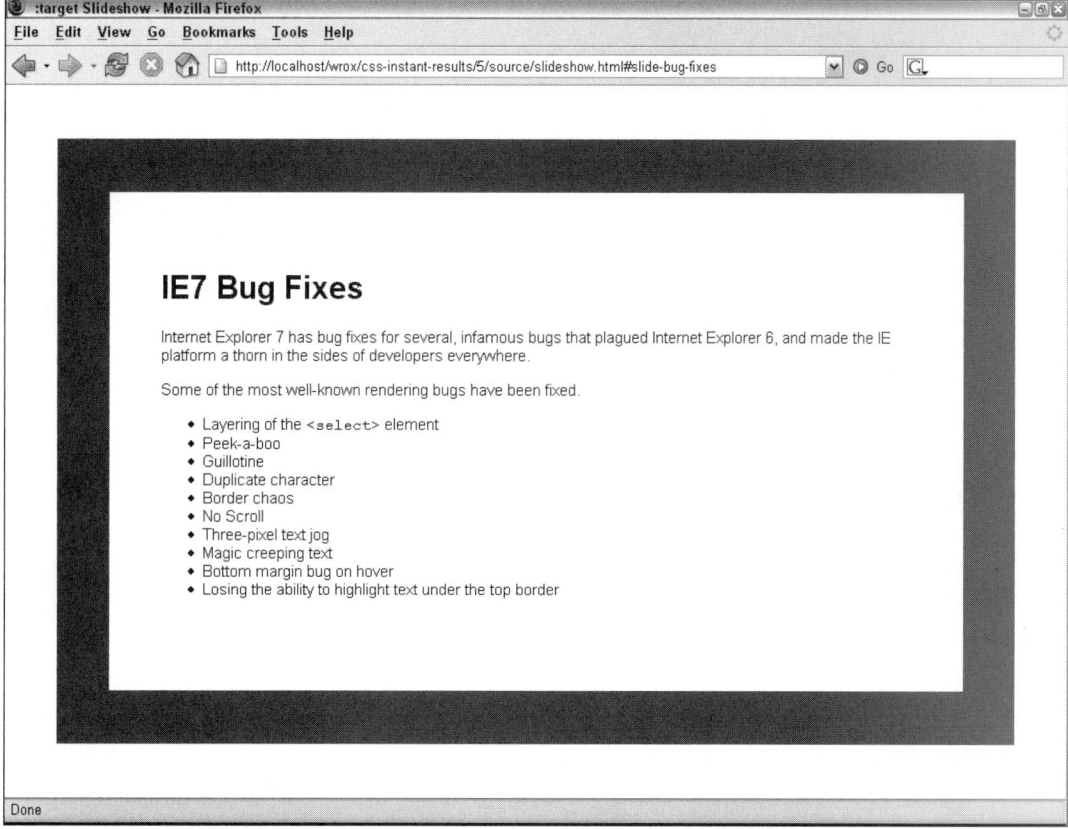

Figure 5-2

Figure 5-3 shows the contents of slide 3, "More IE7 Bug Fixes."

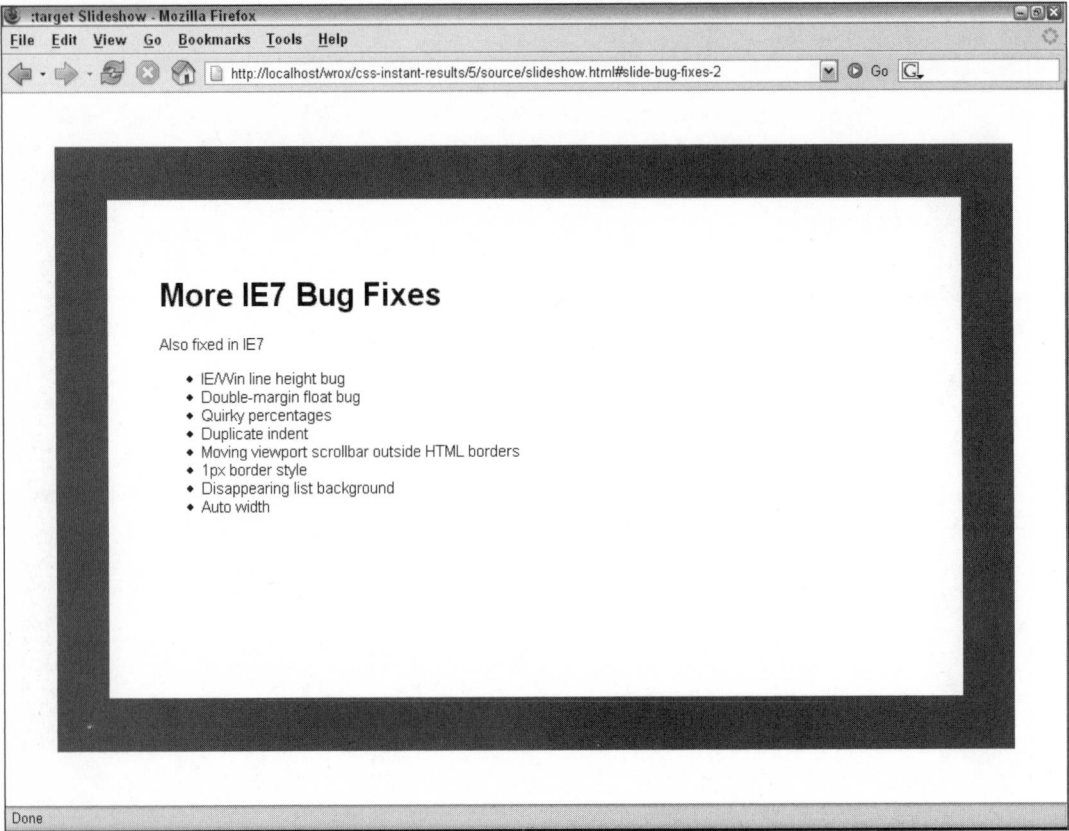

Figure 5-3

Figure 5-4 shows the contents of slide 4, "New CSS Support in IE7."

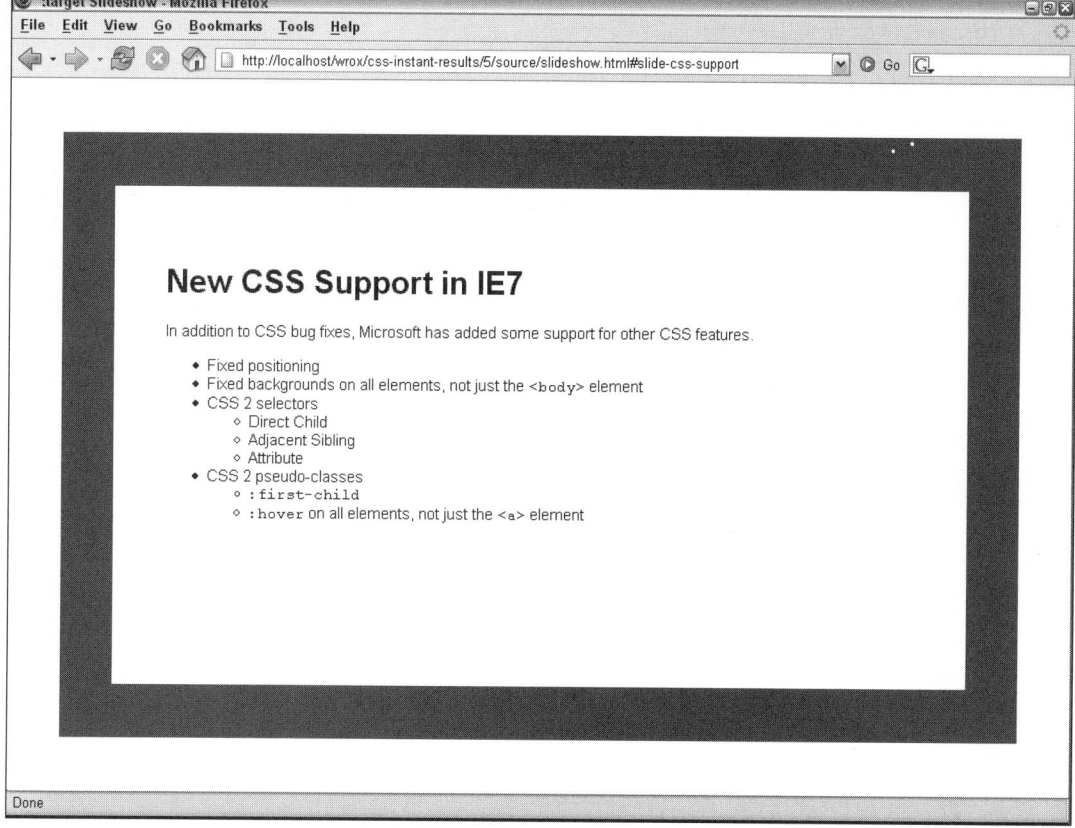

Figure 5-4

Figure 5-5 shows the contents of slide 5, "IE 7 Markup Improvements."

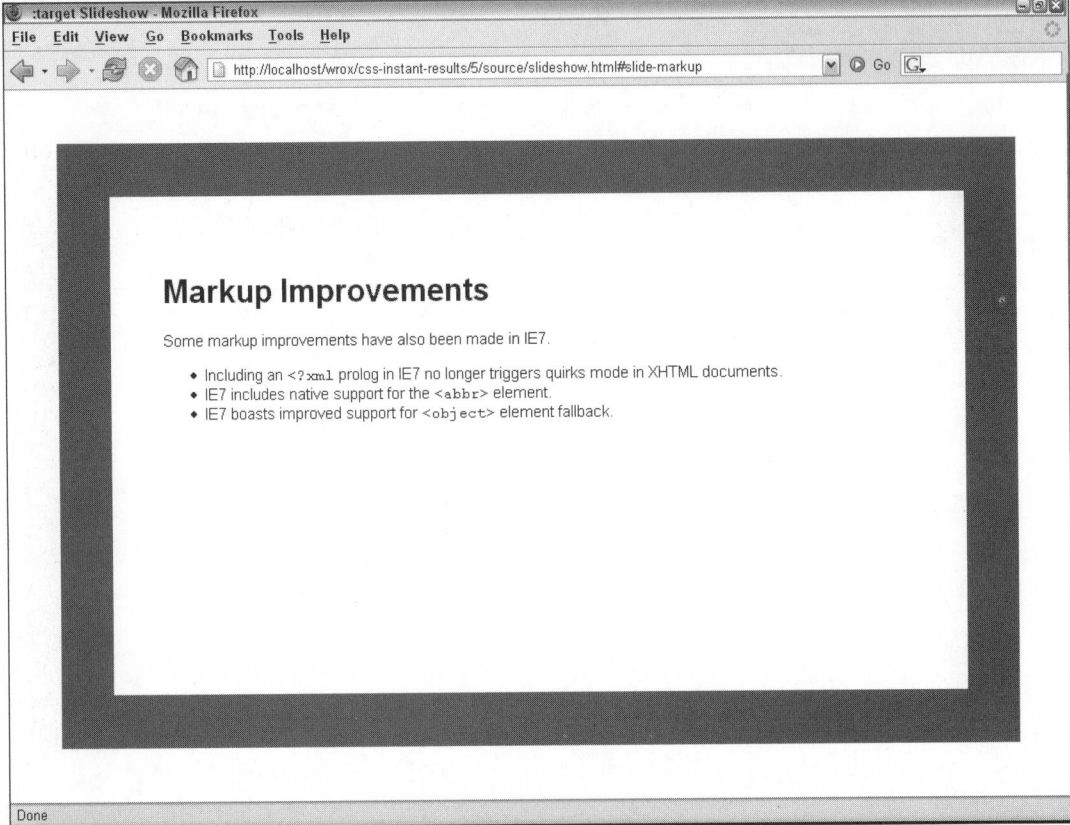

Figure 5-5

Figure 5-6 shows the contents of slide 6, "IE7 Release Date."

Figure 5-6

As you can see, there isn't much to creating a web-based slide show. The rest of this section is a review of the styles applied in `slideshow.css`.

In the first rule you applied a font to the document, setting it to 12 pixels and sans-serif:

```
body {
    font: 12px sans-serif;
}
```

The next style sheet rule applies to any element with a "code" class name. When an element is given a "code" class name, a monospace font is applied to that element:

```
.code {
    font-family: monospace;
}
```

Next, each slide is styled. First, each <div> element with a "slide" class name is hidden with the display: none; declaration. Then each slide <div> is positioned absolutely. By specifying the top: 0; and bottom: 0; combination of offset properties, the height of the <div> element is stretched to a height that is relative to the height of the element the slide <div> element is positioned relative to. Then the left: 0; and right: 0; combination of offset properties stretches the <div> element to a width relative to the width of the element it is positioned relative to. This is necessary because absolutely positioned elements follow the *shrink-to-fit* width and height sizing algorithms. By default, the shrink-to-fit sizing algorithm means that the width and height of the <div> element is determined by the content contained inside of it and it will grow in width or in height only enough to accommodate that content.

Next, the font-size of each slide is increased to 15 pixels, and then a solid blue border, 50 pixels in width, is applied to all sides of each "slide" <div>. Finally, 50 pixels of margin and 50 pixels of padding are applied:

```
div.slide {
    display: none;
    position: absolute;
    top: 0;
    bottom: 0;
    left: 0;
    right: 0;
    font-size: 15px;
    border: 50px solid #369;
    margin: 50px;
    padding: 50px;
}
```

Next comes the mechanism that makes this particular slide show possible. When a <div> with a slide class name is the target of an HTML anchor request, that <div> is given the display: block; declaration. When a <div> isn't the target of an HTML anchor request, the style reverts back to display: none; as specified by the previous rule:

```
div.slide:target {
    display: block;
}
```

The next rule positions the slide show navigation in the lower right-hand corner of the screen with the bottom: 0; and right: 0; combination of offset properties. The "slide-navigation" <div> is made fully transparent with the opacity: 0.0; declaration, which hides the navigation by default. A fixed width of 200 pixels is applied. Then a white background is applied with a 1-pixel solid black border. Finally, 10 pixels of padding and margin are applied:

```
div#slide-navigation {
    position: absolute;
    bottom: 0;
    right: 0;
    opacity: 0.0;
    width: 200px;
    background: white;
    border: 1px solid black;
    padding: 10px;
    margin: 10px;
}
```

In the following rule, the default styles of the `<ul>` element containing the navigation for the slide show are removed with the `margin: 0;`, `padding: 0;`, and `list-style: none;` declarations:

```
div#slide-navigation ul {
    margin: 0;
    padding: 0;
    list-style: none;
}
```

In the next rule, 5 pixels of margin add space between each link for the slide show navigation:

```
div#slide-navigation li {
    margin-top: 5px;
}
```

Then the default underline for each link is removed, and the links themselves are colored black:

```
div#slide-navigation a {
    text-decoration: none;
    color: black;
}
```

Finally, to make the slide show navigation visible when the user's mouse cursor is hovering over it, the next rule resets the opacity property to a value of 1, which makes the "slide-navigation" `<div>` element fully opaque:

```
div#slide-navigation:hover {
    opacity: 1;
}
```

Now you have a quick and easy method to build your own standards-based slide show. The next section describes the caveats associated with this approach.

Testing and Caveats

First and foremost, the slide show as presented doesn't even work in Internet Explorer, or even Opera for that matter. Neither of those browsers support the `:target` pseudo-class or the CSS 3 `opacity` property. At the time of this writing, version 9 of the Opera browser is in development and is said to support the CSS 3 `opacity` property, but as of now no support for the `:target` pseudo-class is planned for Opera 9. At present, I have no fix for Opera; however, it is possible to use JavaScript in Opera 9, detect the anchor portion of the URL, and display the appropriate slide.

Instead of using Dean Edwards' JavaScript, this section demonstrates how to get the slide show working using grassroots Internet Explorer hacks — that is, by using proprietary features and JavaScript.

Figure 5-7 shows the slide show as it now stands in Internet Explorer.

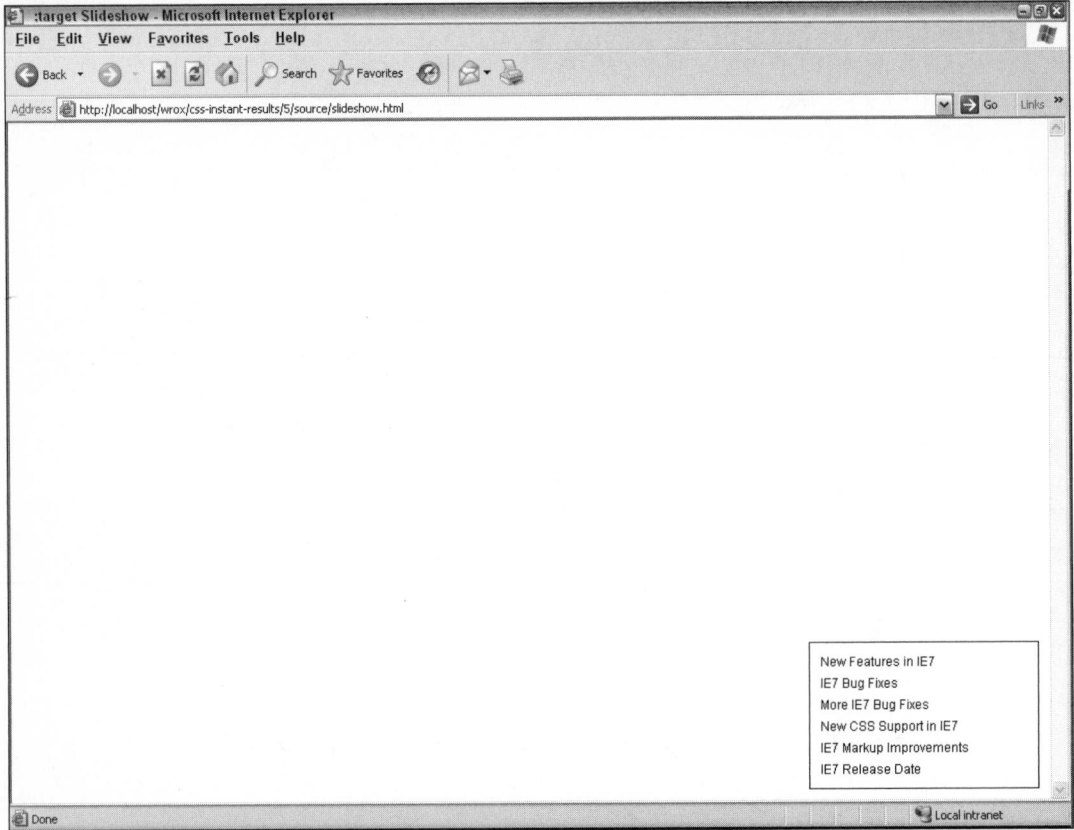

Figure 5-7

To address Internet Explorer's lack of support for the CSS 3 `opacity` property, you use the proprietary `filter` property. The `filter` property is used to provide a variety of graphical effects. The caveat with this property is that it only works in Microsoft Internet Explorer for Windows. Instead of using the `opacity: 0;` declaration to get full transparency, you use the following more verbose declaration for Internet Explorer:

```
filter:progid:DXImageTransform.Microsoft.Alpha(opacity=0);
```

Unlike the CSS 3 `opacity` property, the `filter` property accepts a percentage, so the value you specify in the `opacity=` portion of the syntax is a value between 0 and 100, where 0 is fully transparent and 100 is fully opaque.

To get around Internet Explorer not supporting the CSS 3 `:target` pseudo-class, you use JavaScript to detect the presence of the anchor portion of the URL, then get the anchor portion of the URL and display the correct slide.

To fix the slide show for Internet Explorer and Opera 9, follow these steps:

1. Make the following changes to `slideshow.html`:

```html
<!DOCTYPE html PUBLIC "-//W3C//DTD XHTML 1.0 Strict//EN"
"http://www.w3.org/TR/xhtml1/DTD/xhtml1-strict.dtd">
<html xmlns='http://www.w3.org/1999/xhtml' xml:lang='en'>
    <head>
        <meta http-equiv="Content-Type" content="text/html; charset=UTF-8" />
        <title>:target Slideshow</title>
        <link rel='stylesheet' type='text/css' href='styles/slideshow.other.css' />
        <!-- compliance patch for microsoft browsers -->
        <!--[if lt IE 7]>
            <style type='text/css'>
                div.slide {
                    width:
                        expression(
                            document.getElementById('slideshow').offsetWidth - 300
                        );
                    height:
                        expression(
                            document.getElementById('slideshow').offsetHeight -300
                        );
                }
            </style>
        <![endif]-->
        <script type='text/javascript'>
            switch (navigator.appName)
            {
                case 'Microsoft Internet Explorer':
                case 'Opera':
                {
                    document.write("<script src='slideshow.js'");
                    document.write("type='text/javascript'>");
                    document.write("</" + "script>");
                    break;
                }
            }
        </script>
    </head>
<body id='slideshow'>
        <div id='slide-new-features' class='slide'>
            <h1>New Features in Microsoft Internet Explorer 7</h1>
            <p>
                The latest version of Microsoft's flagship Internet Explorer
                7 browser contains many key enhancements that promise
                to make a web developer's job easier.
            </p>
        </div>
        <div id='slide-bug-fixes' class='slide'>
            <h1>IE7 Bug Fixes</h1>
```

```
<p>
    Internet Explorer 7 has bug fixes for several, infamous bugs that
    plagued Internet Explorer 6, and made the IE platform a thorn in
    the sides of developers everywhere.
</p>
<p>
    Some of the most well-known rendering bugs have been fixed.
</p>
<ul>
    <li>
        Layering of the
        <span class='code'>&lt;select&gt;</span> element
    </li>
    <li>Peek-a-boo</li>
    <li>Guillotine</li>
    <li>Duplicate character</li>
    <li>Border chaos</li>
    <li>No Scroll</li>
    <li>Three-pixel text jog</li>
    <li>Magic creeping text</li>
    <li>Bottom margin bug on hover</li>
    <li>Losing the ability to highlight text under the top border</li>
</ul>
</div>
<div id='slide-bug-fixes-2' class='slide'>
    <h1>More IE7 Bug Fixes</h1>
    <p>Also fixed in IE7</p>
    <ul>
        <li>IE/Win line height bug</li>
        <li>Double-margin float bug</li>
        <li>Quirky percentages</li>
        <li>Duplicate indent</li>
        <li>Moving viewport scrollbar outside HTML borders</li>
        <li>1px border style</li>
        <li>Disappearing list background</li>
        <li>Auto width</li>
    </ul>
</div>
<div id='slide-css-support' class='slide'>
    <h1>New CSS Support in IE7</h1>
    <p>
        In addition to CSS bug fixes, Microsoft has added some support
        for other CSS features.
    </p>
    <ul>
        <li>Fixed positioning</li>
        <li>
            Fixed backgrounds on all elements, not just the
            <span class='code'>&lt;body&gt;</span> element
        </li>
        <li>CSS 2 selectors
            <ul>
                <li>Direct Child</li>
                <li>Adjacent Sibling</li>
                <li>Attribute</li>
            </ul>
        </li>
```

```
                <li>CSS 2 pseudo-classes
                    <ul>
                        <li class='code'>:first-child</li>
                        <li>
                            <span class='code'>:hover</span> on all elements,
                            not just the <span class='code'>&lt;a&gt;</span>
                            element
                        </li>
                    </ul>
                </li>
            </ul>
        </div>
        <div id='slide-markup' class='slide'>
            <h1>Markup Improvements</h1>
            <p>
                Some markup improvements have also been made in IE7.
            </p>
            <ul>
                <li>
                    Including an <span class='code'>&lt;?xml</span> prolog
                    in IE7 no longer triggers quirks mode in XHTML
                    documents.
                </li>
                <li>
                    IE7 includes native support for the
                    <span class='code'>&lt;abbr&gt;</span> element.
                </li>
                <li>
                    IE7 boasts improved support for
                    <span class='code'>&lt;object&gt;</span> element fallback.
                </li>
            </ul>
        </div>
        <div id='slide-ie7-release' class='slide'>
            <h1>IE7 Release Date</h1>
            <p>
                Microsoft has not commited to a definitive release date
                for IE7 at the time of this writing. As of now, only a public
                beta of IE7 has been announced, and is expected for the first
                quarter of 2006.
            </p>
        </div>
        <div id='slide-navigation'>
            <ul id='slide-navigation-inner'>
                <li><a href='#slide-new-features'>New Features in IE7</a></li>
                <li><a href='#slide-bug-fixes'>IE7 Bug Fixes</a></li>
                <li><a href='#slide-bug-fixes-2'>More IE7 Bug Fixes</a></li>
                <li><a href='#slide-css-support'>New CSS Support in IE7</a></li>
                <li><a href='#slide-markup'>IE7 Markup Improvements</a></li>
                <li><a href='#slide-ie7-release'>IE7 Release Date</a></li>
            </ul>
        </div>
    </body>
</html>
```

2. Save the preceding document as `slideshow.other.html`.

3. Make the following modifications to `slideshow.css`:

```css
html {
    height: 100%;
}
body {
    font: 12px sans-serif;
    margin: 0;
    padding: 0;
    height: 100%;
}
.code {
    font-family: monospace;
}
div.slide {
    display: none;
    position: absolute;
    top: 0;
    bottom: 0;
    left: 0;
    right: 0;
    font-size: 15px;
    border: 50px solid #369;
    margin: 50px;
    padding: 50px;
}
div.slide:target {
    display: block;
}
div#slide-navigation {
    position: absolute;
    bottom: 0;
    right: 0;
    opacity: 0.0;
    filter: progid:DXImageTransform.Microsoft.Alpha(opacity=0);
    width: 200px;
    background: white;
    border: 1px solid black;
    padding: 10px;
    margin: 10px;
}
div#slide-navigation ul {
    margin: 0;
    padding: 0;
    list-style: none;
}
div#slide-navigation li {
    margin-top: 5px;
}
div#slide-navigation a {
    text-decoration: none;
    color: black;
}
div#slide-navigation:hover {
    opacity: 1;
}
```

4. Save the preceding as `slideshow.other.css`.

5. In yet another file, add the following JavaScript:

```javascript
var $currentSlide = '';

function slideEvents()
{
    var $li = document.getElementById('slide-navigation-inner').childNodes;

    for (var $i in $li)
    {
        if ($li[$i].childNodes &&
            $li[$i].childNodes[0] &&
            $li[$i].childNodes[0].nodeName == 'A'
        ) {
            $li[$i].childNodes[0].onclick = getSlide;
        }
    }

    getSlide();

    var $navigation = document.getElementById('slide-navigation');

    if (navigator.appName == 'Microsoft Internet Explorer')
    {
        $navigation.onmouseover = function()
        {
            this.style.filter =
                'progid:DXImageTransform.Microsoft.Alpha(opacity=100);';
        };

        $navigation.onmouseout = function()
        {
            this.style.filter =
                'progid:DXImageTransform.Microsoft.Alpha(opacity=0);';
        };
    }
}

function getSlide()
{
    if (this.href)
    {
        var $anchor = this.href.substring(
            this.href.indexOf('#') + 1, this.href.length
        );

        if (document.getElementById($currentSlide))
        {
            document.getElementById($currentSlide).style.display = 'none';
        }

        $currentSlide = $anchor;

        if ($anchor.length && document.getElementById($anchor))
        {
```

```
            document.getElementById($anchor).style.display = 'block';
        }
    }
}

window.onload = slideEvents;
```

6.   Save the preceding document as `slideshow.js`.

If you were successful making the preceding modifications, you'll have a working slide show in Internet Explorer 6, as is shown in Figure 5-8.

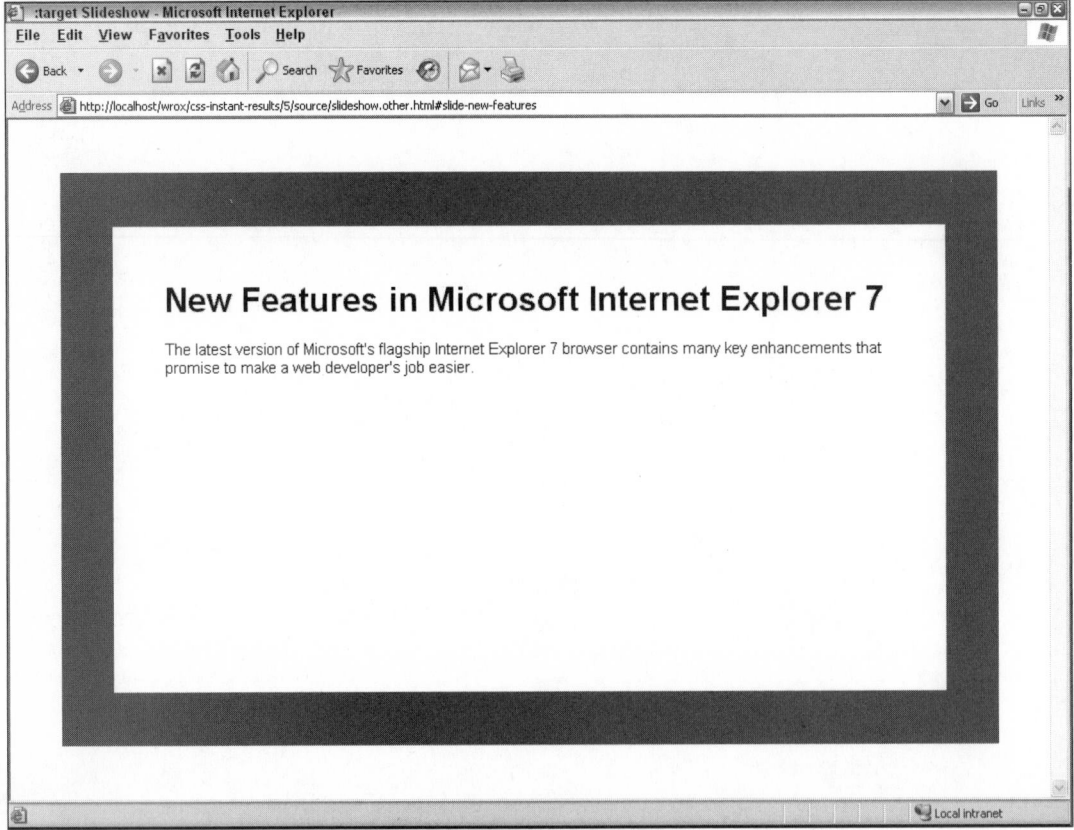

Figure 5-8

You also have a mostly working slide show in Opera 8 (the navigation menu isn't hidden by default), and a functional navigation menu in Opera 9. Figure 5-9 shows the slide show in Opera 8.

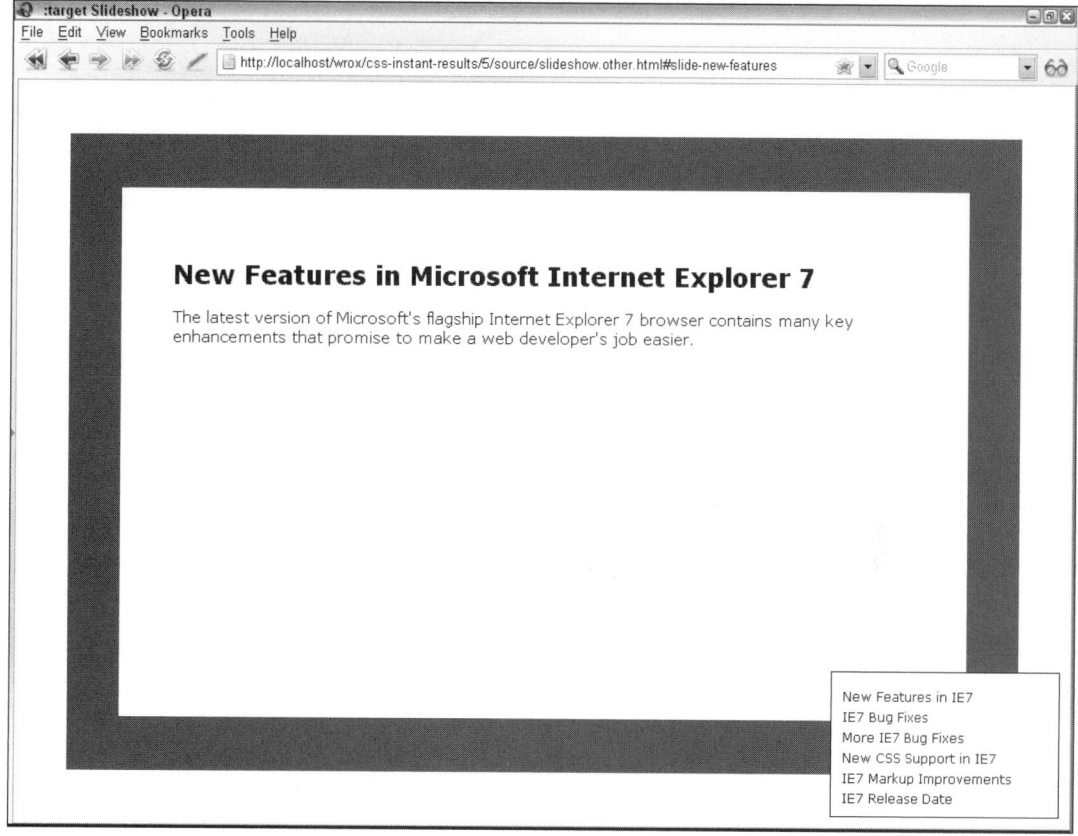

Figure 5-9

The first modifications you made were in `slideshow.html`. The following markup is applied to correct Internet Explorer's lack of support for the combination of offset properties to imply width or height. Because `right: 0;` and `left: 0;` as applied to the same element don't imply width in Internet Explorer, you used Internet Explorer's proprietary `expression()` feature to include JavaScript directly in a style sheet:

```
<!-- compliance patch for microsoft browsers -->
<!--[if lt IE 7]>
    <style type='text/css'>
        div.slide {
            width:
                expression(
                    document.getElementById('slideshow').offsetWidth - 300
                );
```

```
                height:
                    expression(
                        document.getElementById('slideshow').offsetHeight -300
                    );
            }
        </style>
    <![endif]-->
```

The width of `<div>` elements with a "slide" class name is defined by applying `expression()`. To get a width that is based on the viewport, you had to make a few other modifications as well. You applied a `slideshow` id name to the `<body>` element:

```
    <body id='slideshow'>
```

You also added a few rules to `slideshow.css`:

```
html {
    height: 100%;
}
body {
    font: 12px sans-serif;
    margin: 0;
    padding: 0;
    height: 100%;
}
```

By applying the id name `slideshow` to the `<body>` element, you now have a point of reference for defining width based on the dimensions of the viewport. `document.getElementById('slideshow')` references the `<body>` element from the style sheet using JavaScript. The `offsetWidth` property gets the width of the `<body>` element, but it does so using the old, proprietary Internet Explorer box model, where an element's width includes the border and padding of the element, and the content of the element occupies the space that remains after border and padding are applied. Three hundred pixels are subtracted from the value of the `offsetWidth` property, which accounts for the margin, borders, and padding applied to each "slide" `<div>` element. The same is done for the height, but by using the `offsetHeight` property instead. By default, because `<body>` is a block-level element, height for the `<body>` element is calculated using the shrink-to-fit algorithm — its height is determined based on how much content is inside of it. To get an `offsetHeight` value that reflects the height of the viewport window, you set the margin and padding to nothing to remove any default margin or padding. Then you set the height to 100%. Because percentage height is determined based on the height of the parent of the element the percentage measurement is applied to, you also set the height of the `<html>` element to 100%. With a 100% height defined for the `<body>` element, you can now reference the `offsetHeight` property of that element and have a height for the "slide" `<div>` elements that reflect the height of the viewport. Again taking away 300 pixels to account for borders, margin, and padding, you get "slide" `<div>` elements with dimensions based on the viewport.

You applied one more change to `slideshow.css`, the addition of a declaration including the proprietary `filter` property. This declaration hides the navigation menu for the slide show by default:

```
div#slide-navigation {
    position: absolute;
    bottom: 0;
    right: 0;
```

```
        opacity: 0.0;
        filter: progid:DXImageTransform.Microsoft.Alpha(opacity=0);
        width: 200px;
        background: white;
        border: 1px solid black;
        padding: 10px;
        margin: 10px;
}
```

The last modification you made to the slide show was the application of a JavaScript that provides functionality in lieu of support for the CSS 3 :target pseudo-class.

I'm not going into great detail about the basics of JavaScript syntax. As mentioned in Chapter 3, if you need a comprehensive overview of JavaScript, Paul Wilton's *Beginning JavaScript 2nd Edition* is a good place to start.

As also mentioned in Chapter 3, it's difficult to get very far in web development without at some point using JavaScript. What you see next leverages the JavaScript language to provide the same functionality in Opera 9 and Internet Explorer 6 as is provided in Mozilla Firefox.

You begin the JavaScript by setting a variable, $currentSlide, which is used to keep track of which slide the user is currently viewing. This variable is described in further detail later in this section:

```
var $currentSlide = '';
```

Almost everything done in JavaScript is driven by events, such as when the user's mouse moves over a certain element or clicks on a certain element. These events can be captured, and isolated bits of code can be executed when an event happens. The following function, slideEvents(), is executed when the document loads up. When it is executed, it performs several subroutines that get the slide show functioning. It attaches onclick events to each of the <li> elements containing links for the slide show navigation. When one of the <li> elements is clicked, the appropriate slide is displayed. It also hides and reveals the navigation menu, depending on whether the user's mouse is hovering over the portion of the screen where the navigation menu is positioned. The function begins with a function declaration, which includes the function keyword, and the name of the function, slideEvents:

```
function slideEvents()
{
```

The first order of business within the function is to retrieve all of the children of the <ul> element with a slide-navigation-inner id name:

```
var $li = document.getElementById('slide-navigation-inner').childNodes;
```

Using the for/in construct, each of the children <a> elements of the <li> elements receive onclick events. When the <a> element is clicked, the getSlide function is executed. Before that onclick event can be assigned, you must first make sure that the target <li> element has children, has a first child, and that first child is an <a> element. This is done to avoid any potential JavaScript errors:

```
for (var $i in $li)
{
    if ($li[$i].childNodes &&
        $li[$i].childNodes[0] &&
        $li[$i].childNodes[0].nodeName == 'A'
    ) {
        $li[$i].childNodes[0].onclick = getSlide;
    }
}
```

Next is a call to the `getSlide()` function. This is done because a user might navigate to the slide show via a URL that already includes a slide in the anchor portion of the URL:

```
getSlide();
```

Next, the element with a "slide-navigation" is assigned to the `$navigation` variable:

```
var $navigation = document.getElementById('slide-navigation');
```

Then you need to re-create the navigation menu's becoming fully opaque when the user's mouse hovers over it, which you did with the following rule from `slideshow.css`:

```
div#slide-navigation:hover {
    opacity: 1;
}
```

To replicate this with JavaScript, you use the `onmouseover` and `onmouseout` events. First you assign the `onmouseover` event to the `$navigation` variable, which is a reference to the "slide-navigation" `<div>` element. Within the function for the `onmouseover` event, you make sure the browser is Microsoft Internet Explorer with the syntax `navigator.appName == 'Microsoft Internet Explorer'`, which is the only browser that supports the `filter` property. The `this` keyword refers to the element that the `onmouseover` event was applied to, the "slide-navigation" `<div>` element. `this.style.filter` is assigned the value that you want the "slide-navigation" `<div>` to have when the user's mouse hovers over it; 100 sets the opacity to fully opaque:

```
if (navigator.appName == 'Microsoft Internet Explorer')
{
    $navigation.onmouseover = function()
    {
        this.style.filter =
            'progid:DXImageTransform.Microsoft.Alpha(opacity=100);';
    };
```

Having made the "slide-navigation" `<div>` element fully opaque upon the user's mouse hovering over it, you must now add another event that fires off when the user's mouse leaves the boundaries of the element. That is done with the `onmouseout` event, with an identical function applied to the `onmouseout` event. The only difference is the opacity is set to "0" or fully transparent:

```
    $navigation.onmouseout = function()
    {
        this.style.filter =
            'progid:DXImageTransform.Microsoft.Alpha(opacity=0);';
    };
}
```

Now for the bit that makes the slide show work without support for the `:target` pseudo-class. You begin by making a new function declaration using the `function` keyword, followed by the name of the function, `getSlide`:

```
function getSlide()
{
```

The first thing to be done is to get the anchor portion of the URL. The URL for the document is found within the `.href` property. Using the `substring()` method, you can extract only the anchor of the URL. `substring()` needs two bits of information to extract the right portion of the string (these are called parameters, or arguments). `substring()` retrieves a portion of the URL based on the number of characters in the URL. So, you need to know where the anchor begins and where it ends. If the URL has 100 characters total, and the "#" character is the 75th character, you need a way to determine that the "#" character is the 75th character. You do this with `indexOf()` function. `indexOf` needs to know what you're looking for — in this case the "#" character — it then retrieves the position of the "#" within the URL. You don't want the "#" character to be retrieved, though, only the characters that appear after it. To get only those characters, you add one to the value returned by `indexOf`. `substring()` also needs to know the position of the last character you want to get; because you want all of the anchor, you give it the total character count of the URL:

```
if (this.href)
{
    var $anchor = this.href.substring(
        this.href.indexOf('#') + 1, this.href.length
    );
```

You now have the text of the anchor, and consequently, the id name of a particular slide. When users click a link in the navigation you also need some way of hiding the previous slide they were viewing, if there is one. You do this by telling the browser to remember the slide the user is currently looking at, and that is stored in the `$currentSlide` variable. If there is a `$currentSlide`, it is hidden when a new request is made:

```
if (document.getElementById($currentSlide))
{
    document.getElementById($currentSlide).style.display = 'none';
}
$currentSlide = $anchor;
```

Now you can display the slide of the current request. First you check to make sure that there is an anchor, and that there is an element that exists with that id name. If there is, you set the value of the `display` property for that element to `block`:

```
        if ($anchor.length && document.getElementById($anchor))
        {
            document.getElementById($anchor).style.display = 'block';
        }
    }
}
```

The last thing you have to do is get the browser to do all of the preceding things. Because the JavaScript is included between the <head> and </head> tags, and JavaScript is read and possibly executed as the document loads, the elements contained between the <body> and </body> tags don't yet exist. With the following line you tell the browser to execute the slideEvents() function when the document has completed loading:

```
window.onload = slideEvents;
```

Now you have a slide show that works in Internet Explorer 6 and Opera 9.

Custom Borders and Rounded Corners

A common complaint among web designers is the boxy nature of web design. The good news is that several techniques can be utilized to break out of square corners; some can even be utilized to make custom borders as well. In this chapter, you learn how to go about the task of breaking out of square corners, and you see CSS's limited selection of border styles.

The biggest challenge with customizing corners and borders is content of varying width, height, or both. Anyone can make a fixed dimension design, or even simply skip most of the markup and CSS and include a design via an image. I approach this project assuming that competent designers plan for adjustments in resolution or font size and use CSS and markup when appropriate to further accessibility and search engine visibility. The goal of a well-designed implementation of custom borders or rounded corners is a design that doesn't break at a certain resolution or when font size adjustments are made.

Plans are in the works to make custom borders and rounded corners easier to implement. In CSS 3 a new syntax is in development for specifying multiple backgrounds on a single element, and to specify images for different border segments. At the time of this writing only Apple's Safari browser has implemented experimental support for CSS 3 multiple backgrounds, although the CSS 3 backgrounds and borders module is still a draft specification and possibly subject to change. Support in other browsers is less likely until the CSS 3 backgrounds and borders module reaches at least Candidate Recommendation status. There is also the `border-radius` property in CSS 3, which provides functionality for rounding the corners of a box. A property similar to but not the exact equivalent of the `border-radius` property exists, and that is the `-moz-border-radius` property, which works only in browsers that have the gecko rendering engine, such as Mozilla, Mozilla Firefox, and Netscape, among others.

Until browsers support the CSS 3 backgrounds and borders module, web designers must rely on methods that introduce more markup and style sheet rules than will be required with that support.

The next section describes the design concepts of some of the various techniques that are used to make rounded corners or custom borders.

Design

As you saw in Chapters 1, 3, and 4, custom borders and corners sometimes require lots of excess, meaningless markup to be inserted. The best cross-browser method uses the techniques presented in those chapters, because all browsers support backgrounds pretty much equally well. The caveat with that approach is the extra markup. Inserting more `<div>` elements into the markup just introduces more bloat, and when all is said and done the technique isn't too much better than using tables for layout, although I believe that meaningless `<div>` elements are better than `<table>` elements, which I believe should be reserved for organizing tabular data in a semantic way. Removing tables from layout allows them to reclaim some semantics previously obscured by their overuse.

> *In my opinion, the best technique to implement rounded corners and custom borders appears on the web site* 456bereastreet.com. *Developed by Swedish web developer Roger Johansson, this technique keeps the markup simple and free of meaningless elements that clutter and bloat the markup. He uses JavaScript to insert these extra, meaningless elements dynamically, and if JavaScript is disabled, the user sees a less stylish version of the same content. I believe Johansson's approach is superior because it uses JavaScript to enhance the design, but also because it makes the markup cleaner and easier to maintain. I decided not to present Johansson's technique in detail here, because it requires JavaScript. If you would like to learn more about this technique, you can get the tutorial from Johansson's web site at the following URL:* http://www.456bereastreet.com/archive/200505/transparent_custom_corners_and_borders.

For the main project in this chapter, I reiterate the technique that you've seen in previous chapters, but here it's isolated to demonstrate only the markup and CSS required to implement the technique within your own projects.

The next section presents the source code for this project.

Code and Code Explanation

1. Enter the following markup:

```
<!DOCTYPE html PUBLIC "-//W3C//DTD XHTML 1.0 Strict//EN"
"http://www.w3.org/TR/xhtml1/DTD/xhtml1-strict.dtd">
<html xmlns='http://www.w3.org/1999/xhtml' xml:lang='en'>
    <head>
        <meta http-equiv="Content-Type" content="text/html; charset=UTF-8" />
        <title>Custom corners and borders</title>
        <link rel='stylesheet' type='text/css' href='styles/borders.css' />
    </head>
    <body>
        <div class='content'>
            <div class='header'>
                <h1><span>Heading</span></h1>
            </div>
            <div class='outer-body'>
                <div class='body'>
                    <div class='inner-body'>
<p>
      Lorem ipsum dolor sit amet, consectetuer adipiscing elit. Morbi sem.
```

```
    Maecenas neque. Donec bibendum, justo id varius vulputate, eros neque
    scelerisque lectus, a lobortis ipsum enim et nunc. Maecenas sit amet
    urna a turpis pellentesque gravida. Donec a enim vitae felis tempor
    lobortis. Morbi sodales lacinia augue. Cum sociis natoque penatibus
    et magnis dis parturient montes, nascetur ridiculus mus. Praesent
    metus. In hac habitasse platea dictumst. Vestibulum convallis
    scelerisque leo. Cras risus arcu, imperdiet vel, commodo non,
    malesuada in, metus. Aenean commodo adipiscing pede. Suspendisse
    tellus orci, placerat quis, ullamcorper id, consectetuer sed, nisi.
</p>
<p>

    Nullam et orci. Vestibulum ante ipsum primis in faucibus orci luctus
    et ultrices posuere cubilia Curae; Suspendisse suscipit accumsan
    felis. Aliquam in justo ut leo rutrum iaculis. In tempus, sapien
    eget commodo pulvinar, dolor tortor placerat ipsum, id feugiat elit
    massa id nisi. Nulla fringilla adipiscing mauris. Curabitur lacinia,
    orci eu convallis varius, metus felis molestie nibh, sit amet
    scelerisque ligula nulla sed enim. Vestibulum ligula. Nam aliquet.
    Aenean erat ante, suscipit pharetra, vulputate a, aliquam ac, quam.
    Ut lobortis suscipit velit. Morbi pellentesque. Mauris aliquam
    blandit diam. Suspendisse potenti. Ut pede nibh, feugiat nec,
    porttitor sed, malesuada nec, libero. Morbi facilisis, nisl at dictum
    imperdiet, nisl justo adipiscing dui, sed pretium tellus ipsum eu
    velit. Quisque pede lorem, ullamcorper sagittis, venenatis vel,
    venenatis a, orci. Vivamus ante ante, bibendum id, volutpat id,
    tristique vitae, libero. Cras volutpat iaculis purus. Pellentesque
    mi arcu, ultricies non, pharetra in, auctor sit amet, diam.
</p>
<p>

    Pellentesque mollis rutrum leo. Nulla ac enim. Sed auctor est eget leo.
    Vivamus purus tortor, ornare nec, condimentum id, venenatis vel, nulla.
    Pellentesque commodo magna at eros. Suspendisse in massa fringilla est
    blandit sagittis. Duis metus. Praesent tellus ante, bibendum vitae,
    tincidunt sit amet, varius vitae, mauris. Mauris nibh. Donec
    dignissim eleifend quam. Etiam luctus. Integer feugiat, arcu vitae
    molestie dictum, turpis quam porttitor massa, a semper purus mi quis
    odio. Donec sem ligula, sollicitudin nec, lacinia id, sodales vitae,
    sem. Aliquam erat volutpat. Aliquam eros. Quisque in turpis quis ante
    dignissim malesuada. Class aptent taciti sociosqu ad litora torquent
    per conubia nostra, per inceptos hymenaeos.
</p>
<p>

    Class aptent taciti sociosqu ad litora torquent per conubia nostra, per
    inceptos hymenaeos. Cras pellentesque diam a augue pretium ullamcorper.
    Vestibulum dapibus consectetuer pede. Cras id sapien quis magna dictum
    sodales. Ut convallis eleifend massa. Sed semper arcu non lacus. Nullam
    vitae eros. Morbi eu odio. Maecenas in pede. Fusce sem lacus,
    sollicitudin nec, blandit ac, pellentesque et, mauris. Proin sodales.
    Aenean eget risus. Etiam quis augue ac augue hendrerit semper.
    Curabitur auctor sem at tortor.
</p>
<p>

    Proin quam nunc, egestas vulputate, hendrerit id, sagittis et, purus.
    Quisque in purus et massa dapibus pretium. Integer libero mauris,
```

```
        malesuada quis, rutrum hendrerit, tincidunt vitae, justo. Donec
        vehicula. Lorem ipsum dolor sit amet, consectetuer adipiscing elit.
        Donec aliquet. Sed gravida tristique lorem. In laoreet enim sit amet
        libero. Donec nisl nisi, gravida fermentum, consectetuer suscipit,
        malesuada ac, metus. Sed id eros. Curabitur bibendum scelerisque tortor.
        Nulla facilisi. Donec vulputate feugiat odio. Nam vitae lectus. Nullam
        molestie est et dolor. Proin sit amet tellus eu mauris interdum
        volutpat. Nulla at lectus id sem laoreet ornare. Donec nec quam feugiat
        urna elementum tincidunt. Nunc suscipit facilisis mi.
    </p>
                        </div>
                    </div>
                </div>
                <div class='outer-footer'>
                    <div class='footer'>
                        <div class='inner-footer'>
                        </div>
                    </div>
                </div>
            </div>
        </body>
</html>
```

2. Save the preceding as `borders.html`.

3. Enter the following style sheet:

```
body {
    padding: 0;
    margin: 0;
    font: 12px sans-serif;
    background: #fff;
}
div.content {
    color: white;
    background: url('../images/borders_01.png') no-repeat top left;
}
div.header {
    background: url('../images/borders_03.png') no-repeat top right;
}
div.header h1 {
    background: url('../images/borders_02.png') repeat-x top;
    margin: 0 22px 0 22px;
    font-size: 14px;
    height: 26px;
    line-height: 26px;
}
div.header h1 span {
    position: relative;
    top: 10px;
}
div.outer-body {
```

```
        background: url('../images/borders_04.png') repeat-y left;
    }
    div.body {
        background: url('../images/borders_06.png') repeat-y right;
    }
    div.inner-body {
        background: url('../images/borders_05.png');
        margin: 0 22px 0 22px;
    }
    div.inner-body p:first-child {
        margin-top: 0;
        padding-top: 10px;
    }
    div.inner-body p:last-child {
        margin-bottom: 0;
    }
    div.outer-footer {
        background: url('../images/borders_07.png') no-repeat bottom left;
    }
    div.footer {
        background: url('../images/borders_09.png') no-repeat bottom right;
    }
    div.inner-footer {
        background: url('../images/borders_08.png') repeat-x bottom;
        height: 28px;
        margin: 0 22px 0 22px;
    }
```

4. Save the preceding as `borders.css`.

The preceding results in the output shown in Figure 6-1.

This project requires nine different background images: one for each corner, one for each side, and one for the center. You began the process of applying custom borders and corners with adding additional markup to the document; at the very least you needed nine different elements, one for each image. By using backgrounds you have a method that is easier to deploy for a variety of browsers.

The first rule you applied in `borders.css` is relevant for the `<body>` element. First you removed default margin and padding, specified a font, and set the background to white for consistency.

It is always a good idea to set a background on the `<body>` element, because it is possible that a user's browser or operating system may apply a color other than white by default. Specifying a default background color prevents this.

```
body {
    padding: 0;
    margin: 0;
    font: 12px sans-serif;
    background: #fff;
}
```

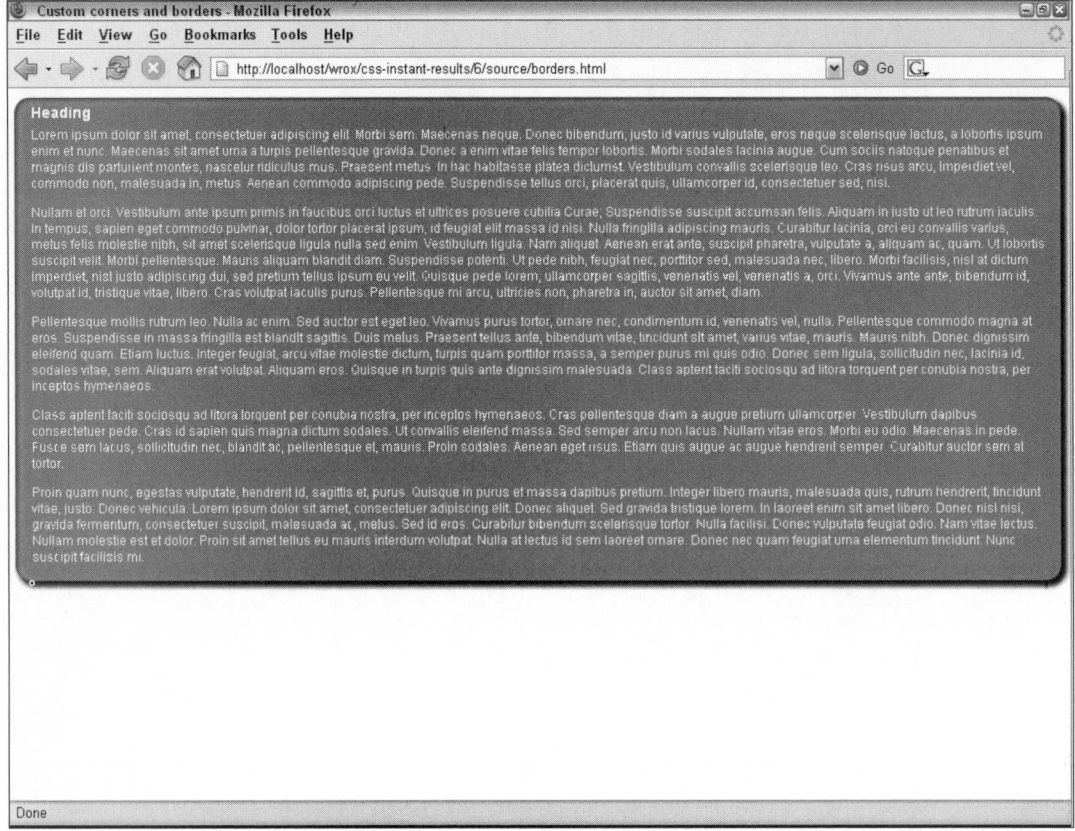

Figure 6-1

The next rule in `borders.css` sets about the business of customizing the corners and borders. Using PhotoShop I sliced an image into nine parts. The first image is applied to the `<div>` with a `content` class name, which houses all of the other elements. The color is set to white to better contrast with the dark background color I have chosen. Then the first background image is specified, non-repeating to the top and left of the `content` `<div>` element:

```
div.content {
    color: white;
    background: url('../images/borders_01.png') no-repeat top left;
}
```

In the next rule, the second image is applied. This time it's the top-right corner that's applied to the `<div>` element with a `header` class name:

```
div.header {
    background: url('../images/borders_03.png') no-repeat top right;
}
```

To ensure that the custom borders and backgrounds continue to do their task at any size, whether by changing the resolution, resizing the browser window, or increasing or decreasing the font size, this technique is designed so that the borders on the sides are repeated. In the next rule, the third image is applied to become the top border. It is repeated along the x-axis, and positioned to the top of the `<h1>` element, which is a descendant of the `<div>` element with a `header` class name. Then to prevent overlap with the `content` and `header` `<div>` elements, left and right margins are applied equal to the width of the images used for the top-left and top-right corners. Then a font-size of 14 pixels is applied. A height of 26 pixels is applied so that the background is always visible, regardless of the size of the content within the `<h1>` element, then `line-height` is also made 26 pixels:

```
div.header h1 {
    background: url('../images/borders_02.png') repeat-x top;
    margin: 0 22px 0 22px;
    font-size: 14px;
    height: 26px;
    line-height: 26px;
}
```

The text in the `<h1>` element doesn't fit in quite right with the height of the `<h1>`, so the position of the text within the `<h1>` element is tweaked by giving the `<span>` element a relative position and then off-setting the element from the top by 10 pixels:

```
div.header h1 span {
    position: relative;
    top: 10px;
}
```

The fourth image is applied next. That image becomes the border for the left side. The background is set to repeat along the y-axis to accommodate content of any length vertically, and to the left of the element with an `outer-body` class name:

```
div.outer-body {
    background: url('../images/borders_04.png') repeat-y left;
}
```

The fifth image follows, and that image becomes the right border. It is also repeated along the y-axis, but is positioned on the right of the element with a `body` class name:

```
div.body {
    background: url('../images/borders_06.png') repeat-y right;
}
```

The sixth image becomes the background for the content in the middle. In some cases it may be possible not to use an image for the center at all, but instead use a solid color. I chose to use an image. The background is set for the `<div>` element with an `inner-body` class name and is set to repeat along both the y- and x-axes. Then as was done for the `<h1>` element previously in the style sheet, you applied left and right margins equal to the width of the background images used for the left and right borders:

```
div.inner-body {
    background: url('../images/borders_05.png');
    margin: 0 22px 0 22px;
}
```

The next rule corrects a gap that appears at the top of the outer-border <div> element and the bottom of the header. Removing the top margin of the first <p> element removes this gap. Then you applied a padding of 10 pixels to make more room for the heading:

```
div.inner-body p:first-child {
    margin-top: 0;
    padding-top: 10px;
}
```

Just like the previous rule for the gap at the top, the next rule removes a gap at the bottom by removing the bottom margin of the last <p> element using the CSS 3 :last-child pseudo-class:

```
div.inner-body p:last-child {
    margin-bottom: 0;
}
```

The seventh image is applied to the <div> element with an outer-footer class name. The seventh background image is specified non-repeating to the bottom left of the outer-footer <div> element:

```
div.outer-footer {
    background: url('../images/borders_07.png') no-repeat bottom left;
}
```

The eighth image is applied to the <div> element with a footer class name. It is applied also non-repeating to the bottom and right of the footer <div> element:

```
div.footer {
    background: url('../images/borders_09.png') no-repeat bottom right;
}
```

Finally, in the last rule appearing in borders.css, you apply the bottom border. Just as you did for the top border in the <h1> element, you applied the ninth image repeating along the x-axis of the <div> element with an inner-footer class name. The inner-footer <div> element then gets a height of 28 pixels, which is the actual height of the image used in the background for this element, and the bottom-left and bottom-right corners. You then finish off the inner-footer <div> element by setting the left and right margins of the inner-footer <div> element to be equal to the width of the images used for the bottom-left and bottom-right corners:

```
div.inner-footer {
    background: url('../images/borders_08.png') repeat-x bottom;
    height: 28px;
    margin: 0 22px 0 22px;
}
```

You may be wondering what the text in the borders.html *document means. This is dummy text used for centuries in the print industry, and in more recent years in web site and software development. The dummy text is written in Latin, and is simply there as filler to see what a template looks like with copy added. If you are interested in learning more about its origin, go to the web site* www.lipsum.com.

In the next section you see the problems with this approach and how to correct them.

Testing and Caveats

In this section you take the final design of the last section and expand the test bed of browsers to include Internet Explorer and Opera.

The design used here has just a couple of deficiencies in other browsers, and this has to do with the use of the `:first-child` and `:last-child` pseudo-classes in the style sheet.

Figure 6-2 shows the project as it appears in Internet Explorer, which supports neither the `:first-child` nor `:last-child` pseudo-classes.

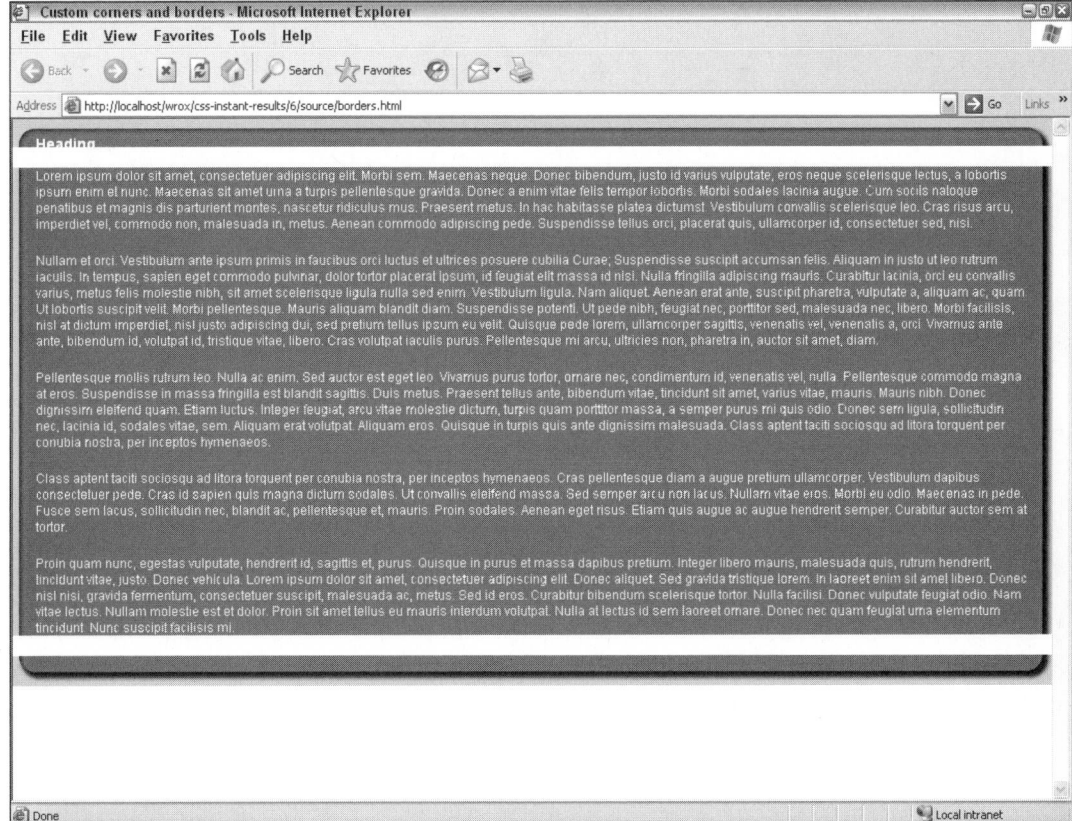

Figure 6-2

Figure 6-3 shows the project as it appears in Opera, which doesn't support the CSS 3 `:last-child` pseudo-class.

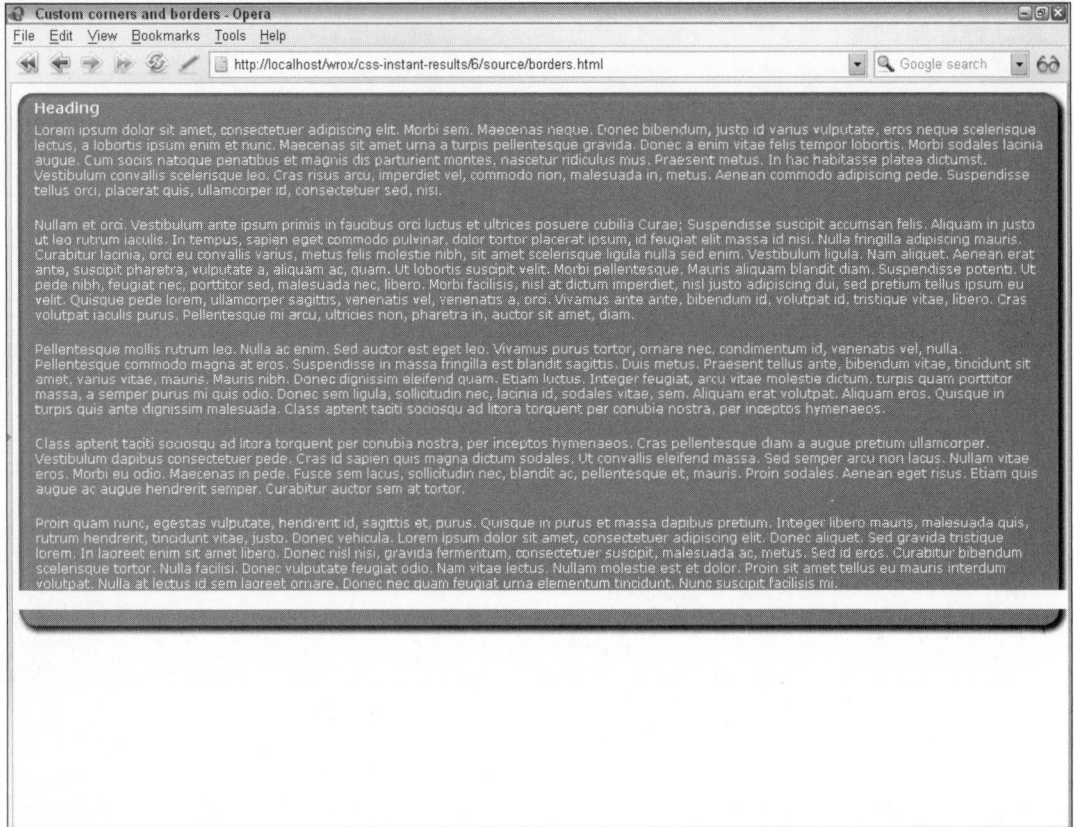

Figure 6-3

One additional problem plagues Internet Explorer. Because the PNG images used for the background images contain alpha channels (transparent portions), the background images appear with the transparent portions gray in Internet Explorer. For this project, the fix isn't quite simple. The PNG images must be updated to have no transparent parts to have the same look and feel in Internet Explorer.

To correct the gaps seen in Figures 6-2 and 6-3, you must first understand why the gaps appear. As you saw in the previous section, the gaps were removed by taking away the top margin of the first <p> element and the bottom margin of the last <p> element. These gaps can be attributed to margin collapsing. The top margin of the first <p> element collapsed with the top margin of the <div> with an inner-body class name, which in turn collapsed with the top margin of the <div> with a body class name, which collapsed with the top margin of the outer-body <div> element. That resulted in a gap between the outer-body <div> element and the header <div> element. The same happened on the bottom, but there it was the bottom margin that collapsed. There are two solutions to the problem, as you have already seen. One is to remove the margin. Because the content within the inner-body <div> may not always be predictable, another, possibly superior method exists, and that is to apply 1 pixel of padding to the inner-body <div> element. After doing so, you get the results shown in Figure 6-4 in Internet Explorer 6, and likewise a similar result in Opera. These corrections appear on the source CD-ROM accompanying this book in the Project 6 folder as borders.fixed.html.

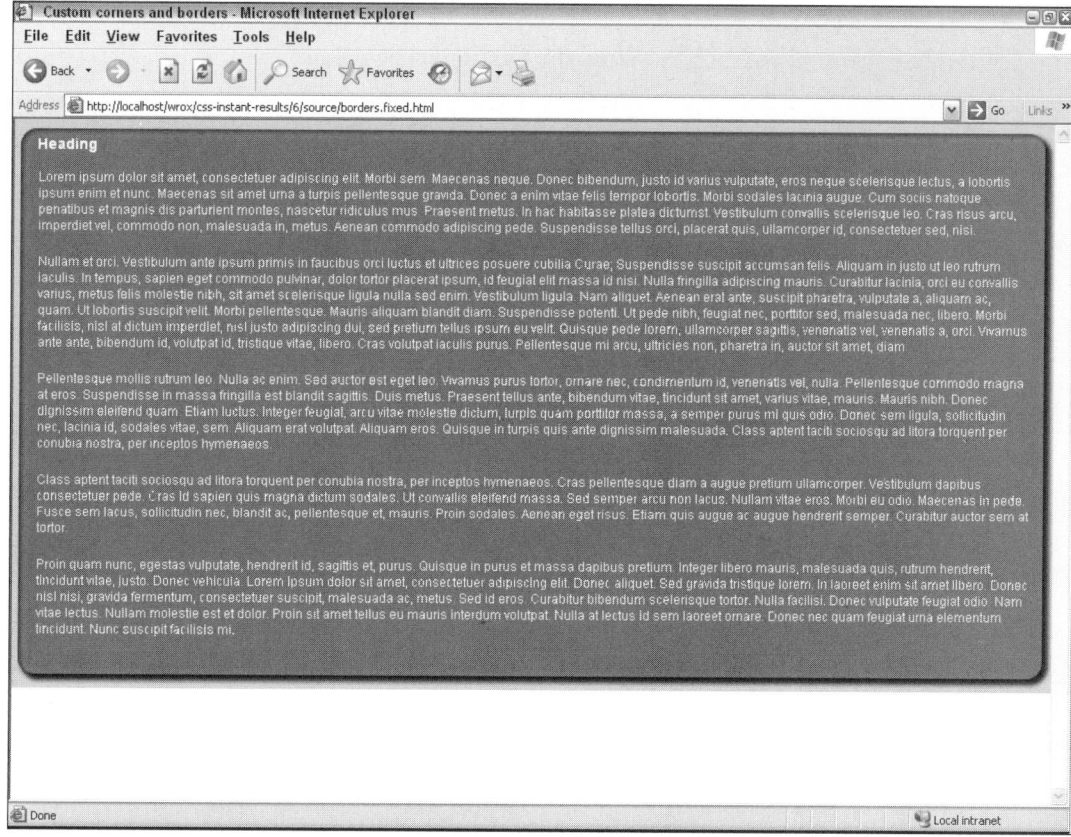

Figure 6-4

The next section explores some alternative approaches for this project.

Using and Modifying the Project

This section presents an alternative approach for custom corners. The approaches used here focus on customizing the corners of an element with a border applied via CSS.

This technique was inspired by Adam Kalsey, whose original version can be found online at `http://kalsey.com/2003/07/rounded_corners_in_css/`.

Kalsey's technique takes a minimalist approach, works in all the popular browsers, and is quite suitable if rounded corners are your only goal.

The approach in this section has been modified to account for elements with borders. To implement this approach, follow these steps:

1. Open `borders.html` and make the following changes:

```
<!DOCTYPE html PUBLIC "-//W3C//DTD XHTML 1.0 Strict//EN"
"http://www.w3.org/TR/xhtml1/DTD/xhtml1-strict.dtd">
<html xmlns='http://www.w3.org/1999/xhtml' xml:lang='en'>
    <head>
        <meta http-equiv="Content-Type" content="text/html; charset=UTF-8" />
        <title>Custom corners and borders</title>
        <link rel='stylesheet' type='text/css' href='styles/borders.kalsey.css' />
        <!-- compliance patch for microsoft browsers -->
        <!--[if lt IE 7]>
            <link rel='stylesheet' type='text/css'
                href='styles/borders.kalsey.ie.css' />
        <![endif]-->
    </head>
    <body>
        <div class='content'>
            <h1 class='top'>
                <span>Header Text</span>
            </h1>
            <img src='images/simple_borders_03.png'
                alt='top right border'
                class='top-right' />
            <div class='body'>
```

```
<p>
    Lorem ipsum dolor sit amet, consectetuer adipiscing elit. Morbi sem.
    Maecenas neque. Donec bibendum, justo id varius vulputate, eros neque
    scelerisque lectus, a lobortis ipsum enim et nunc. Maecenas sit amet
    urna a turpis pellentesque gravida. Donec a enim vitae felis tempor
    lobortis. Morbi sodales lacinia augue. Cum sociis natoque penatibus
    et magnis dis parturient montes, nascetur ridiculus mus. Praesent
    metus. In hac habitasse platea dictumst. Vestibulum convallis
    scelerisque leo. Cras risus arcu, imperdiet vel, commodo non,
    malesuada in, metus. Aenean commodo adipiscing pede. Suspendisse
    tellus orci, placerat quis, ullamcorper id, consectetuer sed, nisi.
</p>
<p>
    Nullam et orci. Vestibulum ante ipsum primis in faucibus orci luctus
    et ultrices posuere cubilia Curae; Suspendisse suscipit accumsan
    felis. Aliquam in justo ut leo rutrum iaculis. In tempus, sapien
    eget commodo pulvinar, dolor tortor placerat ipsum, id feugiat elit
    massa id nisi. Nulla fringilla adipiscing mauris. Curabitur lacinia,
    orci eu convallis varius, metus felis molestie nibh, sit amet
    scelerisque ligula nulla sed enim. Vestibulum ligula. Nam aliquet.
    Aenean erat ante, suscipit pharetra, vulputate a, aliquam ac, quam.
    Ut lobortis suscipit velit. Morbi pellentesque. Mauris aliquam
    blandit diam. Suspendisse potenti. Ut pede nibh, feugiat nec,
    porttitor sed, malesuada nec, libero. Morbi facilisis, nisl at dictum
    imperdiet, nisl justo adipiscing dui, sed pretium tellus ipsum eu
    velit. Quisque pede lorem, ullamcorper sagittis, venenatis vel,
    venenatis a, orci. Vivamus ante ante, bibendum id, volutpat id,
    tristique vitae, libero. Cras volutpat iaculis purus. Pellentesque
    mi arcu, ultricies non, pharetra in, auctor sit amet, diam.
</p>
```

```
<p>
    Pellentesque mollis rutrum leo. Nulla ac enim. Sed auctor est eget leo.
    Vivamus purus tortor, ornare nec, condimentum id, venenatis vel, nulla.
    Pellentesque commodo magna at eros. Suspendisse in massa fringilla est
    blandit sagittis. Duis metus. Praesent tellus ante, bibendum vitae,
    tincidunt sit amet, varius vitae, mauris. Mauris nibh. Donec
    dignissim eleifend quam. Etiam luctus. Integer feugiat, arcu vitae
    molestie dictum, turpis quam porttitor massa, a semper purus mi quis
    odio. Donec sem ligula, sollicitudin nec, lacinia id, sodales vitae,
    sem. Aliquam erat volutpat. Aliquam eros. Quisque in turpis quis ante
    dignissim malesuada. Class aptent taciti sociosqu ad litora torquent
    per conubia nostra, per inceptos hymenaeos.
</p>
<p>
    Class aptent taciti sociosqu ad litora torquent per conubia nostra, per
    inceptos hymenaeos. Cras pellentesque diam a augue pretium ullamcorper.
    Vestibulum dapibus consectetuer pede. Cras id sapien quis magna dictum
    sodales. Ut convallis eleifend massa. Sed semper arcu non lacus. Nullam
    vitae eros. Morbi eu odio. Maecenas in pede. Fusce sem lacus,
    sollicitudin nec, blandit ac, pellentesque et, mauris. Proin sodales.
    Aenean eget risus. Etiam quis augue ac augue hendrerit semper.
    Curabitur auctor sem at tortor.
</p>
<p>
    Proin quam nunc, egestas vulputate, hendrerit id, sagittis et, purus.
    Quisque in purus et massa dapibus pretium. Integer libero mauris,
    malesuada quis, rutrum hendrerit, tincidunt vitae, justo. Donec
    vehicula. Lorem ipsum dolor sit amet, consectetuer adipiscing elit.
    Donec aliquet. Sed gravida tristique lorem. In laoreet enim sit amet
    libero. Donec nisl nisi, gravida fermentum, consectetuer suscipit,
    malesuada ac, metus. Sed id eros. Curabitur bibendum scelerisque tortor.
    Nulla facilisi. Donec vulputate feugiat odio. Nam vitae lectus. Nullam
    molestie est et dolor. Proin sit amet tellus eu mauris interdum
    volutpat. Nulla at lectus id sem laoreet ornare. Donec nec quam feugiat
    urna elementum tincidunt. Nunc suscipit facilisis mi.
</p>
            </div>
            <div class='bottom'>
                <img src='images/simple_borders_09.png'
                    alt='bottom right border'
                    class='bottom-right' />
            </div>
        </div>
    </body>
</html>
```

2. Save this approach as `borders.kalsey.html`.

3. Keeping the rule for the `<body>` element from the original `borders.css`, enter the following new style sheet:

```
body {
    padding: 0;
    margin: 0;
    font: 12px sans-serif;
    background: #fff;
}
```

```
div.content {
    background: #7c92b3;
    border: 1px solid black;
    color: white;
    margin: 10px;
    position: relative;
}
div.body {
    padding: 10px;
}
div.content h1 {
    background: url('../images/simple_borders_01.png') no-repeat top left;
    margin: -1px 0 0 -1px;
    font-size: 14px;
}
div.content h1 span {
    position: relative;
    left: 10px;
    top: 10px;

}
img.top-right {
    position: absolute;
    top: -1px;
    right: -1px;
}
div.bottom {
    background: url('../images/simple_borders_07.png') no-repeat bottom left;
    height: 15px;
    margin: 0 0 -1px -1px;
}
img.bottom-right {
    position: absolute;
    bottom: -1px;
    right: -1px;
}
```

4. Save the preceding style sheet as `borders.kalsey.css`.

5. Enter yet another style sheet:

```
div.content {
    height: 1%;
    z-index: 1;
    background-color: #7087AB;
}
div.content h1 {
    position: relative;
    z-index: 2;
    left: -1px;
    margin-left: 0;
}
img.top-right {
    right: -2px;
}
img.bottom-right {
```

```
        right: -3px;
    }
    div.bottom {
        position: relative;
        z-index: 2;
        left: -1px;
        bottom: -1px;
        margin: 0;
    }
```

6. Save the preceding style sheet as `borders.kalsey.ie.css`.

In Mozilla Firefox, the modifications you made result in the output shown in Figure 6-5.

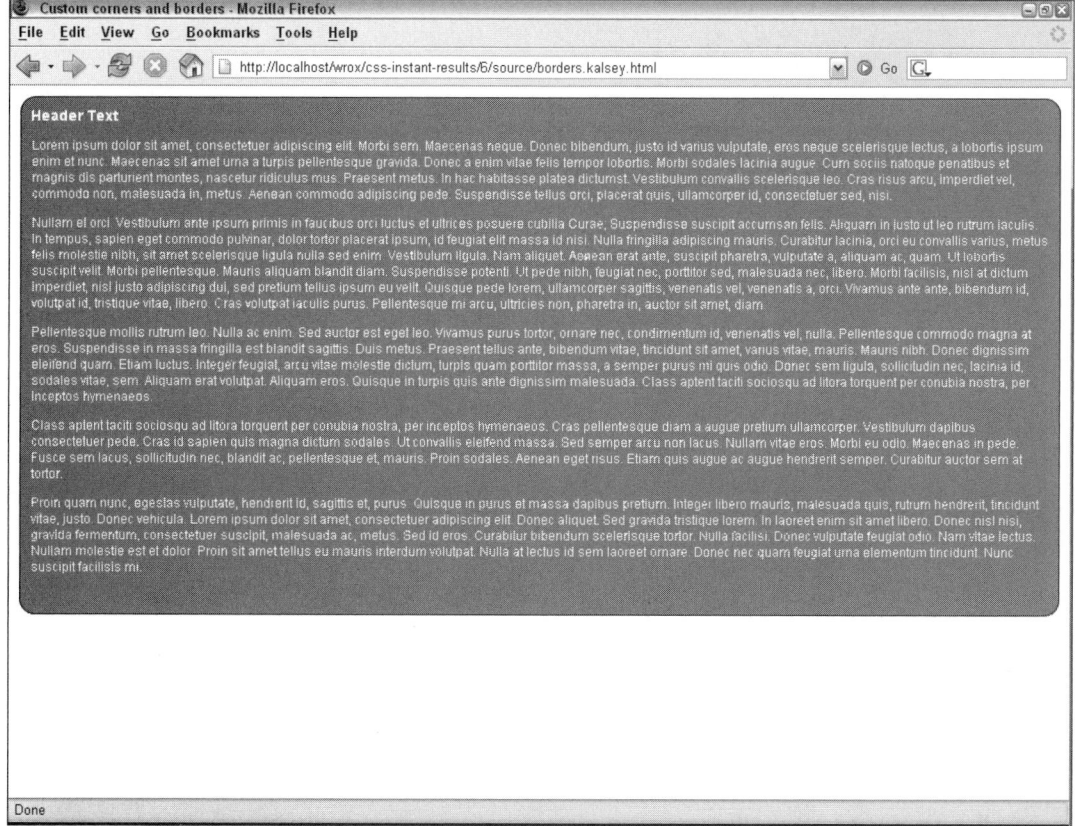

Figure 6-5

These modifications resulted in slightly less markup in the document, though it is not nearly as lean as in Kalsey's tutorial, because this approach required a border around the content.

The first rule in `borders.kalsey.css` applies to the `<div>` element with a `content` class name. You gave it a blue background and set a 1-pixel, solid black border around it. Then you made the text white, and spaced it out from the edges of the viewport with 10 pixels of margin. Finally, you gave it a relative position so that elements within it that are absolutely positioned would position relative to it:

```
div.content {
    background: #7c92b3;
    border: 1px solid black;
    color: white;
    margin: 10px;
    position: relative;
}
```

To give the copy some breathing room, you applied 10 pixels of padding to the <div> element with a body class name:

```
div.body {
    padding: 10px;
}
```

Next, the <h1> element receives styling. The first declaration makes the rounded corner on the left side. The position of the <h1> element must be tweaked so that its left and top overlap the content <div> element by 1 pixel. That makes the top-left corner seamless with the border specified for the content <div> element. Finally, you set the font size to 14 pixels in the last declaration:

```
div.content h1 {
    background: url('../images/simple_borders_01.png') no-repeat top left;
    margin: -1px 0 0 -1px;
    font-size: 14px;
}
```

In the following rule you adjust the position of the text within the <h1> element, which is wrapped with a generic <span> element. The <span> element is given a relative position and is offset from the top and left 10 pixels:

```
div.content h1 span {
    position: relative;
    left: 10px;
    top: 10px;
}
```

Then you positioned the top right image, which appears in an <img /> element. The <img /> element is given an absolute position and offset from the top and right minus 1 pixel, so that it too overlaps with the content <div> element and gives the appearance of a seamless rounded border:

```
img.top-right {
    position: absolute;
    top: -1px;
    right: -1px;
}
```

The next element to be styled is the <div> element with a bottom class name. It is given a background image for the bottom-left corner, which is set non-repeating. Then you give it a height of 15 pixels to be sure the `<div>` has the same height as the background images. Then you offset the bottom and left margins minus 1 pixel to overlap the `bottom` `<div>` element with the `content` `<div>` element:

```
div.bottom {
    background: url('../images/simple_borders_07.png') no-repeat bottom left;
    height: 15px;
    margin: 0 0 -1px -1px;
}
```

Now bottom-right corner also appears in an `<img />` element. The `<img />` element for the bottom-right corner is also positioned absolutely and offset by minus 1 pixel on the bottom and right sides to overlap it with the `content` `<div>` element:

```
img.bottom-right {
    position: absolute;
    bottom: -1px;
    right: -1px;
}
```

As it stands now, the document doesn't fair so well in Internet Explorer. Figure 6-6 shows the document in Internet Explorer before applying the IE-only style sheet.

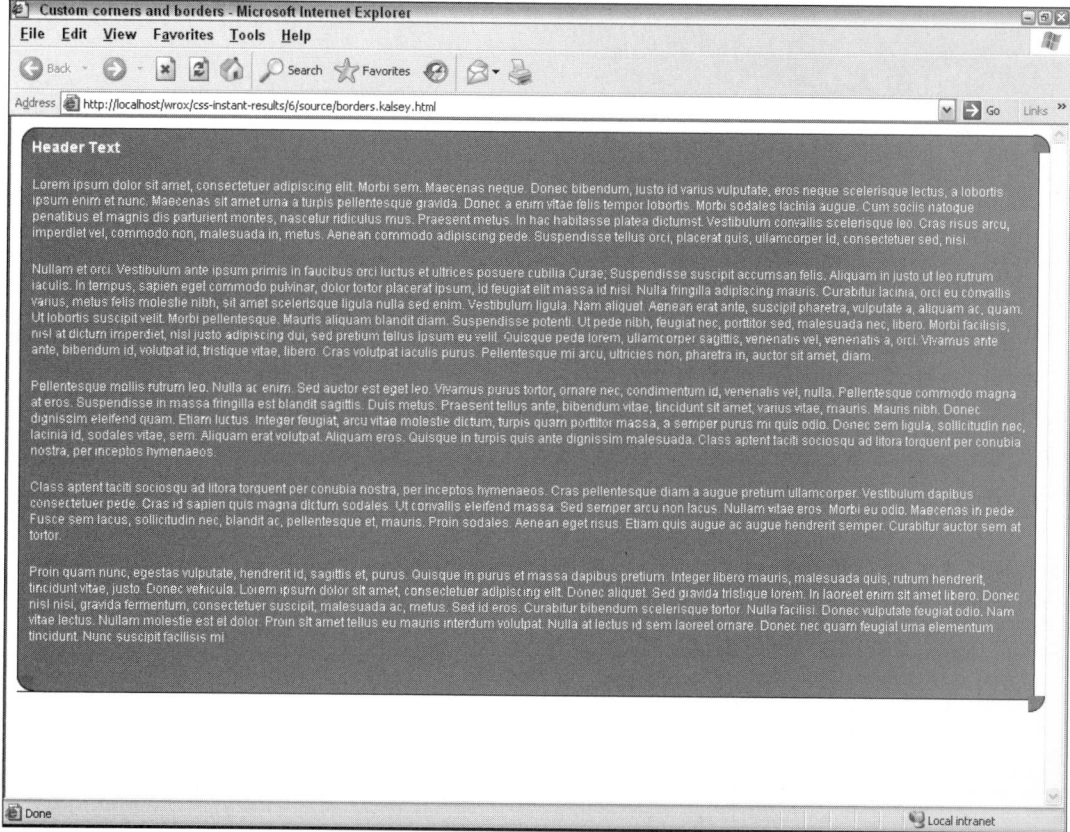

Figure 6-6

To correct the problems shown in Figure 6-6, you applied a new style sheet within Microsoft-proprietary conditional comments.

In the first rule in `borders.kalsey.ie.css`, you first applied a height of 1% to the `<div>` element with a `content` class name. This forces Internet Explorer to rethink its decisions about the placement of the elements positioned relative to the `content` `<div>` and brings better consistency. Explorer also has some issues with layering between the `content` `<div>` and the `<h1>` within it. To correct this you set explicit z-index values. Finally, Internet Explorer doesn't agree that the background color specified for the `content` `<div>` element is the same as the color in the PNG images. To correct this, you supply Internet Explorer a different color value:

```
div.content {
    height: 1%;
    z-index: 1;
    background-color: #7087AB;
}
```

The top-left corner doesn't match up with the border in Internet Explorer, and it turns out that modifying the margin is futile in Internet Explorer, so the margin is set to zero, and the position of the `<h1>` element is modified by giving it a relative position and offsetting from the left minus 1 pixel:

```
div.content h1 {
    position: relative;
    z-index: 2;
    left: -1px;
    margin-left: 0;
}
```

Internet Explorer also doesn't agree with the `<img />` elements positioned on the right sides. To correct this, the top-right image is offset from the right minus 2 pixels, and the bottom right image is offset from the right by 3 pixels:

```
img.top-right {
    right: -2px;
}
img.bottom-right {
    right: -3px;
}
```

The `<div>` element with a `bottom` class name suffered from the same problems as the `<h1>` element. To fix this you set the margin to zero, positioned the `bottom` `<div>` element relatively, gave it a z-index value higher than that of the `content` `<div>`, and offset it from the left and bottom minus 1 pixel:

```
div.bottom {
    position: relative;
    z-index: 2;
    left: -1px;
    bottom: -1px;
    margin: 0;
}
```

With the IE style sheet applied you get the results shown in Figure 6-7.

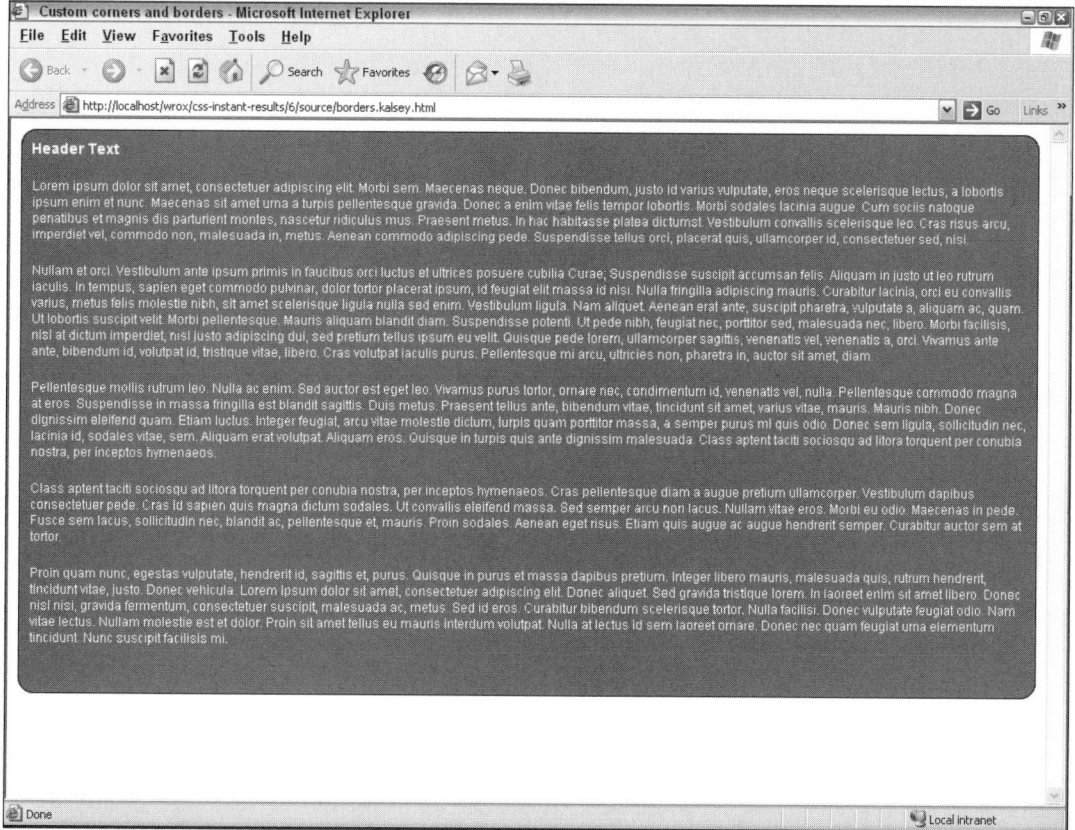

Figure 6-7

And you are now back on par with Firefox and its brethren.

Applying CSS to a Webmail Application

In this chapter you see how to approach the presentational aspects of a web-based mail application. When I was approached with the idea for this book, my editor asked me to come up with several projects that could be easily reused and integrated with little or no additional work. The first thought that came to my mind was *that is all good and well if you're writing about something like JavaScript, or a server-side programming language such as PHP or ASP.NET. It doesn't take much to see how one could write reusable projects with those languages.* With CSS it is a little different. CSS handles the presentational aspects of a web page. Most people have their own creative ideas about how they want to use CSS in their web projects, because generally speaking, companies and individuals want to create web sites that reflect their own unique personalities, position in an industry, and so on. To appease my editor, and to provide something useful for the book, I decided to provide complete projects inasmuch as I could — basic templates for making things like tabs, multi-column layouts, and rounded corners. That is, the most frequently asked "How do I do this with CSS?" questions. But those topics won't fill the whole book. Faced with a dilemma of what to write about, I thought about what I typically do in my own day-to-day job as a web application developer. Every day I write some hodgepodge of PHP, JavaScript, CSS, and markup — no surprise, that's the "web application" part of my job title. So I came to the conclusion: what better to write about than some of the applications that I work on from day to day? One such application is a web-based mail application. Ok, so you aren't going to get a fully functional webmail application, but CSS plays a large role in web application development too. The project in this chapter covers the presentational aspects of a webmail application.

I've seen my share of shoddy web-based mail applications; ugly icons, poor layout and design. The webmail layout presented in this chapter is hardly earth-shattering itself, and it should come as no surprise that graphic development is not my area of expertise. No, expertise in graphic development software is not a prerequisite for being an expert in Cascading Style Sheets! Putting that aside, the webmail application in this project is intended to look and feel like a Mac OS X application. You'll also see some similarities between the webmail application in this chapter and the web-based file management application presented in Chapter 9.

Using the project in this chapter, you'll be able to do one or more of the following:

❑   See what goes into the layout of a webmail application, and perhaps build one of your own.

❑   Use the markup and style sheets presented here, and apply JavaScript and a server-side programming language to complete the project and make a fully functional web-based mail application.

❑   Simply learn more about what types of challenges you may face in creating this particular layout.

A web-based mail application is by no means a simple undertaking, though when all is said and done there isn't much to the presentational aspects of creating one. The following are the design goals for the webmail application:

❑   There should be buttons for common mail operations: reply, reply to all, forward, compose a new message, address book, and delete.

❑   The webmail application should have at least two windows for viewing information about a mailbox. One window should contain mailboxes and folders, and the other window should contain message summary information — the subject line, the sender, whether or not a message has attachments, and the date the message was sent.

The next section covers some of the things to consider in the design of the webmail application.

Design

My opinion is and has always been that a web-based mail application should look and function as much like a native desktop application as possible. Services such as Google's Gmail are examples of web-based mail applications that have embraced this design concept. In Gmail's case the fact that it functions more like a native desktop application was met with much fanfare and is one reason for the service's success. Desktop mail applications all follow similar design principles. The icons may vary, but placement of typical mail-related operations and the user-interface for viewing messages is very similar from application to application. Figure 7-1 is a screenshot from Microsoft Office 2003.

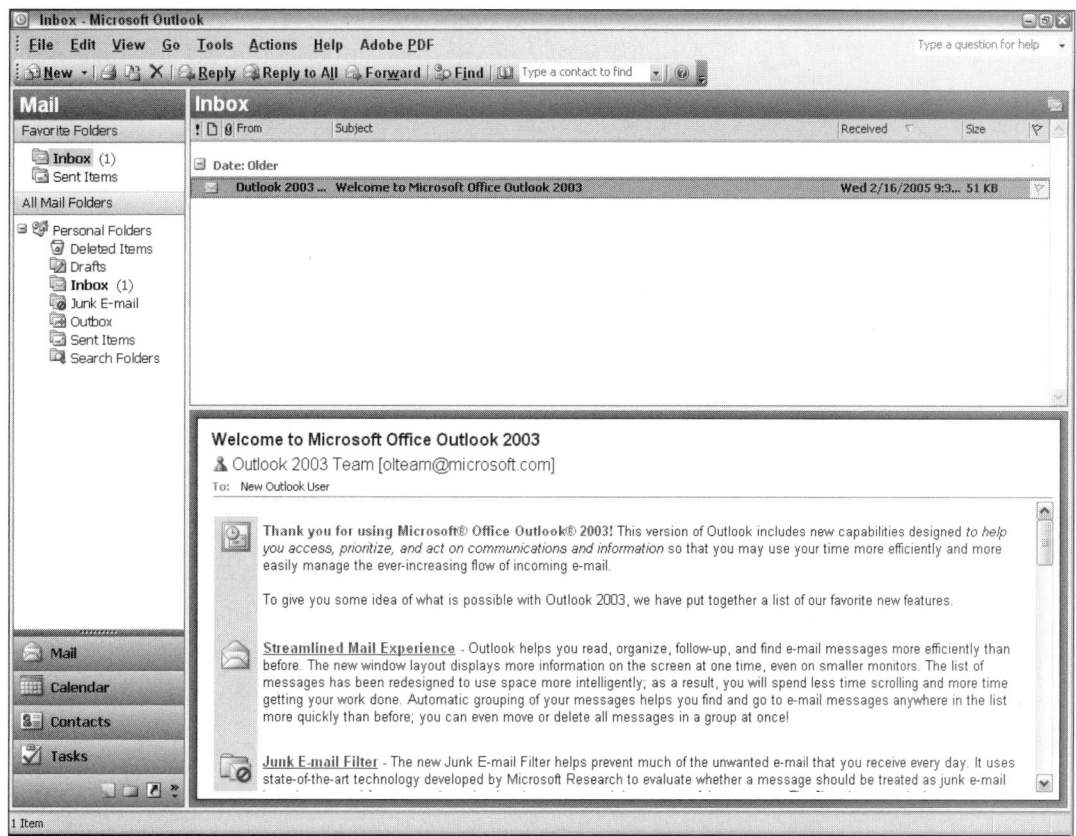

Figure 7-1

Figure 7-2 is a screenshot from Mozilla Thunderbird.

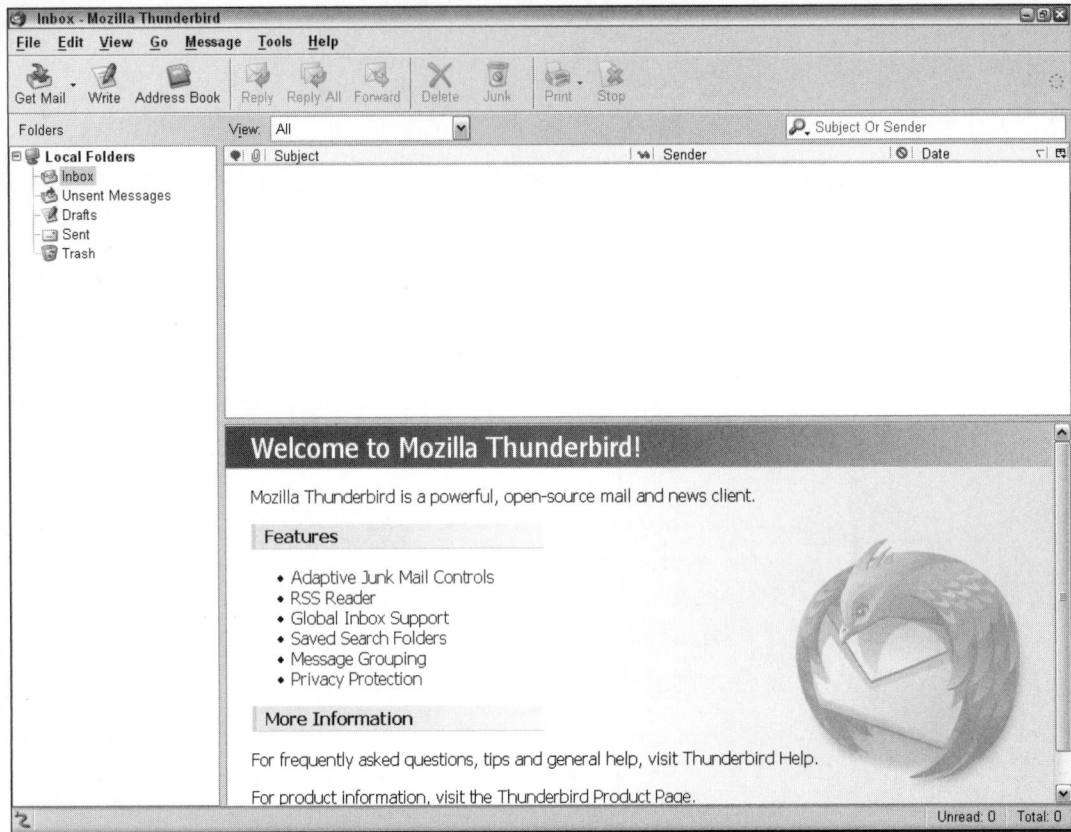

Figure 7-2

What's clear from Figures 7-1 and 7-2 is that mail applications tend to place mailboxes and folders on the left, and messages on the right. Eudora and Mac OS X Mail also follow this scheme. Because desktop applications tend to agree on where to place folders, buttons, and messages, your web-based mail program would benefit from this de facto standard mail application layout.

Most developers would be tempted to use frames to lay out a web-based mail application to match the layout of popular desktop mail applications. Frames intensify the complexity of developing an application. For this web application you would have to partition the document into three different frames — four, if you're including a message preview pane. A web-based mail application should have no more than one frame, and that frame should only be included if a message preview pane is required. Messages must appear in a separate window because most messages today contain HTML, and because these are complete HTML documents, they are ideal for frames. The rest of the application can be laid out with mere CSS in a single document.

You have two routes to take if frame-like design is required using CSS and markup, but they depend on the layout:

❑   Fixed positioning is appropriate if a portion of the document remains in place while another portion of the document scrolls. This is also superior to frames for several reasons. There is only one document to manage. If a dynamic layer such as a drop-down menu is required, a frame design won't work because a layer cannot leave the frame that contains it. Frames are also not accessible for people using speech synthesis browsers.

❑ Absolute positioning, in addition to the `overflow: auto;` declaration, is appropriate if only the contents of the layer (or pseudo-frame, if you prefer) scroll or no scrolling is involved.

As you saw for columns in Chapter 2, pseudo-frames are created with CSS and markup using a stretching technique that involves the use of offset positioning properties in tandem to imply width. That is, `left: 0;` and `right: 0;` present in a rule that also includes a `position: absolute;` or `position: fixed;` declaration imply width. The element is stretched to the width of the element that it's positioned relative to. These principles are used to create a left window for message folders, and a right folder for message summary information.

Message folders in this application are laid out using simple, unordered lists, and the message summaries are included in a simple HTML table.

Now that you've seen an overview of what components come together for the styling of a webmail application, the next section presents the source code and an explanation of how the CSS comes together with the markup to produce the final results.

Code and Code Explanation

To style a web-based mail application, follow these steps:

1. Enter the following markup:

```
<!DOCTYPE html PUBLIC "-//W3C//DTD XHTML 1.0 Strict//EN"
"http://www.w3.org/TR/xhtml1/DTD/xhtml1-strict.dtd">
<html xmlns='http://www.w3.org/1999/xhtml' xml:lang='en'>
    <head>
        <meta http-equiv='content-type' content='text/html; charset=utf-8' />
        <meta http-equiv='content-language' content='en-us' />
        <title>Mail</title>
        <link rel='stylesheet' type='text/css' href='styles/mail.css' />
    </head>
    <body>
        <div id='mail-tools'>
            <table>
                <tbody>
                    <tr>
                        <td class='reply'>
                            <img src='images/reply.png'
                                alt='Reply' title='Reply' />
                        </td>
                        <td class='reply-all'>
                            <img src='images/reply_all.png'
                                alt='Reply All' title='Reply All' />
                        </td>
                        <td class='forward'>
                            <img src='images/forward.png'
                                alt='Forward' title='Forward' />
```

```
                        </td>
                        <td class='compose'>
                            <img src='images/compose.png'
                                alt='Compose' title='Compose' />
                        </td>
                        <td class='address-book'>
                            <img src='images/address_book.png'
                                alt='Address Book' title='Address Book' />
                        </td>
                        <td class='delete'>
                            <img src='images/delete.png'
                                alt='Delete' title='Delete' />
                        </td>
                    </tr>
                </tbody>
            </table>
        </div>
        <div id='mailboxes'>
            <ul>
                <li class='mailbox'>
                    richard@localhost
                    <ul class='folders'>
                        <li class='inbox'>
                            Inbox <span class='inbox-count'>5</span>
                            <ul class='folders'>
                                <li>
                                    <span>p2p.wrox.com</span>
                                    <ul>
                                        <li><span>BegCSS</span></li>
                                        <li class='selected-folder'>
                                            <span>CSS</span>
                                        </li>
                                        <li><span>HTML_Code</span></li>
                                        <li><span>Javascript</span></li>
                                        <li><span>Javascript_how</span></li>
                                        <li><span>PHP_How</span></li>
                                        <li><span>Other</span></li>
                                    </ul>
                                </li>
                                <li><span>W3C-CSS</span></li>
                                <li><span>IE7</span></li>
                            </ul>
                        </li>
                        <li class='drafts'>
                            Drafts
                            <span class='drafts-count'>1</span>
                        </li>
                        <li class='sent'>Sent</li>
                        <li class='trash'>Trash</li>
                    </ul>
                </li>
                <li class='mailbox'>
                    webmaster@localhost
                    <ul class='folders'>
                        <li class='inbox'>
                            Inbox <span class='inbox-count'>3</span>
```

```
                        </li>
                        <li class='drafts'>
                            Drafts
                            <span class='drafts-count'>2</span>
                        </li>
                        <li class='sent'>Sent</li>
                        <li class='trash'>Trash</li>
                    </ul>
                </li>
            </ul>
        </div>
        <div id='messages'>
            <table>
                <colgroup>
                    <col id='mail-attachments-col' />
                    <col id='mail-subject-col' />
                    <col id='mail-sender-col' />
                    <col id='mail-date-col' />
                </colgroup>
                <thead>
                    <tr>
                        <th><img src='images/paperclip.png' alt='paperclip' /></th>
                        <th>Subject</th>
                        <th>Sender</th>
                        <th>Date</th>
                    </tr>
                </thead>
                <tbody>
                    <tr>
                        <td class='mail-attachment'></td>
                        <td class='mail-subject'>
                            <a href='#'>[CSS] CSS and frameset capabilities</a>
                        </td>
                        <td class='mail-sender'>
                            <a href='#' title='&lt;donotreply@wrox.com&gt;'>
                                Wrox P2P Forum Subscriptions
                            </a>
                        </td>
                        <td class='mail-date'>11:58 AM</td>
                    </tr>
                    <tr>
                        <td class='mail-attachment'></td>
                        <td class='mail-subject'>
                            <a href='#'>[CSS] aspx inside of css</a>
                        </td>
                        <td class='mail-sender'>
                            <a href='#' title='&lt;donotreply@wrox.com&gt;'>
                                Wrox P2P Forum Subscriptions
                            </a>
                        </td>
                        <td class='mail-date'>4:45 AM</td>
                    </tr>
                    <tr>
                        <td class='mail-attachment'></td>
                        <td class='mail-subject'>
```

163

```
                    <a href='#'>[CSS] aspx inside of css</a>
            </td>
            <td class='mail-sender'>
                <a href='#' title='&lt;donotreply@wrox.com&gt;'>
                    Wrox P2P Forum Subscriptions
                </a>
            </td>
            <td class='mail-date'>2:12 PM</td>
        </tr>
        <tr>
            <td class='mail-attachment'></td>
            <td class='mail-subject'>
                <a href='#'>
                    [CSS] fixing header, and first column of table.
                </a>
            </td>
            <td class='mail-sender'>
                <a href='#' title='&lt;donotreply@wrox.com&gt;'>
                    Wrox P2P Forum Subscriptions
                </a>
            </td>
            <td class='mail-date'>October 27, 2005 5:32 AM</td>
        </tr>
        <tr>
            <td class='mail-attachment'></td>
            <td class='mail-subject'>
                <a href='#'>
                    [CSS] fixing header, and first column of table.
                </a>
            </td>
            <td class='mail-sender'>
                <a href='#' title='&lt;donotreply@wrox.com&gt;'>
                    Wrox P2P Forum Subscriptions
                </a>
            </td>
            <td class='mail-date'>October 21, 2005 7:09 AM</td>
        </tr>
        <tr>
            <td class='mail-attachment'></td>
            <td class='mail-subject'>
                <a href='#'>
                    [CSS] fixing header, and first column of table.
                </a>
            </td>
            <td class='mail-sender'>
                <a href='#' title='&lt;donotreply@wrox.com&gt;'>
                    Wrox P2P Forum Subscriptions
                </a>
            </td>
            <td class='mail-date'>October 21, 2005 7:11 AM</td>
        </tr>
        <tr>
            <td class='mail-attachment'></td>
            <td class='mail-subject'>
                <a href='#'>
                    [CSS] fixing header, and first column of table.
```

```
                </a>
            </td>
            <td class='mail-sender'>
                <a href='#' title='&lt;donotreply@wrox.com&gt;'>
                    Wrox P2P Forum Subscriptions
                </a>
            </td>
            <td class='mail-date'>October 21, 2005 8:09 AM</td>
        </tr>
        <tr>
            <td class='mail-attachment'></td>
            <td class='mail-subject'>
                <a href='#'>
                    [CSS] fixing header, and first column of table.
                </a>
            </td>
            <td class='mail-sender'>
                <a href='#' title='&lt;donotreply@wrox.com&gt;'>
                    Wrox P2P Forum Subscriptions
                </a>
            </td>
            <td class='mail-date'>October 21, 2005 8:25 AM</td>
        </tr>
        <tr>
            <td class='mail-attachment'></td>
            <td class='mail-subject'>
                <a href='#'>
                    [CSS] fixing header, and first column of table.
                </a>
            </td>
            <td class='mail-sender'>
                <a href='#' title='&lt;donotreply@wrox.com&gt;'>
                    Wrox P2P Forum Subscriptions
                </a>
            </td>
            <td class='mail-date'>October 21, 2005 8:33 AM</td>
        </tr>
    </tbody>
</table>
</div>
</body>
</html>
```

2. Save the preceding markup as `mail.html`.

3. Enter the following style sheet:

```
html,
body {
    width: 100%;
    height: 100%;
    margin: 0;
    padding: 0;
    font: 12px sans-serif;
    background: url('../images/brushed_metal.png');
}
```

```
a {
    color: #369;
    text-decoration: none;
}
div#mail-tools {
    padding: 8px 0 0 8px;
}
td.compose {
    padding-left: 25px;
}
td.address-book {
    padding-right: 25px;
}
div#mailboxes,
div#messages {
    position: absolute;
    top: 0;
    bottom: 0;
    border: 1px solid rgb(128, 128, 128);
    overflow: auto;
}
div#mailboxes {
    left: 0;
    width: 200px;
    margin: 52px 0 10px 10px;
    background: #fff;
}
div#messages {
    left: 0;
    right: 0;
    margin: 52px 10px 10px 220px;
    background: url('../images/stripes.png');
}
div#messages > table {
    width: 100%;
    border-collapse: collapse;
}
div#messages > table th {
    background: rgb(249, 250, 253);
    border-bottom: 1px solid rgb(200, 200, 200);
    text-align: left;
    padding: 2px 4px;
}
div#messages > table th + th {
    border-left: 1px solid rgb(200, 200, 200);
}
col#mail-sender-col,
col#mail-date-col,
col#mail-attachments-col {
    width: 1%;
}
td.mail-sender,
td.mail-date {
    white-space: nowrap;
    padding: 0 4px;
}
```

```
div#messages > table tbody tr {
    height: 20px;
}
div#messages > table tbody tr:hover {
    background: #369;
    color: #fff;
}
div#messages > table tbody tr:hover a {
    color: #fff;
}
td.mail-subject {
    background: url('../images/16x16/2381.png') no-repeat left;
    padding-left: 20px;
    white-space: nowrap;
}
div#mailboxes ul {
    list-style: none;
    margin: 0;
    padding: 10px;
}
li.mailbox {
    padding: 5px 0 0 0;
    font-weight: bold;
}
li.mailbox + li.mailbox {
    border-top: 1px solid rgb(200, 200, 200);
}
li.mailbox * {
    font-weight: normal;
}
li.mailbox > ul > li {
    padding-left: 20px;
    min-height: 20px;
}
li.inbox {
    background: url('../images/inbox.png') no-repeat top left;
}
li.drafts {
    background: url('../images/drafts.png') no-repeat top left;
}
li.sent {
    background: url('../images/sent.png') no-repeat top left;
}
li.trash {
    background: url('../images/trash.png') no-repeat top left;
}
span.inbox-count,
span.drafts-count {
    font-weight: bold;
}
span.inbox-count::before,
span.drafts-count::before {
    content: '(';
}
span.inbox-count::after,
span.drafts-count::after {
```

```
        content: ')';
    }
ul.folders ul.folders li {
    background: url('../images/folder.png') no-repeat top left;
    padding-left: 20px;

}
ul.folders ul.folders ul {
    position: relative;
    left: -20px;
}
li.selected-folder > span {
    background: #369;
    color: #fff;
}
ul.folders ul.folders span:hover {
    background: #369;
    color: white;
}
```

4. Save the preceding style sheet as `mail.css`.

The result is shown in Figure 7-3.

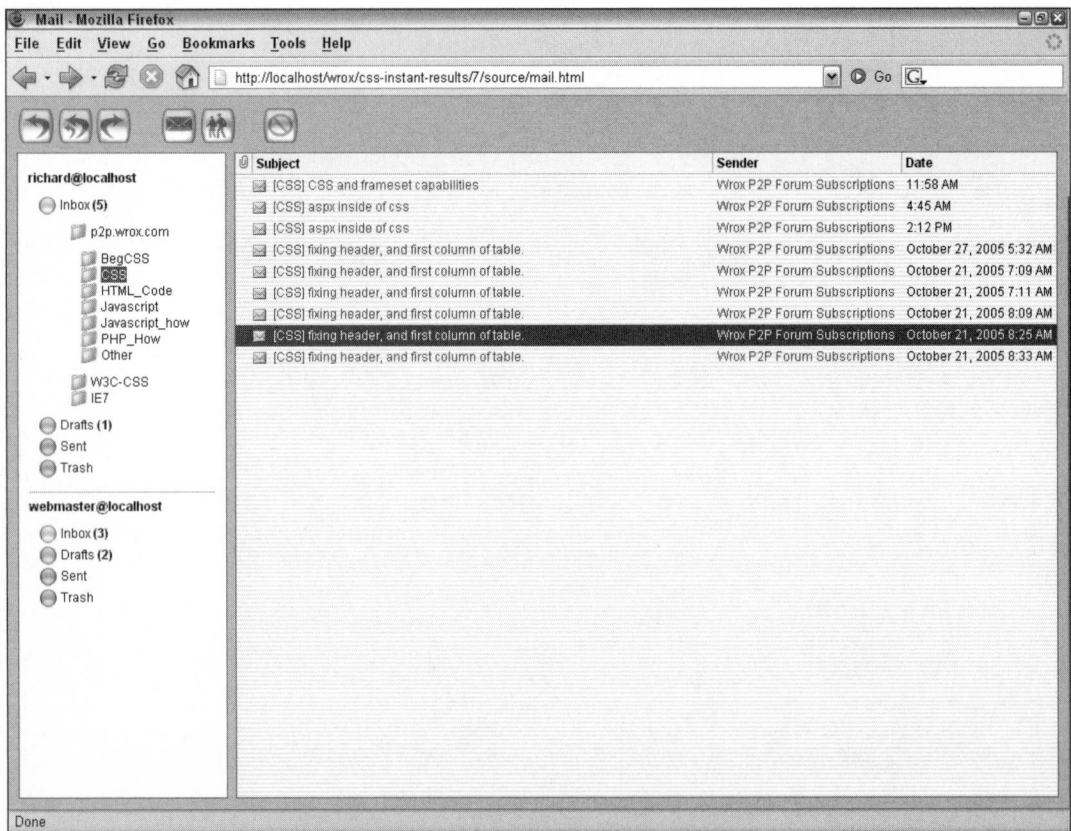

Figure 7-3

168

As you can see from the preceding source code, there isn't much to get started with a web-based mail application. Granted what I have provided is minimalist and doesn't include the other aspects of web-based mail, such as composing a message, viewing an address book, configuration menus, and so on.

The remainder of this section reviews each rule applied in `mail.css` and explains why each rule is required.

The first rule appearing in `mail.css` applies to the `<html>` and `<body>` elements. These are given 100% width and height because by default, block elements only expand vertically enough to facilitate the statically positioned content that appears within. Because the `<div>` elements for mailbox folders and the window for message summaries are positioned absolutely, they have no effect on the height of the `<html>` and `<body>` elements, but their dimensions must be based on the width and height of the `<html>` and `<body>` elements to make pseudo-frame windows that resize with the browser window. The next two declarations remove default margin or padding. The `<html>` element has no default margin or padding, but the `<body>` element may have one or the other depending on the browser. In Opera it's padding, in Mozilla Firefox and IE it's margin.

```
html,
body {
    width: 100%;
    height: 100%;
    margin: 0;
    padding: 0;
    font: 12px sans-serif;
    background: url('../images/brushed_metal.png');
}
```

The next declaration sets the font to 12-pixel, generic sans-serif for the entire document. Finally, a background image is set; `brushed_metal.png` is intended to help the mail application look like Mac OS X applications, such as Mac OS X Mail. The image is set to repeat on the x- and y-axes.

The next rule sets styling for links. With the following rule, links are made blue and the default underline is removed:

```
a {
    color: #369;
    text-decoration: none;
}
```

The next rule refers to the `<div>` just after the opening `<body>` element, which has a `mail-tools` id name. This `<div>` contains a `<table>` element, which in turn houses the buttons for the mail application. It is given 8 pixels of padding on the top and 8 pixels of padding on the left to provide some space between the top and left borders of the viewport and the content inside of the `<div>`:

```
div#mail-tools {
    padding: 8px 0 0 8px;
}
```

The next two rules refer to `<td>` elements that house buttons for mail application controls, specifically the Compose and Address Book buttons. Twenty-five pixels of padding are applied to the left of the

`<td>` element containing the compose button, and 25 pixels are applied to the right of the `<td>` element containing the Address Book button. This provides some separation between the different types of controls:

```
td.compose {
    padding-left: 25px;
}
td.address-book {
    padding-right: 25px;
}
```

The next rule applies to the `<div>` with a `mailboxes` id name, which houses mailbox folders and the `<div>` with a `messages` id name, which houses message summary information and applies some styles that are shared between the two `<div>` elements. First the `position: absolute;` declaration is applied; because these two elements are children of the `<body>` element, the two `<div>` elements are positioned relative to the `<body>` element. The `top: 0;` and `bottom: 0;` declarations cause the `<div>` elements to stretch their height based on the height of the `<body>` element, which as you saw earlier in this section has width and height based on its parent, the `<html>` element, which in turn has width and height based on the width and height of the browser's viewport. The `top: 0;` and `bottom: 0;` combination of properties lets the `mailboxes` and `messages` `<div>` elements have vertical dimensions that are dependent on the height of the viewport. Next, each `<div>` element is given a 1-pixel, solid gray border. The last declaration, `overflow: auto;`, causes each `<div>` to have scrollbars if the content contained within exceeds the dimensions of the `<div>`:

```
div#mailboxes,
div#messages {
    position: absolute;
    top: 0;
    bottom: 0;
    border: 1px solid rgb(128, 128, 128);
    overflow: auto;
}
```

The next rule refers to the `<div>` with a `mailboxes` id name also. It receives the `left: 0;` declaration to position it on the left side of the window, then it gets a fixed width of 200 pixels. Margin is adjusted to accommodate the buttons at the top of the viewport. Setting the top margin to 52 pixels prevents the `<div>` from overlapping those buttons. The bottom and left margins are set to 10 pixels to add some space between the left and bottom borders of the viewport and the left and bottom borders of the `<div>`. Finally, the `<div>` receives a white background:

```
div#mailboxes {
    left: 0;
    width: 200px;
    margin: 52px 0 10px 10px;
    background: #fff;
}
```

In the next rule, the `<div>` with a `messages` id name is referenced by itself. The first two declarations, `left: 0;` and `right: 0;`, stretch the `<div>` as wide as the viewport, then the margin is adjusted for this `<div>` as it was in the last rule. Fifty-two pixels of top margin prevent the `<div>` from overlapping the buttons at the top of the mail application, then 10 pixels are applied to the right and bottom sides to provide some space between the right and bottom borders of the `<div>` and the right and bottom borders of the viewport. Two hundred and twenty pixels of margin are applied to the left side to prevent the `<div>` from overlapping with the `mailboxes` `<div>`, which appears on its left. The last declaration specifies the `stripes.png` image, which is set to repeat along the x- and y-axes:

```
div#messages {
    left: 0;
    right: 0;
    margin: 52px 10px 10px 220px;
    background: url('../images/stripes.png');
}
```

The following rule is applied to the `<table>` element that contains message summary information such as the subject, sender, whether a message has attachments, and the date the message was sent. First the `<table>` element is set to 100% width, so that it is as wide as the `messages` `<div>` is. The second declaration, `border-collapse: collapse;`, removes default spacing from between table cells:

```
div#messages > table {
    width: 100%;
    border-collapse: collapse;
}
```

After setting up the table, in the next rule you apply styles to the table's header elements. Each `<th>` is given an off-white background, and a 1-pixel, solid gray bottom border. Text in `<th>` elements is typically center-aligned by default; the `text-align: left;` declaration is included to force the text to left align. Finally, 2 pixels of padding are applied to the top and bottom of each `<th>` element, and 4 pixels of padding are applied to the left and right of each `<th>` element:

```
div#messages > table th {
    background: rgb(249, 250, 253);
    border-bottom: 1px solid rgb(200, 200, 200);
    text-align: left;
    padding: 2px 4px;
}
```

The next rule places a border between each `<th>` element. By using the selector `div#messages > table th + th`, you select every `<th>` element except the first. This is done to make sure that there is only a left border on all `<th>` elements except the first, otherwise there would be a left border on the first `<th>` element:

```
div#messages > table th + th {
    border-left: 1px solid rgb(200, 200, 200);
}
```

With the next rule, the columns for attachments, sender, and date are set to be as small as possible with a `width: 1%;` declaration. Because `<table>` elements don't honor explicit widths, and actually treat width and height more like minimum width and height, this makes these columns take up as little space as possible, and the Subject column take up the space that remains:

```
col#mail-sender-col,
col#mail-date-col,
col#mail-attachments-col {
    width: 1%;
}
```

171

Because the Sender and Date columns were made as small as possible, causing the text to wrap, the `white-space: nowrap;` declaration is set to prevent text wrapping. Also, because of the size of each column, the text of the Sender column runs up right next to the Date column, so 4 pixels of padding are added to the left and right sides to space out the text of each column a bit:

```
td.mail-sender,
td.mail-date {
    white-space: nowrap;
    padding: 0 4px;
}
```

Setting the height of each `<tr>` element to 20 pixels in the next rule provides some spacing between each message in the messages window:

```
div#messages > table tbody tr {
    height: 20px;
}
```

The next rule is applied if the user's mouse cursor is hovering over a message in his mailbox. It applies a blue background and white text:

```
div#messages > table tbody tr:hover {
    background: #369;
    color: #fff;
}
```

Because the preceding rule applies a blue background with white text when the user's mouse is hovering over a message in his mailbox, the links also change color. The following rule changes the links to white in that scenario:

```
div#messages > table tbody tr:hover a {
    color: #fff;
}
```

The next rule applies to the Subject column of the "messages" view. First an envelope icon is applied, which was hijacked from Microsoft Outlook 2003. To prevent the text of the subject from overlapping with the envelope icon, 20 pixels of left padding are applied. Finally, as was the case for the date and sender columns, the text is prevented from wrapping with the `white-space: nowrap;` declaration:

```
td.mail-subject {
    background: url('../images/16x16/2381.png') no-repeat left;
    padding-left: 20px;
    white-space: nowrap;
}
```

The next series of rules applies to the mailbox folders on the left side of the application. First some defaults for all `<ul>` elements contained in the `mailboxes` `<div>` element. The default list bullets are removed with the `list-style: none;` declaration. Default margin is removed with the `margin: 0;` declaration, and then 10 pixels of padding are applied to each `<ul>` element:

```
div#mailboxes ul {
    list-style: none;
    margin: 0;
```

```
    padding: 10px;
}
```

The top-level `<li>` elements that contain the email addresses are each given a `mailbox` class name. Five pixels of top padding are applied to provide some space between the top mailbox and the top border of the `mailboxes` `<div>` element, and also between each mailbox. Then, the text of each email address is made bold with the `font-weight: bold;` declaration:

```
li.mailbox {
    padding: 5px 0 0 0;
    font-weight: bold;
}
```

Using the selector `li.mailbox + li.mailbox` in the next rule causes there to be a 1-pixel, solid gray border between each mailbox:

```
li.mailbox + li.mailbox {
    border-top: 1px solid rgb(200, 200, 200);
}
```

Because you set the text of each email address to be bold in a preceding rule, the following rule overrides inheritance by resetting the `font-weight` property to `normal` for all descendants of the `<li>` elements with `mailbox` class names:

```
li.mailbox * {
    font-weight: normal;
}
```

The next rule prepares the `<li>` elements with `inbox`, `drafts`, `sent`, and `trash` class names to receive icons. First the left padding is set to 20 pixels to prevent the text of each `<li>` element from overlapping the icon, and a minimum height of 20 pixels is set to prevent the icon from being clipped if the `<li>` element's height isn't large enough to accommodate it:

```
li.mailbox > ul > li {
    padding-left: 20px;
    min-height: 20px;
}
```

The next series of rules places icons for the `<li>` elements with `inbox`, `drafts`, `sent`, and `trash` class names — a different colored orb for each `<li>` element set non-repeating to the top and left of each one:

```
li.inbox {
    background: url('../images/inbox.png') no-repeat top left;
}
li.drafts {
    background: url('../images/drafts.png') no-repeat top left;
}
li.sent {
    background: url('../images/sent.png') no-repeat top left;
}
li.trash {
    background: url('../images/trash.png') no-repeat top left;
}
```

The next rule sets the message count for the Inbox and Drafts folders to bold:

```
span.inbox-count,
span.drafts-count {
    font-weight: bold;
}
```

Because not all people may want parentheses around their message count, the next two rules allow that to be customized from the style sheet using the ::before and ::after pseudo-elements and the content property:

```
span.inbox-count::before,
span.drafts-count::before {
    content: '(';
}
span.inbox-count::after,
span.drafts-count::after {
    content: ')';
}
```

The next rule applies a folder icon to subfolders of the inbox folder. As was the case for icons in preceding rules, the background is set non-repeating top and left, then left padding is adjusted to keep the text of the folder name from overlapping with the folder icon:

```
ul.folders ul.folders li {
    background: url('../images/folder.png') no-repeat top left;
    padding-left: 20px;
}
```

The position of subfolders is adjusted with the next rule by including the position: relative; declaration, and negative offsetting from the left of 20 pixels:

```
ul.folders ul.folders ul {
    position: relative;
    left: -20px;
}
```

Users may appreciate the folder they are currently viewing being highlighted in the directory structure on the left. That is done with the following rule. It sets the <span> child of the selected folder to have a blue background and white text:

```
li.selected-folder > span {
    background: #369;
    color: #fff;
}
```

Finally, the last rule, like the previous, gives <span> elements a blue background and white text, but this time only when the user's mouse is hovering over one of them:

```
ul.folders ul.folders span:hover {
    background: #369;
    color: white;
}
```

Now that you have seen how the presentational aspects of the mail application come together with the markup, in the next section you look at our old friend Internet Explorer and what needs to be tweaked to make the design shine just as well in Internet Explorer 6 as it does in other browsers.

Testing and Caveats

In this section you take the final product from the previous section and test it more rigorously, which involves having a look at the project in Internet Explorer for Windows.

As you might have guessed, as it now stands the mail application doesn't look like anything resembling a professionally designed web page in Internet Explorer. The good news is there isn't much required to bring Internet Explorer up to par with Mozilla Firefox.

Figure 7-4 shows what the mail application now looks like in Internet Explorer 6.

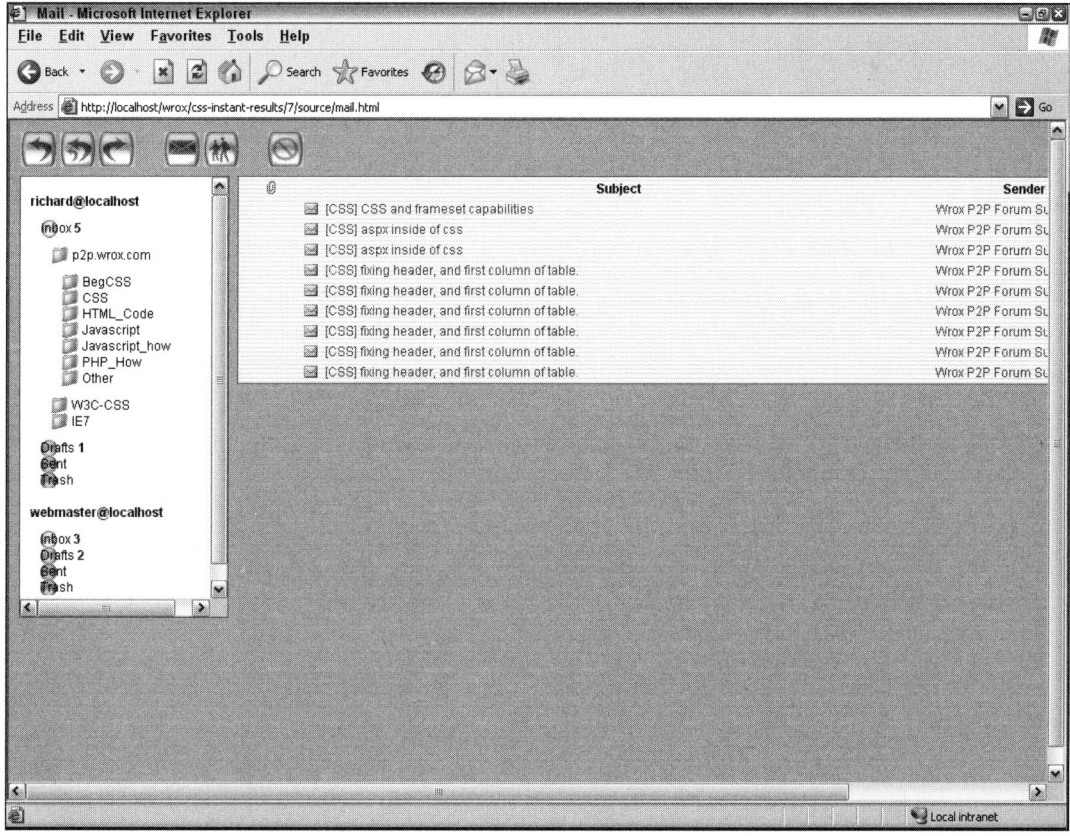

Figure 7-4

Is this another job for Dean Edwards' fantastic IE7 JavaScript? Sure. Figure 7-5 shows what the mail application looks like with Dean's IE7 applied to it.

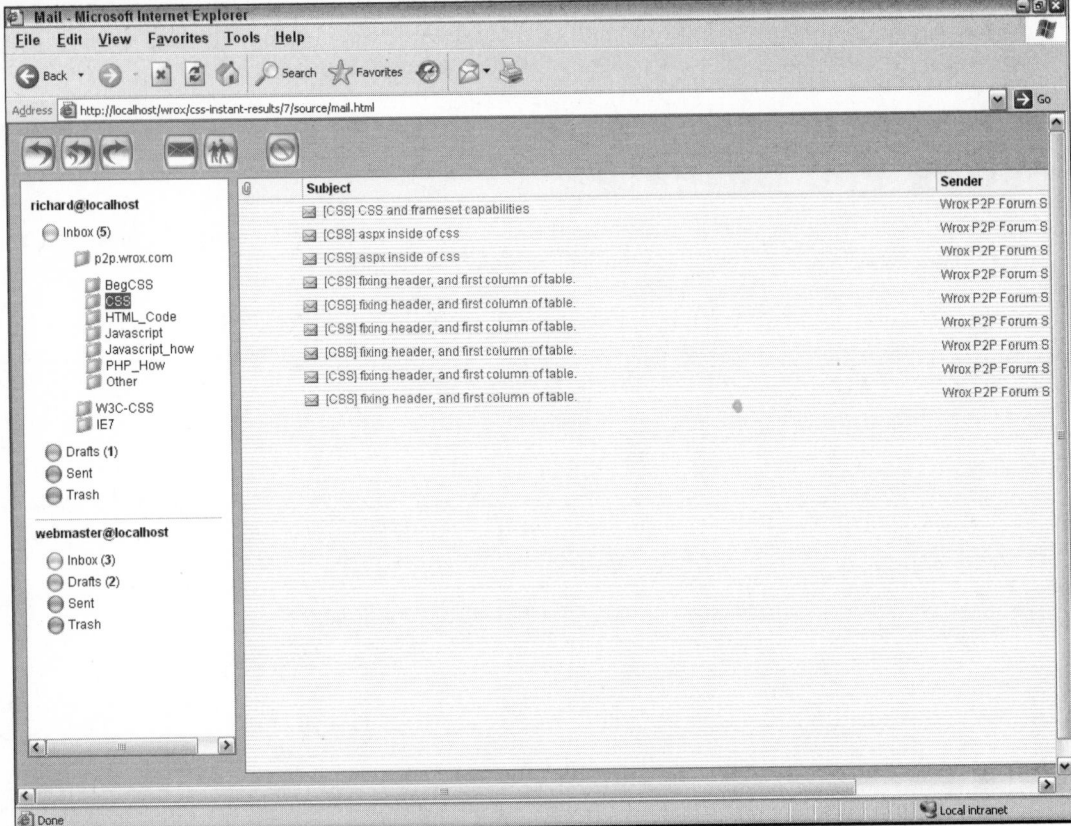

Figure 7-5

The mail application is still not quite there, even with Dean's IE7 JavaScript applied. This application exposes some bugs in IE7 (at the time of this writing at least — I'm certain Dean is working on a fix even as I type away) that have to do with the use of margin in addition to using the combination of offset properties to imply width or height.

In Figure 7-5, you see the following problems with the rendering:

❑   The left margin specified on the messages `<div>` element, which also has the left and right combination of offset properties to imply width, is not subtracted from the width as it is in Firefox.

❑   The attachments column is too wide.

❑   The icons at the top are PNG images with transparent portions; IE does not handle transparent PNG images out of the box.

❑   When hovering over a message, the blue background doesn't appear in the Subject column.

❑   The mailboxes `<div>` is just a smidge too short.

❑   There are vertical and horizontal scrollbars for the viewport.

The rendering problems listed here aren't showstoppers for the mail application. To remedy these problems, follow these steps:

1. Open `mail.html` and make the following changes:

```html
<!DOCTYPE html PUBLIC "-//W3C//DTD XHTML 1.0 Strict//EN"
"http://www.w3.org/TR/xhtml1/DTD/xhtml1-strict.dtd">
<html xmlns='http://www.w3.org/1999/xhtml' xml:lang='en'>
    <head>
        <meta http-equiv='content-type' content='text/html; charset=utf-8' />
        <meta http-equiv='content-language' content='en-us' />
        <title>Mail</title>
        <link rel='stylesheet' type='text/css' href='styles/mail.css' />
        <!-- compliance patch for microsoft browsers -->
        <!--[if lt IE 7]>
            <script src="/ie7/ie7-standard-p.js" type="text/javascript">
            </script>
            <link rel='stylesheet' type='text/css' href='styles/mail.ie.css' />
        <![endif]-->
    </head>
<body id='mail'>
    <div id='mail-tools'>
        <table>
            <tbody>
                <tr>
                    <td class='reply'>
                        <img src='images/reply-trans.png'
                            alt='Reply' title='Reply' />
                    </td>
                    <td class='reply-all'>
                        <img src='images/reply_all-trans.png'
                            alt='Reply All' title='Reply All' />
                    </td>
                    <td class='forward'>
                        <img src='images/forward-trans.png'
                            alt='Forward' title='Forward' />
                    </td>
                    <td class='compose'>
                        <img src='images/compose-trans.png'
                            alt='Compose' title='Compose' />
                    </td>
                    <td class='address-book'>
                        <img src='images/address_book-trans.png'
                            alt='Address Book' title='Address Book' />
                    </td>
                    <td class='delete'>
                        <img src='images/delete-trans.png'
                            alt='Delete' title='Delete' />
                    </td>
                </tr>
            </tbody>
        </table>
    </div>
    <div id='mailboxes'>
        <ul>
```

2.   Save the modified file as `mail.ie.html`.

3.   Enter the following style sheet:

```
col#mail-attachments-col {
    width: 1px;
}
div#messages > table tbody tr:hover td.mail-subject {
    background: #369 url('../images/16x16/2381.png') no-repeat left;
}
div#messages {
    width: expression(
        document.getElementById('mail').offsetWidth - 235
    );
}
div#messages,
div#mailboxes {
    height: expression(
        document.getElementById('mail').offsetHeight - 65
    );
}
```

4.   Save the new style sheet as `mail.ie.css`.

The modifications result in the output shown in Figure 7-6.

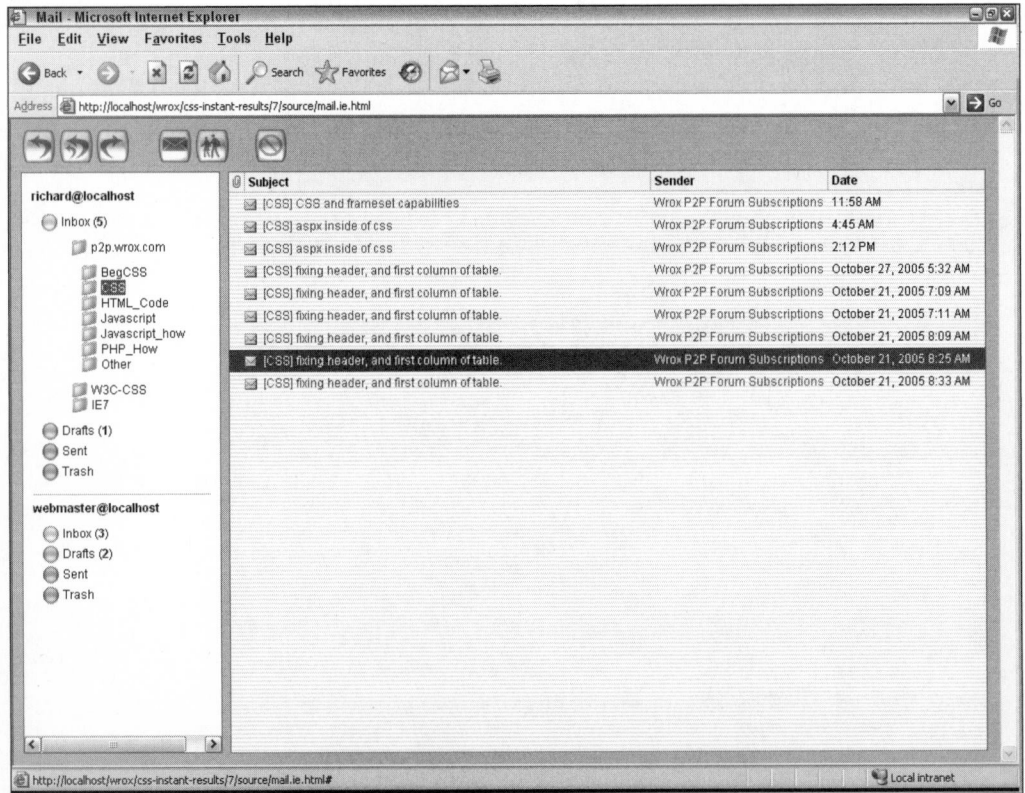

Figure 7-6

The modifications you made bring Internet Explorer up to par in its rendering with Firefox, Opera, and Safari.

The first modifications give each of those transparent PNG images a "-trans" prefix. The "-trans" prefix is used by Dean Edwards' IE7 JavaScript as a filter that alerts IE7 to which PNG images need a special transparent PNG hack applied. In Chapter 9 you see how this hack functions inside and out; for this project the "-trans" prefix is a quick and dirty way to get around Internet Explorer's lack of native PNG transparency support.

The remainder of this section examines each of the rules in menu.ie.css in further detail, and explains why they work.

In the first rule you have applied a width: 1px; declaration to the mail attachments column. Specifying width: 1px; for all columns causes IE to ignore the white-space: nowrap; declaration on the Sender and Date columns, so those columns keep the width: 1%; declaration originally specified in menu.css, and the Attachments column gets width: 1px;:

```
col#mail-attachments-col {
    width: 1px;
}
```

The next rule corrects IE not applying a blue background to the Subject column upon mousingover the messages that appear there. It turns out this is because there is a background specified for that column, the envelope icon. To correct the problem, the <td> with a mail-subject class name is selected when the user mousesover the parent <tr> element, then the blue used for the parent <tr> element is specified explicitly for the child <td> as well (in addition to the envelope icon):

```
div#messages > table tbody tr:hover td.mail-subject {
    background: #369 url('../images/16x16/2381.png') no-repeat left;
}
```

Next, the width of the messages <div> is corrected. The technique used here is the same as you saw in Chapter 2, in the section titled "Good Old-Fashioned Internet Explorer Hacking" — the Microsoft-proprietary expression() feature is used to include JavaScript directly in the style sheet. You applied a mail id name to the <body> element, which is what is referenced here using the getElementById() method. The offsetWidth property is used to get the width of the <body> element, then 235 pixels are subtracted, which includes the width of the mailboxes <div> and the margin on the left and right sides of that <div> element:

```
div#messages {
    width: expression(
        document.getElementById('mail').offsetWidth - 235
    );
}
```

In the last rule appearing in mail.ie.css you correct the height of both the messages and mailboxes <div> elements. Here again, you use the expression() feature to get the offsetHeight property of the <body> element, subtract 65 pixels, which adjusts the height of each <div> element to account for the space at the top of the document for buttons and the margin beneath each <div> element:

```
div#messages,
div#mailboxes {
    height: expression(
        document.getElementById('mail').offsetHeight - 65
    );
}
```

Having tamed Internet Explorer, the next section presents some alternative approaches to the mail application.

Using and Modifying the Project

In this section you see the following approaches to the web-based mail application:

❑   Adding a preview pane for messages via an inline frame.

❑   Restructuring the document in the three-column format of Microsoft Outlook 2003.

Adding a preview pane is a relatively simple undertaking: just add an inline frame, then apply some styling to resize the messages <div> to accommodate it. You see how this is done in the next section.

Adding a Message Preview Pane

Because messages can be in HTML or plain text format, the message preview pane must be an inline frame to keep it sequestered as an independent document. To add a message preview pane, follow these steps:

1.   Make the following modifications to mail.ie.html:

```
<!DOCTYPE html PUBLIC "-//W3C//DTD XHTML 1.0 Frameset//EN"
"http://www.w3.org/TR/xhtml1/DTD/xhtml1-frameset.dtd">
<html xmlns='http://www.w3.org/1999/xhtml' xml:lang='en'>
    <head>
        <meta http-equiv='content-type' content='text/html; charset=utf-8' />
        <meta http-equiv='content-language' content='en-us' />
        <title>Mail</title>
        <link rel='stylesheet' type='text/css'
            href='styles/mail.messagePreview.css' />
        <!-- compliance patch for microsoft browsers -->
        <!--[if lt IE 7]>
            <script src="/ie7/ie7-standard-p.js" type="text/javascript">
            </script>
            <link rel='stylesheet' type='text/css'
                href='styles/mail.ie.messagePreview.css' />
        <![endif]-->
    </head>
    <body id='mail'>
        <div id='mail-tools'>
            <table>
                <tbody>
```

2. Continue modifying `mail.ie.html`, adding the following markup:

```
            <tr>
                <td class='mail-attachment'></td>
                <td class='mail-subject'>
                    <a href='#'>
                        [CSS] fixing header, and first column of table.
                    </a>
                </td>
                <td class='mail-sender'>
                    <a href='#' title='&lt;donotreply@wrox.com&gt;'>
                        Wrox P2P Forum Subscriptions
                    </a>
                </td>
                <td class='mail-date'>October 21, 2005 8:33 AM</td>
            </tr>
        </tbody>
    </table>
</div>
<iframe id='message-preview'
        name='message_preview'
        src=''
        frameborder='0'
        marginwidth='0'
        marginheight='0'></iframe>
</body>
</html>
```

3. Save the modified document as `mail.messagePreview.html`.

4. Make the following changes to `mail.css`:

```css
div#mailboxes,
div#messages {
    position: absolute;
    top: 0;
    bottom: 0;
    border: 1px solid rgb(128, 128, 128);
    overflow: auto;
}
div#mailboxes {
    left: 0;
    width: 200px;
    margin: 52px 0 10px 10px;
    background: #fff;
}
div#messages {
    left: 0;
    right: 0;
    margin: 52px 10px 300px 220px;
    background: url('../images/stripes.png');
}
div#messages > table {
    width: 100%;
    border-collapse: collapse;
}
```

5. Continue making changes to `mail.css`. Add the following rule:

```css
ul.folders ul.folders ul {
    position: relative;
    left: -20px;
}
li.selected-folder > span {
    background: #369;
    color: #fff;
}
ul.folders ul.folders span:hover {
    background: #369;
    color: white;
}
iframe#message-preview {
    position: absolute;
    border: 1px solid rgb(128, 128, 128);
    bottom: 0;
    left: 0;
    right: 0;
    margin: 0 10px 10px 220px;
    height: 280px;
    background: #fff;
}
```

6. Save the file as `mail.messagePreview.css`.

7. Make the following modifications to `mail.ie.css`:

```css
col#mail-attachments-col {
    width: 1px;
}
div#messages > table tbody tr:hover td.mail-subject {
    background: #369 url('../images/16x16/2381.png') no-repeat left;
}
div#messages {
    width: expression(
        document.getElementById('mail').offsetWidth - 235
    );
    height: expression(
        document.getElementById('mail').offsetHeight - 355
    );
}
div#mailboxes {
    height: expression(
        document.getElementById('mail').offsetHeight - 65
    );
}
iframe#message-preview {
    width: expression(
        document.getElementById('mail').offsetWidth - 235
    );
}
```

8. Save the file as `mail.ie.messagePreview.css`.

In Firefox you see the output shown in Figure 7-7.

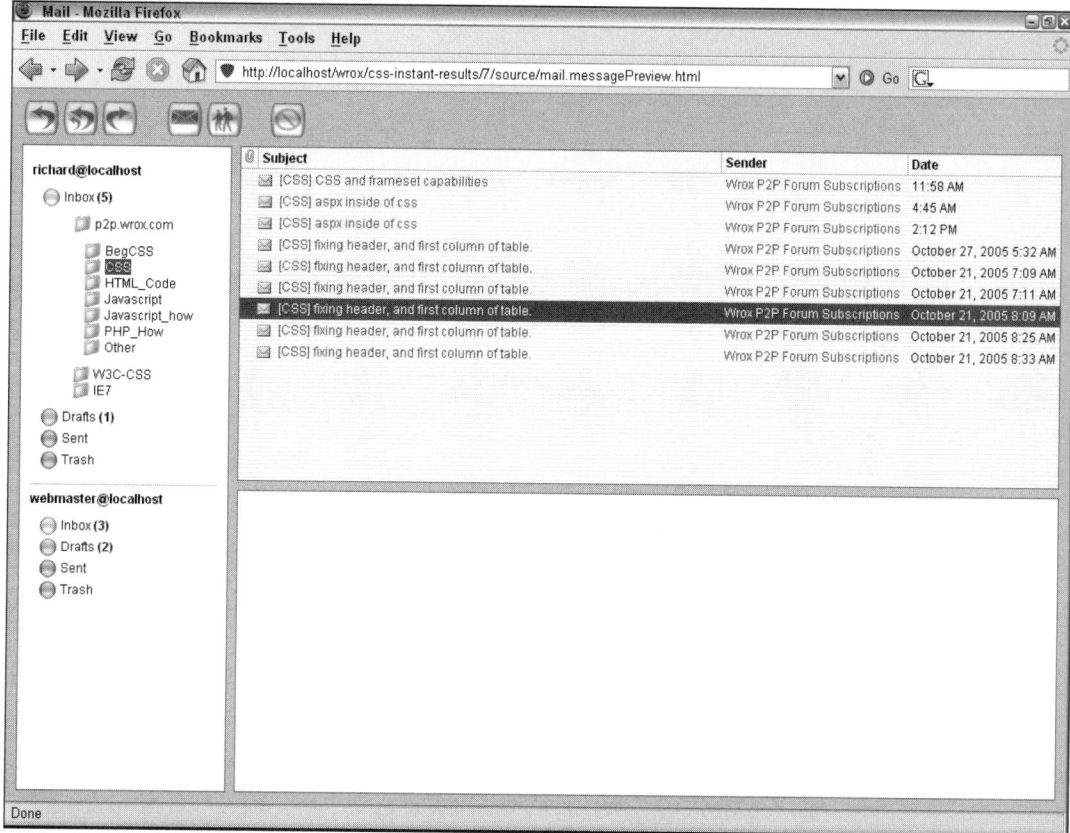

Figure 7-7

In Internet Explorer you see the output shown in Figure 7-8.

Adding a message preview pane to the mail application was a fairly straightforward undertaking. First, because the document contains an inline frame, you changed the Document Type Declaration to the XHTML frameset Document Type Declaration. Then you modified the file path of the style sheets to reflect the new file names. Near the end of the document, after the closing `</div>` tag for the `messages` `<div>`, you added an `<iframe>` element, which will be used to preview messages. In `mail.css`, you made room for the new `<iframe>` element, by modifying the following rule:

```
div#messages {
    left: 0;
    right: 0;
    margin: 52px 10px 300px 220px;
    background: url('../images/stripes.png');
}
```

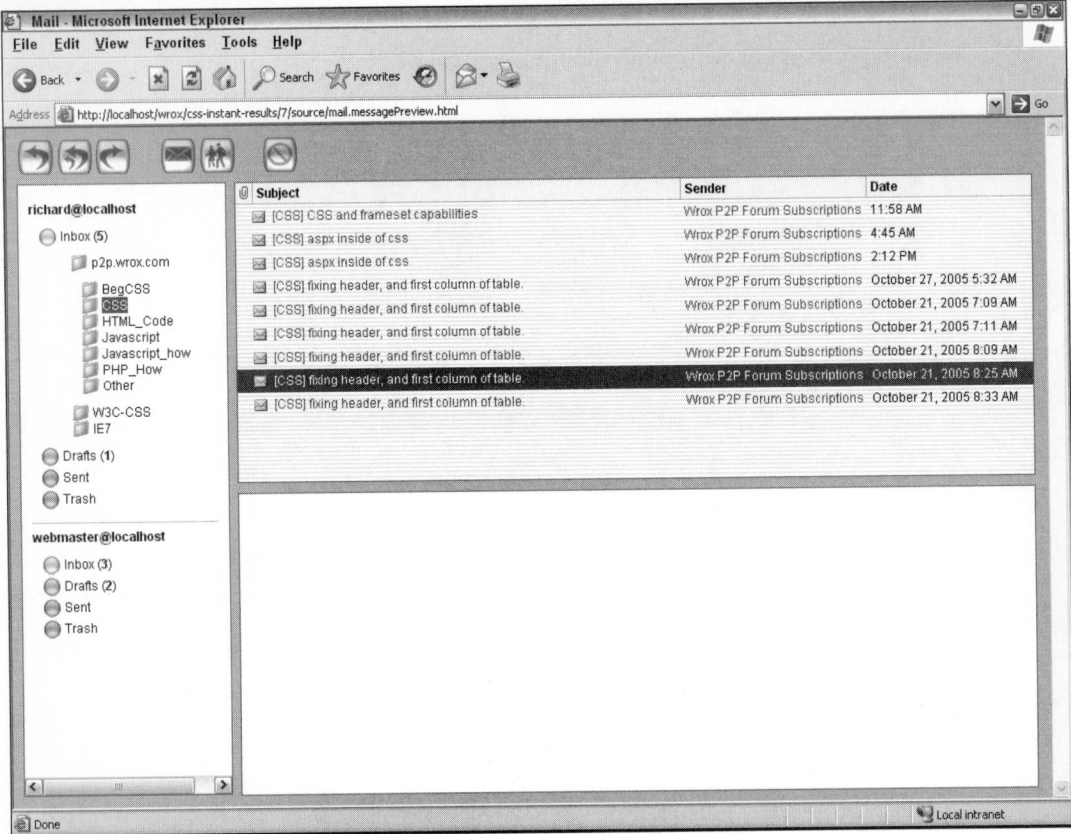

Figure 7-8

The bottom margin is made much bigger to make room in the area of the viewport that the `<iframe>` element occupies.

Then a new rule is applied to position the `<iframe>` element. It is positioned absolutely and given a solid gray border identical to that of the `mailboxes` and `messages` `<div>` elements. It is positioned to the bottom of the viewport with the `bottom: 0;` declaration and stretched for the width of the viewport with the combination of `left: 0;` and `right: 0;` offset properties. Then margin is specified to space it out 10 pixels from the right and bottom borders of the viewport. Next, 220 pixels of left margin are specified to prevent the `<iframe>` element from overlapping the `mailboxes` `<div>` element to its left. The `<iframe>` element then receives a height of 280 pixels and a white background:

```
iframe#message-preview {
    position: absolute;
    border: 1px solid rgb(128, 128, 128);
    bottom: 0;
    left: 0;
```

```
        right: 0;
        margin: 0 10px 10px 220px;
        height: 280px;
        background: #fff;
}
```

The final adjustments that you made address new inconsistencies in Internet Explorer.

First you must adjust the height of the messages <div> element:

```
div#messages {
    width: expression(
        document.getElementById('mail').offsetWidth - 235
    );
    height: expression(
        document.getElementById('mail').offsetHeight - 355
    );
}
```

In the preceding rule the Microsoft-proprietary expression() feature is used to adjust the height of the messages <div> element in an effort to prevent it from overlapping the new <iframe> element that has been added. The value of 355 is the equivalent to the space above the messages <div> element that the buttons appear in, the height of the <iframe> element, and the other extra vertical space such as margins that must be subtracted from the height of the messages element to keep everything in check.

The last modification you made to mail.ie.messagePreview.css was to add a new rule for the <iframe> element:

```
iframe#message-preview {
    width: expression(
        document.getElementById('mail').offsetWidth - 235
    );
}
```

The width of the <iframe> element must also be adjusted, so that it takes up all the space available to it horizontally between the mailboxes <div> and the right border of the viewport. You subtract 235 pixels from the width of the <body> element to accommodate the width of the mailboxes <div>, which results in the <iframe> rendering the same in Internet Explorer as it does in Firefox.

In the next section you see how to get a three-column layout like that in Microsoft Office 2003.

Three-Column Layout a la Microsoft Outlook 2003

This section outlines how to modify the project so that it has a three-column layout, like that found in Microsoft's Outlook 2003. Figure 7-9 is a screenshot of Microsoft Outlook 2003 with the three-column view.

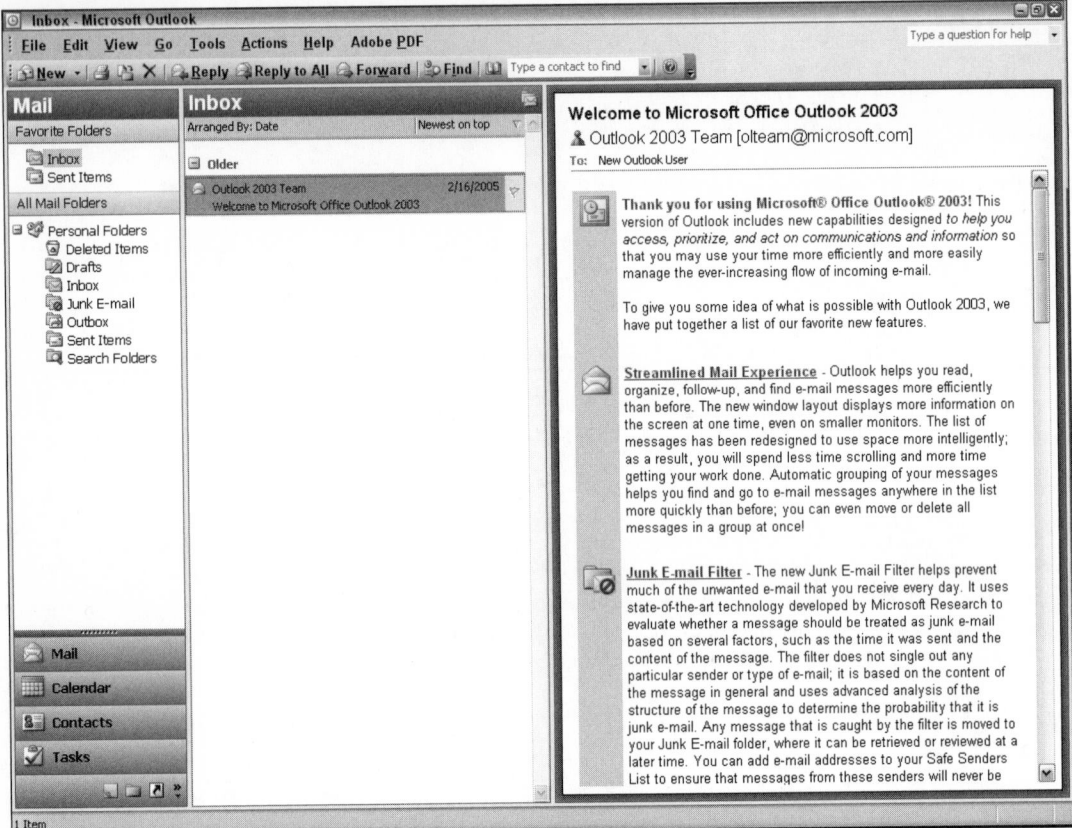

Figure 7-9

To make a mail application layout like that of Microsoft Outlook 2003, follow these steps:

1. Make the following modifications to `mail.messagePreview.html`:

```
<!DOCTYPE html PUBLIC "-//W3C//DTD XHTML 1.0 Frameset//EN"
"http://www.w3.org/TR/xhtml1/DTD/xhtml1-frameset.dtd">
<html xmlns='http://www.w3.org/1999/xhtml' xml:lang='en'>
    <head>
        <meta http-equiv='content-type' content='text/html; charset=utf-8' />
        <meta http-equiv='content-language' content='en-us' />
        <title>Mail</title>
        <link rel='stylesheet' type='text/css' href='styles/mail.outlook2k3.css' />
        <!-- compliance patch for microsoft browsers -->
        <!--[if lt IE 7]>
            <script src="/ie7/ie7-standard-p.js" type="text/javascript">
            </script>
            <link rel='stylesheet' type='text/css'
                href='styles/mail.ie.outlook2k3.css' />
        <![endif]-->
    </head>
```

```
<body id='mail'>
    <div id='mail-tools'>
        <table>
            <tbody>
                <tr>
                    <td class='reply'>
                        <img src='images/reply-trans.png'
                            alt='Reply' title='Reply' />
                    </td>
                    <td class='reply-all'>
                        <img src='images/reply_all-trans.png'
                            alt='Reply All' title='Reply All' />
                    </td>
                    <td class='forward'>
                        <img src='images/forward-trans.png'
                            alt='Forward' title='Forward' />
                    </td>
                    <td class='compose'>
                        <img src='images/compose-trans.png'
                            alt='Compose' title='Compose' />
                    </td>
                    <td class='address-book'>
                        <img src='images/address_book-trans.png'
                            alt='Address Book' title='Address Book' />
                    </td>
                    <td class='delete'>
                        <img src='images/delete-trans.png'
                            alt='Delete' title='Delete' />
                    </td>
                </tr>
            </tbody>
        </table>
    </div>
    <div id='mailboxes'>
        <ul>
            <li class='mailbox'>
                richard@localhost
                <ul class='folders'>
                    <li class='inbox'>
                        Inbox <span class='inbox-count'>5</span>
                        <ul class='folders'>
                            <li>
                                <span>p2p.wrox.com</span>
                                <ul>
                                    <li><span>BegCSS</span></li>
                                    <li class='selected-folder'>
                                        <span>CSS</span></li>
                                    <li><span>HTML_Code</span></li>
                                    <li><span>Javascript</span></li>
                                    <li><span>Javascript_how</span></li>
                                    <li><span>PHP_How</span></li>
                                    <li><span>Other</span></li>
                                </ul>
                            </li>
```

```
                    <li><span>W3C-CSS</span></li>
                    <li><span>IE7</span></li>
                </ul>
            </li>
            <li class='drafts'>Drafts
                <span class='drafts-count'>1</span>
            </li>
            <li class='sent'>Sent</li>
            <li class='trash'>Trash</li>
        </ul>
    </li>
    <li class='mailbox'>
        webmaster@localhost
        <ul class='folders'>
            <li class='inbox'>
                Inbox <span class='inbox-count'>3</span>
            </li>
            <li class='drafts'>
                Drafts
                <span class='drafts-count'>2</span>
            </li>
            <li class='sent'>Sent</li>
            <li class='trash'>Trash</li>
        </ul>
    </li>
</ul>
</div>
<div id='messages'>
    <div class='message'>
        <span class='mail-date'>11:58 AM</span>
        <div class='mail-sender'>
            <a href='#' title='&lt;donotreply@wrox.com&gt;'>
                Wrox P2P Forum Subscriptions
            </a>
        </div>
        <div class='mail-subject'>
            <a href='#'>[CSS] CSS and frameset capabilities</a>
        </div>
    </div>
    <div class='message'>
        <span class='mail-date'>4:45 AM</span>
        <div class='mail-sender'>
            <a href='#' title='&lt;donotreply@wrox.com&gt;'>
                Wrox P2P Forum Subscriptions
            </a>
        </div>
        <div class='mail-subject'>
            <a href='#'>[CSS] aspx inside of css</a>
        </div>
    </div>
    <div class='message'>
        <span class='mail-date'>2:12 PM</span>
        <div class='mail-sender'>
            <a href='#' title='&lt;donotreply@wrox.com&gt;'>
                Wrox P2P Forum Subscriptions
            </a>
```

```
            </div>
            <div class='mail-subject'>
                <a href='#'>[CSS] aspx inside of css</a>
            </div>
    </div>
    <div class='message'>
        <span class='mail-date'>October 27, 2005 5:32 AM</span>
        <div class='mail-sender'>
            <a href='#' title='&lt;donotreply@wrox.com&gt;'>
                Wrox P2P Forum Subscriptions
            </a>
        </div>
        <div class='mail-subject'>
            <a href='#'>[CSS] fixing header, and first column of table.</a>
        </div>
    </div>
    <div class='message'>
        <span class='mail-date'>October 21, 2005 7:09 AM</span>
        <div class='mail-sender'>
            <a href='#' title='&lt;donotreply@wrox.com&gt;'>
                Wrox P2P Forum Subscriptions
            </a>
        </div>
        <div class='mail-subject'>
            <a href='#'>[CSS] fixing header, and first column of table.</a>
        </div>
    </div>
    <div class='message'>
        <span class='mail-date'>October 21, 2005 7:11 AM</span>
        <div class='mail-sender'>
            <a href='#' title='&lt;donotreply@wrox.com&gt;'>
                Wrox P2P Forum Subscriptions
            </a>
        </div>
        <div class='mail-subject'>
            <a href='#'>[CSS] fixing header, and first column of table.</a>
        </div>
    </div>
    <div class='message'>
        <span class='mail-date'>October 21, 2005 8:09 AM</span>
        <div class='mail-sender'>
            <a href='#' title='&lt;donotreply@wrox.com&gt;'>
                Wrox P2P Forum Subscriptions
            </a>
        </div>
        <div class='mail-subject'>
            <a href='#'>[CSS] fixing header, and first column of table.</a>
        </div>
    </div>
    <div class='message'>
        <span class='mail-date'>October 21, 2005 8:25 AM</span>
        <div class='mail-sender'>
            <a href='#' title='&lt;donotreply@wrox.com&gt;'>
                Wrox P2P Forum Subscriptions
            </a>
```

```
                    </div>
                    <div class='mail-subject'>
                        <a href='#'>[CSS] fixing header, and first column of table.</a>
                    </div>
                </div>
                <div class='message'>
                    <span class='mail-date'>October 21, 2005 8:33 AM</span>
                    <div class='mail-sender'>
                        <a href='#' title='&lt;donotreply@wrox.com&gt;'>
                            Wrox P2P Forum Subscriptions
                        </a>
                    </div>
                    <div class='mail-subject'>
                        <a href='#'>[CSS] fixing header, and first column of table.</a>
                    </div>
                </div>
            </div>
        </div>
        <iframe id='message-preview'
                name='message_preview'
                frameborder='0'
                marginwidth='0'
                marginheight='0'></iframe>
    </body>
</html>
```

2. Save the modified file as `mail.outlook2k3.html`.

3. Make the following changes to `mail.messagePreview.css`:

```css
html,
body {
    width: 100%;
    height: 100%;
    margin: 0;
    padding: 0;
    font: 12px sans-serif;
    background: url('../images/brushed_metal.png');
}
a {
    color: #369;
    text-decoration: none;
}
div#mail-tools {
    padding: 8px 0 0 8px;
}
img#mailbox-image {
    margin-right: 10px;
    float: right;
}
td.compose {
    padding-left: 25px;
}
td.address-book {
    padding-right: 25px;
```

```
}
div#mailboxes,
div#messages {
    position: absolute;
    top: 0;
    bottom: 0;
    border: 1px solid rgb(128, 128, 128);
    overflow: auto;
}
div#mailboxes {
    left: 0;
    width: 200px;
    margin: 52px 0 10px 10px;
    background: #fff;
}
div#messages {
    left: 0;
    right: 0;
    margin: 52px 0 10px 220px;
    width: 375px;
    background: url('../images/stripes.png');
}
div#messages > table {
    width: 100%;
    border-collapse: collapse;
}
div#messages > table th {
    background: rgb(249, 250, 253);
    border-bottom: 1px solid rgb(200, 200, 200);
    text-align: left;
    padding: 2px 4px;
}
div#messages > table th + th {
    border-left: 1px solid rgb(200, 200, 200);
}
col#mail-sender-col,
col#mail-date-col,
col#mail-attachments-col {
    width: 1%;
}
td.mail-sender,
td.mail-date {
    white-space: nowrap;
    padding: 0 4px;
}
div#messages > table tbody tr {
    height: 20px;
}
div#messages > table tbody tr:hover {
    background: #369;
    color: #fff;
}
div#messages > table tbody tr:hover a {
```

```
        color: #fff;
}
td.mail-subject {
    background: url('../images/16x16/2381.png') no-repeat left;
    padding-left: 20px;
    white-space: nowrap;
}
div.message {
    background: url('../images/16x16/2381.png') no-repeat 2px 10px;
    padding: 2px 5px 2px 20px;
    margin-bottom: 5px;
}
div.message:hover {
    background: #369 url('../images/16x16/2381.png') no-repeat 2px 10px;
    color: white;
}
div.message:hover a {
    color: white;
}
div.mail-sender a {
    color: black;
}
span.mail-date {
    float: right;
}
div#mailboxes ul {
    list-style: none;
    margin: 0;
    padding: 10px;
}
li.mailbox {
    padding: 5px 0 0 0;
    font-weight: bold;
}
li.mailbox + li.mailbox {
    border-top: 1px solid rgb(200, 200, 200);
}
li.mailbox * {
    font-weight: normal;
}
li.mailbox > ul > li {
    padding-left: 20px;
    min-height: 20px;
}
li.inbox {
    background: url('../images/inbox.png') no-repeat top left;
}
li.drafts {
    background: url('../images/drafts.png') no-repeat top left;
}
li.sent {
    background: url('../images/sent.png') no-repeat top left;
}
li.trash {
    background: url('../images/trash.png') no-repeat top left;
}
```

```css
span.inbox-count,
span.drafts-count {
    font-weight: bold;
}
span.inbox-count::before,
span.drafts-count::before {
    content: '(';
}
span.inbox-count::after,
span.drafts-count::after {
    content: ')';
}
ul.folders ul.folders li {
    background: url('../images/folder.png') no-repeat top left;
    padding-left: 20px;

}
ul.folders ul.folders ul {
    position: relative;
    left: -20px;
}
li.selected-folder > span {
    background: #369;
    color: #fff;
}
ul.folders ul.folders span:hover {
    background: #369;
    color: white;
}
iframe#message-preview {
    position: absolute;
    border: 1px solid rgb(128, 128, 128);
    top: 0;
    bottom: 0;
    left: 0;
    right: 0;
    margin: 52px 10px 10px 605px;
    background: #fff;
}
```

4. Save the changes in a new file as `mail.outlook2k3.css`.

5. Open `mail.ie.messagePreview.css` and make the following changes:

```css
col#mail-attachments-col {
    width: 1px;
}
div#messages > table tbody tr:hover td.mail-subject {
    background: #369 url('../images/16x16/2381.png') no-repeat left;
}
div#mailboxes,
div#messages,
iframe#message-preview {
    height: expression(
```

```
              document.getElementById('mail').offsetHeight - 65
    );
}
iframe#message-preview {
    width: expression(
        document.getElementById('mail').offsetWidth - 615
    );
}
```

6. Save the file as `mail.ie.outlook2k3.css`.

Loading up `mail.outlook2k3.html` in Firefox 1.5 gives the output shown in Figure 7-10.

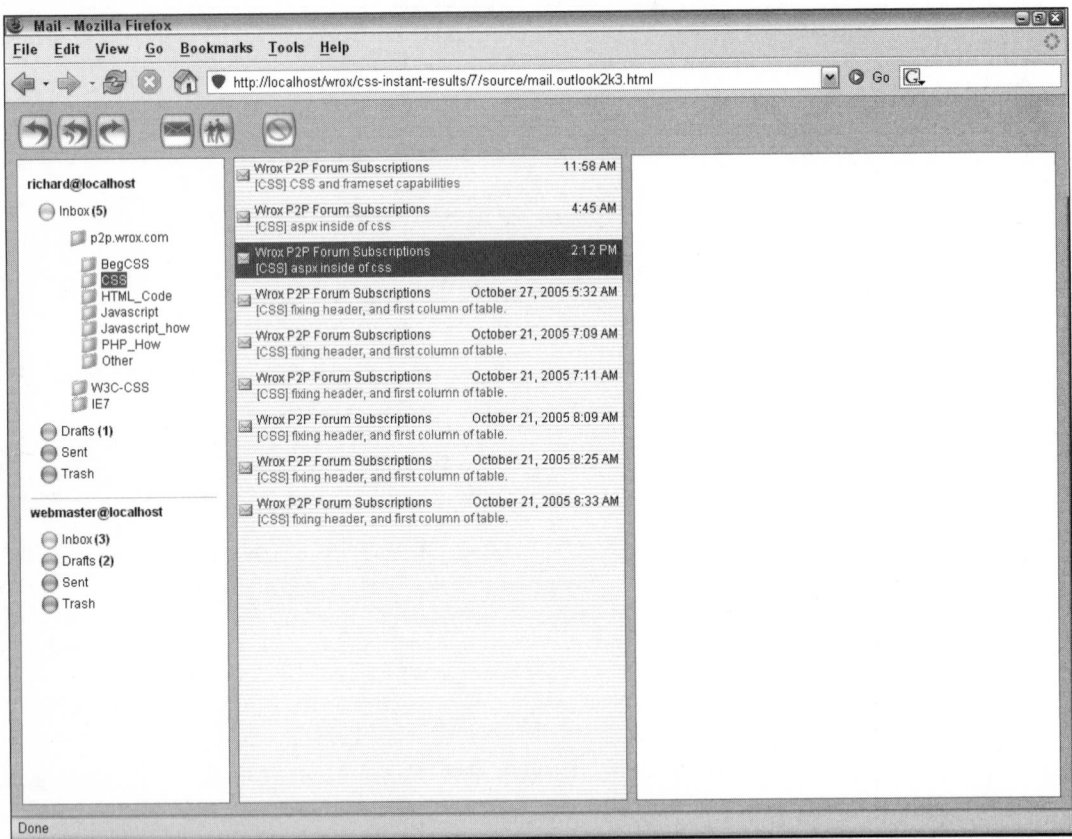

Figure 7-10

Loading up `mail.outlook2k3.html` in Internet Explorer 6 gives the output shown in Figure 7-11.

This time the modifications were a bit more extensive. Now it is possible using a server-side program to offer users multiple methods of viewing their mailbox contents.

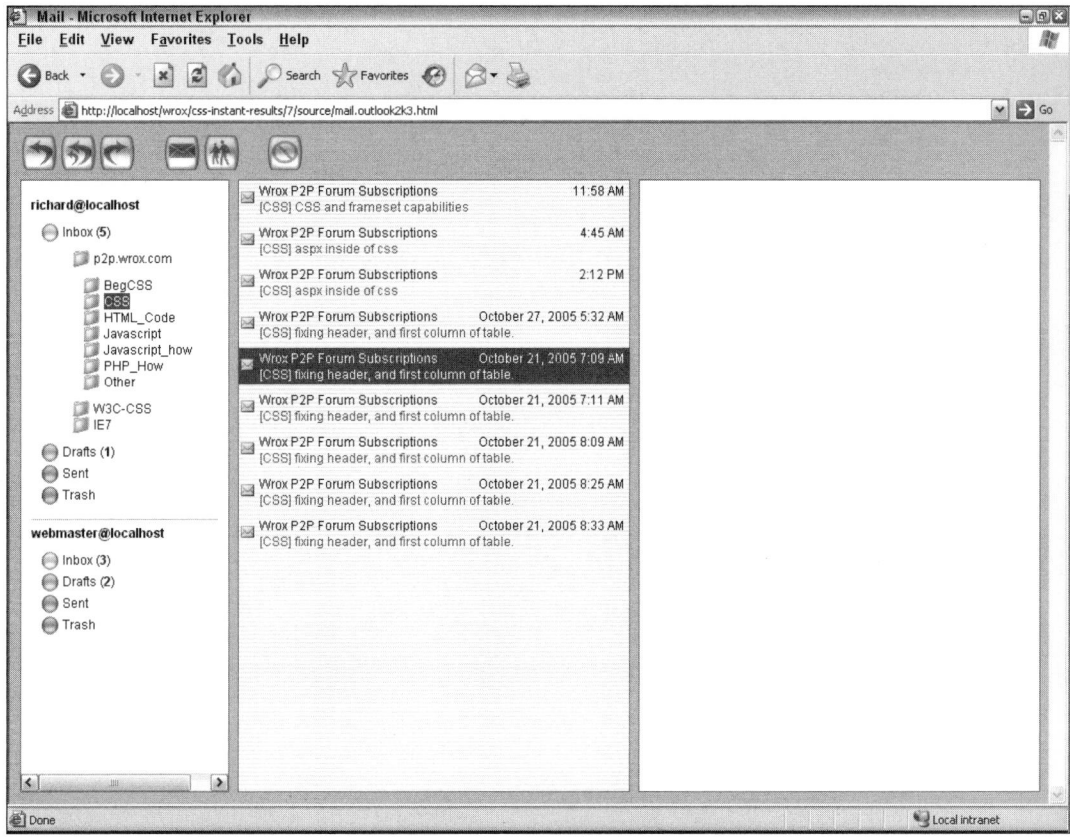

Figure 7-11

The first modifications you made were to the markup. First the style sheets had to be updated to reflect the new file names. Then you restructured the markup removing the `<table>` that originally housed message summary information, and replaced that with `<div>` elements, which allowed for the message summary information to be formatted in a manner more consistent with Outlook 2003. After restructuring the markup you set about to make changes to the style sheets. The first modification you made was to the following rule:

```
div#messages {
    left: 0;
    right: 0;
    margin: 52px 0 10px 220px;
    width: 375px;
    background: url('../images/stripes.png');
}
```

The `messages` `<div>` element was given a fixed width of 375 pixels, and the margins were adjusted. You kept the top margin of 52 pixels (to prevent the `messages` `<div>` element from overlapping with the buttons at the top), no right margin, 10 pixels of bottom margin (to add space between the bottom border of the messages `<div>` and the bottom border of the viewport), and 220 pixels of left margin to keep the messages `<div>` from overlapping with the mailboxes `<div>`.

The next series of rules that you applied formatted the restructured message summaries. The first rule applies to the `<div>` with a message class name, which wrapped each individual message summary. First the envelope icon is set non-repeating, 2 pixels from the left and 10 pixels from the top. Then padding is applied. Two pixels of padding are applied to the top and bottom, 5 pixels on the right and 20 pixels on the left, to accommodate the icon and prevent the content within the `<div>` element from overlapping with the background. Then 5 pixels of bottom margin are applied to space each message summary out from the others:

```
div.message {
    background: url('../images/16x16/2381.png') no-repeat 2px 10px;
    padding: 2px 5px 2px 20px;
    margin-bottom: 5px;
}
```

Just as you did in the original project, you make the background of the message `<div>` element blue and the text white when the user's mouse hovers over a message summary:

```
div.message:hover {
    background: #369 url('../images/16x16/2381.png') no-repeat 2px 10px;
    color: white;
}
```

Next, the links within the message `<div>` element must also be made white when the user's mouse hovers over a message summary, otherwise the text would be invisible because the color of links is the same color as the color of the background hover:

```
div.message:hover a {
    color: white;
}
```

In the following rule you set the color of the link for the Sender to black, which I felt was necessary to add contrast between the Sender text and that of the Subject text:

```
div.mail-sender a {
    color: black;
}
```

The last rule to be modified was that for the `<iframe>` element. It is given the `top: 0;` declaration, where previously it had only the `bottom: 0;` declaration. Then you modified the margin for the `<iframe>` element to accommodate both the mailboxes and messages `<div>` elements, which both appear to its left, and also to accommodate the buttons at the top of the document:

```
iframe#message-preview {
    position: absolute;
    border: 1px solid rgb(128, 128, 128);
    top: 0;
    bottom: 0;
    left: 0;
    right: 0;
```

```
    margin: 52px 10px 10px 605px;
    background: #fff;
}
```

The last modifications you made enable the three-column layout to work in Internet Explorer as well as it does in Firefox.

Because the mailboxes, messages, and message-preview elements all have the same height, you added selectors to the following rule:

```
div#mailboxes,
div#messages,
iframe#message-preview {
    height: expression(
        document.getElementById('mail').offsetHeight - 65
    );
}
```

The last modification you made adjusts the <iframe> element's width to accommodate the mailboxes and messages elements:

```
iframe#message-preview {
    width: expression(
        document.getElementById('mail').offsetWidth - 615
    );
}
```

Styling Input Forms

This chapter leads you through styling an input form. This involves creating a form with a look and feel that is unique to your own web site (instead of the default look and feel provided by your browser) by using custom buttons and input fields that use images for backgrounds. The project presented in this chapter also contains many elements of projects from previous chapters. In addition to styling input forms, you'll see a real-world implementation of the tabs project from Chapter 1, the multi-column project from Chapter 2, and rounded corners from Chapter 6. These elements come together in a page taken from p2p.wrox.com, the Wrox Programmer to Programmer forum web site where Wrox readers go for help with their technical questions about Wrox books and the languages covered by those books. Specifically, this project uses the p2p.wrox.com user registration form. I've rewritten the page so that it conforms to strict XHTML syntax, and written a style sheet to make the document resemble the original as closely as possible. With this project you'll be able to observe not only how to style an input form, but also how other projects featured in this book can come together in a real web site, complete with corporate branding, while still following very closely the basic principles presented in the original projects. You also learn about the challenges you might face in making a cross-browser, cross-platform document that renders in as many browsers on as many operating systems as possible.

The goals of the input form project are as follows:

- ❑ All text, password, and textarea fields must have a unique look.

- ❑ The underlying markup must make use of semantic HTML elements, such as `<fieldset>`, `<legend>`, `<label>`, and the `accesskey` attribute for accessibility.

- ❑ The custom HTML form must fit into Wrox's corporate branding, and exhibit the look and feel distinctive to Wrox.

- ❑ The registration form recoded in XHTML and CSS must match its original counterpart as closely as possible.

The next section discusses the design parameters of this project and some of the challenges faced in creating it.

Design

Many in the web development community oppose styling input forms. The principal argument typically has to do with usability; the user expects input forms to look consistent between web sites. However, the spectrum of styles possible combined with the unfortunate fact that not everyone has A+ user-interface design capabilities can make for a potentially inaccessible experience for site-goers.

The default look and feel of a form usually mimics how the operating system styles input forms. There are some exceptions. Opera has its own default look and feel for input forms no matter what the operating system. Input fields in Firefox on Windows and Mac OS X closely resemble those of Windows and Internet Explorer. Safari, naturally, uses Mac OS X's "Aqua" to render input fields, which are pretty much the same as those you find in other Mac OS X applications that also use Aqua.

For Safari, there is a fundamental limitation that prevents this project from functioning at all. At the time of this writing, Safari does not allow input fields to be styled. The tricks used here will have no effect in Safari 1.3 and 2.0. Recent development builds of Safari, however, do have the ability to style certain input fields, and Safari's developers continue to improve this aspect of Safari.

> *Safari developer Dave Hyatt and others on the Safari team regularly blog about Safari updates, bug fixes, and new features in the Safari Team's weblog, Surfin Safari. You can check in for yourself at* `http://webkit.opendarwin.org` *to keep up-to-date on new features in the Safari browser.*

The requirements for the core project presented here are relatively simple — really nothing more than applying a few background images and disabling default styles present in input controls. The context in which the input form resides, however, is a bit more complicated, as it brings together several projects presented in earlier chapters — the tabs project from Chapter 1 and the multi-column project from Chapter 2. I chose to use these projects here to demonstrate their usefulness in a real-live web site. As presented in Chapters 1 and 2, they used only very generic XHTML containers.

As I began this project, I considered copying and pasting the source code from the Wrox web site, then decided that moving from that table-riddled, old-school HTML design to a modern XHTML design would require a complete overhaul of the underlying code. Nothing could be reused except for the images.

Figure 8-1 shows a screenshot of the Wrox new user registration page at the time of this writing.

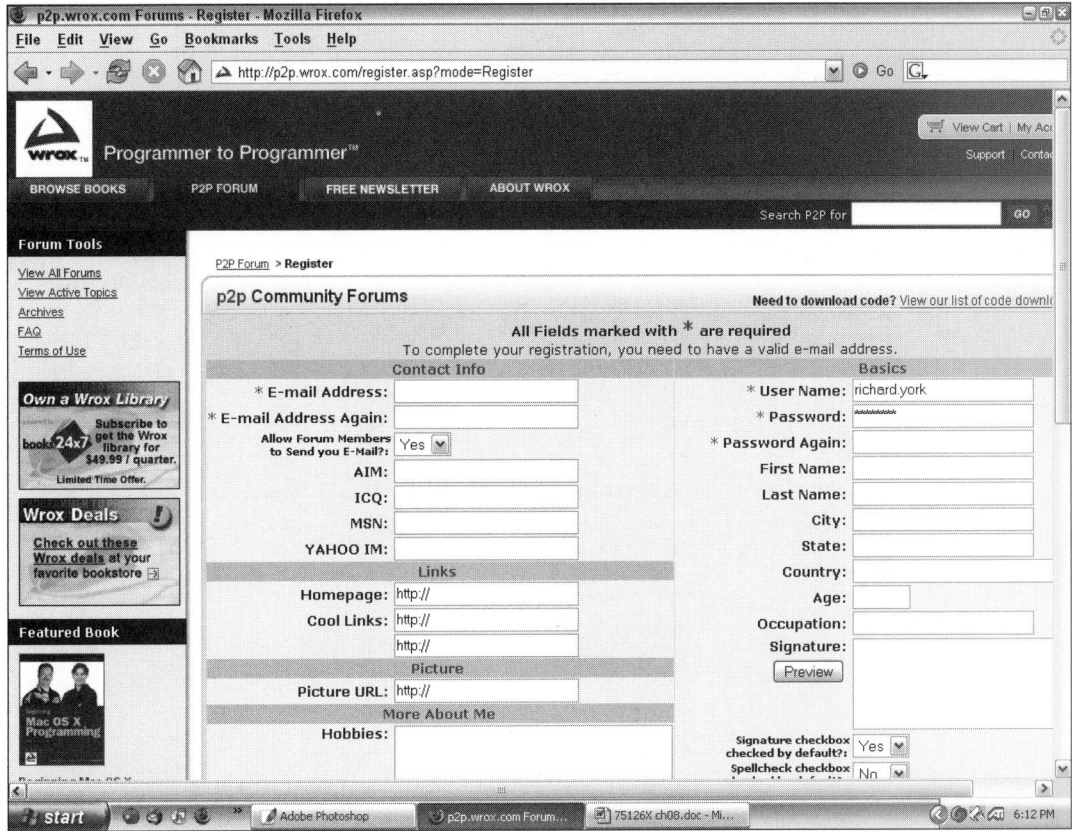

Figure 8-1

In Figure 8-1, you see that the current registration form doesn't even fit into a computer with a 1024 × 768 resolution, the resolution at which all of this book's screenshots are taken. When you finish this project, the registration form will fit comfortably in a 1024 × 768 screen resolution, and even reduce gracefully to 800 × 600.

Figure 8-2 shows a screenshot of the source code of the same document.

Figure 8-2

When you finish this project, the source code of this document will look nothing like Figure 8-2. It will be clean, maintainable, extendable, and smaller in size. Old-school HTML attributes like `width`, `height`, `background`, `bgcolor`, and so on will no longer exist in the document. The only tables you'll find in the document will be those that house the form controls.

The next section presents the code and code explanation for the Wrox P2P registration page.

Code and Code Explanation

To see how the Wrox Programmer to Programmer web site registration form is styled using XHTML and CSS, follow these steps:

1. Enter the following markup. Remember, the markup is provided in the source CD-ROM accompanying this book. The following can be found in the Chapter 8 folder as `register.html`:

```
<!DOCTYPE html PUBLIC "-//W3C//DTD XHTML 1.0 Strict//EN"
"http://www.w3.org/TR/xhtml1/DTD/xhtml1-strict.dtd">
<html xmlns='http://www.w3.org/1999/xhtml' xml:lang='en' id='p2p-wrox-com'>
```

```
<head>
  <meta http-equiv="Content-Type" content="text/html; charset=UTF-8" />
  <title>p2p.wrox.com Forums - Register</title>
  <link rel='stylesheet' type='text/css' href='styles/p2p-header.css' />
  <link rel='stylesheet' type='text/css' href='styles/p2p-body.css' />
  <link rel='stylesheet' type='text/css' href='styles/p2p-form.css' />
  <link rel='shortcut icon' href='images/favicon.ico' type='image/x-icon' />
</head>
<body id='top'>
  <div id='wrapper'>
    <div id='header'>
      <div id='h-logo'>
        <a href='#'>
          <img src='images/logo.gif' alt='Wrox Programmer to Programmer' />
        </a>
      </div>
      <div id='h-cart'>
        <div>
          <a href='#'>View Cart</a> |
          <a href='#'>My Account</a>
        </div>
      </div>
      <div id='h-links'>
        <a href='#'>Support</a> |
        <a href='#'>Contact Us</a>
      </div>
    </div>
    <ul id='tabs'>
      <li class='browse-books'>
        <a href='#'>
          <img src='images/browsebooks.gif' alt='Browse Books' />
        </a>
      </li>
      <li class='p2p-forum'>
        <a href='#'>
          <img src='images/p2pcommunity_on.gif' alt='P2P Forum' />
        </a>
      </li>
      <li class='free-newsletter'>
        <a href='#'>
          <img src='images/free_news.gif' alt='Free Newsletter' />
        </a>
      </li>
      <li class='about-wrox'>
        <a href='#'>
          <img src='images/aboutwrox.gif' alt='About Wrox' />
        </a>
      </li>
    </ul>
    <form action='javascript:void(0);' method='post'>
      <div id='search'>
        <a href='#'>Advanced<br />Search</a>
        <label for='p2p-search'>Search P2P for</label>
        <input name='search' id='p2p-search' size='20' value='' type='text' />
        <input src='images/go_p2p.gif' alt='go' type='image' />
      </div>
```

```
        </form>
        <div id='column'>
          <div class='box tools'>
            <h4>Forum Tools</h4>
            <ul>
              <li><a href='#'>View All Forums</a></li>
              <li><a href='#'>View Active Topics</a></li>
              <li><a href='#'>Archives</a></li>
              <li><a href='#'>FAQ</a></li>
              <li><a href='#'>Terms of Use</a></li>
            </ul>
          </div>
          <div class='box ads'>
            <p>
              <a href='#'>
                <img src='images/ad1.jpg' alt='Own a Wrox Library...' />
              </a>
            </p>
            <p>
              <a href='#'>
                <img src='images/ad2.gif' alt='Wrox deals...' />
              </a>
            </p>
          </div>
          <div class='box featured'>
            <h4>Featured Book</h4>
            <p class='featured-book'>
              <a href='#'>
                <img src='images/book.jpg' alt='Beginning Mac OS X Programming' />
              </a>
              <a href='#'>Beginning Mac OS X Programming</a>
            </p>
          </div>
          <div class='box ads'>
            <p>
              <a href='#'>
                <img src='images/ad3.gif' alt='Wrox Tech Jobs...' />
              </a>
            </p>
          </div>
        </div>
        <div id='breadcrumbs'>
          <ul>
            <li><a href='#'>P2P Forum</a></li>
            <li class='here'>Register</li>
          </ul>
        </div>
        <div id='content'>
          <h1>
            <span class='inner'>
                Need to download code?
                <a href='#'>View our list of code downloads.</a>
            </span>
            <span style='color: #c03;'>p2p</span> Community Forums
          </h1>
          <div id='body'>
```

```
            <div id='innerbody'>
<!-- Begin Content -->
<p>
  <span style='font-weight: bold;'>
    All Fields marked with
    <span class='required'>*</span> are required.
  </span><br />
  To complete your registration, you need to have a valid e-mail
  address.
</p>
<form action='javascript: void(0);' method='post'>
<div class='column1'>
  <fieldset>
    <legend>Contact Info</legend>
    <table class='form'>
      <colgroup>
        <col />
        <col />
      </colgroup>
      <tbody>
        <tr>
          <td class='label'>
            <label for='email'>
              <span class='required'>*</span>
              E-mail Address:
            </label>
          </td>
          <td class='input'>
            <input name='email'
                   id='email' size='25' maxlength='50' value='' class='i' />
          </td>
        </tr>
        <tr>
          <td class='label'>
            <label for='email-confirm'>
              <span class='required'>*</span>
              E-mail Address Again:
            </label>
          </td>
          <td class='input'>
            <input name='email_confirm'
                   id='email-confirm'
                   size='25' maxlength='50' value='' class='i' />
          </td>
        </tr>
        <tr>
          <td class='label'>
            <label for='receive-email'>
              Allow Forum Members<br />
              to Send you E-Mail?:
            </label>
          </td>
          <td class='input'>
            <select name='receive_email' id='receive-email' class='y-n'>
              <option value='1' selected='selected'>Yes</option>
              <option value='0'>No</option>
```

```
                </select>
              </td>
          </tr>
          <tr>
            <td class='label'>
              <label for='aim'>AIM:</label>
            </td>
            <td class='input'>
              <input name='aim'
                     id='aim' size='25' maxlength='50' value='' class='i' />
            </td>
          </tr>
          <tr>
            <td class='label'>
              <label for='icq'>ICQ:</label>
            </td>
            <td class='input'>
              <input name='icq'
                     id='icq' size='25' maxlength='50' value='' class='i' />
            </td>
          </tr>
          <tr>
            <td class='label'>
              <label for='msn'>MSN:</label>
            </td>
            <td class='input'>
              <input name='msn'
                     id='msn' size='25' maxlength='50' value='' class='i' />
            </td>
          </tr>
          <tr>
            <td class='label'>
              <label for='yahoo'>YAHOO IM:</label>
            </td>
            <td class='input'>
              <input name='yahoo'
                     id='yahoo' size='25' maxlength='50' value='' class='i' />
            </td>
          </tr>
        </tbody>
      </table>
</fieldset>
<fieldset>
  <legend>Links</legend>
  <table class='form'>
    <colgroup>
      <col />
      <col />
    </colgroup>
    <tbody>
      <tr>
        <td class='label'>
          <label for='homepage'>Homepage:</label>
        </td>
        <td class='input'>
          <input name='homepage'
```

```
                               id='homepage'
                               size='25' maxlength='255' value='http://' class='i' />
                </td>
             </tr>
             <tr>
                <td class='label' rowspan='2'>
                   <label for='link1'>Cool Links:</label>
                </td>
                <td class='input'>
                   <input name='link1'
                          id='link1'
                          size='25' maxlength='255' value='http://' class='i' />
                </td>
             </tr>
             <tr>
                <td class='input'>
                   <input name='link2'
                          id='link2'
                          size='25' maxlength='255' value='http://' class='i' />
                </td>
             </tr>
          </tbody>
       </table>
    </fieldset>
    <fieldset>
       <legend>Picture</legend>
       <table class='form'>
          <colgroup>
             <col />
             <col />
          </colgroup>
          <tbody>
             <tr>
                <td class='label'>
                   <label for='picture-url'>Picture URL:</label>
                </td>
                <td class='input'>
                   <input name='picture_url'
                          id='picture-url'
                          size='25' maxlength='255' value='http://' class='i' />
                </td>
             </tr>
          </tbody>
       </table>
    </fieldset>
    <fieldset>
       <legend>More About Me</legend>
       <table class='form'>
          <colgroup>
             <col />
             <col />
          </colgroup>
          <tbody>
             <tr>
                <td class='label'>
```

```
              <label for='hobbies'>Hobbies:</label>
            </td>
            <td class='input'>
              <textarea name='hobbies' id='hobbies' cols='30' rows='4'></textarea>
            </td>
          </tr>
          <tr>
            <td class='label'>
              <label for='quote'>Favorite Quote:</label>
            </td>
            <td class='input'>
              <textarea name='quote' id='quote' cols='30' rows='4'></textarea>
            </td>
          </tr>
          <tr>
            <td class='label'>
              <label for='bio'>Bio:</label>
            </td>
            <td class='input'>
              <textarea name='bio' id='bio' cols='30' rows='4'></textarea>
            </td>
          </tr>
        </tbody>
      </table>
    </fieldset>
</div>
<div class='column2'>
  <fieldset>
    <legend>Basics</legend>
    <table class='form'>
      <colgroup>
        <col />
        <col />
      </colgroup>
      <tbody>
        <tr>
          <td class='label'>
            <label for='username'>
              <span class='required'>*</span>
              User Name:
            </label>
          </td>
          <td class='input'>
            <input name='username' id='username' size='25' value='' class='i' />
          </td>
        </tr>
        <tr>
          <td class='label'>
            <label for='password'>
              <span class='required'>*</span>
              Password:
            </label>
          </td>
          <td class='input'>
            <input type='password'
                   name='password' id='password' size='25' value='' class='i' />
```

```
        </td>
      </tr>
      <tr>
        <td class='label'>
          <label for='pd-confirm'>
            <span class='required'>*</span>
            Password Again:
          </label>
        </td>
        <td class='input'>
          <input type='password'
                 name='pd_confirm'
                 id='pd-confirm' size='25' value='' class='i' />
        </td>
      </tr>
      <tr>
        <td class='label'>
          <label for='first-name'>First Name:</label>
        </td>
        <td class='input'>
          <input name='first_name'
                 id='first-name' size='25' value='' class='i' />
        </td>
      </tr>
      <tr>
        <td class='label'>
          <label for='last-name'>Last Name:</label>
        </td>
        <td class='input'>
          <input name='last_name' id='last-name' size='25' value='' class='i' />
        </td>
      </tr>
      <tr>
        <td class='label'>
          <label for='city'>City:</label>
        </td>
        <td class='input'>
          <input name='city' id='city' size='25' value='' class='i' />
        </td>
      </tr>
      <tr>
        <td class='label'>
          <label for='state'>State:</label>
        </td>
        <td class='input'>
          <input name='state' id='state' size='25' value='' class='i' />
        </td>
      </tr>
      <tr>
        <td class='label'>
          <label for='county'>County:</label>
        </td>
        <td class='input'>
          <input name='county' id='county' size='25' value='' class='i' />
        </td>
```

```
        </tr>
        <tr>
          <td class='label'>
            <label for='age'>Age:</label>
          </td>
          <td class='input'>
            <input name='age' id='age' size='2' value='' class='a' />
          </td>
        </tr>
         <tr>
          <td class='label'>
            <label for='occupation'>Occupation:</label>
          </td>
          <td class='input'>
            <input name='occupation'
                   id='occupation' size='25' value='' class='i' />
          </td>
        </tr>
        <tr>
          <td class='label'>
            <label for='signature'>Signature:</label>
          </td>
          <td class='input'>
            <textarea name='signature'
                      id='signature' cols='30' rows='4'></textarea>
          </td>
        </tr>
        <tr>
          <td class='label'>
            <label for='signature-default'>
              Signature checkbox<br />checked by default?:
            </label>
          </td>
          <td class='input'>
            <select name='signature_default' id='signature-default' class='y-n'>
              <option value='1' selected='selected'>Yes</option>
              <option value='0'>No</option>
            </select>
          </td>
        </tr>
        <tr>
          <td class='label'>
            <label for='spellcheck-default'>
              Spellcheck checkbox<br />checked by default?:
            </label>
          </td>
          <td class='input'>
            <select name='spellcheck_default' id='spellcheck-default' class='y-n'>
              <option value='1'>Yes</option>
              <option value='0' selected='selected'>No</option>
            </select>
          </td>
        </tr>
        <tr>
          <td class='label'>
            <label for='timezone'>Your TimeZone:</label>
```

```
          </td>
        <td class='input'>
          <select name='timezone' id='timezone'>
            <option value='' selected='selected'>
              Use the server time (EST)
            </option>
            <option value='-12'>(GMT - 12:00)</option>
            <option value='-11'>(GMT - 11:00)</option>
            <option value='-10'>(GMT - 10:00) Hawaii</option>
            <option value='-9'>(GMT - 09:00) Alaska</option>
            <option value='-8'>(GMT - 08:00) Pacific Time (US)</option>
            <option value='-7'>(GMT - 07:00) Mountain Time (US)</option>
            <option value='-6'>(GMT - 06:00) Central Time (US)</option>
            <option value='-5'>(GMT - 05:00) Eastern Time (US)</option>
            <option value='-4'>(GMT - 04:00)</option>
            <option value='-3'>(GMT - 03:00)</option>
            <option value='-2'>(GMT - 02:00)</option>
            <option value='-1'>(GMT - 01:00)</option>
            <option value='0'>(GMT) Greenwich Mean Time</option>
            <option value='1'>(GMT + 01:00)</option>
            <option value='2'>(GMT + 02:00)</option>
            <option value='3'>(GMT + 03:00)</option>
            <option value='4'>(GMT + 04:00)</option>
            <option value='5'>(GMT + 05:00)</option>
            <option value='6'>(GMT + 06:00)</option>
            <option value='7'>(GMT + 07:00)</option>
            <option value='8'>(GMT + 08:00)</option>
            <option value='9'>(GMT + 09:00)</option>
            <option value='10'>(GMT + 10:00)</option>
            <option value='11'>(GMT + 11:00)</option>
            <option value='12'>(GMT + 12:00)</option>
            <option value='13'>(GMT + 13:00)</option>
          </select>
        </td>
      </tr>
      <tr>
        <td class='label'>
          <label for='dst'>Adjust for Daylight<br />Savings Time?:</label>
        </td>
        <td class='input'>
          <select name='dst' id='dst' class='y-n'>
            <option value='1'>Yes</option>
            <option value='0' selected='selected'>No</option>
          </select> * Must choose a timezone
        </td>
      </tr>
    </tbody>
  </table>
</fieldset>
<fieldset>
  <legend>Subscription Preferences</legend>
  <table class='form'>
    <colgroup>
      <col />
      <col />
    </colgroup>
```

```
          <tbody>
            <tr>
              <td class='label'>
                <label for='email-self'>
                  Receive Your Postings:
                </label>
              </td>
              <td class='input'>
                <select name='email_self' id='email-self'>
                  <option value='0' selected='selected'>
                    No, don't send my postings to me
                  </option>
                  <option value='1'>Yes, send me my postings</option>
                </select>
              </td>
            </tr>
            <tr>
              <td class='label'>
                <label for='topic-default'>
                  Topic Subscribe checkbox<br />
                  checked by default for<br />
                  topics you create?:
                </label>
              </td>
              <td class='input'>
                <select name='topic_default' id='topic-default' class='y-n'>
                  <option value='1'>Yes</option>
                  <option value='0' selected='selected'>No</option>
                </select>
              </td>
            </tr>
          </tbody>
        </table>
      </fieldset>
</div>
<div class='buttons'>
  <a href='#' class='back'>Back To Forum</a>
  <input value='Submit' name='submit' type='submit' />
</div>
</form>
</div>
<!-- End Content -->
        </div>
      </div>
    </div>
    <div id='footer'>
      <a href="http://www.wrox.com/go/copyright">Copyright &copy; 2000-2005</a> by
      <a href="http://www.wiley.com">John Wiley &amp; Sons, Inc.</a>
      or related companies.
      All rights reserved. Please read our
      <a href="http://www.wrox.com/go/privacy">Privacy Policy</a>.
    </div>
  </body>
</html>
```

2. Save the preceding as `register.html`.

3. Enter the following style sheet. The following can be found on the source CD-ROM accompanying the book in the styles folder, in the Chapter 8 folder as `p2p-header.css`:

```css
body {
    margin: 0;
    padding: 0;
    font: 11px Arial, Helvetica, sans-serif;
}
a:link {
    color: #903;
}
a:visited {
    color: #603;
}
a:hover {
    color: #c03;
    text-decoration: none
}
a:active {
    color:#903;
    text-decoration:none
}
img {
    border: none;
}
div#wrapper {
    position: relative;
    min-height: 1000px;
}
div#header {
    background-color: #c03;
    position: relative;
}
div#header a {
    text-decoration: none;
    margin: 0 4px;
}
div#h-cart {
    position: absolute;
    top: 23px;
    right: 15px;
    background: url('../images/css_background.gif') no-repeat center;
    width: 170px;
    height: 25px;
}
div#h-cart div {
    position: absolute;
    top: 6px;
    left: 35px;
    color: #8c8c8c;
}
div#h-links {
```

```
        position: absolute;
        top: 54px;
        right: 27px;
}
div#h-links a {
        color: white;
}
ul#tabs {
        height: 23px;
        list-style-type: none;
        margin: -4px 0 0 0;
        position: relative;
        padding: 0;
        background: url('../images/background.gif') repeat-x top;
        border-bottom: 1px solid #6c6c6c;
}
ul#tabs li {
        position: absolute;
        top: 1px;
        left: 0;
}
ul#tabs li.p2p-forum {
        left: 141px;
}
ul#tabs li.free-newsletter {
        left: 287px;
}
ul#tabs li.about-wrox {
        left: 445px;
}
form {
        margin: 0;
        padding: 0;
}
div#search {
        background-color: #333;
        text-align: right;
        color: #fff;
        height: 27px;
}
div#search a {
        float: right;
        line-height: 11px;
        margin: 0 10px 0 5px;
        text-align: left;
        text-decoration: none;
        color: rgb(128, 128, 128);
}
div#search a:hover {
        color: #fff;
}
div#search * {
        vertical-align: middle;
}
```

4. Save the preceding style sheet as `p2p-header.css`.

5. Enter the following style sheet:

```css
div#column {
    position: absolute;
    top: 129px;
    bottom: 0;
    left: 0;
    width: 175px;
    background: url('../images/gradient_left.gif') repeat-y center;
}
div#column h4 {
    color: white;
    background-color: #000;
    margin: 0 4px 0 0;
    padding: 5px 0 5px 10px;
    font-size: 13px;
}
div.box ul {
    margin: 0;
    padding: 5px 0 5px 10px;
    list-style-type: none;
}
div.box li {
    margin: 5px 0 0 0;
}
div.box.ads {
    text-align: center;
}
div.box.featured a {
    margin: 10px;
    display: block;
    color: rgb(128, 128, 128);
    font-weight: bold;
}
div#breadcrumbs {
    margin-left: 200px;
}
div#breadcrumbs ul {
    margin: 25px 0 4px 0;
    padding: 0;
    list-style-type: none;
    overflow: auto;
}
div#breadcrumbs li {
    float: left;
}
div#breadcrumbs li + li::before {
    font-family: monospace;
    content: '>';
    margin: 0 5px;
    font-weight: bold;
}
div#breadcrumbs a {
```

```
        color: rgb(128, 128, 128);
}
div#breadcrumbs a:hover {
        color: #c03;
}
div#breadcrumbs li.here {
    font-weight: bold;
}
div#content {
    clear: both;
    margin: 0 0 0 185px;
}
div#content h1 {
    background: url('../images/top_left.gif') no-repeat top left;
    font-size: 16px;
    height: 30px;
    padding: 10px 0 0 15px;
    margin: 0 25px 0 0;
}
div#content h1 span.inner {
    background: url('../images/top_right.gif') no-repeat top right;
    float: right;
    font-size: 11px;
    position: relative;
    height: 22px;
    margin: -10px -11px 0 0;
    padding: 18px 10px 0 0;
}
div#content h1 span.inner a {
    font-weight: normal;
}
div#body {
    background: #e5e5e5;
    min-height: 400px;
    margin-right: 14px;
    border: 1px solid #ccc;
}
div#footer {
    background: #fff url('../images/gradient_bottom.gif') repeat-x top;
    padding: 5px 0 5px 10px;
    font-size: 12px;
    height: 50px;
}
```

6. Save the preceding style sheet as `p2p-body.css`.

7. Enter the following style sheet for the P2P registration input form:

```
div#innerbody {
    max-width: 1000px;
    min-width: 790px;
    margin: auto;
    padding: 10px;
}
div#innerbody > p * {
    font-size: 13px;
```

```
        vertical-align: middle;
}
div#innerbody span.required {
    color: #c03;
    font-size: 24px;
    font-weight: bold;
}
div.column1 {
    float: left;
    width: 49%;
}
div.column2 {
    position: relative;
    width: 49%;
    margin-left: 50%;
}
fieldset {
    border: 1px solid #ccc;
    background-color: #f5f5f5;
}
legend {
    color: #c03;
    font-weight: bold;
    font-size: 13px;
}
table.form {
    width: 100%;
}
table.form col {
    width: 50%;
}
td.label {
    text-align: right;
    vertical-align: top;
    font-weight: bold;
}
td.label * {
    vertical-align: middle;
}
div#innerbody input.i,
div#innerbody textarea {
    border: 0px solid transparent;
    font: 14px Arial, Helvetica, sans-serif;
}
div#innerbody input.i {
    width: 196px;
    height: 18px;
    padding: 2px 0 0 4px;
    background: url('../images/input.png') no-repeat;
}
div#innerbody input.a {
    width: 40px;
    height: 18px;
    padding: 2px 0 0 4px;
    background: url('../images/input-a.png') no-repeat;
```

```
}
div#innerbody textarea {
    padding: 2px;
    height: 96px;
    width: 236px;
    background: url('../images/textarea.png') no-repeat;
}
div.buttons {
    clear: both;
    overflow: auto;
}
div.buttons a {
    float: left;
}
div.buttons input {
    float: right;
}
```

8. Save the preceding style sheet as `p2p-form.css`.

This mountain of code results in the output shown in Figure 8-3.

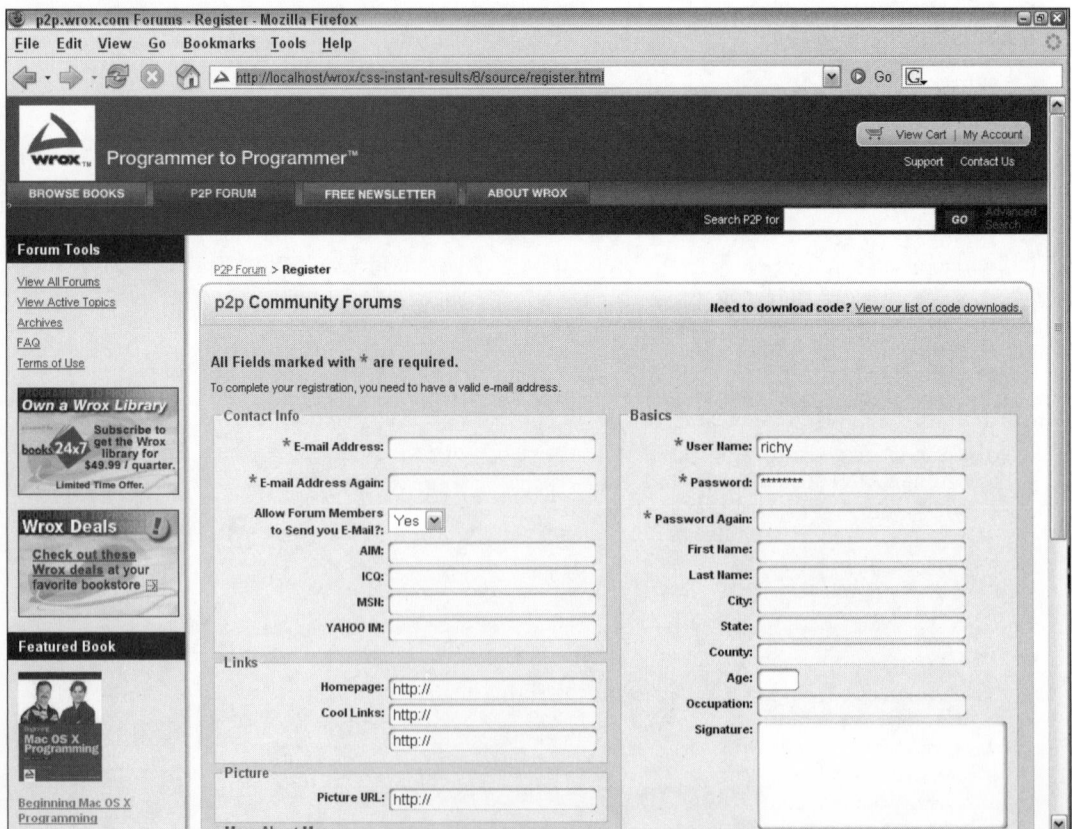

Figure 8-3

In Figure 8-3, you see that the text inputs and the textarea inputs have all been given a unique look and feel via the inclusion of CSS backgrounds. Because this was a rather large project encompassing many different design principles, this section reviews each piece that came together to produce the output you see in Figure 8-3.

You begin by styling the header portion of the registration form (which contains the Wrox P2P logo), shopping cart, additional navigation links, tabs, and search form.

The logo, shopping cart icon, and other navigational links are enclosed in a `<div>` with a `header` id name. Then the individual components are sequestered in their own `<div>` containers, and named for what each item's purpose is, respectively:

```
<div id='wrapper'>
  <div id='header'>
    <div id='h-logo'>
      <a href='#'>
        <img src='images/logo.gif' alt='Wrox Programmer to Programmer' />
      </a>
    </div>
    <div id='h-cart'>
      <div>
        <a href='#'>View Cart</a> |
        <a href='#'>My Account</a>
      </div>
    </div>
    <div id='h-links'>
      <a href='#'>Support</a> |
      <a href='#'>Contact Us</a>
    </div>
  </div>
```

In the style sheet named `p2p-header.css`, several rules define the look and feel of this portion of the document. The first several rules of the `p2p-header.css` document define some generic styles:

```
body {
    margin: 0;
    padding: 0;
    font: 11px Arial, Helvetica, sans-serif;
}
a:link {
    color: #903;
}
a:visited {
    color: #603;
}
a:hover {
    color: #c03;
    text-decoration: none
}
a:active {
    color:#903;
    text-decoration:none
}
```

```
img {
    border: none;
}
```

The default margin and padding are removed from the `<body>` element to bring the dimensions of the header `<div>` element flush with the browser's viewport borders. Links are then given different colors depending on their state: a dark red for unvisited links, an even darker red for visited links, and a lighter red for links the user's mouse is hovering over or clicking on. Finally, borders are removed from `<img>` elements.

The next style defines the `<div>` element that encompasses all of the document's content, with the exception of the footer. This `<div>` element is aptly named `wrapper`. This `<div>` element enables you to create the two-column layout without affecting the footer. It provides a point of reference with which to position the left column, and even though it also wraps the header, it could have just as easily wrapped only the two columns:

```
div#wrapper {
    position: relative;
    min-height: 1000px;
}
```

First you apply the `position: relative;` declaration, which allows the left column to position relative to the wrapper `<div>` instead of relative to the browser's viewport. Then, a `min-height: 1000px` declaration is provided to ensure that the wrapper `<div>` will always be at least 1000 pixels high. Providing a minimum height ensures that the left column won't get too small for its content, because the left column's height will be based on the height of the wrapper `<div>` element.

The next rule applies to the `<div>` element that wraps the Wrox logo, shopping cart, and navigational links:

```
div#header {
    background-color: #c03;
    position: relative;
}
```

This `<div>` element is given the "Wrox" red background and a `position: relative;` declaration. With a relative position, now the shopping cart and navigational links can be positioned relative to the header.

Next, those links are styled:

```
div#header a {
    text-decoration: none;
    margin: 0 4px;
}
```

The underline is removed and some additional space is applied to the left and right of each link with the `margin: 0 4px;` declaration.

The `<div>` wrapping the cart links is positioned absolutely, but relative to the header `<div>` element in the next rule:

```
div#h-cart {
    position: absolute;
    top: 23px;
    right: 15px;
    background: url('../images/css_background.gif') no-repeat center;
    width: 170px;
    height: 25px;
}
```

A graphic containing the shopping cart logo and gray oval is applied to the background, and is positioned precisely where the original was in Figure 8-1. The width and height of the h-cart <div> element is made to match the width and height of the background image. Within the h-cart <div> element is yet another <div> element that contains the "View Cart" and "My Account" links. This <div> element is also positioned absolutely:

```
div#h-cart div {
    position: absolute;
    top: 6px;
    left: 35px;
    color: #8c8c8c;
}
```

A light gray color is then specified for the vertical bar that separates the two links. Similarly, the links for "Support" and "Contact Us" are also absolutely positioned and also given a white color, instead of the dark red that's specified by default:

```
div#h-links {
    position: absolute;
    top: 54px;
    right: 27px;
}
div#h-links a {
    color: white;
}
```

Next, are the four tabs: Browse Books, P2P Forum, Free Newsletter, and About Wrox:

```
<ul id='tabs'>
  <li class='browse-books'>
    <a href='#'>
      <img src='images/browsebooks.gif' alt='Browse Books' />
    </a>
  </li>
  <li class='p2p-forum'>
    <a href='#'>
      <img src='images/p2pcommunity_on.gif' alt='P2P Forum' />
    </a>
  </li>
  <li class='free-newsletter'>
    <a href='#'>
      <img src='images/free_news.gif' alt='Free Newsletter' />
    </a>
```

```
        </li>
        <li class='about-wrox'>
          <a href='#'>
            <img src='images/aboutwrox.gif' alt='About Wrox' />
          </a>
        </li>
      </ul>
```

As was done in Chapter 1, these are encompassed by a `<ul>` element, and then each individual `<li>` element is given a unique class name to control the position of each tab:

```
ul#tabs {
    height: 23px;
    list-style-type: none;
    margin: -4px 0 0;
    position: relative;
    padding: 0;
    background: url('../images/background.gif') repeat-x top;
    border-bottom: 1px solid #6c6c6c;
}
```

The `<ul>` element is given an explicit height, which makes the background image visible. Because the `<li>` elements are positioned absolutely, they have no effect on the height of the `<ul>` element. The background image is repeated along the x-axis horizontally. The top margin is adjusted to match the original page in Figure 8-1 as much as possible, then other margin and default padding are removed, in addition to the default list style. Finally, a gray bottom border is applied.

The individual tabs then receive styling:

```
ul#tabs li {
    position: absolute;
    top: 1px;
    left: 0;
}
ul#tabs li.p2p-forum {
    left: 141px;
}
ul#tabs li.free-newsletter {
    left: 287px;
}
ul#tabs li.about-wrox {
    left: 445px;
}
```

The first rule sets up styles common to all of the tabs. Each subsequent `<li>` element is then positioned absolutely on a trial-and-error basis, until the result looks close to the original. You may be wondering, how does the "P2P Forum" tab overlap the border? This is done by the image being 1 pixel more in height than the others—CSS layering at its finest.

Next is the search box. Naturally, the search box is wrapped in a `<form>` element that signals the beginning of the form. Next, a `<div>` container wraps the form controls, and is the element to receive the dark gray background. The `<div>` element could be omitted and the same result achieved by applying the styles to the `<form>` element; however, to validate as strict XHTML, the `<form>` element may contain only certain elements as its immediate child. Specifically it may contain only `<p>`, `<h1>`, `<h2>`, `<h3>`, `<h4>`, `<h5>`, `<h6>`, `<div>`, `<pre>`, `<address>`, `<fieldset>`, `<ins>`, `<del>`.

```
<form action='javascript:void(0);' method='post'>
  <div id='search'>
    <a href='#'>Advanced<br />Search</a>
    <label for='p2p-search'>Search P2P for</label>
    <input name='search' id='p2p-search' size='20' value='' type='text' />
    <input src='images/go_p2p.gif' alt='go' type='image' />
  </div>
</form>
```

Because human error is a factor in any project, it's a good idea to get in the habit of checking your work with the W3 validation service at `http://validator.w3.org`. For the previous snip of markup, Figure 8-4 shows what the W3 validator produces when the `<div>` is omitted.

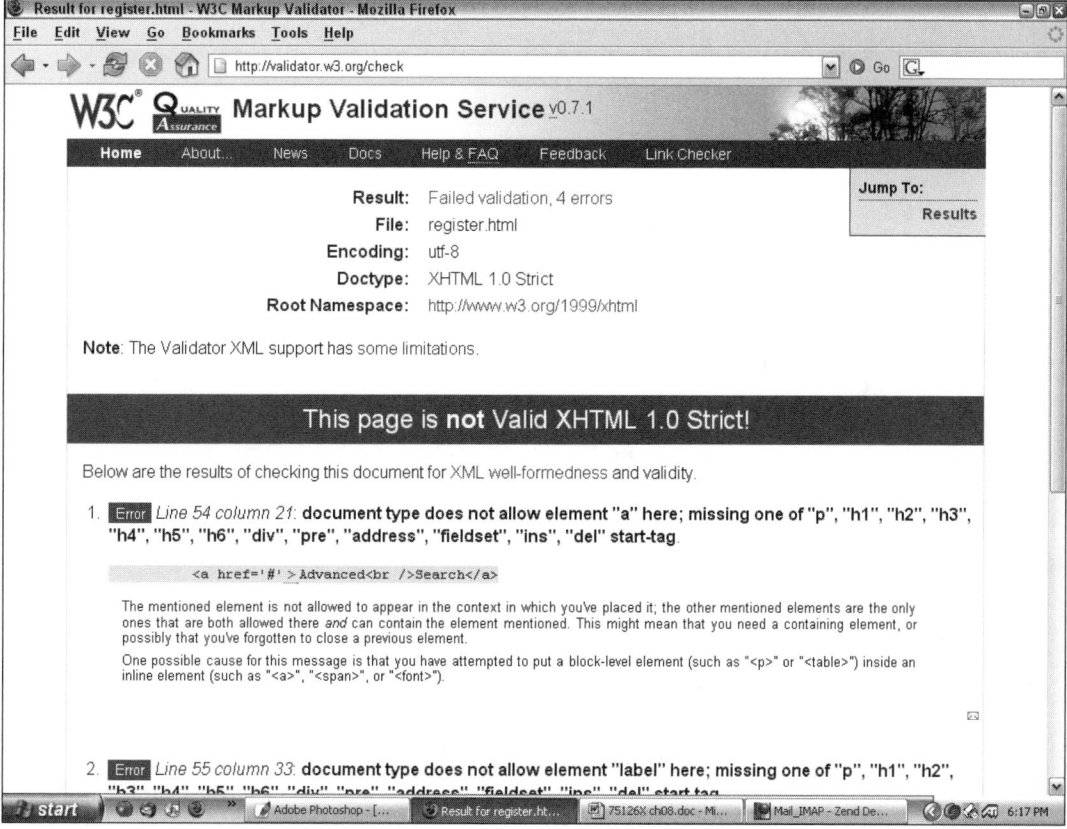

Figure 8-4

Figure 8-5 shows what the W3 validator produces when the `<div>` is included, and the XHTML validates.

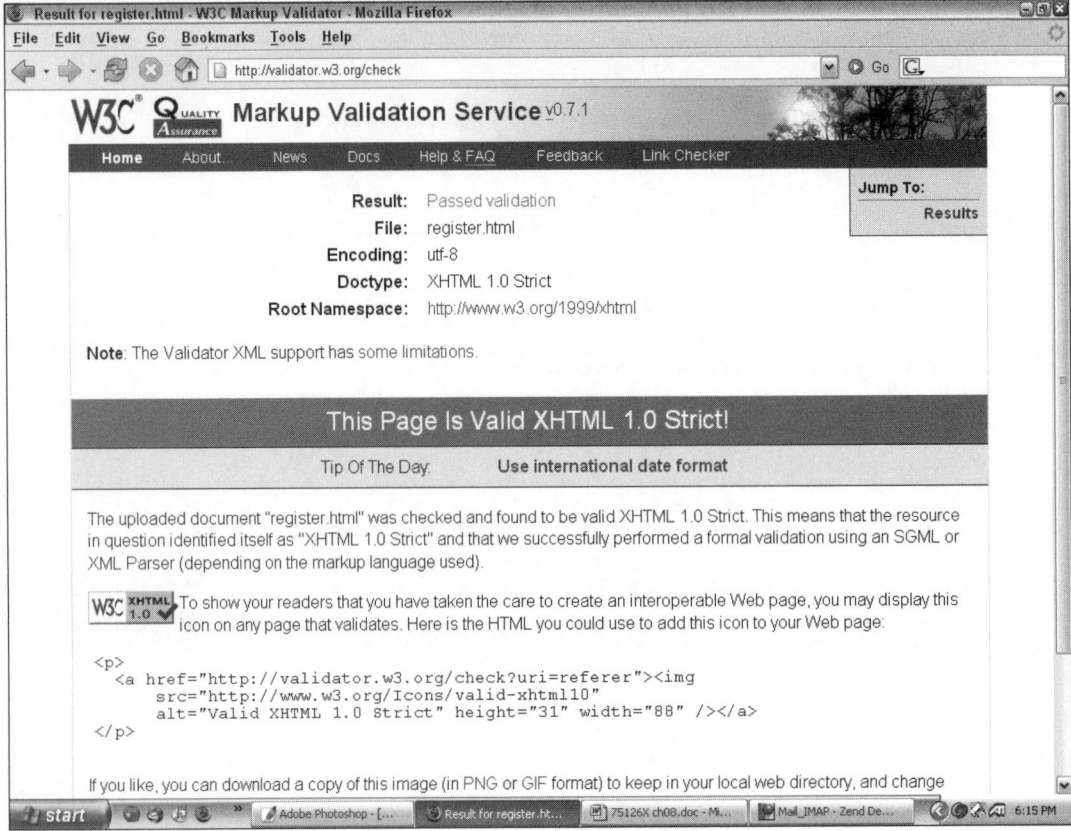

Figure 8-5

The style sheet rules for the search box are simple and to the point. The first rule removes any default margin or padding from the `<form>` element:

```
form {
    margin: 0;
    padding: 0;
}
```

Next, the `<div>` contained within the search `<form>`, which itself houses the form controls, is given a dark gray background with the declaration `background-color: #333`. The text is aligned to the right, made white in color, and finally the `<div>` is given an explicit height of 27 pixels:

```
div#search {
    background-color: #333;
    text-align: right;
    color: #fff;
    height: 27px;
}
```

The "Advanced Search" link is styled next. It is floated to the right to make the <a> element a block-level element, which is useful for providing margin to control its placement according to block-level box model rules, rather than inline box model rules. This also allows the line break between "Advanced" and "Search" to happen without affecting the label and form controls. Without floating the <a> element, the word "Search" would appear on a new line below the form label and input controls. The line-height is also adjusted to 11 pixels, which is the same size as the font size; this brings the styling of this link closer to the original P2P registration form shown in Figure 8-1. The text is aligned to the left. Because the search <div> is set to align to the right, and because you made the <a> element a block-level element by floating it, the text inside of it can be left aligned. The default underline is removed with the text-decoration : none; declaration, and lastly, the link text is made a lighter gray in color so it can be visible against the darker gray background:

```
div#search a {
    float: right;
    line-height: 11px;
    margin: 0 10px 0 5px;
    text-align: left;
    text-decoration: none;
    color: rgb(128, 128, 128);
}
```

After styling the link to match the Advanced Search link in Figure 8-1, another rule is added for mousing over the link. When the user's mouse comes over the link it will be made white:

```
div#search a:hover {
    color: #fff;
}
```

Finally, to make everything inside of the search <div> align vertically, a wild card universal selector is used to select all descendants of the <div> element, and the declaration vertical-align: middle; is applied to one and all:

```
div#search * {
    vertical-align: middle;
}
```

Remember that the vertical-align property can be applied only to inline or table-cell elements. Because all of the children of the <div> element are inline-level elements (with the exception of the Advanced Search link, which you made block-level by floating it), this technique works.

The search box is followed by the left column, which contains some site navigation and some advertisements:

```
<div id='column'>
  <div class='box tools'>
    <h4>Forum Tools</h4>
    <ul>
      <li><a href='#'>View All Forums</a></li>
      <li><a href='#'>View Active Topics</a></li>
      <li><a href='#'>Archives</a></li>
      <li><a href='#'>FAQ</a></li>
      <li><a href='#'>Terms of Use</a></li>
    </ul>
  </div>
</div>
```

```
        <div class='box ads'>
          <p>
            <a href='#'>
              <img src='images/ad1.jpg' alt='Own a Wrox Library...' />
            </a>
          </p>
          <p>
            <a href='#'>
              <img src='images/ad2.gif' alt='Wrox deals...' />
            </a>
          </p>
        </div>
        <div class='box featured'>
          <h4>Featured Book</h4>
          <p class='featured-book'>
            <a href='#'>
              <img src='images/book.jpg' alt='Beginning Mac OS X Programming' />
            </a>
            <a href='#'>Beginning Mac OS X Programming</a>
          </p>
        </div>
        <div class='box ads'>
          <p>
            <a href='#'>
              <img src='images/ad3.gif' alt='Wrox Tech Jobs...' />
            </a>
          </p>
        </div>
      </div>
```

The whole lot is wrapped by a `<div>` with the id name `column`, then each section of the column is broken down into `<div>` elements which all have multiple class names. The class name `box` is common to all four `<div>` elements. The second class name is narrowed down to what more-specific role the box plays in the document. Two boxes are ads, so the second class name for those is `ads`. The first box contains links for forum navigation, so its second class name is `tools`. The last box contains a featured Wrox book, so its second class name is `featured`. The naming conventions allow you to style the bits of content within each box based on what the box contains.

The first style sheet rule from `p2p-body.css` styles the `column` `<div>`. It is positioned absolutely, and stretched the height of the wrapper `<div>` element by specifying the declarations `top: 129px;` and `bottom: 0`. The elements that together comprise the headers of the document — the logo, tabs, and search box — have a height of 129 pixels:

```
div#column {
    position: absolute;
    top: 129px;
    bottom: 0;
    left: 0;
    width: 175px;
    background: url('../images/gradient_left.gif') repeat-y center;
}
```

The `left: 0;` declaration places the column `<div>` on the left side of the wrapper `<div>`, and finally the image `gradient_left.gif` is repeated along the y-axis of the column `<div>`.

The next rule styles the text of the left column headings Forum Tools and Featured Book. These are given black backgrounds with white text, and then the margin and padding are adjusted to match the original form shown in Figure 8-1. The last declaration in the rule sets the font size to 13 pixels:

```
div#column h4 {
    color: white;
    background-color: #000;
    margin: 0 4px 0 0;
    padding: 5px 0 5px 10px;
    font-size: 13px;
}
```

Subsequent rules are for the left column links: View All Forums, View Active Topics, and so on. These links are contained in an unordered list. The list is first stripped of its default styling, and its padding is adjusted to position the links similarly to what you observed in Figure 8-1:

```
div.box ul {
    margin: 0;
    padding: 5px 0 5px 10px;
    list-style-type: none;
}
```

The second rule styling the links places 5 pixels of space between each link vertically:

```
div.box li {
    margin: 5px 0 0 0;
}
```

The <div> boxes containing ads are easy to style — the ad images are merely aligned to the center of the <div> containing them:

```
div.box.ads {
    text-align: center;
}
```

The last <div> to receive styling is the <div> containing the featured Wrox book:

```
div.box.featured a {
    margin: 10px;
    display: block;
    color: rgb(128, 128, 128);
    font-weight: bold;
}
```

The links contained in the <div> with both box and featured class names are made block elements. This helps to position the image and the link containing the title of the book. The link is given a darker gray color and is made bold.

The next markup in the document is an implementation of a user-interface concept commonly known as *bread crumbs*. Bread crumbs are used to illustrate to the user where in a web site's navigational hierarchy they are currently located. This turns out to be a series of links that flow with the categorization the current page resides in. The first link represents the broadest category; other links represent categories downward to the page where the user is currently located. The current page shouldn't be a link, because the user is already at that location. Bread crumbs in the Wrox P2P registration page are represented in an unordered list:

```
<div id='breadcrumbs'>
  <ul>
    <li><a href='#'>P2P Forum</a></li>
    <li class='here'>Register</li>
  </ul>
</div>
```

The `<div>` containing bread crumb links is the first element to be styled. It is given left margin equal to the width of the left column, and then some:

```
div#breadcrumbs {
    margin-left: 200px;
}
```

The next element to be styled is the `<ul>` element containing each individual bread crumb. Its default list styling is removed, along with default margin or padding applied by the browser, which makes the rendering consistent across platforms because some browsers apply margin by default and others apply padding. Some space is also added to the top margin to move the bread crumbs further down from the `<div>` containing the search box above it, and to the bottom margin, to space it from the `<div>` containing content below it. Finally, the `overflow: auto;` declaration forces the height of the `<ul>` element to be the same as the `<li>` elements contained inside of it. This is necessary because the `<li>` elements are left-floated. Because they are left-floated, they have no effect on the dimensions of the `<ul>` element that contains them — that is until the `overflow` property is given a value other than `visible`, the default. When the `overflow` property contains a value other than `visible`, the `<ul>` container's dimensions become the height of the highest floated element it contains — if it contains floated content — and the floated content exceeds its boundaries. Without the `overflow` property, the `<ul>` element would need to have an explicit height provided, otherwise the bottom margin applied to it would need to be a much higher value to have any effect (for example, the height of the highest `<li>` element contained inside of it, and then some). With the `overflow` property, it is possible to have bread crumbs that are more than one line, which would also give the `<ul>` element the possibility of a variable height — that is not possible with other approaches:

```
div#breadcrumbs ul {
    margin: 25px 0 4px 0;
    padding: 0;
    list-style-type: none;
    overflow: auto;
}
```

Each `<li>` element is next floated to the left to make all of the `<li>` elements appear on the same line. A similar result could be achieved by giving each `<li>` element a `display: inline;` declaration. I happen to prefer floating:

```
div#breadcrumbs li {
    float: left;
}
```

A *greater-than* symbol appears between each bread crumb. You used the combination of the adjacent sibling selector and the `::before` pseudo-element to include this symbol in the document. The result of this is that every `<li>` element except the first has a greater-than symbol before it. Some margin is applied to the left and right of each greater-than symbol. Then the font is made monospace and bold:

```
div#breadcrumbs li + li::before {
    font-family: monospace;
    content: '>';
    margin: 0 5px;
    font-weight: bold;
}
```

The bread crumb links are then made gray. . .

```
div#breadcrumbs a {
    color: rgb(128, 128, 128);
}
```

. . .and red when the user's mouse hovers over them:

```
div#breadcrumbs a:hover {
    color: #c03;
}
```

The current location is then made bold:

```
div#breadcrumbs li.here {
    font-weight: bold;
}
```

The bread crumbs are followed by the markup that contains the document content. The markup begins with a `<div>` with an id name of `content`, which in turn wraps all of the content that appears in the right column between the bread crumbs and the footer. The first element within the content `<div>` is the page heading, and it appears in an `<h1>` element. It contains the text "p2p Community Forums" and a link for code downloads, followed by a `<div>` with a `body` id name which contains the registration form itself:

```
<div id='content'>
  <h1>
    <span class='inner'>
       Need to download code?
       <a href='#'>View our list of code downloads.</a>
    </span>
    <span style='color: #c03;'>p2p</span> Community Forums
  </h1>
  <div id='body'>
```

The first element to be styled in this lot is the content `<div>`. It is given a `clear: both;` declaration, preventing it from floating up beside the left-floated bread crumbs, which is not necessary in any browser but Internet Explorer. Because the `<ul>` element containing bread crumbs is given an overflow value other than `visible`, this is the same as clearing the floats in standards-savvy browsers. Left margin is also applied to prevent the content from being overlapped by the left column:

```
div#content {
    clear: both;
    margin: 0 0 0 185px;
}
```

Additionally, the <h1> element is provided with styles. The first declaration sets the background of the element with an image containing the left rounded corner that you observed in the output in Figure 8-3. The font size of an <h1> element is rather large by default, so this is reset to 16 pixels. The <h1> is then given an explicit height, which helps to position the background containing the custom borders. Padding and margin then position the text within:

```
div#content h1 {
    background: url('../images/top_left.gif') no-repeat top left;
    font-size: 16px;
    height: 30px;
    padding: 10px 0 0 15px;
    margin: 0 25px 0 0;
}
```

A <span> element contains the code download link. It is given the other half of the background containing custom borders. Slicing the background into two pieces allows the content to have a variable width and to scale up with larger resolutions. It is floated to the right and then positioned into place using the height property, margin, and padding. The position: relative; declaration is included to curtail any ill-effects in Explorer (such as the peek-a-boo bug), and the font size is set to 11 pixels:

```
div#content h1 span.inner {
    background: url('../images/top_right.gif') no-repeat top right;
    float: right;
    font-size: 11px;
    position: relative;
    height: 22px;
    margin: -10px -11px 0 0;
    padding: 18px 10px 0 0;
}
```

The next rule removes the bold font from the code download link:

```
div#content h1 span.inner a {
    font-weight: normal;
}
```

The <div> element with a body id name contains the registration form. It is given a gray background and a 1-pixel wide, solid gray border. A minimum height is set to ensure that the body <div> is always visible, even if it doesn't contain content. A right margin is then applied to line up the border of the body <div> with the border in the background images specified for the <h1> element, and the <span> containing the code download link:

```
div#body {
    background: #e5e5e5;
    min-height: 400px;
    margin-right: 14px;
    border: 1px solid #ccc;
}
```

The last bit of code referenced in the `p2p-body.css` style sheet references the footer `<div>`, which contains copyright information and a link to Wrox's privacy policy:

```
<div id='footer'>
  <a href="http://www.wrox.com/go/copyright">Copyright &copy; 2000-2005</a> by
  <a href="http://www.wiley.com">John Wiley &amp; Sons, Inc.</a>
  or related companies.
  All rights reserved. Please read our
  <a href="http://www.wrox.com/go/privacy">Privacy Policy</a>.
</div>
```

The footer `<div>` is fairly straightforward. It contains a background that repeats along the x-axis for the width of the document. Some padding is introduced to space the content of the `<div>` from the edges of the `<div>`. The font size is set to 12 pixels, and an explicit height is specified to provide some spacing between the text and the bottom of the document:

```
div#footer {
    background: #fff url('../images/gradient_bottom.gif') repeat-x top;
    padding: 5px 0 5px 10px;
    font-size: 12px;
    height: 50px;
}
```

The registration form begins with a `<div>` element named `innerbody`. I've lumped this element in with the registration form because it is an element that can have a different purpose from page to page in a Wrox P2P template; that is, it may or may not have minimum or maximum dimensional constraints placed on it. After the `innerbody` `<div>` element, the form begins with a `<p>` element containing text that dictates that all form controls markup with a red asterisk are required fields, and a valid email address is required to complete registration:

```
          <div id='innerbody'>
<!-- Begin Content -->
<p>
  <span style='font-weight: bold;'>
    All Fields marked with
    <span class='required'>*</span> are required.
  </span><br />
  To complete your registration, you need to have a valid e-mail
  address.
</p>
```

The `innerbody` `<div>` is the first element to be styled in the `p2p-form.css` style sheet. It is given minimum and maximum width constraints, which prevents the form from becoming unreadable at extreme screen resolution thresholds:

```
div#innerbody {
    max-width: 1000px;
    min-width: 790px;
    margin: auto;
    padding: 10px;
}
```

Subsequently, all descendants of the <p> element are selected. This boils down to the two <span> elements that follow:

```
<span style='font-weight: bold;'>
   All Fields marked with
   <span class='required'>*</span> are required.
</span>
```

Each is vertically aligned to the middle and given a font size of 13 pixels:

```
div#innerbody > p * {
    font-size: 13px;
    vertical-align: middle;
}
```

Next, all of those red asterisks are styled. Each asterisk is wrapped by a <span> element with a required class name. These are each given a 24-pixel, red, bold font:

```
div#innerbody span.required {
    color: #c03;
    font-size: 24px;
    font-weight: bold;
}
```

Following that rule is the <form> element containing the controls that make up the registration form. The form is split in half, with half going into the <div> with a column1 class name and the other half going into the <div> with a column2 class name. Each part of the form is further broken down within each of these column <div> elements. <fieldset> and <legend> elements define each sub-partition of the registration form. Then, within each <fieldset> element, after the <legend>, a <table> element contains the form controls and labels:

```
<form action='javascript: void(0);' method='post'>
<div class='column1'>
  <fieldset>
    <legend>Contact Info</legend>
    <table class='form'>
      <colgroup>
        <col />
        <col />
      </colgroup>
      <tbody>
        <tr>
          <td class='label'>
            <label for='email'>
              <span class='required'>*</span>
              E-mail Address:
            </label>
          </td>
          <td class='input'>
            <input name='email'
                   id='email' size='25' maxlength='50' value='' class='i' />
          </td>
```

The two columns are positioned using floating. The first `<div>` is floated to the left, which places the two columns side-by-side. Each is given a width of 49%. The width is specified at 49% to defeat a bug in Internet Explorer, which doesn't understand that 50% + 50% = 100%. At 50% width, IE still places the second column below the first.

A `position: relative;` is specified to side-step unwelcome CSS rendering bugs such as Explorer's peek-a-boo bug. The second column is given a right margin of 50% to keep all of its content on the right of the first column:

```
div.column1 {
    float: left;
    width: 49%;
}
div.column2 {
    position: relative;
    width: 49%;
    margin-left: 50%;
}
```

The next elements to be styled are the `<fieldset>` and `<legend>` elements. It is not possible to style the `<fieldset>` and `<legend>` elements to match the old P2P Wrox registration form exactly, which did not contain these elements. The problem is with the styling that browsers allow the `<legend>` element to receive. Firefox, not surprisingly, allows the `<legend>` element to be positioned using margin or relative positioning and the four offset properties. Internet Explorer also allows `<legend>` to be positioned, but has some bugs, as you see in the next section. Opera and Safari do not allow the `<legend>` element's position to be modified. If it were not for these limitations, the `<fieldset>` element could be given a darker gray, thick, top border, the `<legend>` a background of the same color, and margin to modify its position to match the styling in Figure 8-1. Even doing this, it would not be possible to center the `<legend>` element. The nail in the coffin for this approach is one Explorer bug that defeats the possibility of a reproducing the thick gray box around the `<legend>` element in Figure 8-1. In Explorer, a border appears around the `<legend>` element, even when none is specified explicitly, and it is given a background to match the `<fieldset>`'s border. To preserve proper form semantics, and to make the form as accessible as possible, it should have both `<fieldset>` and `<legend>` elements; the solution, it seems, is to work with what browsers do allow. The `<legend>` is given a red, bold, 13-pixel font, and the `<fieldset>` is given a solid gray border and a lighter gray background:

```
fieldset {
    border: 1px solid #ccc;
    background-color: #f5f5f5;
}
legend {
    color: #c03;
    font-weight: bold;
    font-size: 13px;
}
```

Following `<fieldset>` and `<legend>` are the styles for the table containing form controls. Each form `<table>` is given a 100% width, which is done because by default `<table>` elements follow the shrink-to-fit width sizing algorithm, and only expand enough to accommodate their content. Having applied a 100% width, each `<table>` will always be as wide as the element that contains it:

```
table.form {
    width: 100%;
}
```

Now that the `<table>` has a 100% width, its two columns can each be given half of that width, which is specified in the next rule:

```
table.form col {
    width: 50%;
}
```

After each column is given a 50% width, each `<td>` element with a `label` class name is styled. The font is made bold, and the text aligned to the top and right of each cell:

```
td.label {
    text-align: right;
    vertical-align: top;
    font-weight: bold;
}
```

As was done in previous rules, the all descendants of label `<td>` elements are selected and vertically align to the middle:

```
td.label * {
    vertical-align: middle;
}
```

Next each `<input>` and `<textarea>` are styled. Each `<input>` of the same length is given an `i` class name. This is done because a form this complex can have text inputs of varying lengths. This approach to custom styling input forms requires a custom background to be created separately for each size of input field.

First default styles are stripped from the `<input>` and `<textarea>` fields. This is done by giving the border a zero width. The font is then adjusted to 14 pixels sans-serif:

```
div#innerbody input.i,
div#innerbody textarea {
    border: 0px solid transparent;
    font: 14px Arial, Helvetica, sans-serif;
}
```

Each `<input>` field is given the exact dimensions of the background image inserted. The height, width, and padding combined equal the dimensions of the background image. The background image is then specified and positioned top left (the default value of the background-position property):

```
div#innerbody input.i {
    width: 196px;
    height: 18px;
    padding: 2px 0 0 4px;
    background: url('../images/input.png') no-repeat;
}
```

The next rule is pretty much identical to the rule for all the other input fields, except the dimensions are adjusted to accommodate the smaller "Age" field, and a smaller background image, input-a.png, is used for the smaller input field:

```
div#innerbody input.a {
    width: 40px;
    height: 18px;
    padding: 2px 0 0 4px;
    background: url('../images/input-a.png') no-repeat;
}
```

The same is done for <textarea> fields — height, width, and padding are all specified to be in harmony with the background image specified:

```
div#innerbody textarea {
    padding: 2px;
    height: 96px;
    width: 236px;
    background: url('../images/textarea.png') no-repeat;
}
```

There's not much to styling form controls. The <select> element can also be given a background in this way, but browser support for styling the <select> element is not consistent, and because the most popular browser, Internet Explorer, does not allow the <select> element to be completely styled, it is omitted here. Checkbox, file inputs, and radio controls can also be completely customized, but the customization of these inputs requires JavaScript, and as such is outside of the scope of this book.

The last elements in the P2P registration form to be styled is the <div> containing the form submission button, and a link back to the forum's default page. This <div> is aptly given a buttons class name. It is given the clear: both; declaration to prevent the buttons <div> from ever coming up beside the column <div> in the registration form that is floated to the left. It is also given an overflow: auto; declaration to give it the same height as the highest floated element that it contains:

```
div.buttons {
    clear: both;
    overflow: auto;
}
```

Finally, the link with the text "Back to Forum" and the submit button are floated to the left and right, respectively:

```
div.buttons a {
    float: left;
}
div.buttons input {
    float: right;
}
```

The next section presents some additional hacks to make the Wrox P2P registration page shine in Internet Explorer.

Testing and Caveats

In this section you take the completed project of the last section and test it in Internet Explorer.

In a project as lengthy and complicated as the Wrox P2P new user registration form, there are bound to be a few incompatibilities. A few of these incompatibilities have already been addressed, but Explorer shows a document that is far from looking like a professional technical book publisher's web site. Figure 8-6 shows a screenshot of the Wrox P2P new user registration form without any hacking applied.

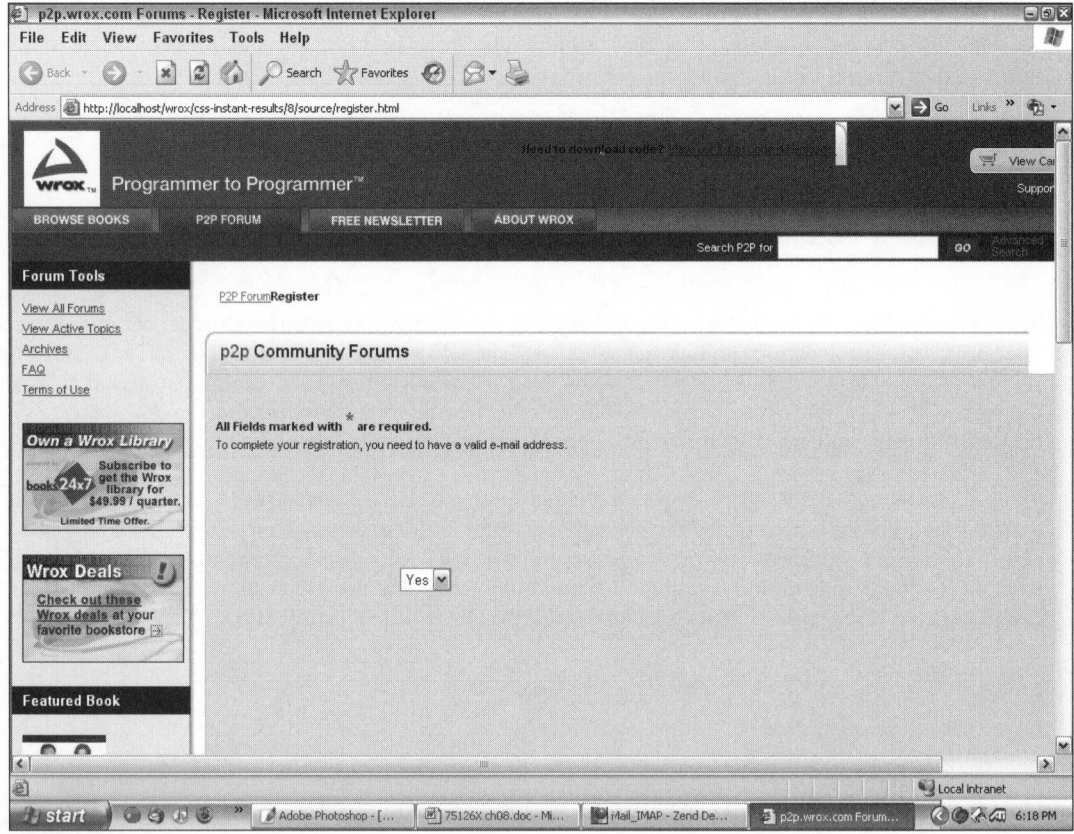

Figure 8-6

To make the Wrox P2P new user registration form appear as sparkling and shiny as it does in Firefox, follow these steps:

1. As with previous projects, Dean Edwards' IE7 JavaScript is applied to bring more consistency to the project. Add the IE7 conditional commented JavaScript to the `register.html` document:

```
<!DOCTYPE html PUBLIC "-//W3C//DTD XHTML 1.0 Strict//EN"
"http://www.w3.org/TR/xhtml1/DTD/xhtml1-strict.dtd">
<html xmlns='http://www.w3.org/1999/xhtml' xml:lang='en' id='p2p-wrox-com'>
```

```
<head>
  <meta http-equiv="Content-Type" content="text/html; charset=UTF-8" />
  <title>p2p.wrox.com Forums - Register</title>
  <link rel='stylesheet' type='text/css' href='styles/p2p-header.css' />
  <link rel='stylesheet' type='text/css' href='styles/p2p-body.css' />
  <link rel='stylesheet' type='text/css' href='styles/p2p-form.css' />
  <link rel='shortcut icon' href='images/favicon.ico' type='image/x-icon' />
    <!-- compliance patch for microsoft browsers -->
    <!--[if lt IE 7]>
        <script src="/ie7/ie7-standard-p.js" type="text/javascript"></script>
    <![endif]-->
</head>
```

2. Save the document as `register-ie.html`.

Having applied the IE7 JavaScript, you get output similar to that in Figure 8-7.

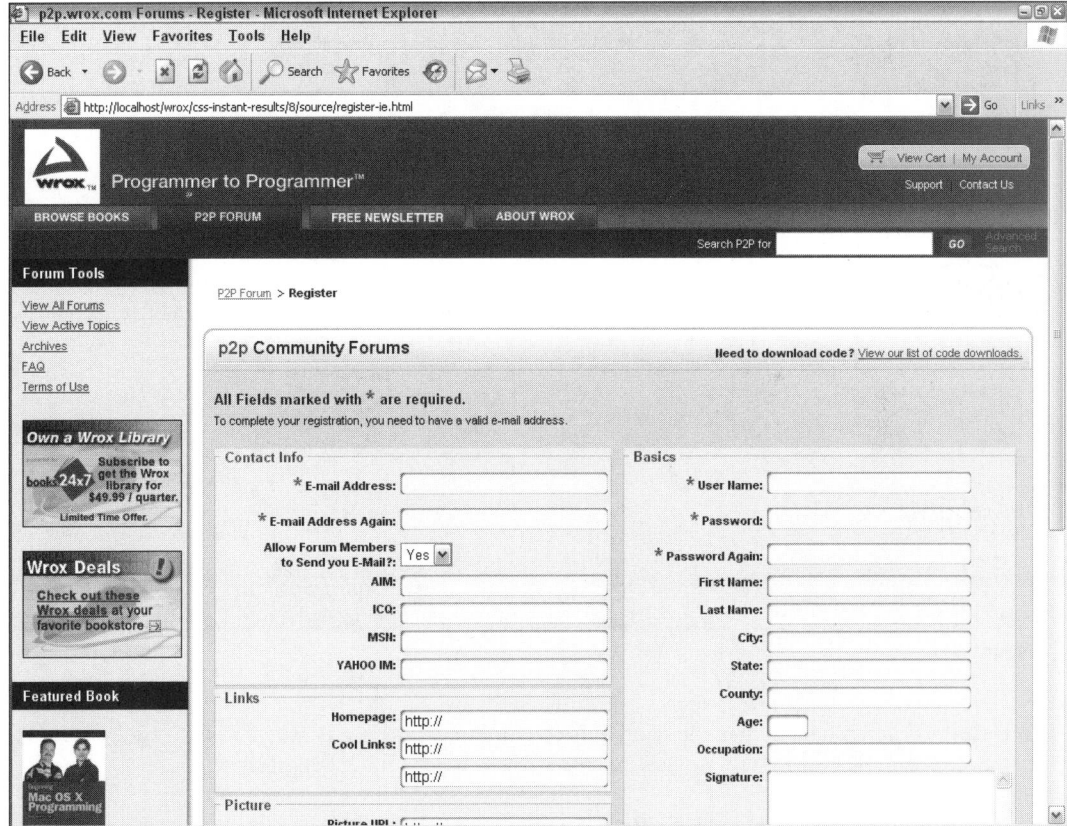

Figure 8-7

The project still is not perfect in Internet Explorer:

- ❑ The top bar containing the logo goes too far to the right.
- ❑ The `<legend>` elements are not positioned correctly.
- ❑ There is too much space between the bread crumbs and the content.

There is also one more bug that isn't so obvious. This bug is demonstrated in Figure 8-8.

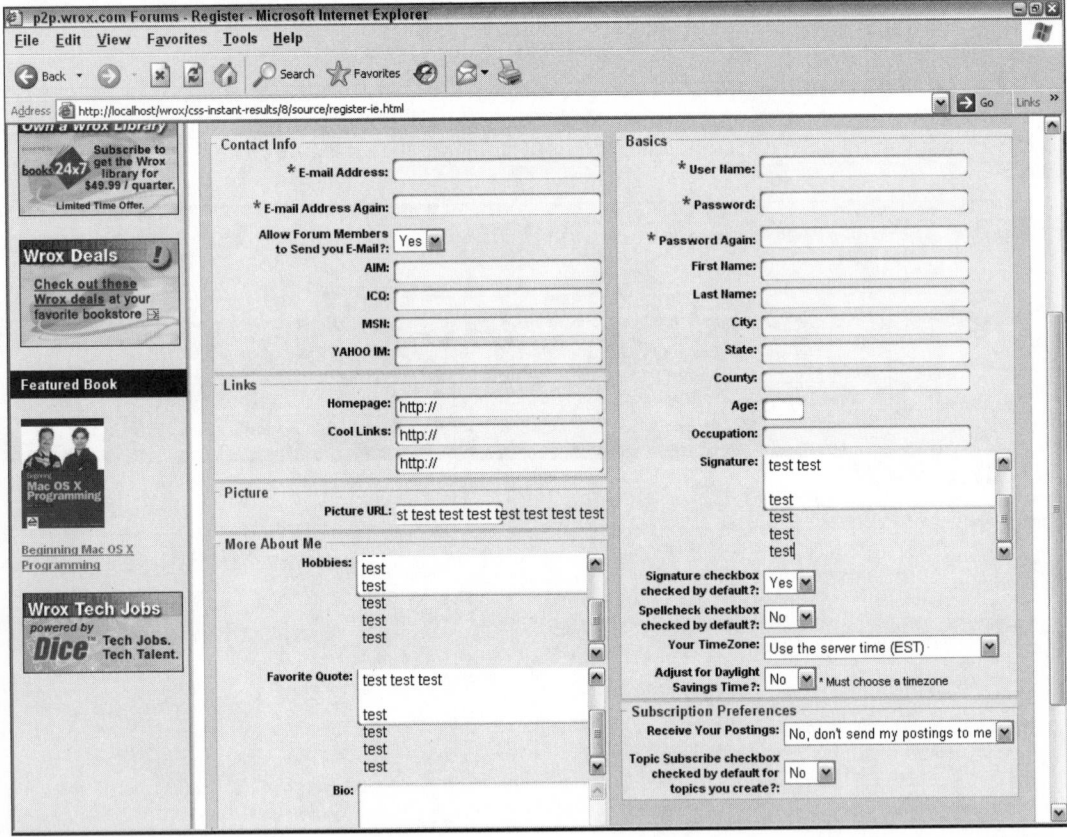

Figure 8-8

In Figure 8-8, you see that when the text fields containing backgrounds are filled with enough text to cause scrolling, the background moves. To correct these bugs, follow these steps:

1. Modify `register-ie.html`, applying the following markup:

```
<!DOCTYPE html PUBLIC "-//W3C//DTD XHTML 1.0 Strict//EN"
"http://www.w3.org/TR/xhtml1/DTD/xhtml1-strict.dtd">
<html xmlns='http://www.w3.org/1999/xhtml' xml:lang='en' id='p2p-wrox-com'>
```

```
<head>
  <meta http-equiv="Content-Type" content="text/html; charset=UTF-8" />
  <title>p2p.wrox.com Forums - Register</title>
  <link rel='stylesheet' type='text/css' href='styles/p2p-header.css' />
  <link rel='stylesheet' type='text/css' href='styles/p2p-body.css' />
  <link rel='stylesheet' type='text/css' href='styles/p2p-form.css' />
  <link rel='shortcut icon' href='images/favicon.ico' type='image/x-icon' />
      <!-- compliance patch for microsoft browsers -->
      <!--[if lt IE 7]>
          <script src="/ie7/ie7-standard-p.js" type="text/javascript"></script>
          <link rel='stylesheet' type='text/css' href='styles/p2p-ie.css' />
      <![endif]-->
</head>
```

2. Save the preceding markup as `register-ie-hacks.html`.

3. Enter the following style sheet into your text editor:

```
div#header {
    /* The Holly Hack fixes positioning
       of the cart links */
    height: 1%;
}
div#content {
    margin-top: -20px;
}
div#innerbody input.i {
    background: url('../images/input.png') no-repeat fixed;
}
div#innerbody input.a {
    background: url('../images/input-a.png') no-repeat fixed;
}
div#innerbody textarea {
    background: url('../images/textarea.png') no-repeat fixed;
    padding-right: 20px;
}
fieldset {
    position: relative;
    margin-bottom: 10px;
}
legend {
    /* This seems the only way to get Explorer
       to position the <legend> correctly */
    position: absolute;
    top: -10px;
}
```

4. Save the new style sheet as `p2p-ie.css`.

This results in the output shown in Figure 8-9.

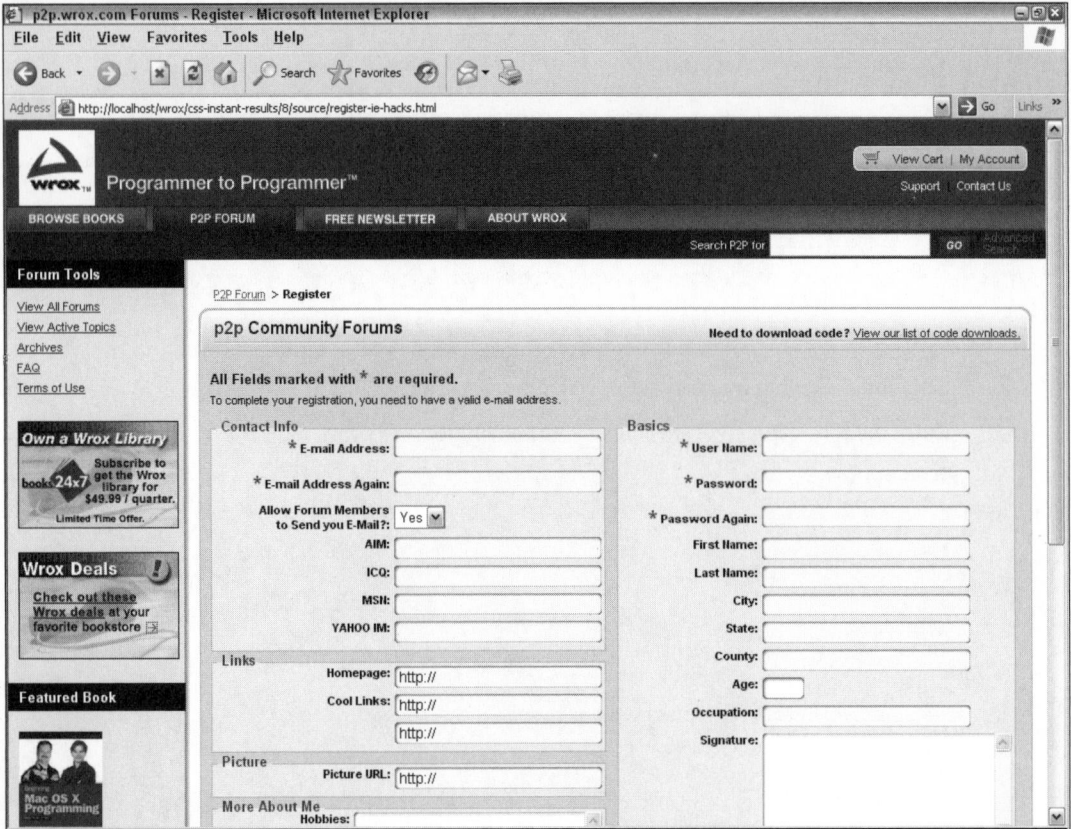

Figure 8-9

The hacks required to get Explorer on the same page, so to speak, as other browsers are relatively simple. Given the symptoms exhibited in Figures 8-7 and 8-8, the resulting conditional comment style sheet is simple and to the point. First a "Holly" hack is applied to the header <div> element:

```
div#header {
    /* The Holly Hack fixes positioning
       of the cart links */
    height: 1%;
}
```

The Holly Hack is named for developer Holly Bergevin, who along with another fellow named "Big John" maintain the online browser bug site extraordinaire "Position is Everything" at http://www.positioniseverything.net. The Holly Hack is a technique used to force an element in Explorer to acquire the "layout" algorithm, which is used internally within Internet Explorer's Trident rendering engine. While I could write an entire chapter about "layout" in Explorer, the simple, to the point explanation is that elements without layout define their dimensions based on the last element to have layout—for instance, auto width on a block element is determined by that element's parent, and that element's parent may also have an auto width which is itself determined by that element's parent, and so on.

Layout in Explorer is an internal algorithm used to implement rendering scenarios like this: elements with layout serve as the reference point to render children and descendants whose dimensions position are reliant upon that element's dimensions. The Holly Hack forces a new point of reference to be created, which corrects the incorrect positioning of the navigational links in the header of the registration form.

You can learn more about Internet Explorer's proprietary hasLayout feature from the following URL: http://www.satzansatz.de/cssd/onhavinglayout.html.

The next hack corrects the spacing between the bread crumbs and the content <div>. The top margin is simply set to negative 20 pixels to force the content <div> up farther:

```
div#content {
    margin-top: -20px;
}
```

After correcting the space between the bread crumbs and the content <div>, the next hack fixes those scrolling backgrounds in the <input> and <textarea> elements. Applying the fixed keyword to the background property prevents the background of the <input> and <textarea> element from scrolling:

```
div#innerbody input.i {
    background: url('../images/input.png') no-repeat fixed;
}
div#innerbody input.a {
    background: url('../images/input-a.png') no-repeat fixed;
}
div#innerbody textarea {
    background: url('../images/textarea.png') no-repeat fixed;
    padding-right: 20px;
}
```

Finally, the top border of the <fieldset> element and the position of the <legend> element are corrected with the following two rules. Applying a bottom margin to the <fieldset> element pushes its top border up to where it belongs, and a position: relative; declaration positions the absolutely positioned <legend> element relative to the <fieldset> element, and it is then wiggled into place using the top: -10px declaration:

```
fieldset {
    position: relative;
    margin-bottom: 10px;
}
legend {
    /* This seems the only way to get Explorer
       to position the <legend> correctly */
    position: absolute;
    top: -10px;
}
```

With the Wrox P2P new user registration form fixed and working properly in Internet Explorer, the next chapter discusses user interface design.

User-Interface
for a Web-based File Viewer

In this chapter you see some techniques for styling a user interface (UI) for a web-based file viewer application. *UI* can refer to anything from a web site's navigation to a series of controls that come together to allow a complex web application to function. The file navigation application in this project is designed to resemble Mac OS X's Aqua user interface. If you have never seen Mac OS X, Aqua makes use of horizontal pinstripe backgrounds (or sometimes brushed metal backgrounds), and buttons with lighting effects making the buttons appear to have water inside—hence the Aqua name. This is what gives the Mac operating system its unique look and feel. Figure 9-1 is a screenshot of Mac OS X Finder.

For this project you'll be using the graphics, markup, and style sheets of an open source (Free-BSD licensed) project I've been developing, which I call "Hierophant" (which has not been released to the general public at the time of this writing), an open source PHP-driven framework and content management system (CMS). In case you're curious, the term "Hierophant" refers to ancient Greek priests, who are said to have had the ability to make the mysterious or esoteric easy to understand (by one definition). I chose this name because I wanted to write a complex PHP framework that made complex and sometimes difficult tasks easy for the average user.

This application is called "hFinder" because it provides much of the functionality that Mac OS X's Finder or Windows Explorer provides, only it provides file management functionality through a browser as opposed to Finder, which is part of the Mac operating system. Because the real application is a complex interweaving of technologies beyond the scope of this book, namely PHP, MySQL, and JavaScript, I'm only including the style sheets, graphics, and markup. The event-driven functionality is discussed only in theory, and only what is relevant to applying style sheets to the underlying markup.

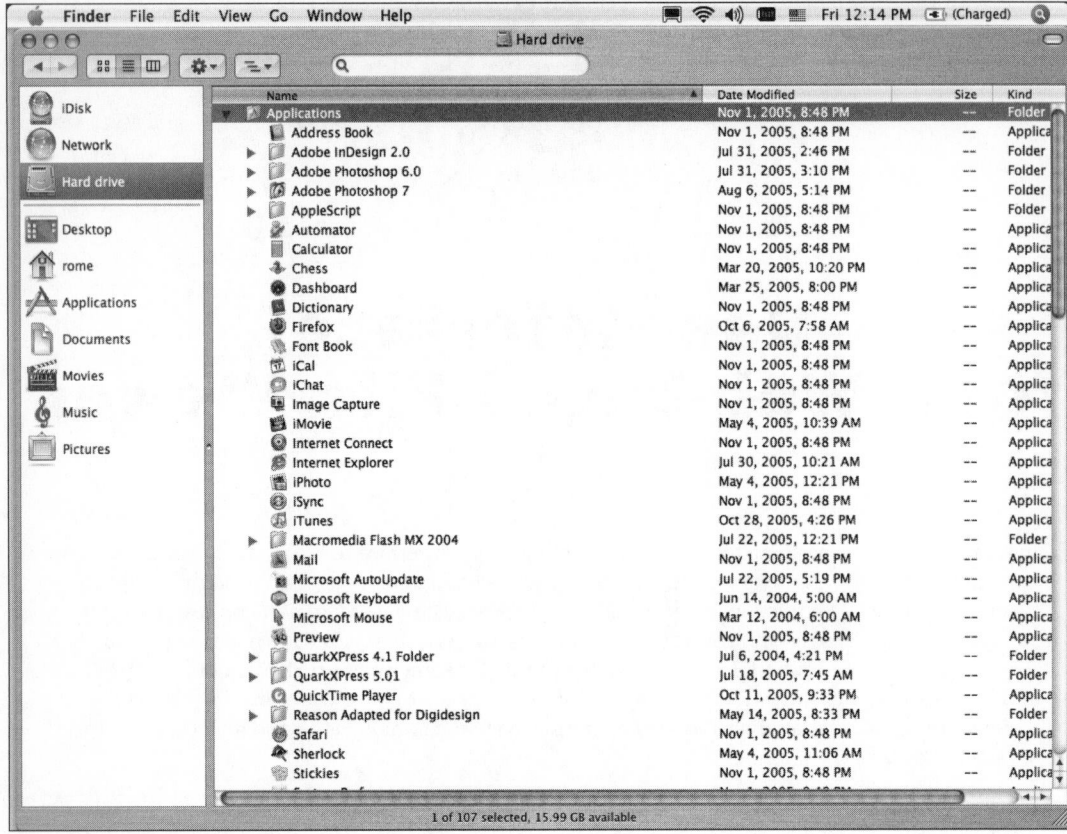

Figure 9-1

The purpose of hFinder is to make everything associated with file management a breeze for the novice user, with a look and feel the average user is likely to already be familiar and comfortable with, because the widgets used in hFinder are designed to mirror native operating system file management functionality.

Here are the goals of hFinder:

❑ The project must be reusable, because other parts of the Hierophant framework may also require file management functionality, but not necessarily all of the controls found in hFinder. For instance, designing a web-based file management application may also be useful in designing other applications. A web-based what-you-see-is-what-you-get (WYSIWYG) HTML editor may require an "open" or "save as" dialog, where it would be useful for the user to see a graphical representation of files on the server.

❑ The application must support multiple methods of viewing a file's information, such as lists, details, thumbnails, icons, columns, and so on. The application should attempt to implement as many views that the user would be familiar with as possible (for example, both those common to Windows and to Macintosh) for maximum usability. The result is a hybrid of Mac OS X Finder and Windows Explorer. If all views are not supported, it must at least be easy to extend with new methods at a later time.

❑ The application must have two views side-by-side: in the left view, a tree representation of the directories on the server, and on the right, the contents of the selected directory. This is exactly the functionality that Windows Explorer provides.

❑ Each file must have an accompanying icon. HTML files have a web browser icon, directories have folder icons, and so on.

❑ The left tree view must have arrows next to the directories to indicate that the folder contains other folders.

❑ The application must have a toolbar for common functions that would be associated with browsing files; for instance, buttons for going forward and back, refreshing, and so on.

❑ The application must have menus for other common operations, such as to upload a new file, create a directory, change the view of the current directory, modify preferences, and so on.

Having seen the goals of the hFinder application, the next section discusses what CSS features play a role in creating the hFinder application.

Design

It is not uncommon in the real world for a team of people to be given separate portions of a project when developing an application. One person may oversee presentational layout, another might create the graphics, another may oversee JavaScript, and still another may handle the server-side programming (PHP, ASP, Java, Ruby, and so on). The hFinder application is an ideal candidate for such team-oriented delegation, though in reality it was designed by only a single person — me!

Applying CSS to the hFinder application is the most complex project presented in this book. The hFinder application, like the p2p.wrox.com user registration form in Chapter 8, puts into practice many of the concepts that you've already seen in earlier projects, such as drop-down menus and multi-column layout, but it also presents some unique challenges that have not yet been covered.

The next section presents the source code for hFinder, followed by an explanation of the source code by feature. The individual features of the hFinder project are as follows:

❑ Drop-down navigational menus (File, View, Help) and a context menu (for right-clicking over a file)

❑ Toolbar for browse buttons (back, forward, refresh, and so on)

❑ Pure-CSS popup windows (for uploading a file or modifying a file's properties)

❑ A directory tree for navigating directories

❑ A directory window for viewing the contents of a directory

Because the application is so complex, the entire source code is presented first, followed by a detailed explanation of how it comes together, modularized by the various methods mentioned in the preceding list.

Code and Code Explanation

The following is the complete source for the hFinder application. The source code for the hFinder application can be obtained from the CD-ROM accompanying this book, or online at www.wrox.com. Because of the length of the source code files, following the source code is an explanation of the different aspects of this project.

1. Enter the following markup:

```
<!DOCTYPE html PUBLIC "-//W3C//DTD XHTML 1.0 Transitional//EN"
"http://www.w3.org/TR/2002/REC-xhtml1-20020801/DTD/xhtml1-transitional.dtd">
<html xmlns='http://www.w3.org/1999/xhtml' xml:lang='en'>
    <head>
        <meta http-equiv='content-type' content='text/html; charset=utf-8' />
        <meta http-equiv='content-language' content='en-us' />
        <title>hFinder File Management Application</title>
        <!-- compliance patch for microsoft browsers -->
        <!--[if lt IE 7]>
            <script src="/ie7/ie7-standard.js"
                    type="text/javascript"></script>
            <script src="/ie7/ie7-css3-selectors.js"
                    type="text/javascript"></script>
            <link rel='stylesheet'
                type='text/css'
                href='styles/hFinder.ie.css' />
            <link rel='stylesheet'
                type='text/css'
                href='styles/tree.ie.css' />
            <script type='text/javascript'
                    src='js/png.js'></script>
        <![endif]-->
        <link rel='stylesheet' type='text/css' href='styles/hFinder.css' />
    <!--

        Hierophant Framework

        http://www.smilingsouls.net/hierophant
        (c) Copyright 1998-2005 Richard York, All rights Reserved

        Use and redistribution are subject to the terms of the license.
        http://www.smilingsouls.net/hierophant/license

    -->
    </head>
    <body>
        <ul id='hfinder-menu'>
            <li class='hfinder-menu-item' id='hfinder-menu-file'>
                File
                <ul>
                    <li id='hfinder-menu-new-file'>
                        <span>New File</span>
                    </li>
                    <li id='hfinder-menu-new-directory' class='sep'>
                        <span>New Directory</span>
                    </li>
                    <li id='hfinder-menu-close'>
```

```
                <span>Close</span></li>
            </ul>
        </li>
        <li class='hfinder-menu-item' id='hfinder-menu-view'>
            View
            <ul>
                <li id='hfinder-menu-thumbnail'>
                    <span>Thumbnails</span>
                </li>
                <li id='hfinder-menu-tile'>
                    <span>Tiles</span>
                </li>
                <li id='hfinder-menu-icon'>
                    <span>Icons</span>
                </li>
                <li id='hfinder-menu-details'>
                    <span>Details</span>
                </li>
                <li id='hfinder-menu-list' class='sep'>
                    <span>List</span>
                </li>
                <li id='hfinder-menu-default-view'>
                    <span>Set Current as Default</span>
                </li>
            </ul>
        </li>
        <li class='hfinder-menu-item' id='hfinder-menu-admin'>
            Admin
            <ul>
                <li id='hfinder-menu-home-directory' class='sep'>
                    <span>Home Directory</span>
                </li>
                <li id='hfinder-menu-manage-users'>
                    <span>Manage Users</span>
                </li>
                <li id='hfinder-menu-manage-groups'>
                    <span>Manage Groups</span>
                </li>
            </ul>
        </li>
        <li class='hfinder-menu-item' id='hfinder-menu-help'>
            Help
            <ul>
                <li id='hfinder-help-contents'>
                    <span>Help Contents</span>
                </li>
            </ul>
        </li>
    </ul>
    <div id='hfinder-toolbar'>
        <table style='width: 100%; border-collapse: collapse;'>
            <tbody>
                <tr>
                    <td style='width: 35px;'>
                        <img src='images/back.png'
```

```
                        alt='Back'
                        title='Back'
                        class='hfinder-toolbar-control'
                        id='hfinder-back' />
            </td>
            <td style='width: 35px;'>
                <img src='images/forward.png'
                        alt='Forward'
                        title='Forward'
                        class='hfinder-toolbar-control'
                        id='hfinder-forward' />
            </td>
            <td style='width: 35px;'>
                <img src='images/refresh.png'
                        alt='Refresh'
                        title='Refresh'
                        class='hfinder-toolbar-control'
                        id='hfinder-refresh' />
            </td>
            <td style='width: 35px;'>
                <img src='images/home.png'
                        alt='Home'
                        title='Home'
                        class='hfinder-toolbar-control'
                        id='hfinder-home' />
            </td>
            <td style='vertical-align: middle;'>
                <input type='text'
                        style='width: 98%;'
                        value='/'
                        id='hfinder-location-input' />
            </td>
            <td style='width: 35px;'>
                <img src='images/go.png'
                        alt='Go'
                        title='Go to this location.'
                        class='hfinder-toolbar-control'
                        id='hfinder-location-go' />
            </td>
            <td style='width: 35px;'>
                <img src='images/directory.png'
                        alt='New Directory'
                        title='New Directory'
                        class='hfinder-toolbar-control'
                        id='hfinder-new-directory' />
            </td>
            <td style='width: 35px;'>
                <img src='images/file.png'
                        alt='New File'
                        title='New File'
                        class='hfinder-toolbar-control'
                        id='hfinder-new-file' />
            </td>
        </tr>
    </tbody>
```

```
            </table>
        </div>
        <div id='hfinder-tree'>
            <ul class='file-tree'>
                <li>
                    <div class='file-tree-directory file-tree-root'
                        id='tree-dir-1'>
                        <span>Hard drive</span>
                    </div>
                    <ul id='directory-1' class='file-tree-dir-list'>
                        <li>
                            <div class='file-tree-directory'
                                id='tree-dir-3645'>
                                <span>account</span>
                            </div>
                            <img src='images/right.png'
                                class='file-has-children'
                                id='tree-3645'
                                alt='+'
                                title='Click to expand.' />
                        </li>
                        <li>
                            <div class='file-tree-directory'
                                id='tree-dir-31'>
                                <span>cp</span>
                            </div>
                        </li>
                        <li>
                            <div class='file-tree-directory'
                                id='tree-dir-3785'>
                                <span>daemon</span>
                            </div>
                        </li>
                        <li>
                            <div class='file-tree-directory'
                                id='tree-dir-3677'>
                                <span>file</span>
                            </div>
                        </li>
                        <li>
                            <div class='file-tree-directory'
                                id='tree-dir-26'>
                                <span>forum</span>
                            </div>
                        </li>
                        <li>
                            <div class='file-tree-directory'
                                id='tree-dir-3651'>
                                <span>home</span>
                            </div>
                            <img src='images/right.png'
                                class='file-has-children'
                                id='tree-3651'
                                alt='+'
                                title='Click to expand.' />
```

```
        </li>
        <li>
            <div class='file-tree-directory'
                id='tree-dir-3681'>
                <span>images</span>
            </div>
            <img src='images/right.png'
                class='file-has-children'
                id='tree-3681'
                alt='+'
                title='Click to expand.' />
        </li>
        <li>
            <div class='file-tree-directory'
                id='tree-dir-3690'>
                <span>js</span>
            </div>
            <img src='images/right.png'
                class='file-has-children'
                id='tree-3690'
                alt='+'
                title='Click to expand.' />
        </li>
        <li>
            <div class='file-tree-directory'
                id='tree-dir-30'>
                <span>listener</span>
            </div>
        </li>
        <li>
            <div class='file-tree-directory'
                id='tree-dir-29'>
                <span>logout</span>
            </div>
        </li>
        <li>
            <div class='file-tree-directory'
                id='tree-dir-3682'>
                <span>media</span>
            </div>
            <img src='images/right.png'
                class='file-has-children'
                id='tree-3682'
                alt='+'
                title='Click to expand.' />
        </li>
        <li>
            <div class='file-tree-directory'
                id='tree-dir-3667'>
                <span>network</span>
            </div>
        </li>
        <li>
            <div class='file-tree-directory'
                id='tree-dir-3735'>
                <span>products</span>
```

```
                                </div>
                                <img src='images/right.png'
                                    class='file-has-children'
                                    id='tree-3735'
                                    alt='+'
                                    title='Click to expand.' />
                        </li>
                        <li>
                            <div class='file-tree-directory'
                                id='tree-dir-28'>
                                <span>register</span>
                            </div>
                        </li>
                        <li>
                            <div class='file-tree-directory'
                                id='tree-dir-3784'>
                                <span>search</span>
                            </div>
                        </li>
                    </ul>
                </li>
            </ul>
        </div>
        <div id='hfinder-files'>
            <div id='dir-3645'
                class='file-details file-directory'
                title='account'>
                <div>
                    <div class='file-icon-wrapper'>
                        <img src='images/32x32/MacOSXAqua_012.png'
                            class='file-details-img'
                            alt='folder' />
                    </div>
                    <div class='file-details-caption file-caption-wrapper'>
                        <span class='file-name'>account</span>
                    </div>
                </div>
            </div>
            <div id='dir-31'
                class='file-details file-directory'
                title='cp'>
                <div>
                    <div class='file-icon-wrapper'>
                        <img src='images/32x32/MacOSXAqua_012.png'
                            class='file-details-img'
                            alt='folder' />
                    </div>
                    <div class='file-details-caption file-caption-wrapper'>
                        <span class='file-name'>cp</span>
                    </div>
                </div>
            </div>
            <div id='dir-3785'
                class='file-details file-directory'
                title='daemons'>
                <div>
```

```
            <div class='file-icon-wrapper'>
                <img src='images/32x32/MacOSXAqua_012.png'
                    class='file-details-img'
                    alt='folder' />
            </div>
            <div class='file-details-caption file-caption-wrapper'>
                <span class='file-name'>daemons</span>
            </div>
        </div>
    </div>
</div>
<div id='dir-3677'
    class='file-details file-directory'
    title='file'>
    <div>
        <div class='file-icon-wrapper'>
            <img src='images/32x32/MacOSXAqua_012.png'
                class='file-details-img'
                alt='folder' />
        </div>
        <div class='file-details-caption file-caption-wrapper'>
            <span class='file-name'>file</span>
        </div>
    </div>
</div>
<div id='dir-26'
    class='file-details file-directory'
    title='forum'>
    <div>
        <div class='file-icon-wrapper'>
            <img src='images/32x32/MacOSXAqua_012.png'
                class='file-details-img'
                alt='folder' />
        </div>
        <div class='file-details-caption file-caption-wrapper'>
            <span class='file-name'>forum</span>
        </div>
    </div>
</div>
<div id='dir-3651'
    class='file-details file-directory'
    title='home'>
    <div>
        <div class='file-icon-wrapper'>
            <img src='images/32x32/MacOSXAqua_012.png'
                class='file-details-img'
                alt='folder' />
        </div>
        <div class='file-details-caption file-caption-wrapper'>
            <span class='file-name'>home</span>
        </div>
    </div>
</div>
<div id='dir-3681'
    class='file-details file-directory'
    title='images'>
```

```
        <div>
            <div class='file-icon-wrapper'>
                <img src='images/32x32/MacOSXAqua_012.png'
                    class='file-details-img'
                    alt='folder' />
            </div>
            <div class='file-details-caption file-caption-wrapper'>
                <span class='file-name'>images</span>
            </div>
        </div>
    </div>
    <div id='dir-3690'
        class='file-details file-directory'
        title='js'>
        <div>
            <div class='file-icon-wrapper'>
                <img src='images/32x32/MacOSXAqua_012.png'
                    class='file-details-img'
                    alt='folder' />
            </div>
            <div class='file-details-caption file-caption-wrapper'>
                <span class='file-name'>js</span>
            </div>
        </div>
    </div>
    <div id='dir-30'
        class='file-details file-directory'
        title='listener'>
        <div>
            <div class='file-icon-wrapper'>
                <img src='images/32x32/MacOSXAqua_012.png'
                    class='file-details-img'
                    alt='folder' />
            </div>
            <div class='file-details-caption file-caption-wrapper'>
                <span class='file-name'>listener</span>
            </div>
        </div>
    </div>
    <div id='dir-29'
        class='file-details file-directory'
        title='logout'>
        <div>
            <div class='file-icon-wrapper'>
                <img src='images/32x32/MacOSXAqua_012.png'
                    class='file-details-img'
                    alt='folder' />
            </div>
            <div class='file-details-caption file-caption-wrapper'>
                <span class='file-name'>logout</span>
            </div>
        </div>
    </div>
    <div id='dir-3682'
        class='file-details file-directory'
```

```
                    title='media'>
            <div>
                <div class='file-icon-wrapper'>
                    <img src='images/32x32/MacOSXAqua_012.png'
                        class='file-details-img'
                        alt='folder' />
                </div>
                <div class='file-details-caption file-caption-wrapper'>
                    <span class='file-name'>media</span>
                </div>
            </div>
        </div>
        <div id='dir-3667'
            class='file-details file-directory'
            title='network'>
            <div>
                <div class='file-icon-wrapper'>
                    <img src='images/32x32/MacOSXAqua_012.png'
                        class='file-details-img'
                        alt='folder' />
                </div>
                <div class='file-details-caption file-caption-wrapper'>
                    <span class='file-name'>network</span>
                </div>
            </div>
        </div>
        <div id='dir-3735'
            class='file-details file-directory'
            title='products'>
            <div>
                <div class='file-icon-wrapper'>
                    <img src='images/32x32/MacOSXAqua_012.png'
                        class='file-details-img'
                        alt='folder' />
                </div>
                <div class='file-details-caption file-caption-wrapper'>
                    <span class='file-name'>products</span>
                </div>
            </div>
        </div>
        <div id='dir-28'
            class='file-details file-directory'
            title='register'>
            <div>
                <div class='file-icon-wrapper'>
                    <img src='images/32x32/MacOSXAqua_012.png'
                        class='file-details-img'
                        alt='folder' />
                </div>
                <div class='file-details-caption file-caption-wrapper'>
                    <span class='file-name'>register</span>
                </div>
            </div>
        </div>
        <div id='dir-3784'
```

```
                    class='file-details file-directory'
                    title='search'>
                <div>
                    <div class='file-icon-wrapper'>
                        <img src='images/32x32/MacOSXAqua_012.png'
                            class='file-details-img'
                            alt='search' />
                    </div>
                    <div class='file-details-caption file-caption-wrapper'>
                        <span class='file-name'>search</span>
                    </div>
                </div>
            </div>
            <div id='reg-112'
                    class='file-details file-registry-doc'
                    title='File Not Found'>
                <div>
                    <div class='file-icon-wrapper'>
                        <img src='images/32x32/21.png'
                            title='text/html'
                            alt='text/html'
                            class='file-details-img' />
                    </div>
                    <div class='file-details-caption file-caption-wrapper'>
                        <span class='file-name' id='freg-112'>404.html</span>
                        <h4>File Not Found</h4>
                        <p class='file-details-text'>
                            This is a custom 404 error document.
                        </p>
                    </div>
                </div>
            </div>
            <div id='reg-1'
                    class='file-details file-registry-doc'
                    title='Welcome'>
                <div>
                    <div class='file-icon-wrapper'>
                        <img src='images/32x32/21.png'
                            alt='text/html'
                            title='text/html'
                            class='file-details-img' />
                    </div>
                    <div class='file-details-caption file-caption-wrapper'>
                        <span class='file-name' id='freg-1'>index.html</span>
                        <h4>Welcome</h4>
                        <p class='file-details-text'>
                            This is the default page for the website.
                        </p>
                    </div>
                </div>
            </div>
        </div>
<div id='hfinder-contextmenu'>
    <ul>
        <li id='context-open' class='sep'>
```

```
                    <span style='font-weight: bold;'>Open</span>
            </li>
            <li id='context-control-panel'>
                <span>Control Panel</span>
            </li>
            <li id='context-title-description' class='sep'>
                <span>Modify Title and Description</span>
            </li>
            <li id='context-delete'>
                <span>Delete</span>
            </li>
            <li id='context-rename' class='sep'>
                <span>Rename</span>
            </li>
            <li id='context-properties'>
                <span>Properties</span>
            </li>
            <li id='context-permissions'>
                <span>Permissions</span>
            </li>
        </ul>
    </div>
    <div id='file-upload'>
        <div class='file-titlebar'>Upload a File</div>
        <form method='post'
            id='hfinder-upload-form'
            enctype='multipart/form-data'
            action='javascript:void(0);'
            target='hfinder-file'>
            <input type='hidden' name='dir' value='' id='hfinder-dir' />
            <table style='width: 100%;'>
                <colgroup>
                    <col style='width: 25%;'>
                    <col style='width: 75%;'>
                </colgroup>
                <tbody style='text-align: left;'>
                    <tr>
                        <td>
                            <label for='hfinder-meta-title'>
                                Title:
                            </label>
                        </td>
                        <td>
                            <input type='text'
                                style='width: 98%;'
                                name='meta_title'
                                id='hfinder-meta-title' />
                        </td>
                    </tr>
                    <tr>
                        <td style='vertical-align: top;'>
                            <label for='hfinder-meta-description'>
                                File Description:
                            </label>
                        </td>
```

```
                            <td>
                                <textarea rows='4'
                                          cols='15'
                                          style='width: 98%;'
                                          name='meta_description'
                                          id='hfinder-meta-description'></textarea>
                            </td>
                        </tr>
                        <tr>
                            <td>
                                <label for='hfinder-upload'>
                                    Select a file:
                                </label>
                            </td>
                            <td>
                                <input type='file'
                                       name='content'
                                       id='hfinder-upload' />
                            </td>
                        </tr>
                        <tr>
                            <td style='text-align: right;' colspan='2'>
                                <input type='submit'
                                       title='Upload File'
                                       value='Upload'
                                       id='hfinder-file-upload' />
                                <input type='submit'
                                       value='Cancel'
                                       id='hfinder-file-cancel' />
                            </td>
                        </tr>
                    </tbody>
                </table>
            </form>
        </div>
        <iframe id='hfinder-file' name='hfinder-file' src=''></iframe>
        <div id='file-modify-attributes'>
            <div class='file-titlebar'>Modify Title and Description</div>
            <form method='post' action='javascript:void(0);'>
                <input type='hidden' name='dir' value='' id='hfinder-dir' />
                <table style='width: 100%;'>
                    <colgroup>
                        <col style='width: 25%;'>
                        <col style='width: 75%;'>
                    </colgroup>
                    <tbody style='text-align: left;'>
                        <tr>
                            <td>
                                <label for='file-modify-meta-title'>
                                    Title:
                                </label>
                            </td>
                            <td>
                                <input type='text'
                                       style='width: 98%;'
```

```
                                    name='meta_title'
                                    id='file-modify-meta-title'
                                    disabled='disabled' />
                        </td>
                    </tr>
                    <tr>
                        <td style='vertical-align: top;'>
                            <label for='file-modify-meta-description'>
                                File Description:
                            </label>
                        </td>
                        <td>
                            <textarea rows='4'
                                      cols='15'
                                      style='width: 98%;'
                                      name='meta_description'
                                      id='file-modify-meta-description'
                                      disabled='disabled'></textarea>
                        </td>
                    </tr>
                    <tr>
                        <td style='text-align: right;' colspan='2'>
                            <input type='hidden'
                                   id='file-modify-id'
                                   name='file_modify_id'
                                   value='' />
                            <input type='submit'
                                   id='file-modify-save'
                                   title='Save'
                                   value='Save'
                                   disabled='disabled' />
                            <input type='submit'
                                   id='file-modify-cancel'
                                   value='Cancel'
                                   disabled='disabled' />
                        </td>
                    </tr>
                </tbody>
            </table>
        </form>
    </div>
  </body>
</html>
```

2. Save the markup as hFinder.html.

3. Enter the following style sheet, which includes other style sheets that are separated by the portion of the application being styled. The styles contained in this style sheet set up basic layout and position the various columns and modules that house controls:

```
@import 'menus.css';
@import 'views.css';
@import 'tree.css';
@import 'popup.css';

body,
```

```css
html {
    width: 100%;
    height: 100%;
    min-width: 500px;
    min-height: 300px;
}
body {
    padding: 0;
    margin: 0;
    background: url('../images/brushed_metal.png');
    -moz-user-select: none;
}
div#hfinder-toolbar {
    position: absolute;
    top: 0;
    left: 0;
    right: 0;
    margin: 28px 10px 0 10px;
}
div#hfinder-tree {
    position: absolute;
    top: 0;
    bottom: 0;
    left: 0;
    margin: 73px 0 10px 10px;
    width: 190px;
    background: white;
    overflow: auto;
    border: 1px solid rgb(128, 128, 128);
    z-index: 1;
}
div#hfinder-files {
    margin: 73px 10px 10px 210px;
    position: absolute;
    top: 0;
    bottom: 0;
    left: 0;
    right: 0;
    border: 1px solid rgb(128, 128, 128);
    background: white url('../images/stripes.png');
    z-index: 1;
    overflow: auto;
}
```

4. Save as `hFinder.css`.

5. Enter the following style sheet, which styles the various menus:

```css
ul#hfinder-menu {
    list-style: none;
    margin: 0;
    padding: 2px;
    font: 12px sans-serif;
    height: 19px;
}
ul#hfinder-menu li.hfinder-menu-item {
```

```
        float: left;
        padding: 3px;
        margin: 0 3px;
        position: relative;
}
ul#hfinder-menu li.hfinder-menu-item:hover {
        background: rgb(128, 128, 128);
        color: white;
}
ul#hfinder-menu li.hfinder-menu-item:hover > ul {
        visibility: visible;
}
div#hfinder-contextmenu {
        /*visibility: hidden;*/
        position: absolute;
        z-index: 4;
        right: 25px;
        bottom: 25px;
}
li#context-title-description {
        display: none;
}
div#hfinder-contextmenu ul,
ul#hfinder-menu ul {
        font: 12px sans-serif;
        color: black;
        background: white url('../images/stripes.png');
        width: 16em;
        list-style: none;
        margin: 0;
        padding: 2px;
        border: 1px solid rgb(128, 128, 128);
        opacity: 0.9;
}
ul#hfinder-menu ul {
        position: absolute;
        visibility: hidden;
        top: 18px;
        left: 0;
        z-index: 2;
}
li.sep {
        border-bottom: 1px solid rgb(200, 200, 200);
        margin-bottom: 2px;
}
div#hfinder-contextmenu ul > li,
ul#hfinder-menu ul > li {
        padding: 3px 5px;
}
div#hfinder-contextmenu ul > li > span,
ul#hfinder-menu ul > li > span,
div#directory-view ul > li > span {
        padding: 0 0 0 15px;
}
div#hfinder-contextmenu ul > li:hover,
```

```
ul#hfinder-menu ul > li:hover {
    background: #369;
    color: white;
}
```

6. Save as menus.css.

7. Enter the following style sheet, which styles the directory tree:

```
ul.file-tree,
ul.file-tree ul {
    list-style: none;
    font: 12px sans-serif;
    white-space: nowrap;
    margin: 5px 0 0 0;
    padding: 0 0 0 15px;
}
ul.file-tree li {
    padding: 4px 0;
    position: relative;
}
ul.file-tree-dir-list li:hover > div > span {
    background: #369;
    color: white;
}
div.file-tree-directory.file-tree-root {
    background: url('../images/hard_drive.png') no-repeat left center;
    height: 32px;
    padding: 0 0 4px 34px;
    border: 1px solid white;
    border-bottom: 2px solid rgb(200, 200, 200);
}
div.file-tree-directory.file-tree-root span {
    display: block;
    margin-top: 10px;
}
ul.file-tree div {
    margin: -5px 0 0 -10px;
    background: url('../images/folder.png') no-repeat left center;
    padding-left: 20px;
}
img.file-has-children {
    position: absolute;
    top: -2px;
    left: -25px;
}
```

8. Save the preceding style sheet as tree.css.

9. The next style sheet styles the various methods of viewing directory contents:

```
div.file-thumbnail,
div.file-icon,
div.file-tile,
div.file-list,
div.file-details.file-directory {
```

```
        float: left;
        position: relative;
        overflow: hidden;
        font: 13px sans-serif;
        margin: 3px;
        padding: 4px;
        cursor: pointer;
}
div.file-thumbnail img {
        padding: 35px;
        border: 1px solid rgb(232, 232, 232);
}
div.file-thumbnail div.file-image-thumb-wrapper {
        width:  118px;
        height: 118px;
        border: 1px solid rgb(232, 232, 232);
        padding-top: 4px;
}
div.file-thumbnail img.file-image-thumb {
        padding: 0;
        border: none;
}
div.file-list {
        width: 250px;
        height: 20px;
}
div.file-details {
        margin: 3px;
        padding: 4px;
        font: 12px sans-serif;
        cursor: pointer;
}
div.file-thumbnail {
        width: 120px;
        height: 155px;
}
div.file-thumbnail > div {
        text-align: center;
}
div.file-thumbnail span.file-name {
        position: absolute;
        bottom: 10px;
        left: 0;
        width: 120px;
        text-align: center;
}
div.file-icon {
        width: 100px;
        height: 60px;
        text-align: center;
}
div.file-details.file-directory,
div.file-tile {
        width: 200px;
        height: 40px;
}
```

```
div.file-details.file-registry-doc {
    clear: both;
    float: none;
}
div.file-tile > div > div.file-caption-wrapper,
div.file-details.file-directory > div > div.file-caption-wrapper,
div.file-list > div > div.file-caption-wrapper {
    position: absolute;
    top: 10px;
    left: 42px;
}
div.file-list > div > div.file-caption-wrapper {
    top: 3px;
    left: 25px;
}
div.file-details.file-registry-doc > div > div.file-caption-wrapper > span {
    float: right;
}
div.file-details.file-registry-doc h4 {
    margin: 0 0 0 40px;
    border-bottom: 1px dotted black;
}
div.file-details.file-registry-doc p {
    margin: 3px 0 0 40px;
}
div.file-details div.file-icon-wrapper,
div.file-tile div.file-icon-wrapper,
div.file-list div.file-icon-wrapper {
    float: left;
}
div.file-highlight-on,
div.file-details.file-highlight-on {
    background: url('images/stripes_darker.png');
    padding: 4px;
}
div.file-highlight-off,
div.file-details.file-highlight-off {
    background: transparent;
    padding: 4px;
    border: none;
}
```

10. Save the preceding style sheet as `views.css`.

11. The next style sheet contains styles for the pure-CSS popup windows:

```
div.file-titlebar {
    padding: 2px 5px;
    font-weight: bold;
    border-bottom: 1px solid rgb(128, 128, 128);
    margin-bottom: 3px;
    font: 16px sans-serif;
}
div#file-upload,
div#file-modify-attributes {
    position: absolute;
```

```
        width: 600px;
        height: 250px;
        top: 50%;
        left: 50%;
        margin: -125px 0 0 -300px;
        border: 3px solid rgb(128, 128, 128);
        background: url('../images/brushed_metal.png');
        z-index: 5;
        display: none;
}
div#file-upload {
        display: block;
}
div#file-upload label,
div#file-modify-attributes label {
        font: 12px sans-serif;
        display: block;
        text-align: right;
}
input#hfinder-location-input {
        font: 12px sans-serif;
        padding: 2px;
}
input#hfinder-location-input:focus,
input#hfinder-location-input:hover {
        outline: 2px solid rgb(203, 245, 254);
        -moz-outline: 2px solid rgb(203, 245, 254);
}
input[type='text'],
textarea {
        border: 1px solid rgb(128, 128, 128);
}
iframe#hfinder-file {
        z-index: 20;
        position: absolute;
        bottom: 0;
        left: 0;
        width: 100%;
        height: 100px;
        background: white;
        display: none;
}
```

12.   Save the last style sheet as popup.css.

The code results in the output shown in Figure 9-2.

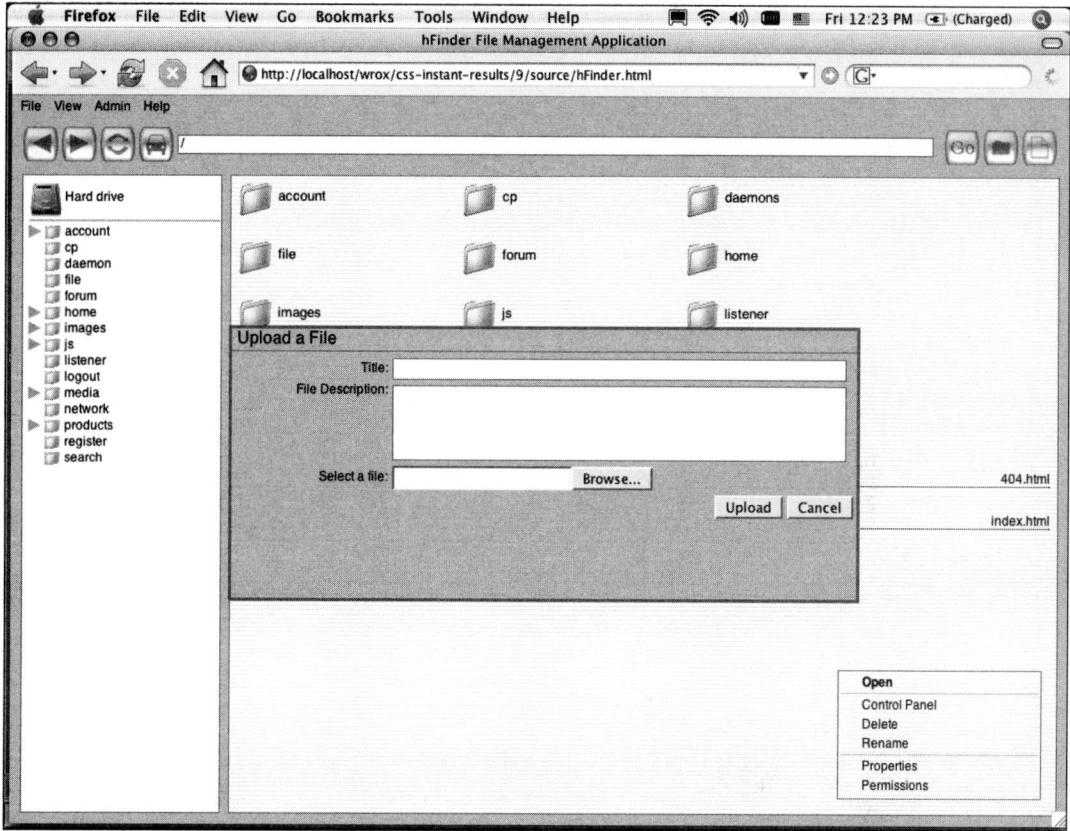

Figure 9-2

Figure 9-2 shows the file upload popup windows and the context menu, which are controls that should be hidden until needed. Figure 9-3 shows the hFinder application with the file upload popup and the context menu hidden.

Now that you've seen the result of styling of the hFinder application, the following section provides an explanation of how the styling comes together with the markup to achieve the results shown in Figures 9-2 and 9-3.

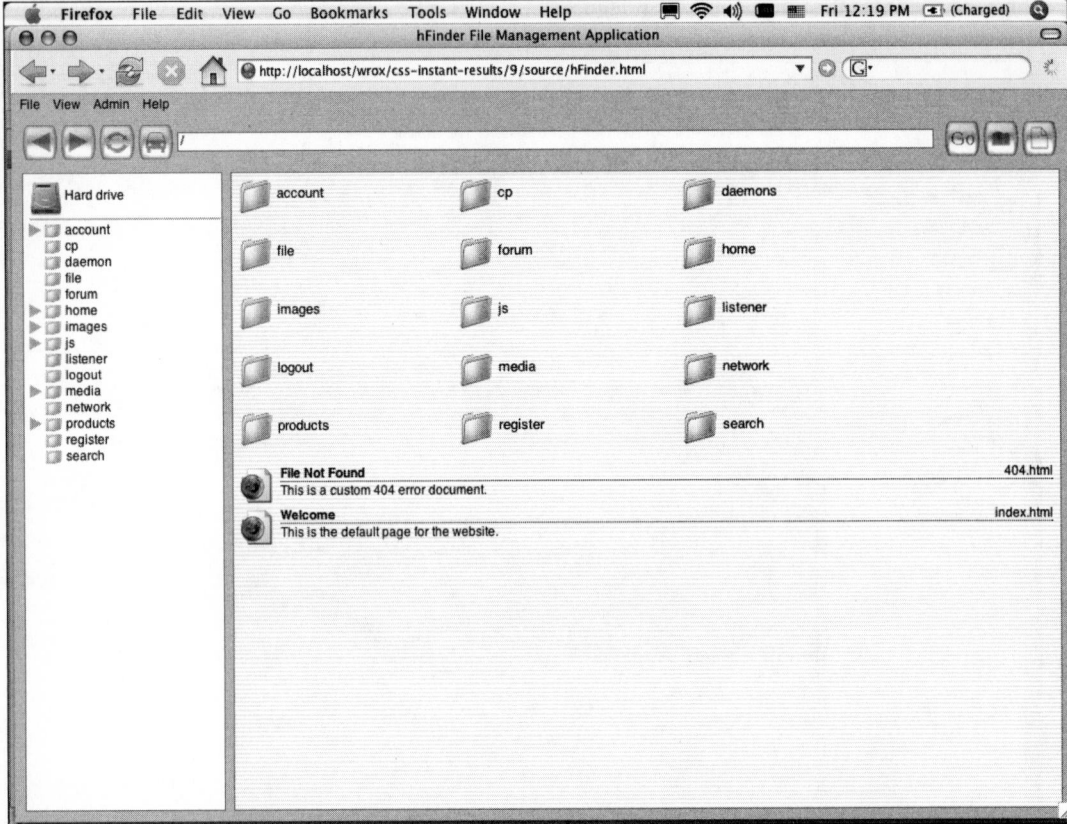

Figure 9-3

Laying the Foundation

The file hFinder.css deals specifically with the following markup, which has been edited to show what is relevant:

```
    </head>
      <body>
        <div id='hfinder-toolbar'>
        </div>
        <div id='hfinder-tree'>
        </div>
        <div id='hfinder-files'>
        </div>
      </body>
    </html>
```

With the style sheet hFinder.css applied, the results shown in Figure 9-4 are achieved.

Figure 9-4

The first styles that appear in hFinder.css are @import rules for the other modules of the application:

```
@import 'menus.css';
@import 'views.css';
@import 'tree.css';
@import 'popup.css';
```

Everything in hFinder.css deals with the foundation of the look and feel of the hFinder application. The first rule makes the <html> and <body> elements take up 100% of the width and height of the browser's viewport. This is needed to give the tree view and directory contents a size relative to the viewport — when the window is resized these portions of the document also resize. Minimum constraints are also provided to prevent the design from being broken when the browser window is really small:

```
body,
html {
    width: 100%;
    height: 100%;
    min-width: 500px;
    min-height: 300px;
}
```

The next rule removes default `margin` and `padding`, then specifies the brushed metal background for the whole browser window. The last declaration in this rule is proprietary to Gecko browsers. `moz-user-select: none;` prevents the user from selecting text in the window. In effect it makes the selection invisible. Selection is prevented in the application because when mouse click events are attached via JavaScript, the browser may make a selection when the user did not intend to make one. However, because the application developer (or savvy users) may want to make a selection, a selection is still made, but it is invisible. Right-clicking over an invisible selection (or command + A, or CTRL + A) in Mozilla Firefox still provides the option "view selection source," which is useful when portions of the document are changing via JavaScript, as would be the case if this application were fully functional. An identical effect can be achieved using the proprietary `::-moz-selection` pseudo-element, by including the declarations `background: transparent;` and `color: inherit;`. In Internet Explorer, preventing a user selection requires JavaScript. In fact, for the sake of a complete, cross-browser method, the following is the JavaScript Internet Explorer requires to provide the same feature:

```
<script type='text/javascript'>
    document.onselectstart = function() {return false;};
</script>
```

Whereas in Mozilla and Gecko-derivatives an invisible selection is still made using the CSS method, in IE no selection at all is possible using this method:

```
body {
    padding: 0;
    margin: 0;
    background: url('../images/brushed_metal.png');
    -moz-user-select: none;
}
```

The next rule positions the toolbar, which is a `<div>` with an "hfinder-toolbar" id name. The `<div>` is positioned absolutely to the top of the viewport, then stretched along the width of the viewport using the `left: 0;` and `right: 0;` declarations. Then 28 pixels of margin are applied to the top of the `<div>` to prevent it from overlapping with the menus that appear above it, and 10 pixels of margin are applied to the left and right sides of the `<div>` to provide some space between the toolbar and the left and right sides of the viewport:

```
div#hfinder-toolbar {
    position: absolute;
    top: 0;
    left: 0;
    right: 0;
    margin: 28px 10px 0 10px;
}
```

The next rule positions the `<div>` that contains the tree representation of the directory structure (it has an hfinder-tree id name). The `<div>` is first positioned absolutely, then stretched along the height of the viewport, using the `top: 0;` and `bottom: 0;` declarations, then positioned to the left of the viewport using the `left: 0;` declaration. Margin is then applied to the top of the `<div>`—73 pixels, which prevents the tree view from overlapping with the menus and the toolbar, and 10 pixels of margin are provided to the bottom and left sides of the `<div>` to space it from the left and bottom sides of the viewport. Following the offset properties, the `<div>` is given an explicit width of 190 pixels and a white background. The `overflow: auto;` declaration is provided to prevent the contents of the `<div>` from flowing over the boundaries of the `<div>`; if there is more content than available space, scrollbars will appear accordingly. Next a 1-pixel solid gray border is applied, and finally a z-index sets the position of the <div> along the z-axis as first in the stacking order:

```
div#hfinder-tree {
    position: absolute;
    top: 0;
    bottom: 0;
    left: 0;
    margin: 73px 0 10px 10px;
    width: 190px;
    background: white;
    overflow: auto;
    border: 1px solid rgb(128, 128, 128);
    z-index: 1;
}
```

The next rule to be introduced positions the <div> displaying contents of a directory. Like the previous rule, this <div> is positioned absolutely, but it is stretched in all four directions using the four offset properties. Then margin is used to fine-tune the position of the <div> — again, 73 pixels of space prevent the directory contents from overlapping the menu and the toolbar at the top of the application window. Ten pixels of margin are provided on the bottom and right sides of the <div> to space it from the bottom and right sides of the viewport. Finally, 210 pixels of space are provided for the left margin to prevent the <div> from overlapping with the tree view. A 1-pixel solid gray border is provided and a pinstripe background is specified, which repeats both on the x- and y-axis. A z-index provides the placement of the <div> on the z-axis, and lastly, the overflow: auto; declaration causes scrollbars to appear if the contents of the <div> are greater than its dimensions:

```
div#hfinder-files {
    position: absolute;
    top: 0;
    bottom: 0;
    left: 0;
    right: 0;
    margin: 73px 10px 10px 210px;
    border: 1px solid rgb(128, 128, 128);
    background: white url('../images/stripes.png');
    z-index: 1;
    overflow: auto;
}
```

With a foundation in place, the next section describes how the menus were styled.

Applying Menus

This section describes how the styles in menus.css were applied to the following snippet of markup. The first snippet is the menus at the top of the document — the File, View, Admin, and Help menus:

```
<body>
    <ul id='hfinder-menu'>
        <li class='hfinder-menu-item' id='hfinder-menu-file'>
            File
            <ul>
```

```
                    <li id='hfinder-menu-new-file'>
                        <span>New File</span>
                    </li>
                    <li id='hfinder-menu-new-directory' class='sep'>
                        <span>New Directory</span>
                    </li>
                    <li id='hfinder-menu-close'>
                        <span>Close</span></li>
                </ul>
            </li>
            <li class='hfinder-menu-item' id='hfinder-menu-view'>
                View
                <ul>
                    <li id='hfinder-menu-thumbnail'>
                        <span>Thumbnails</span>
                    </li>
                    <li id='hfinder-menu-tile'>
                        <span>Tiles</span>
                    </li>
                    <li id='hfinder-menu-icon'>
                        <span>Icons</span>
                    </li>
                    <li id='hfinder-menu-details'>
                        <span>Details</span>
                    </li>
                    <li id='hfinder-menu-list' class='sep'>
                        <span>List</span>
                    </li>
                    <li id='hfinder-menu-default-view'>
                        <span>Set Current as Default</span>
                    </li>
                </ul>
            </li>
            <li class='hfinder-menu-item' id='hfinder-menu-admin'>
                Admin
                <ul>
                    <li id='hfinder-menu-home-directory' class='sep'>
                        <span>Home Directory</span>
                    </li>
                    <li id='hfinder-menu-manage-users'>
                        <span>Manage Users</span>
                    </li>
                    <li id='hfinder-menu-manage-groups'>
                        <span>Manage Groups</span>
                    </li>
                </ul>
            </li>
            <li class='hfinder-menu-item' id='hfinder-menu-help'>
                Help
                <ul>
                    <li id='hfinder-help-contents'>
                        <span>Help Contents</span>
                    </li>
                </ul>
            </li>
        </ul>
```

```
<div id='hfinder-toolbar'>
</div>
<div id='hfinder-tree'>
</div>
<div id='hfinder-files'>
</div>
```

The next snippet is the context menu, which in the JavaScript-enabled application appears when the user right-clicks over a file or directory. The styles applied to the context menu are nearly identical to those applied to the menus at the top of the document:

```
<div id='hfinder-contextmenu'>
    <ul>
        <li id='context-open' class='sep'>
            <span style='font-weight: bold;'>Open</span>
        </li>
        <li id='context-control-panel'>
            <span>Control Panel</span>
        </li>
        <li id='context-title-description' class='sep'>
            <span>Modify Title and Description</span>
        </li>
        <li id='context-delete'>
            <span>Delete</span>
        </li>
        <li id='context-rename' class='sep'>
            <span>Rename</span>
        </li>
        <li id='context-properties'>
            <span>Properties</span>
        </li>
        <li id='context-permissions'>
            <span>Permissions</span>
        </li>
    </ul>
</div>
</body>
```

The first style sheet rule is applied to the `<ul>` element with an `hfinder-menu` id name. This `<ul>` element houses the menus at the top of the document — File, View, Admin, and Help. The first declaration, `list-style-type: none;`, removes the bullets for each list item, which appear by default in unordered lists. The margin is set to zero to remove default margin, and padding is set to 2 pixels, just to add a bit of space. A 12-pixel, generic sans-serif font is then specified, and a fixed height of 19 pixels is specified, which is done because the `<li>` items contained by the `<ul>` element are floated, and because they are floated they are not considered when the height of the `<ul>` element is calculated:

```
ul#hfinder-menu {
    list-style: none;
    margin: 0;
    padding: 2px;
    font: 12px sans-serif;
    height: 19px;
}
```

The next rule sets the position of each top-level list item, that is, the ones with the text "File," "View," "Admin," and "Help." Each <li> element is floated to the left, then 3 pixels of padding are applied to provide some spacing between the border of each list item and the text contained within. Next, 3 pixels of margin are applied to the left and right sides of each <li> element, which places 3 pixels of space between the left border of the <ul> element containing all four <li> elements, and 6 pixels of space between each individual <li> element:

```
ul#hfinder-menu li.hfinder-menu-item {
    float: left;
    padding: 3px;
    margin: 0 3px;
    position: relative;
}
```

The next rule sets the background and text color of the top-level <li> elements when a user's mouse hovers over. Each top-level <li> element has been given an hfinder-menu-item class name. The background is set to gray, and the text color is set to white:

```
ul#hfinder-menu li.hfinder-menu-item:hover {
    background: rgb(128, 128, 128);
    color: white;
}
```

The next bit is included only for styling purposes. It makes the menus visible when a user's mouse hovers over one of those <li> elements. In the completed JavaScript-enabled hFinder application, the display of the menus is handled by JavaScript. The reason for this is two-fold: first, a bug in Firefox 1.0 (fixed in Firefox 1.5) causes the menus to disappear prematurely when the user's mouse cursor reaches a portion of the menu that is layered above another element that has the overflow property set to a value other than visible. This bug is defeated when JavaScript-enabled menus are used instead of pure-CSS menus. The second reason is in the hFinder application, which is designed to feel like a desktop application. The menus are "click to open," as they would be if this were a true desktop application. You saw in Chapter 4 that such menus are possible via manipulation of the :target pseudo-class. This application is ideal for the use of the :target pseudo-class. Because the body of the document can never scroll, it isn't subject to the caveats of that approach (the document will scroll or jump slightly if the body has enough content to scroll). For this application, I simply decided that because most other aspects of the application require JavaScript already, making the menus JavaScript-driven is more appropriate:

```
ul#hfinder-menu li.hfinder-menu-item:hover > ul {
    visibility: visible;
}
```

The next rule applies to the <div> element with an hfinder-contextmenu class name. This menu is dynamically displayed and positioned with a JavaScript oncontextmenu event handler in the final application. As is the case with desktop applications, it enables a web designer to offer a custom menu of options when the user clicks the right mouse button. In this case the options pertain to the directories and files being displayed. The first declaration is commented out. visibility: hidden; hides the context menu; this declaration is disabled so that you can see the effects of styling the context menu. Next the menu is positioned absolutely, relative to the browser's viewport. Finally the right and bottom offset properties are specified, although these values are present purely for testing purposes because the JavaScript dynamically sets the correct position of the context menu based on what item the user has right-clicked:

```
div#hfinder-contextmenu {
    /*visibility: hidden;*/
    position: absolute;
    z-index: 4;
    right: 25px;
    bottom: 25px;
}
```

The next rule refers to an option in the context menu that is not displayed by default. In a context menu it is very likely that some options that are available for directories are not available for files. That is the case here. The Modify Title and Description option is available only for files. The JavaScript in the final application determines whether this option is available when the user right-clicks over an item:

```
li#context-title-description {
    display: none;
}
```

Next is a rule shared by both the context menu and the drop-down menus at the top of the document. Some styles are redundant because they were already specified for the top-level `<ul>` element, which was the first rule of the menus.css style sheet. They are specified again here because the context menu did not share those declarations. Again a 12-pixel, sans-serif font is specified, and the horizontal pin-stripe background. A width of 16 em is specified, which sets the width to 12 × 16 (12-pixel font size times 16 em), or 192 pixels. This width lets the horizontal size of a menu increase or decrease with the user's font preferences. Next, `list-style: none;` is again used to remove the default list bullets. Setting the margin to zero removes the default margin, and 2 pixels of padding space each list item within from the edges of the `<ul>` element. A 1-pixel solid gray border is specified, and finally the menus are made semi-transparent in browsers that support the CSS 3 `opacity` property by setting the `opacity` property to 0.9, where 1 is fully opaque, and 0 is fully transparent:

```
div#hfinder-contextmenu ul,
ul#hfinder-menu ul {
    font: 12px sans-serif;
    color: black;
    background: white url('../images/stripes.png');
    width: 16em;
    list-style: none;
    margin: 0;
    padding: 2px;
    border: 1px solid rgb(128, 128, 128);
    opacity: 0.9;
}
```

In the subsequent rule the `<ul>` elements that make up the drop-down menus at the top are positioned absolutely, relative to their parent `<li>` elements. A `z-index` of two is set to specify the stacking order along the invisible z-axis. The `visibility` property is set to hidden so that the menus are not visible by default. Each `<ul>` element is positioned offset from the top border of their parent `<li>` element by 18 pixels, and then zero pixels from the left border of their parent `<li>` elements:

```
ul#hfinder-menu ul {
    position: absolute;
    z-index: 2;
    visibility: hidden;
```

```
        top: 18px;
        left: 0;
    }
```

In the next rule all `<li>` elements with a `sep` class name are given a solid gray bottom border, in addition to 2 pixels of margin, which spaces that border from the `<li>` element that follows. This style is used on certain `<li>` elements to provide visual separation between items in a menu and lets menu options be organized in a meaningful way:

```
li.sep {
    border-bottom: 1px solid rgb(200, 200, 200);
    margin-bottom: 2px;
}
```

The next rule fine-tunes the position of the text of each menu option. The `padding` property is set, which applies 3 pixels between the top and bottom border of each `<li>` element, and the `<span>` element within (which contains the menu option text) and 5 pixels of padding are applied between the left and right borders of each `<li>` element, and the left and right borders of the `<span>` element contained therein:

```
div#hfinder-contextmenu ul > li,
ul#hfinder-menu ul > li {
    padding: 3px 5px;
}
```

Each `<span>` element also receives some padding: 15 pixels are applied to the left side of each `<span>` element. This is intended to make room for icons, should any be added in the future:

```
div#hfinder-contextmenu ul > li > span,
ul#hfinder-menu ul > li > span,
div#directory-view ul > li > span {
    padding: 0 0 0 15px;
}
```

In the last rule appearing in `menus.css`, each `<li>` element is made a shade of blue and given white text when the user's mouse hovers over a `<li>` element:

```
div#hfinder-contextmenu ul > li:hover,
ul#hfinder-menu ul > li:hover {
    background: #369;
    color: white;
}
```

With menus in place, the next section describes how the markup and styles appearing in the stylesheet `tree.css` come together to make a directory tree.

Styling a Directory Tree

Like the menus, and most structures of organization sequence, the directory tree is marked up using unordered lists, although for this application an ordered list may make just as much sense, if not more, even though the list markers are never seen. The styles in `tree.css` apply to the following snippet of markup from `hFinder.html`:

```
<ul class='file-tree'>
    <li>
        <div class='file-tree-directory file-tree-root'
            id='tree-dir-1'>
            <span>Hard drive</span>
        </div>
        <ul id='directory-1' class='file-tree-dir-list'>
            <li>
                <div class='file-tree-directory'
                    id='tree-dir-3645'>
                    <span>account</span>
                </div>
                <img src='images/right.png'
                    class='file-has-children'
                    id='tree-3645'
                    alt='+'
                    title='Click to expand.' />
            </li>
            <li>
                <div class='file-tree-directory'
                    id='tree-dir-31'>
                    <span>cp</span>
                </div>
            </li>
            <li>
                <div class='file-tree-directory'
                    id='tree-dir-3785'>
                    <span>daemon</span>
                </div>
            </li>
            <li>
                <div class='file-tree-directory'
                    id='tree-dir-3677'>
                    <span>file</span>
                </div>
            </li>
            <li>
                <div class='file-tree-directory'
                    id='tree-dir-26'>
                    <span>forum</span>
                </div>
            </li>
            <li>
                <div class='file-tree-directory'
                    id='tree-dir-3651'>
                    <span>home</span>
                </div>
                <img src='images/right.png'
                    class='file-has-children'
                    id='tree-3651'
                    alt='+'
                    title='Click to expand.' />
            </li>
            <li>
                <div class='file-tree-directory'
                    id='tree-dir-3681'>
```

```
                    <span>images</span>
                </div>
                <img src='images/right.png'
                    class='file-has-children'
                    id='tree-3681'
                    alt='+'
                    title='Click to expand.' />
        </li>
        <li>
            <div class='file-tree-directory'
                id='tree-dir-3690'>
                <span>js</span>
            </div>
            <img src='images/right.png'
                class='file-has-children'
                id='tree-3690'
                alt='+'
                title='Click to expand.' />
        </li>
        <li>
            <div class='file-tree-directory'
                id='tree-dir-30'>
                <span>listener</span>
            </div>
        </li>
        <li>
            <div class='file-tree-directory'
                id='tree-dir-29'>
                <span>logout</span>
            </div>
        </li>
        <li>
            <div class='file-tree-directory'
                id='tree-dir-3682'>
                <span>media</span>
            </div>
            <img src='images/right.png'
                class='file-has-children'
                id='tree-3682'
                alt='+'
                title='Click to expand.' />
        </li>
        <li>
            <div class='file-tree-directory'
                id='tree-dir-3667'>
                <span>network</span>
            </div>
        </li>
        <li>
            <div class='file-tree-directory'
                id='tree-dir-3735'>
                <span>products</span>
            </div>
            <img src='images/right.png'
                class='file-has-children'
                id='tree-3735'
```

```
                                    alt='+'
                                    title='Click to expand.' />
                    </li>
                    <li>
                        <div class='file-tree-directory'
                             id='tree-dir-28'>
                            <span>register</span>
                        </div>
                    </li>
                    <li>
                        <div class='file-tree-directory'
                             id='tree-dir-3784'>
                            <span>search</span>
                        </div>
                    </li>
                </ul>
            </li>
        </ul>
```

The tree structure in the preceding snippet of markup shows only top-level directories. Directories that contain other directories inside of them have gray arrows to the left. Those directories are not displayed by default. In fact, subdirectories don't even appear in the markup because the subdirectories are retrieved via JavaScript in the final application.

The first rule appearing in `tree.css` styles the `<ul>` elements contained in the tree, both top-level and nested. After the default bullets are removed with `list-style: none;`, the font is set to 12 pixels, generic sans-serif. The `white-space: nowrap;` declaration prevents the text contained in descendant nodes from being wrapped (because the `white-space` property is inherited). Finally, as is always the case with `<ul>` elements, the default margin is removed with `margin: 0;`. The last rule is very important, because it creates the "tree" effect. The left padding is set to 15 pixels, which causes each nested `<ul>` element to appear 15 pixels further to the right than its closest ancestral `<ul>` element:

```css
ul.file-tree,
ul.file-tree ul {
    list-style: none;
    font: 12px sans-serif;
    white-space: nowrap;
    margin: 5px 0 0;
    padding: 0 0 0 15px;
}
```

In the subsequent rule, 4 pixels of padding are set on each `<li>` element to place space between their top and bottom borders and the top and bottom borders of the content contained within them. This rule also sets zero padding for the left and right sides. The `position: relative;` declaration is supplied to cause each gray arrow image to be positioned relative to its parent `<li>` element:

```css
ul.file-tree li {
    padding: 4px 0;
    position: relative;
}
```

277

The next rule causes `<span>` elements containing the name of a directory to have a blue background and white text when users hover their mouse cursor over its grandparent `<li>` element:

```
ul.file-tree-dir-list li:hover > div > span {
    background: #369;
    color: white;
}
```

The next rule pertains to the `<div>` element that has both a `file-tree-directory` class name and a `file-tree-root` class name. This `<div>` element has the Mac hard drive icon as its background, which is set non-repeating, left and center in the `<div>`. The `<div>` is given an explicit height of 32 pixels, which was determined from the height of the `hard_drive.png` image. Padding is used to control the position of the child `<span>` element contained within this `<div>`. Four pixels of padding add space between the bottom of the `<li>` element and the bottom of the `<span>` element. To prevent the `<span>` from overlapping with the `hard_drive.png` background image, 34 pixels of left padding is specified. The `border: 1px solid white;` declaration is included to override margin collapsing. Without the `border: 1px solid white;` declaration, the 10 pixels of top margin specified on the child `<span>` element would collapse with the 5 pixels of top margin specified on the `<ul>` element. This could also have been remedied by specifying a larger margin on the child `<span>` element. Which you use is a matter of personal preference. The last declaration of the rule sets the bottom border to 2 pixels, solid gray (overriding the bottom, 1-pixel, solid white border specified by the previous declaration). Then in the next rule for the child `<span>` element, the `<span>` element is made a block-level element with the `display: block;` declaration:

```
div.file-tree-directory.file-tree-root {
    background: url('../images/hard_drive.png') no-repeat left center;
    height: 32px;
    padding: 0 0 4px 34px;
    border: 1px solid white;
    border-bottom: 2px solid rgb(200, 200, 200);
}
div.file-tree-directory.file-tree-root span {
    display: block;
    margin-top: 10px;
}
```

The next rule styles `<div>` elements appearing in each `<li>` element. The first declaration fine-tunes the position of the `<div>` elements, the top margin is set to –5 pixels, which causes each `<div>` to move 5 pixels up, and –10 pixels causes each `<div>` to move 10 pixels to the left. Then each `<div>` receives a folder background that is positioned left and center, non-repeating. Finally, 20 pixels of left padding prevent the contents of the `<span>` element from overlapping the `folder.png` background image:

```
ul.file-tree div {
    margin: -5px 0 0 -10px;
    background: url('../images/folder.png') no-repeat left center;
    padding-left: 20px;
}
```

The last rule appearing in `tree.css` positions the gray arrow image that indicates whether a directory has children directories. Each image is given an appropriate `file-has-children` class name. Each image is positioned absolutely: `top: -2px;` indicates the image is positioned 2 pixels above the parent

`<li>` element's top border, and `left: -25px;` indicates that each image is positioned 25 pixels outside of the parent `<li>` element's left border:

```
img.file-has-children {
    position: absolute;
    top: -2px;
    left: -25px;
}
```

Now that you have seen how to style a directory tree, the next section describes how the stylistic aspects of multiple methods of viewing a directory's contents are achieved.

Styling Multiple Methods of Viewing a Directory's Contents

This section describes how to style multiple methods of viewing a directory's contents. So far you've seen the result of the Details view. In all the style sheets, `views.css` provides for five methods of viewing a directory's contents: Thumbnails, Tiles, Icons, Details, and List (which, of course, correspond to the options in the Views drop-down menu). The styles in `views.css` apply to the following snippet of markup from `hFinder.html`:

```
<div id='dir-3645'
    class='file-details file-directory'
    title='account'>
    <div>
        <div class='file-icon-wrapper'>
            <img src='images/32x32/MacOSXAqua_012.png'
                class='file-details-img'
                alt='folder' />
        </div>
        <div class='file-details-caption file-caption-wrapper'>
            <span class='file-name'>account</span>
        </div>
    </div>
</div>
<div id='dir-31'
    class='file-details file-directory'
    title='cp'>
    <div>
        <div class='file-icon-wrapper'>
            <img src='images/32x32/MacOSXAqua_012.png'
                class='file-details-img'
                alt='folder' />
        </div>
        <div class='file-details-caption file-caption-wrapper'>
            <span class='file-name'>cp</span>
        </div>
    </div>
</div>
<div id='dir-3785'
    class='file-details file-directory'
    title='daemons'>
    <div>
```

```
                    <div class='file-icon-wrapper'>
                        <img src='images/32x32/MacOSXAqua_012.png'
                            class='file-details-img'
                            alt='folder' />
                    </div>
                    <div class='file-details-caption file-caption-wrapper'>
                        <span class='file-name'>daemons</span>
                    </div>
                </div>
            </div>
            <div id='dir-3677'
                class='file-details file-directory'
                title='file'>
                <div>
                    <div class='file-icon-wrapper'>
                        <img src='images/32x32/MacOSXAqua_012.png'
                            class='file-details-img'
                            alt='folder' />
                    </div>
                    <div class='file-details-caption file-caption-wrapper'>
                        <span class='file-name'>file</span>
                    </div>
                </div>
            </div>
            <div id='dir-26'
                class='file-details file-directory'
                title='forum'>
                <div>
                    <div class='file-icon-wrapper'>
                        <img src='images/32x32/MacOSXAqua_012.png'
                            class='file-details-img'
                            alt='folder' />
                    </div>
                    <div class='file-details-caption file-caption-wrapper'>
                        <span class='file-name'>forum</span>
                    </div>
                </div>
            </div>
            <div id='dir-3651'
                class='file-details file-directory'
                title='home'>
                <div>
                    <div class='file-icon-wrapper'>
                        <img src='images/32x32/MacOSXAqua_012.png'
                            class='file-details-img'
                            alt='folder' />
                    </div>
                    <div class='file-details-caption file-caption-wrapper'>
                        <span class='file-name'>home</span>
                    </div>
                </div>
            </div>
            <div id='dir-3681'
                class='file-details file-directory'
                title='images'>
```

```
            <div>
                <div class='file-icon-wrapper'>
                    <img src='images/32x32/MacOSXAqua_012.png'
                        class='file-details-img'
                        alt='folder' />
                </div>
                <div class='file-details-caption file-caption-wrapper'>
                    <span class='file-name'>images</span>
                </div>
            </div>
        </div>
        <div id='dir-3690'
            class='file-details file-directory'
            title='js'>
            <div>
                <div class='file-icon-wrapper'>
                    <img src='images/32x32/MacOSXAqua_012.png'
                        class='file-details-img'
                        alt='folder' />
                </div>
                <div class='file-details-caption file-caption-wrapper'>
                    <span class='file-name'>js</span>
                </div>
            </div>
        </div>
        <div id='dir-30'
            class='file-details file-directory'
            title='listener'>
            <div>
                <div class='file-icon-wrapper'>
                    <img src='images/32x32/MacOSXAqua_012.png'
                        class='file-details-img'
                        alt='folder' />
                </div>
                <div class='file-details-caption file-caption-wrapper'>
                    <span class='file-name'>listener</span>
                </div>
            </div>
        </div>
        <div id='dir-29'
            class='file-details file-directory'
            title='logout'>
            <div>
                <div class='file-icon-wrapper'>
                    <img src='images/32x32/MacOSXAqua_012.png'
                        class='file-details-img'
                        alt='folder' />
                </div>
                <div class='file-details-caption file-caption-wrapper'>
                    <span class='file-name'>logout</span>
                </div>
            </div>
        </div>
        <div id='dir-3682'
            class='file-details file-directory'
```

```
           title='media'>
       <div>
           <div class='file-icon-wrapper'>
               <img src='images/32x32/MacOSXAqua_012.png'
                   class='file-details-img'
                   alt='folder' />
           </div>
           <div class='file-details-caption file-caption-wrapper'>
               <span class='file-name'>media</span>
           </div>
       </div>
   </div>
   <div id='dir-3667'
       class='file-details file-directory'
       title='network'>
       <div>
           <div class='file-icon-wrapper'>
               <img src='images/32x32/MacOSXAqua_012.png'
                   class='file-details-img'
                   alt='folder' />
           </div>
           <div class='file-details-caption file-caption-wrapper'>
               <span class='file-name'>network</span>
           </div>
       </div>
   </div>
   <div id='dir-3735'
       class='file-details file-directory'
       title='products'>
       <div>
           <div class='file-icon-wrapper'>
               <img src='images/32x32/MacOSXAqua_012.png'
                   class='file-details-img'
                   alt='folder' />
           </div>
           <div class='file-details-caption file-caption-wrapper'>
               <span class='file-name'>products</span>
           </div>
       </div>
   </div>
   <div id='dir-28'
       class='file-details file-directory'
       title='register'>
       <div>
           <div class='file-icon-wrapper'>
               <img src='images/32x32/MacOSXAqua_012.png'
                   class='file-details-img'
                   alt='folder' />
           </div>
           <div class='file-details-caption file-caption-wrapper'>
               <span class='file-name'>register</span>
           </div>
       </div>
   </div>
```

```
<div id='dir-3784'
    class='file-details file-directory'
    title='search'>
    <div>
        <div class='file-icon-wrapper'>
            <img src='images/32x32/MacOSXAqua_012.png'
                class='file-details-img'
                alt='search' />
        </div>
        <div class='file-details-caption file-caption-wrapper'>
            <span class='file-name'>search</span>
        </div>
    </div>
</div>
<div id='reg-112'
    class='file-details file-registry-doc'
    title='File Not Found'>
    <div>
        <div class='file-icon-wrapper'>
            <img src='images/32x32/21.png'
                title='text/html'
                alt='text/html'
                class='file-details-img' />
        </div>
        <div class='file-details-caption file-caption-wrapper'>
            <span class='file-name' id='freg-112'>404.html</span>
            <h4>File Not Found</h4>
            <p class='file-details-text'>
                This is a custom 404 error document.
            </p>
        </div>
    </div>
</div>
<div id='reg-1'
    class='file-details file-registry-doc'
    title='Welcome'>
    <div>
        <div class='file-icon-wrapper'>
            <img src='images/32x32/21.png'
                alt='text/html'
                title='text/html'
                class='file-details-img' />
        </div>
        <div class='file-details-caption file-caption-wrapper'>
            <span class='file-name' id='freg-1'>index.html</span>
            <h4>Welcome</h4>
            <p class='file-details-text'>
                This is the default page for the website.
            </p>
        </div>
    </div>
</div>
```

In the preceding snippet of markup, each directory file is contained in a `<div>` element. The id names of each `<div>` element are used to uniquely identify which file is which, allowing the JavaScript in the final application to react appropriately to user events associated with the application's controls for operations like accessing, renaming, deleting, or otherwise modifying something about a file. Then various class names are inserted to provide hooks for styling the various methods of viewing a directory's contents. The purpose of each class name becomes obvious when you see why each rule in `views.css` is included.

To observe Thumbnails view, modify the markup to the following, making the changes highlighted and removing the `<h4>` and `<p>` elements for the title and description of the file:

```
<div id='reg-1'
    class='file-thumbnail file-registry-doc'
    title='Welcome'>
    <div>
        <div class='file-icon-wrapper'>
            <img src='images/48x48/21.png'
                alt='text/html'
                title='text/html'
                class='file-thumbnail-img' />
        </div>
        <div class='file-thumbnail-caption file-caption-wrapper'>
            <span class='file-name' id='freg-1'>index.html</span>
        </div>
    </div>
</div>
```

Repeat the process for each file: replace the word `details` in each class name with `thumbnail`, and change the icon image path from `images/32x32` to `images/48x48`. The result should look something like that shown in Figure 9-5. A file is provided on the source CD-ROM, with all of the work already done (in the Chapter 9 folder, named `hFinder.thumbnails.html`).

For Tiles and Icons views, only the class names change:

```
<div id='reg-1'
    class='file-tile file-registry-doc'
    title='Welcome'>
    <div>
        <div class='file-icon-wrapper'>
            <img src='images/32x32/21.png'
                alt='text/html'
                title='text/html'
                class='file-tile-img' />
        </div>
        <div class='file-tile-caption file-caption-wrapper'>
            <span class='file-name' id='freg-1'>index.html</span>
        </div>
    </div>
</div>
```

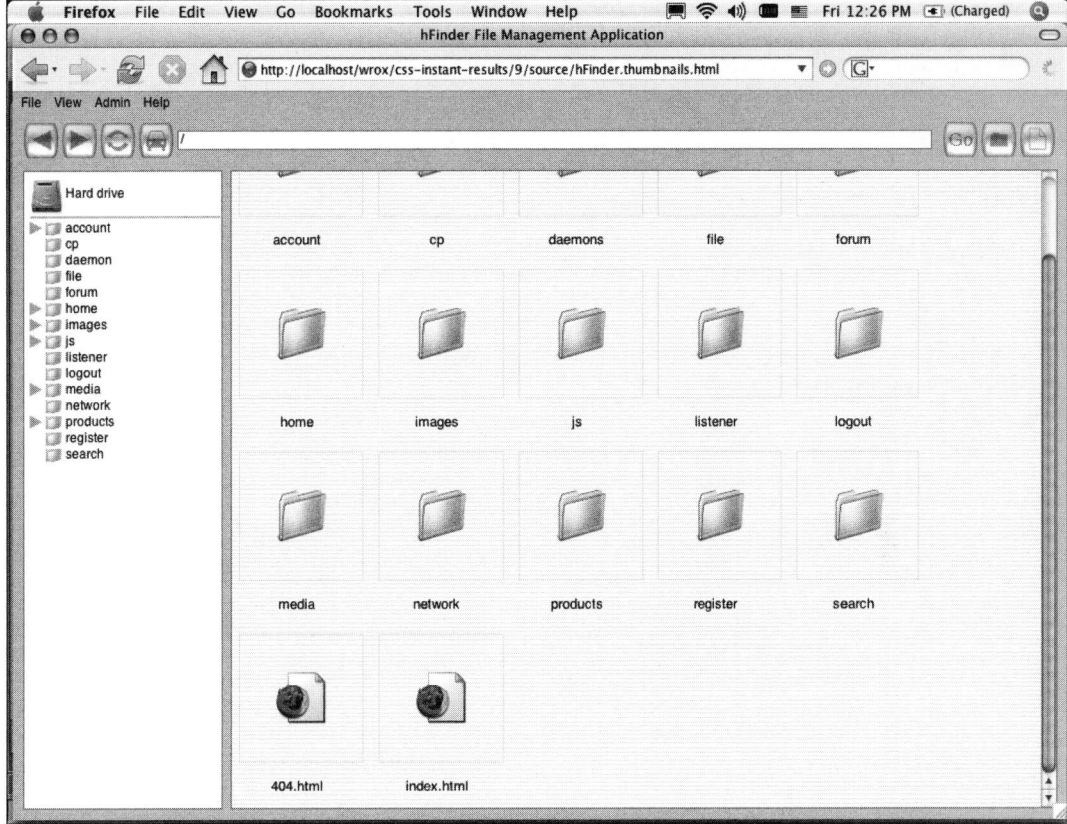

Figure 9-5

As was the case for Thumbnails view, for the Tiles and Icons views, the word details in the class name is changed to tile or icon, depending on the view desired. These files appear on the source CD-ROM as hFinder.tiles.html and hFinder.icons.html.

For Tiles view, the modifications result in something like that appearing in Figure 9-6.

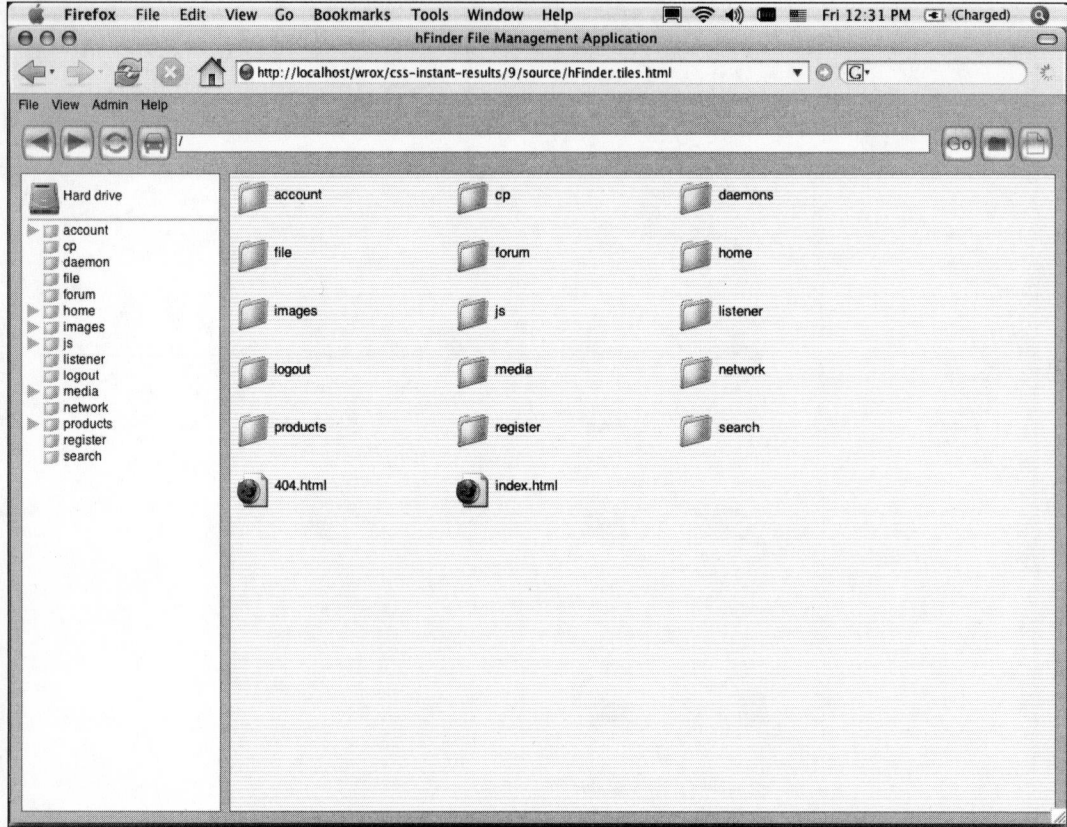

Figure 9-6

For Icons view, the modifications result in something like that appearing in Figure 9-7.

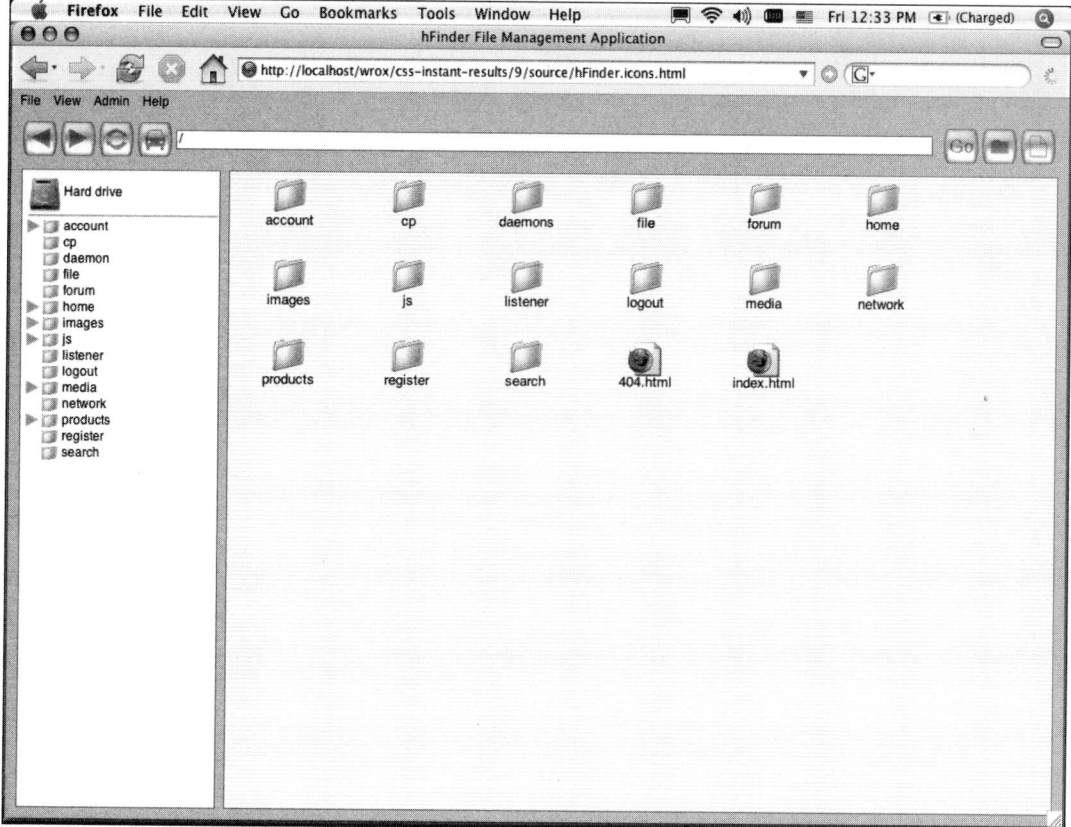

Figure 9-7

For List view the process is the same as for previous views: replace the word details in each class name with list, and as was the case for Thumbnails view, the image path is also altered. This time instead of 32x32, 16x16 is used to invoke icons with dimensions of 16 by 16 pixels. This file appears on the source CD-ROM as hFinder.list.html:

```
<div id='reg-1'
      class='file-list file-registry-doc'
      title='Welcome'>
    <div>
        <div class='file-icon-wrapper'>
            <img src='images/32x32/21.png'
                 alt='text/html'
                 title='text/html'
                 class='file-list-img' />
        </div>
        <div class='file-list-caption file-caption-wrapper'>
            <span class='file-name' id='freg-1'>index.html</span>
        </div>
    </div>
</div>
```

The results of the modifications for List view are shown in the output in Figure 9-8.

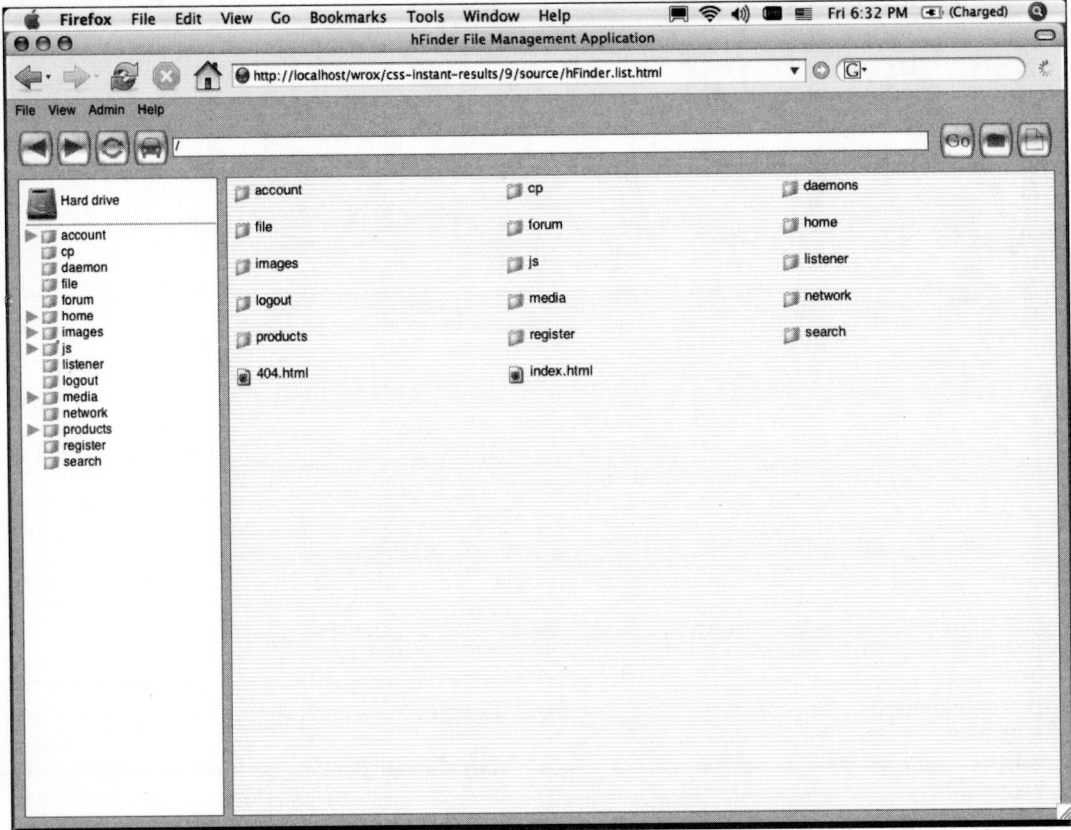

Figure 9-8

More views can be invented, though to be of any use they would likely require entirely different structural markup to be used. You see an example of applying custom views later in this chapter.

The first rule in `views.css` sets some rules that are common between Thumbnails, Icons, Tiles, List, and Details views. First the appropriate `<div>` element is selected. All files and directories in all views are selected, except for files in the Details view. For the Details view only the directories receive the declarations contained within the rules. The distinction allows the directories to appear side-by-side and the files to include title and description information. The `float: left;` declaration enables each file to appear side-by-side, when available space allows it. The `position: relative;` declaration accommodates descendant elements that are positioned absolutely (in some views). Hiding overflow is also important, because some file names can be very long, and when file names are long they will go outside of the fixed-width boundaries of the `<div>` element and overlap with other files. `overflow: hidden;` hides that overflow and prevents file names from overlapping other files. Then the font size is specified as 13 pixels, generic sans-serif. Three pixels of margin are specified, which appear between each file and directory. Four pixels of padding spaces the contents of each `<div>` from the borders of the `<div>` itself. Finally, the `cursor: pointer;` makes the user's cursor icon change to give the user the impression that each file is a clickable entity:

```
div.file-thumbnail,
div.file-icon,
div.file-tile,
div.file-list,
div.file-details.file-directory {
    float: left;
    position: relative;
    overflow: hidden;
    font: 13px sans-serif;
    margin: 3px;
    padding: 4px;
    cursor: pointer;
}
```

In Thumbnails view, two types of images can be expected. The first are those with default application icons that are consistently 48 by 48 pixels. The following rule sets a padding of 35 pixels, and a 1-pixel solid gray border for this type of icon:

```
div.file-thumbnail img {
    padding: 35px;
    border: 1px solid rgb(232, 232, 232);
}
```

The second type of thumbnail icons are a preview of a file (an image, PDF, and so on) with dimensions that are not predictable. For the sake of consistency, the styles should appear similar for these images and their fixed-width, 48-x-48-pixel counterparts. The declarations of the following rule achieve this by setting the dimensions of a `<div>` with a class name of `file-image-thumb-wrapper` to 118 by 118 pixels, including 1-pixel solid gray border, and 4 pixels of top padding to space the preview thumbnail image from the top border of the `file-image-thumb-wrapper` `<div>` element:

```
div.file-thumbnail div.file-image-thumb-wrapper {
    width:   118px;
    height:  118px;
    border: 1px solid rgb(232, 232, 232);
    padding-top: 4px;
}
```

Because those preview thumbnail images have varying dimensions, and you previously set the border and padding for all descendant images of the "file-thumbnail" `<div>`, that border and padding must be removed for preview-type thumbnail images. This is done in the following rule:

```
div.file-thumbnail img.file-image-thumb {
    padding: 0;
    border: none;
}
```

The next rule sets the height for List view. List view isn't exactly a perfect copy of the List view of Windows XP. You can see the difference in Figure 9-9, which shows a screenshot of Windows XP's List view.

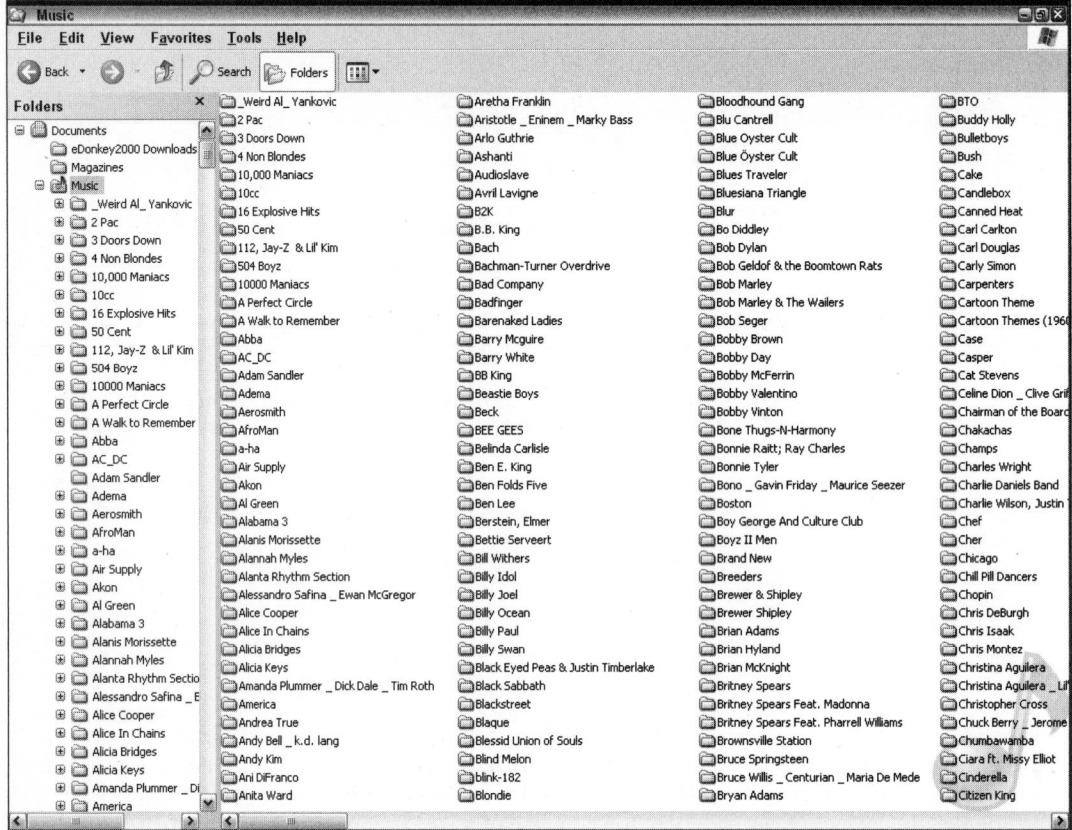

Figure 9-9

In Figure 9-9 you see that files are arranged in invisible columns, and the files appear one after another till the first column is filled. This feat is not possible with the current capabilities of CSS—such a feature requires that it be possible to set columns (as in the CSS 3 columns specification), set column heights, and cause the overflow to only scroll horizontally, rather than vertically (the CSS 3 `overflow-x` and `overflow-y` properties). The CSS 3 columns specification is implemented in an experimental status in Mozilla Firefox 1.5 (the CSS 3 column properties are prefixed with the proprietary "-moz-" prefix). Mozilla Firefox and Internet Explorer support the previously Microsoft-proprietary `overflow-x` and `overflow-y` properties. Because interoperability isn't possible, I didn't attempt to implement a "true" List view. Although List view is beyond the current capabilities of CSS, this type of view is possible using JavaScript to replicate the functionality of Windows XP's List view, but is beyond the scope of this book. For now List view is simply a smaller implementation of Tiles view:

```
div.file-list {
    width: 250px;
    height: 20px;
}
```

The next rule sets some styles that are specific to the Details view, a view that doesn't attempt to mirror Details view in Windows XP. Later in this chapter you learn how to implement a Details view that is true to the Windows XP Details view. In the first rule in `views.css`, you set styles for all views and directories appearing in Details view. The following rule sets styles that are common to both files and directories in Details view (so there is some redundancy between this rule and the first rule). As was the case in the first rule of `views.css`, 3 pixels of margin are specified to separate each file from the other, and 4 pixels of padding to separate the outer border of each `<div>` element from the contents within. Then 12-pixel sans-serif font is specified, followed by `cursor: pointer;` to give the user the impression that each file is a link:

```
div.file-details {
    margin: 3px;
    padding: 4px;
    font: 12px sans-serif;
    cursor: pointer;
}
```

In the next rule for Thumbnails view, each `<div>` is given an explicit width and height that corresponds to the width and height of the contents of each `<div>`:

```
div.file-thumbnail {
    width: 120px;
    height: 155px;
}
```

The thumbnails in Thumbnails view are centered:

```
div.file-thumbnail > div {
    text-align: center;
}
```

The `<span>` containing the file name in Thumbnails view is positioned absolutely, relative to the `file-thumbnail` `<div>`. Each file name is positioned 10 pixels from the bottom, and no pixels from the left, and given a width equal to that of the `file-thumbnail` `<div>`. Finally the text is centered within the `<span>`:

```
div.file-thumbnail span.file-name {
    position: absolute;
    bottom: 10px;
    left: 0;
    width: 120px;
    text-align: center;
}
```

In Icons view the `<div>` is given an explicit width of 100 pixels and an explicit height of 50 pixels, followed by centering the text of the file name:

```
div.file-icon {
    width: 100px;
    height: 60px;
    text-align: center;
}
```

For directories in Details view and both directories and files in Tiles view, each `<div>` is given an explicit width of 200 pixels and a height of 40 pixels:

```
div.file-details.file-directory,
div.file-tile {
    width: 200px;
    height: 40px;
}
```

In Details view, files are not floated beside each other, so `clear: both;` is specified to stop floating from affecting files, and `float: none;` prevents files from being floated at all:

```
div.file-details.file-registry-doc {
    clear: both;
    float: none;
}
```

The next rule positions the file names in Tiles and List views, and directories in Details view. The `<div>` with a `file-caption-wrapper` class name is positioned absolutely, 10 pixels from the top (to vertically center the text), and 42 pixels from the left (to accommodate the 32-x-32-pixel icon):

```
div.file-tile > div > div.file-caption-wrapper,
div.file-details.file-directory > div > div.file-caption-wrapper,
div.file-list > div > div.file-caption-wrapper {
    position: absolute;
    top: 10px;
    left: 42px;
}
```

The next rule overrides the top and left offset properties specified in the previous rule for List view. In List view, because the icons used are smaller (16 × 16 pixels), the `file-caption-wrapper` `<div>` is positioned 3 pixels from the top and 20 pixels from the left:

```
div.file-list > div > div.file-caption-wrapper {
    top: 3px;
    left: 25px;
}
```

In Details view, the file name appears on the right side of the title of the document. This is done with the `float: right;` declaration:

```
div.file-details.file-registry-doc > div > div.file-caption-wrapper > span {
    float: right;
}
```

In Details view the title of the document is contained in an `<h4>` element. The default margin of the `<h4>` element is removed from the top and bottom, and 40 pixels of margin are specified for the left margin to prevent the dotted, black border specified for the bottom of the `<h4>` element from being overlapped by the icon to the left of the `<h4>` element:

```
div.file-details.file-registry-doc h4 {
    margin: 0 0 0 40px;
    border-bottom: 1px dotted black;
}
```

In Details view, the description of the document is contained in a <p> element. Its default top margin is set to 3 pixels to provide some spacing between the text in the <p> element and the bottom border of the <h4> element that precedes it. Then as was the case for the <h4> element, 40 pixels of margin are specified to provide some space between the contents of the <p> element and the icon to the left of it:

```
div.file-details.file-registry-doc p {
    margin: 3px 0 0 40px;
}
```

In Details, Tiles, and List views, the application icon for each file or directory is floated to the left of the text with the float: left; declaration:

```
div.file-details div.file-icon-wrapper,
div.file-tile div.file-icon-wrapper,
div.file-list div.file-icon-wrapper {
    float: left;
}
```

The final two rules within views.css are classes that are dynamically specified via JavaScript. Because an element's class name can be changed via JavaScript, it is also a useful feature for separating scripting and styles. More specifically, it allows you to keep presentational aspects of an application out of JavaScript and in CSS where they belong. The first rule specifies a background image for files, which serves as a visual indication that a file is selected by users moving their mouse over a file or right-clicking over a file:

```
div.file-highlight-on,
div.file-details.file-highlight-on {
    background: url('images/stripes_darker.png');
    padding: 4px;
}
```

The last rule is an extra rule that specifies what should happen when a file is not selected:

```
div.file-highlight-off,
div.file-details.file-highlight-off {
    background: transparent;
    padding: 4px;
    border: none;
}
```

Having seen how different views are created, the next section describes how the CSS popup windows in the hFinder application are created.

CSS Popup Windows

Another feature of the hFinder application is CSS popup windows. Since the advent of popup blockers, it's increasingly desirable to avoid using separate windows for popups. In the hFinder application, however, popup blocking software isn't necessarily relevant, because CSS popup windows in the hFinder application are merely an aesthetic preference.

The styles within popup.css apply to the following snippet of markup. They are controls that allow a new file to be uploaded to the hFinder application, and a utility for editing the title and description of a file (which are visible using the default Details view):

```
<div id='file-upload'>
    <div class='file-titlebar'>Upload a File</div>
    <form method='post'
        id='hfinder-upload-form'
        enctype='multipart/form-data'
        action='javascript:void(0);'
        target='hfinder-file'>
      <input type='hidden' name='dir' value='' id='hfinder-dir' />
      <table style='width: 100%;'>
          <colgroup>
              <col style='width: 25%;'>
              <col style='width: 75%;'>
          </colgroup>
          <tbody style='text-align: left;'>
              <tr>
                  <td>
                      <label for='hfinder-meta-title'>
                          Title:
                      </label>
                  </td>
                  <td>
                      <input type='text'
                          style='width: 98%;'
                          name='meta_title'
                          id='hfinder-meta-title' />
                  </td>
              </tr>
              <tr>
                  <td style='vertical-align: top;'>
                      <label for='hfinder-meta-description'>
                          File Description:
                      </label>
                  </td>
                  <td>
                      <textarea rows='4'
                          cols='15'
                          style='width: 98%;'
                          name='meta_description'
                          id='hfinder-meta-description'></textarea>
                  </td>
              </tr>
              <tr>
                  <td>
                      <label for='hfinder-upload'>
                          Select a file:
                      </label>
                  </td>
                  <td>
                      <input type='file'
                          name='content'
                          id='hfinder-upload' />
                  </td>
              </tr>
              <tr>
                  <td style='text-align: right;' colspan='2'>
                      <input type='submit'
```

```
                                title='Upload File'
                                value='Upload'
                                id='hfinder-file-upload' />
                        <input type='submit'
                                value='Cancel'
                                id='hfinder-file-cancel' />
                    </td>
                </tr>
            </tbody>
        </table>
    </form>
</div>
<iframe id='hfinder-file' name='hfinder-file' src=''></iframe>
<div id='file-modify-attributes'>
    <div class='file-titlebar'>Modify Title and Description</div>
    <form method='post' action='javascript:void(0);'>
        <input type='hidden' name='dir' value='' id='hfinder-dir' />
        <table style='width: 100%;'>
            <colgroup>
                <col style='width: 25%;'>
                <col style='width: 75%;'>
            </colgroup>
            <tbody style='text-align: left;'>
                <tr>
                    <td>
                        <label for='file-modify-meta-title'>
                            Title:
                        </label>
                    </td>
                    <td>
                        <input type='text'
                                style='width: 98%;'
                                name='meta_title'
                                id='file-modify-meta-title'
                                disabled='disabled' />
                    </td>
                </tr>
                <tr>
                    <td style='vertical-align: top;'>
                        <label for='file-modify-meta-description'>
                            File Description:
                        </label>
                    </td>
                    <td>
                        <textarea rows='4'
                                cols='15'
                                style='width: 98%;'
                                name='meta_description'
                                id='file-modify-meta-description'
                                disabled='disabled'></textarea>
                    </td>
                </tr>
                <tr>
                    <td style='text-align: right;' colspan='2'>
                        <input type='hidden'
                                id='file-modify-id'
```

```
                                        name='file_modify_id'
                                        value='' />
                           <input type='submit'
                                  id='file-modify-save'
                                  title='Save'
                                  value='Save'
                                  disabled='disabled' />
                           <input type='submit'
                                  id='file-modify-cancel'
                                  value='Cancel'
                                  disabled='disabled' />
                       </td>
                   </tr>
               </tbody>
           </table>
       </form>
   </div>
```

The first rule appearing in popup.css applies style to the title of the popup window, which appears in the upper left-hand corner of the CSS popup. The first declaration applies some spacing between the borders of the <div> element with a file-titlebar class name and the text within it: 2 pixels on the top and bottom and 5 pixels on the left and right. Then the text in the <div> is made bold, and a 1-pixel, solid gray bottom border is applied. Three pixels of bottom margin apply spacing from the bottom of the title bar and the content that follows it. Finally, a 16-pixel, generic sans-serif font is applied:

```
div.file-titlebar {
    padding: 2px 5px;
    font-weight: bold;
    border-bottom: 1px solid rgb(128, 128, 128);
    margin-bottom: 3px;
    font: 16px sans-serif;
}
```

The next rule positions the popup layers into place. I used the id name of each <div> that is to be made a popup, though I could have just as easily created a "popup" class name, and applied styles via the class name instead.

The popup is positioned perfectly centered both horizontally and vertically using a simple technique. First the popup is given explicit width and height. The width and height can be percentage, pixel, or any type of measurement supported by CSS. There is just one catch — the width and height must be perfectly divisible by two to get the best results. For pixel measurement, the division must result in a round number, not a decimal, because browsers do not support partial pixel measurement. The setting of explicit measurement is one ingredient in the recipe for centering the layer vertically (although other techniques are available).

After setting an explicit width and height, the top and left offset properties are set to 50%. The layer is thus positioned from the top border of the element it is positioned relative to by 50% of that element's height. In this case it is positioned relative to the viewport. So 50% refers to 50% of the viewport's height. Likewise for the left offset property, it is positioned from the left border of the viewport, 50% of the viewport's width. The positioning of the element in itself doesn't center the element vertically or horizontally. To achieve centering, the margin must be tweaked. The top margin is set to a negative value that is equal to half of the value of the element's `height` property, and likewise the left margin is set to a value that is equal to half of the element's `width` property value. With this declaration in place, the layer is now centered both vertically and horizontally.

I chose to go with absolute positioning for this particular layer, because the contents of the document never create viewport scrollbars. For a document that might scroll, fixed positioning would be the best choice because with absolute positioning the layer will scroll with the document. Because these are intended to be popups — more specifically dialogs the user has called to perform a specific action — the popup dialog should remain the focus until the action is completed or the user clicks the Cancel button, at which point the JavaScript enabling the dynamic functionality would hide the dialog.

The next declaration in the rule sets a 3-pixel, solid gray border around the popup, followed by the "brushed metal" background common to Mac OS X applications. Then the z-index is set to position the layer along the invisible z-axis. Finally, the layers are hidden by default with the `display: none;` declaration, because these popups are only displayed when the user wants to perform the action the popup is designed for:

```
div#file-upload,
div#file-modify-attributes {
    position: absolute;
    width: 600px;
    height: 250px;
    top: 50%;
    left: 50%;
    margin: -125px 0 0 -300px;
    border: 3px solid rgb(128, 128, 128);
    background: url('../images/brushed_metal.png');
    z-index: 5;
    display: none;
}
```

For purposes of design and debugging, the next rule sets the display of the file upload dialog to block, to override `display: none;` as specified in the previous rule:

```
div#file-upload {
    display: block;
}
```

In the last rule, the `<label>` elements present in each dialog are styled with 12-pixel, generic sans-serif font. They are also set to block elements with the `display: block;` declaration because `<label>` elements are inline-level elements, by default. Finally the text is aligned to the right of each `<label>` element:

```
div#file-upload label,
div#file-modify-attributes label {
    font: 12px sans-serif;
    display: block;
    text-align: right;
}
```

The next rule refers to the location bar at the top of the hFinder application, nested among the navigation controls. The rules referring to this input are lumped in with those in `popup.css` that also refer to form controls. In the first declaration this input is given a 12-pixel, generic sans-serif font, and 2 pixels of padding to increase the space between the borders of the input and text within it:

```
input#hfinder-location-input {
    font: 12px sans-serif;
    padding: 2px;
}
```

In the next rule the location bar is given an outline when it receives focus, or when the user's mouse hovers over it. The first declaration is the standard CSS 2 `outline` property. The input is given a 2-pixel, solid blue outline. The second declaration is Mozilla-specific, and works for Gecko-derivative browsers prior to the Gecko build used in Mozilla Firefox 1.5. The `-moz-outline` property provides similar functionality to the CSS 2 `outline` property, but doesn't work according to the CSS 2 specification. `-moz-outline` places the outline within the element's borders instead of outside of it, as is specified by CSS 2. Outlines are used to provide emphasis and have no effect on the dimensions of an element, whereas borders are factored into an element's dimensions as part of the CSS box model:

```
input#hfinder-location-input:focus,
input#hfinder-location-input:hover {
    outline: 2px solid rgb(203, 245, 254);
    -moz-outline: 2px solid rgb(203, 245, 254);
}
```

In the next rule, the borders of `<input type='text' />` and `<textarea>` elements are given 1-pixel, solid gray borders to override the browser defaults:

```
input[type='text'],
textarea {
    border: 1px solid rgb(128, 128, 128);
}
```

In the last rule, you see a reference to an `<iframe>` element, which may seem out of place. For an application powered by JavaScript such as this, you may want the user to be able to upload a file without the page reloading. That's where the `<iframe>` comes in. The inline frame can be included in the document, hidden from view, and the upload form can be set to target it for the upload. The `<iframe>` element used here is an example of something with no presentational purpose that may be included in an application, but that requires styling nonetheless. I positioned the `<iframe>` element and gave it some dimensions for debugging purposes. While building the application I'll be able to toggle the display of the `<iframe>` on and off to see what is being output there.

```
iframe#hfinder-file {
    z-index: 20;
    position: absolute;
    bottom: 0;
    left: 0;
    width: 100%;
    height: 100px;
    background: white;
    display: none;
}
```

The next section revisits our neglected friend, Internet Explorer, and explains how to make hFinder work in IE 6.0.

Testing and Caveats

As you have done in previous chapters, in this section you take the final project of the last section as it stands completed and working in Mozilla Firefox and other standards-savvy browsers, and expand the project by testing it in Internet Explorer.

This section also explores the caveats with the design of the hFinder application, and how to get it to display correctly in IE 6.0. Figure 9-10 shows hFinder as it now appears in IE 6 with no fixes applied.

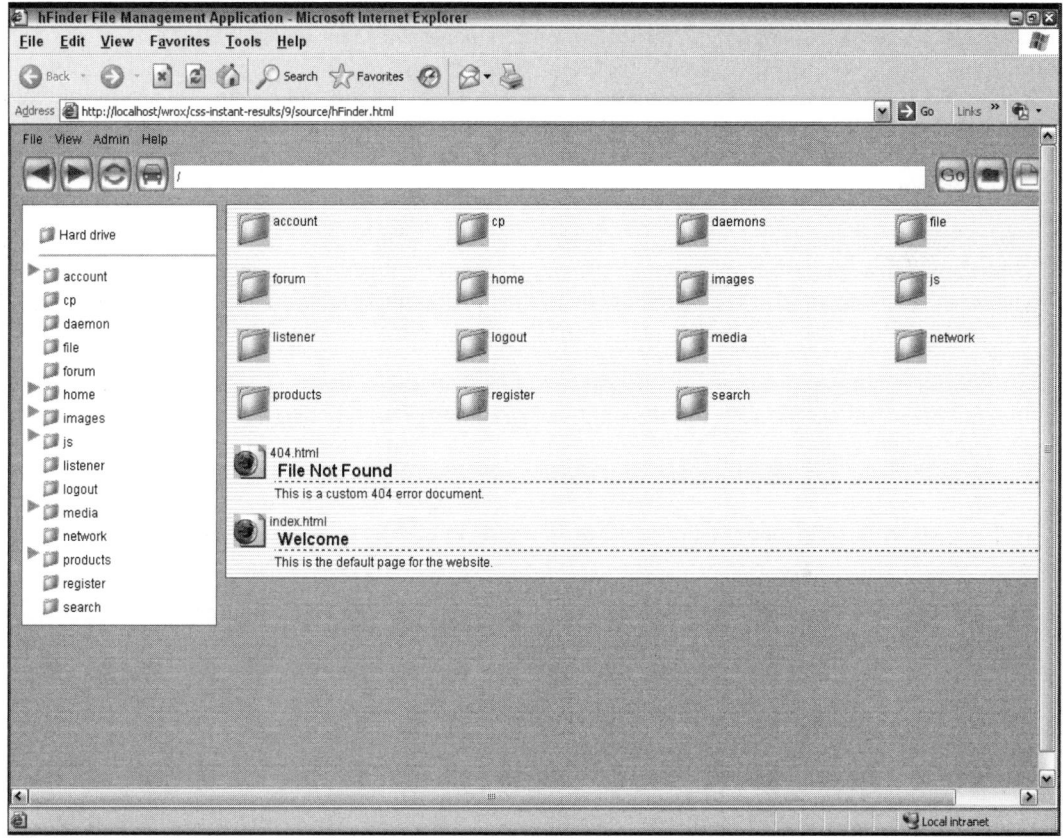

Figure 9-10

In Figure 9-10 you can observe a number of things that are out of place with the Mac Firefox version shown in Figures 9-2 and 9-3. The following are the portions of the document that must be corrected in order to make IE output the same rendering as Mac Firefox:

❑ The toolbar housing Back, Forward, Refresh, and so on is too wide.

❑ IE doesn't recognize the transparent portion of a PNG image as transparent. You can see this shortcoming in the output by the gray boxes around each image with transparent parts.

❑ Instead of the Hard Drive icon at the top of the tree view, a folder icon appears.

❏ The tree view's height isn't as high as the window.

❏ The directory view's width and height are not dependent on the width and height of the view-port (as is the case when the top, right, bottom, and left offset properties are used in tandem to imply width or height).

❏ The directories appearing in the tree view are out of whack — there is too much space between each directory. The arrow isn't aligned with the directory on the right of it.

The toolbar renders too wide because having the location bar input field set to 100% of the width of the `<td>` element it appears in causes the `<div>` that contains this table to render too wide. This is easily corrected however, by supplying Internet Explorer a smaller width for the toolbar.

Next is the issue of Explorer's non-support of PNG transparency. Internet Explorer is capable of render-ing transparent PNG images using the Internet Explorer–proprietary CSS `filter` property. This well-known hack is enabled using a JavaScript to make it easier to implement. This method is presented later in this section.

The problem with displaying the hard drive icon is an issue with Internet Explorer's support of multiple class names on a single element — which it supports correctly. It gets hairy when class names are chained together in a style sheet to refer to the element with multiple class names, which is where Explorer is failing here. This is also easily corrected, because it is fixed by Dean Edwards' IE7 JavaScript.

The tree and directory views do not render properly because of Explorer's lack of support for specifying the four offset properties of a layer in such a way as to imply width or height.

To correct Internet Explorer's rendering of the hFinder application, follow these steps:

1. Make the following modifications to `hFinder.html`:

```
<!DOCTYPE html PUBLIC "-//W3C//DTD XHTML 1.0 Transitional//EN"
"http://www.w3.org/TR/2002/REC-xhtml1-20020801/DTD/xhtml1-transitional.dtd">
<html xmlns='http://www.w3.org/1999/xhtml' xml:lang='en'>
    <head>
        <meta http-equiv='content-type' content='text/html; charset=utf-8' />
        <meta http-equiv='content-language' content='en-us' />
        <title>hFinder File Management Application</title>
        <!-- compliance patch for microsoft browsers -->
        <!--[if lt IE 7]>
            <link rel='stylesheet'
                type='text/css'
                href='styles/hFinder.ie.css' />
            <link rel='stylesheet'
                type='text/css'
                href='styles/tree.ie.css' />
            <script type='text/javascript'
                src='scripts/cssQuery/cssQuery-p.js'></script>
            <script type='text/javascript'
                src='scripts/png.js'></script>
            <script src="/ie7/ie7-standard-p.js" type="text/javascript">
            </script>
        <![endif]-->
        <link rel='stylesheet' type='text/css' href='styles/hFinder.css' />
    </head>
```

```
<body id='hfinder'>
    <ul id='hfinder-menu'>
        <li class='hfinder-menu-item' id='hfinder-menu-file'>
            File
            <ul>
                <li id='hfinder-menu-new-file'>
                    <span>New File</span>
                </li>
                <li id='hfinder-menu-new-directory' class='sep'>
                    <span>New Directory</span>
                </li>
                <li id='hfinder-menu-close'>
                    <span>Close</span></li>
            </ul>
```

2. Save the modified file as `hFinder.ie.html`.

3. Enter the following style sheet:

```
body#hfinder div#hfinder-files {
    width: expression(
        document.getElementById('hfinder').offsetWidth - 225
    );
}
body#hfinder div#hfinder-files,
body#hfinder div#hfinder-tree {
    height: expression(
        document.getElementById('hfinder').offsetHeight - 90
    );
}
div#hfinder-toolbar {
    width: 98%;
}
ul#hfinder-menu {
    position: relative;
}
```

4. Save the preceding style sheet as `hFinder.ie.css`.

5. Enter the following style sheet:

```
ul.file-tree {
    position: relative;
    left: -2px;
}
ul.file-tree li {
    width: 100%;
}
ul.file-tree div {
    position: relative;
    height: 15px;
}
body#hfinder img.file-has-children {
    top: 5px;
}
div#hfinder-tree div.file-tree-directory.file-tree-root {
```

```
    background: url('../images/hard_drive.png') no-repeat left center;
    height: 32px;
    padding: 0 0 4px 34px;
    border: 1px solid white;
    border-bottom: 2px solid rgb(200, 200, 200);
}
```

6. Save the preceding style sheet as `tree.ie.css`.

7. Enter the following JavaScript:

```
hFinderIE = {
    png : function($img)
    {
        var $html =
            '<span ' +
                (($img.id)?         "id='"    + $img.id + "' "         : '') +
                (($img.className)? "class='" + $img.className + "' " : '') +
                (($img.title)?      "title='" + $img.title + "' "      : '') +
                'style="' +
                  'display: inline-block;' +
                  'width: ' + $img.width + 'px;' +
                  'height: ' + $img.height + 'px;' +
                  "filter:progid:DXImageTransform.Microsoft.AlphaImageLoader(src='"
                     + $img.src + "', sizingMethod='scale'); " +
                $img.style.cssText + '" ';

        $html += '></span>';

        $img.outerHTML = $html;
    }
};

window.onload = function()
{
    $imgs = cssQuery('img.hfinder-toolbar-control, div.file-icon-wrapper img');

    for (var $i in $imgs)
    {
        hFinderIE.png($imgs[$i]);
    }
};
```

8. Save the preceding JavaScript as `png.js`.

The preceding changes result in the output shown in Figure 9-11.

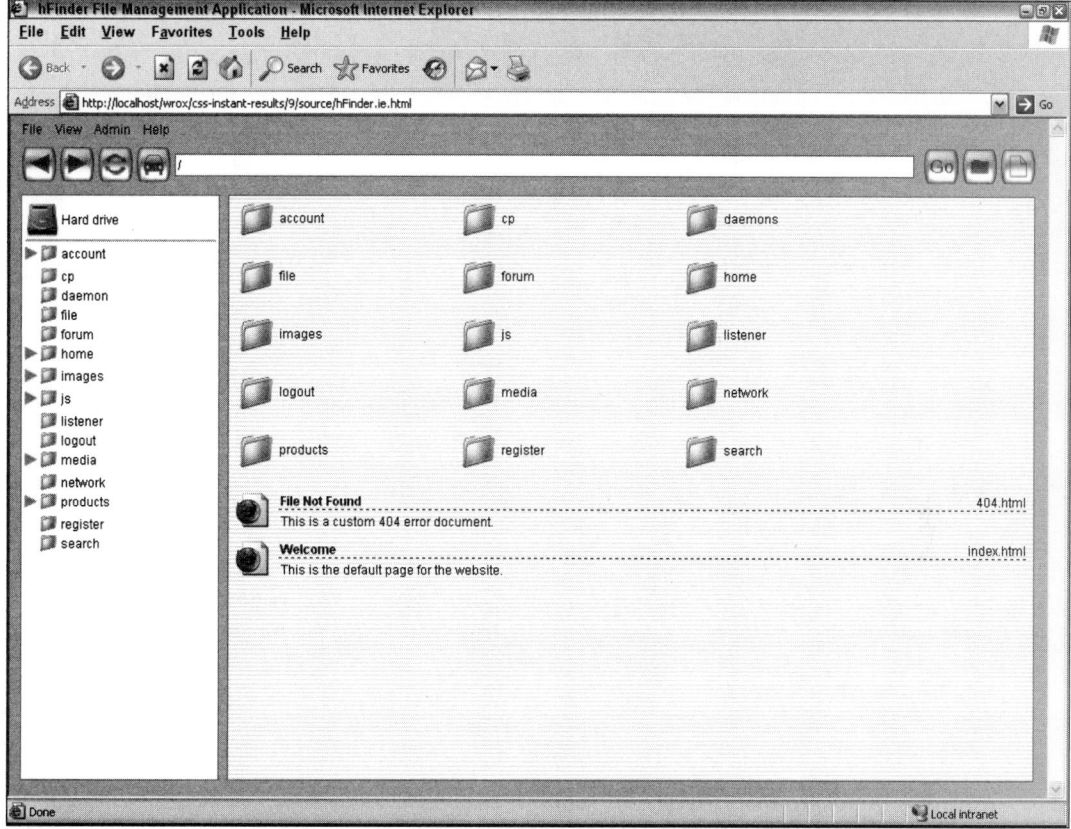

Figure 9-11

In Figure 9-11, you see that Internet Explorer now matches the output observed in Mac Firefox.

Although they might not seem logical, the hacks applied to IE are conceptually simple. The following paragraphs explain each modification.

You begin by altering hFinder.html. The modifications you made were to link up the new style sheets and JavaScript, in addition to applying an id name to the <body> element. Then in hFinder.ie.css the IE first aid begins:

```
body#hfinder div#hfinder-files {
    width: expression(
        document.getElementById('hfinder').offsetWidth - 225
    );
}
```

As you did in the "Good Old-Fashioned Internet Explorer Hacking" section in Chapter 2, you use the proprietary expression() value in conjunction with the width property. Within the expression() value is a snippet of JavaScript that uses the proprietary offsetWidth property to find the "real" width of the `<body>` element (because it has an id name of `hfinder`). Then 225 pixels are subtracted, which equate to about the width of the tree view.

Next, both the height of the tree view and the directory view are set. This time the `offsetHeight` of the `<body>` element is found, and 90 pixels are subtracted, which equate to the height of the menus and toolbar at the top of the document:

```
body#hfinder div#hfinder-files,
body#hfinder div#hfinder-tree {
    height: expression(
        document.getElementById('hfinder').offsetHeight - 90
    );
}
```

The next rule in `hFinder.ie.css` corrects the toolbar that was too wide by giving it a percentage height smaller than 100%:

```
div#hfinder-toolbar {
    width: 98%;
}
```

The final rule in `hFinder.ie.css` corrects a layering issue with the menus. Setting the position of the `<ul>` element with an id name of `hfinder-menu` to relative corrects the problem:

```
ul#hfinder-menu {
    position: relative;
}
```

`tree.ie.css` uses a number of hacks to invoke layout in Internet Explorer — a common remedy for Explorer rendering woes. As mentioned in Chapter 8, layout is invoked by setting position to a value other than `static`, by giving an element a width or height other than `auto`, and by a handful of other properties when specific values are used. Essentially any property/value combination will work that requires Internet Explorer to recalculate an element's dimensions without relying so much on the element's ancestry (as would be the case with the default values of those two particular properties).

The first rule in `tree.ie.css` gives the `<ul>` element with a `file-tree` class name a relative position, and then its position is adjusted 2 pixels to the left:

```
ul.file-tree {
    position: relative;
    left: -2px;
}
```

In the second rule, all `<li>` elements are given a width of 100%, which oddly enough corrects the problem with there being too much space between each directory:

```
ul.file-tree li {
    width: 100%;
}
```

After giving each `<li>` a width of 100%, the directory icons are clipped, and only a small portion of the icon is visible. This is corrected by the next rule, which sets the position to relative and gives each `<div>` a height of 15 pixels. The value of 15 pixels is inconsequential because any height value works:

```
ul.file-tree div {
    position: relative;
    height: 15px;
}
```

Next, the position of the gray arrows is adjusted 5 pixels from the top instead of minus 2, as it was written in the original `tree.css` style sheet:

```
body#hfinder img.file-has-children {
    top: 5px;
}
```

In the last rule you correct the hard drive icon's not appearing in Internet Explorer. The hard drive icon doesn't appear in Internet Explorer because of an issue with specificity. Dean Edwards' IE7 JavaScript corrects Internet Explorer's lack of support for chaining class names by creating and assigning a single class name to any rule that contains chained class names. To fix this, you duplicated the rule in `tree.ie.css`, and added an id selector to the beginning of the selector to increase the specificity of the rule. This could also have been done directly in `tree.css` with an identical result:

```
div#hfinder-tree div.file-tree-directory.file-tree-root {
    background: url('../images/hard_drive.png') no-repeat left center;
    height: 32px;
    padding: 0 0 4px 34px;
    border: 1px solid white;
    border-bottom: 2px solid rgb(200, 200, 200);
}
```

The last file you created was a JavaScript that is used to correct PNG transparency. Within this file there are two functions.

The following JavaScript object contains the functionality that corrects PNG transparency:

```
hFinderIE = {
    png : function($img)
    {
        var $html =
            '<span ' +
                (($img.id)?        "id='"    + $img.id + "' "        : '') +
                (($img.className)? "class='" + $img.className + "' " : '') +
                (($img.title)?     "title='" + $img.title + "' "     : '') +
                'style="' +
                'display: inline-block;' +
                'width: ' + $img.width + 'px;' +
                'height: ' + $img.height + 'px;' +
                "filter:progid:DXImageTransform.Microsoft.AlphaImageLoader(src='"
                    + $img.src + "', sizingMethod='scale'); " +
```

```
                    $img.style.cssText + '" ';

          $html += '></span>';

          $img.outerHTML = $html;
      }
};
```

A JavaScript object is passed to the preceding function. The function assumes this object refers to an `<img />` element. It takes the various attributes of that `<img />` element and copies them to a `<span>` element. The `<span>` element receives the same width, height, id name, class name, and title (if one is specified). Then in addition to width and height, two important styles are applied. The first makes the `<span>` element an inline-block element (to replicate the rendering of an image), and the second applies the proprietary `filter` property.

Essentially, the preceding function takes the following markup for an `<img />` element:

```
<img src="images/back.png"
     alt="Back"
     title="Back"
     class="hfinder-toolbar-control"
     id="hfinder-back" />
```

and replaces it with the following markup:

```
<span title="Back"
      class="hfinder-toolbar-control"
      id="hfinder-back"
      style="display: inline-block;
             width: 34px;
             height: 33px;
             filter:progid:DXImageTransform.Microsoft.AlphaImageLoader(
                 src='images/back.png', sizingMethod='scale'
             );
"></span>
```

The `filter` property provides a method of invoking transparency in PNG images.

The second function appearing in `png.js` is assigned to the `onload` event of the window object. This means the following bit of JavaScript is executed when the window has finished loading all markup and external documents (style sheets, JavaScript, images, and so on). The code can only be executed when the document has finished loading. That prevents the JavaScript from attempting to refer to something that isn't yet loaded, which would cause an error.

Within the function, a reference is made to Dean Edwards' `cssQuery()` function, which you loaded separately. Within the `cssQuery()` function, CSS selectors are used to find the images that need to be corrected for PNG transparency. All images with `hfinder-toolbar-control` class names are includes, in addition to images that are descendants of `<div>` elements with `file-icon-wrapper` class names. The function gathers up all of these images and assigns them to the `$imgs` variable. The `$imgs` variable is then processed using a programming construct called a loop. The loop executes once for each image present in the `$imgs` variable. Then, within the loop, the preceding PNG function is called. That converts each `<img />` element into a `<span>` element, thus correcting Internet Explorer's lack of support for PNG transparency:

```
window.onload = function()
{
    $imgs = cssQuery('img.hfinder-toolbar-control, div.file-icon-wrapper img');

    for (var $i in $imgs)
    {
        hFinderIE.png($imgs[$i]);
    }
};
```

There is another, slightly faster method of fixing PNG transparency in Internet Explorer, but it requires slightly more code:

```
function png($img)
{
    if (navigator.appName == 'Microsoft Internet Explorer')
    {
        var $html =
            '<span ' +
                (($img.id)?        "id='"    + $img.id + "' "        : '') +
                (($img.className)? "class='" + $img.className + "' " : '') +
                (($img.title)?     "title='" + $img.title + "' "     : '') +
                'style="' +
                    'display: inline-block;' +
                    'width: ' + $img.width + 'px;' +
                    'height: ' + $img.height + 'px;' +
                    "filter:progid:DXImageTransform.Microsoft.AlphaImageLoader(src='"
                        + $img.src + "', sizingMethod='scale'); " +
                $img.style.cssText + '" ';

        $html += '></span>';

        $img.outerHTML = $html;
    }
}
```

The preceding code can be included in a JavaScript file that doesn't appear inside of conditional comments. The JavaScript itself will check to make sure that it is Internet Explorer that it is processing PNGs for, because this method is unnecessary for other browsers that do support PNG transparency.

Then, using the preceding function, include the following in the HTML of the document:

```
<img src="images/back.png"
    onload='png(this);'
    alt="Back"
    title="Back"
    class="hfinder-toolbar-control"
    id="hfinder-back" />
```

This method is faster because as soon as the image loads, it is processed for PNG transparency instead of waiting for the entire document to load, as was the case with the other method.

Having repaired rendering in Internet Explorer, the next section describes some additional functionality for the hFinder application.

Using and Modifying the Project

This section explains how to modify the hFinder project for other applications. You see how to modify hFinder in the following ways:

❏   Implement Windows Details view

❏   Modify hFinder so that it resembles a Save As dialog

❏   Create a directory picker dialog from the tree view

As mentioned earlier in this chapter, one of the goals of the hFinder application is to make it reusable for various other aspects of a content management system, and flexible enough to support multiple methods of viewing a directory's contents. The first way you'll modify hFinder is to see what an implementation of Windows Details view looks like.

Windows Details View

This section describes how to implement a new view in the hFinder application, a true-to-Windows Details view. Windows Details view is essentially nothing more than data organized in columns in a table. You can see this in Figure 9-12, which is a screenshot of Windows Details view.

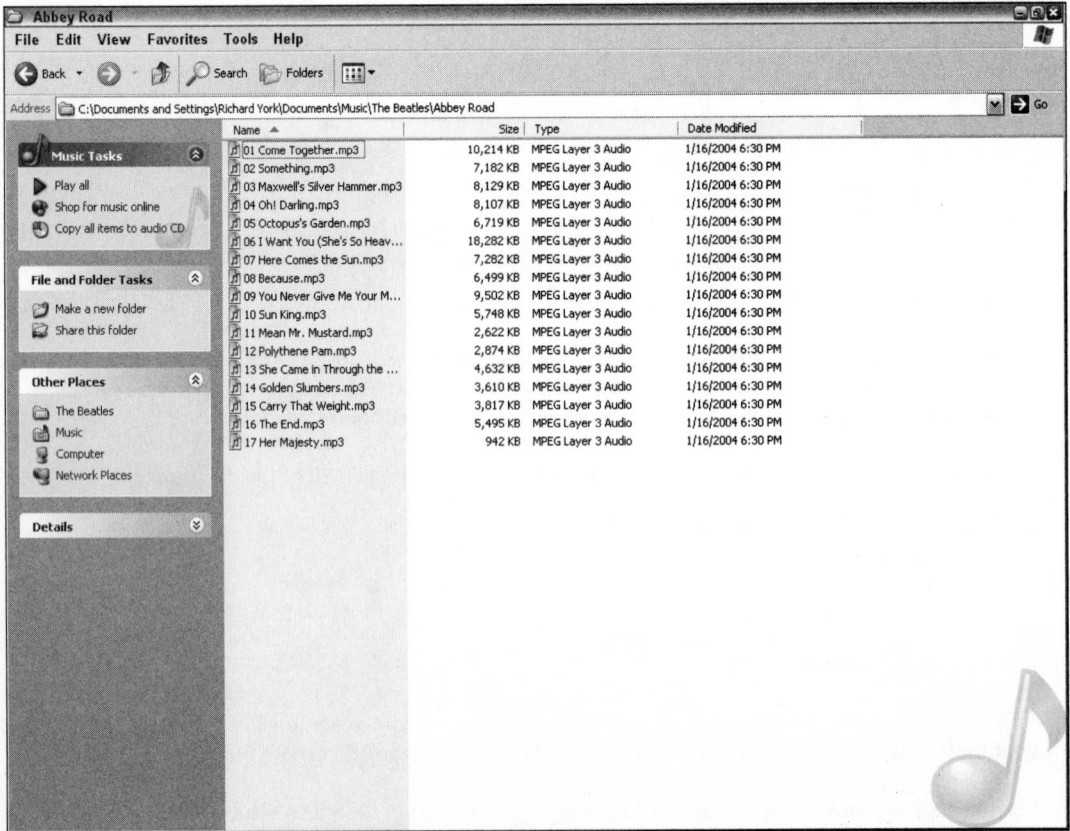

Figure 9-12

As you can see from Figure 9-12 there isn't much to do to implement a Windows-style Details view. It's merely a restructuring of the data into tabular form, and the inclusion of some additional information about a file. To implement the Windows Details view, follow these steps:

1. Make the following modifications to `hFinder.html`:

```html
                </li>
            </ul>
        </li>
    </ul>
</div>
<div id='hfinder-files'>
    <table class='file-wdetails'>
        <colgroup>
            <col style='width: 16px;' />
            <col />
            <col style='width: 10%;' />
            <col style='width: 20%;' />
            <col style='width: 20%;' />
        </colgroup>
        <thead>
            <tr>
                <th></td>
                <th>Name</th>
                <th>Size</th>
                <th>Type</th>
                <th>Last Modified</th>
            </tr>
        </thead>
        <tbody>
            <tr id='dir-3645' class='file-directory' title='account'>
                <td>
                 <img src='images/16x16/MacOSXAqua_012.png' alt='folder' />
                </td>
                <td class='file-name'>account</td>
                <td class='file-size'></td>
                <td class='file-type'>Directory</td>
                <td class='file-last-modified'>11/26/2005 4:28 PM</td>
            </tr>
            <tr id='dir-31' class='file-directory' title='cp'>
                <td>
                 <img src='images/16x16/MacOSXAqua_012.png' alt='folder' />
                </td>
                <td class='file-name'>cp</td>
                <td class='file-size'></td>
                <td class='file-type'>Directory</td>
                <td class='file-last-modified'>11/26/2005 4:30 PM</td>
            </tr>
            <tr id='dir-3785' class='file-directory' title='daemons'>
                <td>
                 <img src='images/16x16/MacOSXAqua_012.png' alt='folder' />
                </td>
                <td class='file-name'>daemons</td>
                <td class='file-size'></td>
                <td class='file-type'>Directory</td>
                <td class='file-last-modified'>11/26/2005 4:33 PM</td>
```

309

```
    </tr>
    <tr id='dir-3677' class='file-directory' title='file'>
        <td>
         <img src='images/16x16/MacOSXAqua_012.png' alt='folder' />
        </td>
        <td class='file-name'>file</td>
        <td class='file-size'></td>
        <td class='file-type'>Directory</td>
        <td class='file-last-modified'>11/26/2005 4:34 PM</td>
    </tr>
    <tr id='dir-26' class='file-directory' title='forum'>
        <td>
         <img src='images/16x16/MacOSXAqua_012.png' alt='folder' />
        </td>
        <td class='file-name'>forum</td>
        <td class='file-size'></td>
        <td class='file-type'>Directory</td>
        <td class='file-last-modified'>11/26/2005 4:35 PM</td>
    </tr>
    <tr id='dir-3651' class='file-directory' title='home'>
        <td>
         <img src='images/16x16/MacOSXAqua_012.png' alt='folder' />
        </td>
        <td class='file-name'>home</td>
        <td class='file-size'></td>
        <td class='file-type'>Directory</td>
        <td class='file-last-modified'>11/26/2005 4:37 PM</td>
    </tr>
    <tr id='dir-3681' class='file-directory' title='images'>
        <td>
         <img src='images/16x16/MacOSXAqua_012.png' alt='folder' />
        </td>
        <td class='file-name'>images</td>
        <td class='file-size'></td>
        <td class='file-type'>Directory</td>
        <td class='file-last-modified'>11/26/2005 4:38 PM</td>
    </tr>
    <tr id='dir-3690' class='file-directory' title='js'>
        <td>
         <img src='images/16x16/MacOSXAqua_012.png' alt='folder' />
        </td>
        <td class='file-name'>js</td>
        <td class='file-size'></td>
        <td class='file-type'>Directory</td>
        <td class='file-last-modified'>11/26/2005 4:39 PM</td>
    </tr>
    <tr id='dir-30' class='file-directory' title='listener'>
        <td>
         <img src='images/16x16/MacOSXAqua_012.png' alt='folder' />
        </td>
        <td class='file-name'>listener</td>
        <td class='file-size'></td>
        <td class='file-type'>Directory</td>
        <td class='file-last-modified'>11/26/2005 4:40 PM</td>
    </tr>
```

```
<tr id='dir-29' class='file-directory' title='logout'>
    <td>
     <img src='images/16x16/MacOSXAqua_012.png' alt='folder' />
    </td>
    <td class='file-name'>logout</td>
    <td class='file-size'></td>
    <td class='file-type'>Directory</td>
    <td class='file-last-modified'>11/26/2005 4:41 PM</td>
</tr>
<tr id='dir-3682' class='file-directory' title='media'>
    <td>
     <img src='images/16x16/MacOSXAqua_012.png' alt='folder' />
    </td>
    <td class='file-name'>media</td>
    <td class='file-size'></td>
    <td class='file-type'>Directory</td>
    <td class='file-last-modified'>11/26/2005 4:42 PM</td>
</tr>
<tr id='dir-3667' class='file-directory' title='network'>
    <td>
     <img src='images/16x16/MacOSXAqua_012.png' alt='folder' />
    </td>
    <td class='file-name'>network</td>
    <td class='file-size'></td>
    <td class='file-type'>Directory</td>
    <td class='file-last-modified'>11/26/2005 4:44 PM</td>
</tr>
<tr id='dir-3735' class='file-directory' title='products'>
    <td>
     <img src='images/16x16/MacOSXAqua_012.png' alt='folder' />
    </td>
    <td class='file-name'>products</td>
    <td class='file-size'></td>
    <td class='file-type'>Directory</td>
    <td class='file-last-modified'>11/26/2005 4:45 PM</td>
</tr>
<tr id='dir-28' class='file-directory' title='register'>
    <td>
     <img src='images/16x16/MacOSXAqua_012.png' alt='folder' />
    </td>
    <td class='file-name'>register</td>
    <td class='file-size'></td>
    <td class='file-type'>Directory</td>
    <td class='file-last-modified'>11/26/2005 4:46 PM</td>
</tr>
<tr id='dir-3784' class='file-directory' title='search'>
    <td>
     <img src='images/16x16/MacOSXAqua_012.png' alt='search' />
    </td>
    <td class='file-name'>search</td>
    <td class='file-size'></td>
    <td class='file-type'>Directory</td>
    <td class='file-last-modified'>11/26/2005 4:47 PM</td>
</tr>
<tr id='reg-112' class='file-registry-doc'
```

```
                          title='File Not Found'>
                       <td>
                           <img src='images/16x16/21.png' alt='text/html' />
                       </td>
                       <td class='file-name' id='freg-112'>404.html</td>
                       <td class='file-size'>900 Bytes</td>
                       <td class='file-type'>text/html</td>
                       <td class='file-last-modified'>11/26/2005 4:49 PM</td>
                    </tr>
                    <tr id='reg-1' class='file-registry-doc' title='Welcome'>
                       <td>
                           <img src='images/16x16/21.png' alt='text/html' />
                       </td>
                       <td class='file-name'>index.html</td>
                       <td class='file-size'>10 KB</td>
                       <td class='file-type'>text/html</td>
                       <td class='file-last-modified'>11/26/2005 4:50 PM</td>
                    </tr>
                </tbody>
            </table>
        </div>
        <div id='hfinder-contextmenu'>
            <ul>
                <li id='context-open' class='sep'>
                    <span style='font-weight: bold;'>Open</span>
                </li>
```

2. Save the modifications you made in a new file called `hFinder.wDetails.html`.

3. Make the following modifications to `views.css`:

```
div.file-highlight-on,
div.file-details.file-highlight-on {
    background: url('images/stripes_darker.png');
    padding: 4px;
}
div.file-highlight-off,
div.file-details.file-highlight-off {
    background: transparent;
    padding: 4px;
    border: none;
}
table.file-wdetails {
    font: 12px sans-serif;
    width: 100%;
}
table.file-wdetails th {
    text-align: left;
}
```

4. Save `views.css`.

The modifications you made result in the output you see in Figure 9-13.

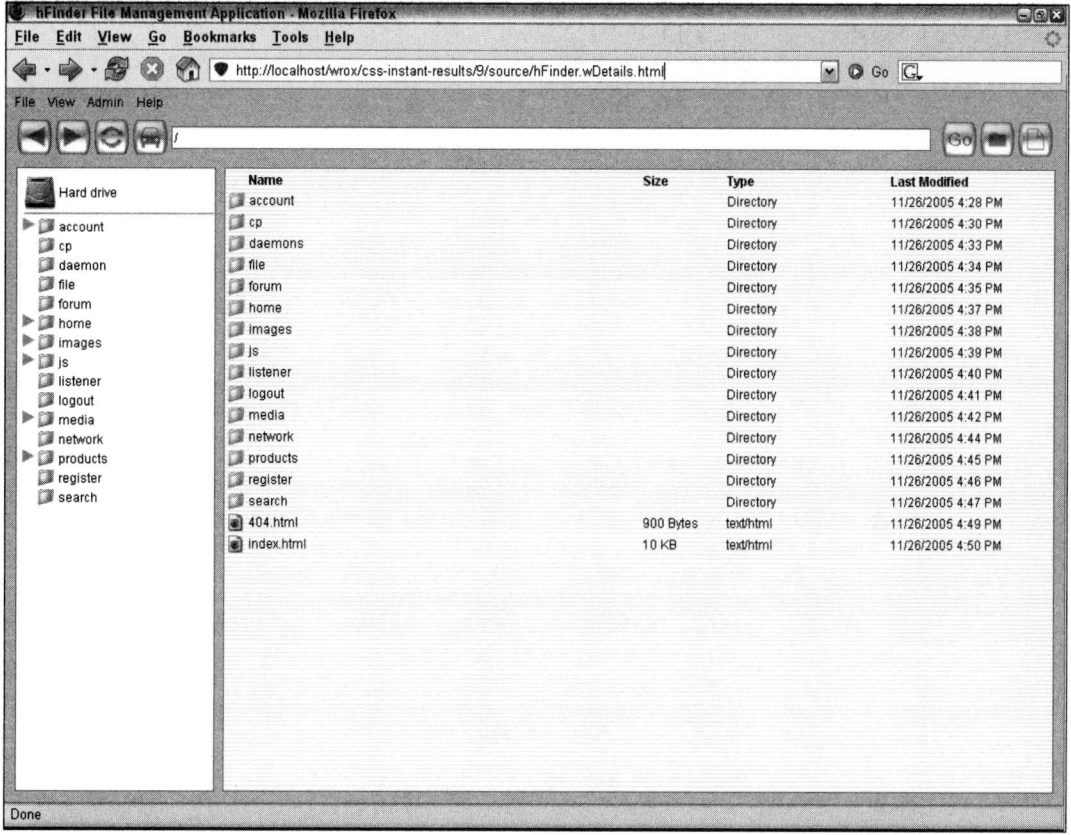

Figure 9-13

The CSS modifications you made were very simple: specify the font, make the `<table>` housing the file details take up all of the space available to it, and align the `<th>` fields to the left.

The next section discusses how to modify hFinder to make a Save As dialog.

Save As Dialog

To make a Save As dialog, the modifications are also relatively simple. To see how it's done, follow these steps:

1. Using the `hFinder.list.html` file on the source CD-ROM, make the following modifications:

```
<!DOCTYPE html PUBLIC "-//W3C//DTD XHTML 1.0 Transitional//EN"
"http://www.w3.org/TR/2002/REC-xhtml1-20020801/DTD/xhtml1-transitional.dtd">
<html xmlns='http://www.w3.org/1999/xhtml' xml:lang='en'>
    <head>
        <meta http-equiv='content-type' content='text/html; charset=utf-8' />
        <meta http-equiv='content-language' content='en-us' />
        <title>hFinder File Management Application</title>
```

```
                <!-- compliance patch for microsoft browsers -->
                <!--[if lt IE 7]>
                    <link rel='stylesheet'
                          type='text/css'
                          href='styles/hFinder.ie.css' />
                    <link rel='stylesheet'
                          type='text/css'
                          href='styles/tree.ie.css' />
                    <script type='text/javascript'
                            src='scripts/cssQuery/cssQuery-p.js'></script>
                    <script type='text/javascript'
                            src='scripts/png.js'></script>
                    <script src="/ie7/ie7-standard-p.js" type="text/javascript">
                    </script>
                <![endif]-->
                <link rel='stylesheet' type='text/css' href='styles/hFinder.css' />
            </head>
    <body id='hfinder-dialog'>
        <div id='hfinder-toolbar'>
            <table style='width: 100%; border-collapse: collapse;'>
                <tbody>
                    <tr>
                        <td style='width: 35px;'>
                            <img src='images/back.png'
                                 alt='Back'
                                 title='Back'
                                 class='hfinder-toolbar-control'
                                 id='hfinder-back' />
                        </td>
                        <td style='width: 35px;'>
                            <img src='images/forward.png'
                                 alt='Forward'
                                 title='Forward'
                                 class='hfinder-toolbar-control'
                                 id='hfinder-forward' />
                        </td>
                        <td style='width: 35px;'>
                            <img src='images/refresh.png'
                                 alt='Refresh'
                                 title='Refresh'
                                 class='hfinder-toolbar-control'
                                 id='hfinder-refresh' />
                        </td>
                        <td style='width: 35px;'>
                            <img src='images/home.png'
                                 alt='Home'
                                 title='Home'
                                 class='hfinder-toolbar-control'
                                 id='hfinder-home' />
                        </td>
                        <td>
                            <div id='file-location'>
                                <div id='file-location-inner'>
                                    <img src='images/drop-arrow.png'
                                         id='file-location-arrow'
                                         alt='arrow' />
```

```
                            <ul>
                                <li title='/'>
                                    <span>Hard drive</span>
                                </li>
                                <!--
                                    You may want to test what happens
                                    when multiple directories are included
                                    to do so, remove the comments around
                                    the following <li> element
                                <li title='/account'>
                                    <span>account</span>
                                </li>
                                -->
                            </ul>
                        </div>
                    </div>
                </td>
                <td style='width: 35px;'>
                    <img src='images/views.png'
                        alt='Change Views'
                        title='Change Views'
                        class='hfinder-toolbar-control'
                        id='hfinder-location-change-views' />
                </td>
                <td style='width: 35px;'>
                    <img src='images/directory.png'
                        alt='New Directory'
                        title='New Directory'
                        class='hfinder-toolbar-control'
                        id='hfinder-new-directory' />
                </td>
                <td style='width: 35px;'>
                    <img src='images/file.png'
                        alt='New File'
                        title='New File'
                        class='hfinder-toolbar-control'
                        id='hfinder-new-file' />
                </td>
            </tr>
        </tbody>
    </table>
</div>
<div id='hfinder-files'>
    <div id='dir-3645'
        class='file-list file-directory'
        title='account'>
        <div>
            <div class='file-icon-wrapper'>
                <img src='images/16x16/MacOSXAqua_012.png'
                    class='file-list-img'
                    alt='folder' />
            </div>
            <div class='file-list-caption file-caption-wrapper'>
                <span class='file-name'>account</span>
            </div>
```

```
            </div>
        </div>
        <div id='dir-31'
            class='file-list file-directory'
            title='cp'>
            <div>
                <div class='file-icon-wrapper'>
                    <img src='images/16x16/MacOSXAqua_012.png'
                        class='file-list-img'
                        alt='folder' />
                </div>
                <div class='file-list-caption file-caption-wrapper'>
                    <span class='file-name'>cp</span>
                </div>
            </div>
        </div>
        <div id='dir-3785'
            class='file-list file-directory'
            title='daemons'>
            <div>
                <div class='file-icon-wrapper'>
                    <img src='images/16x16/MacOSXAqua_012.png'
                        class='file-list-img'
                        alt='folder' />
                </div>
                <div class='file-list-caption file-caption-wrapper'>
                    <span class='file-name'>daemons</span>
                </div>
            </div>
        </div>
        <div id='dir-3677'
            class='file-list file-directory'
            title='file'>
            <div>
                <div class='file-icon-wrapper'>
                    <img src='images/16x16/MacOSXAqua_012.png'
                        class='file-list-img'
                        alt='folder' />
                </div>
                <div class='file-list-caption file-caption-wrapper'>
                    <span class='file-name'>file</span>
                </div>
            </div>
        </div>
        <div id='dir-26'
            class='file-list file-directory'
            title='forum'>
            <div>
                <div class='file-icon-wrapper'>
                    <img src='images/16x16/MacOSXAqua_012.png'
                        class='file-list-img'
                        alt='folder' />
                </div>
                <div class='file-list-caption file-caption-wrapper'>
                    <span class='file-name'>forum</span>
                </div>
```

```
            </div>
        </div>
        <div id='dir-3651'
            class='file-list file-directory'
            title='home'>
            <div>
                <div class='file-icon-wrapper'>
                    <img src='images/16x16/MacOSXAqua_012.png'
                        class='file-list-img'
                        alt='folder' />
                </div>
                <div class='file-list-caption file-caption-wrapper'>
                    <span class='file-name'>home</span>
                </div>
            </div>
        </div>
        <div id='dir-3681'
            class='file-list file-directory'
            title='images'>
            <div>
                <div class='file-icon-wrapper'>
                    <img src='images/16x16/MacOSXAqua_012.png'
                        class='file-list-img'
                        alt='folder' />
                </div>
                <div class='file-list-caption file-caption-wrapper'>
                    <span class='file-name'>images</span>
                </div>
            </div>
        </div>
        <div id='dir-3690'
            class='file-list file-directory'
            title='js'>
            <div>
                <div class='file-icon-wrapper'>
                    <img src='images/16x16/MacOSXAqua_012.png'
                        class='file-list-img'
                        alt='folder' />
                </div>
                <div class='file-list-caption file-caption-wrapper'>
                    <span class='file-name'>js</span>
                </div>
            </div>
        </div>
        <div id='dir-30'
            class='file-list file-directory'
            title='listener'>
            <div>
                <div class='file-icon-wrapper'>
                    <img src='images/16x16/MacOSXAqua_012.png'
                        class='file-list-img'
                        alt='folder' />
                </div>
                <div class='file-list-caption file-caption-wrapper'>
                    <span class='file-name'>listener</span>
                </div>
```

```
            </div>
        </div>
        <div id='dir-29'
            class='file-list file-directory'
            title='logout'>
            <div>
                <div class='file-icon-wrapper'>
                    <img src='images/16x16/MacOSXAqua_012.png'
                        class='file-list-img'
                        alt='folder' />
                </div>
                <div class='file-list-caption file-caption-wrapper'>
                    <span class='file-name'>logout</span>
                </div>
            </div>
        </div>
        <div id='dir-3682'
            class='file-list file-directory'
            title='media'>
            <div>
                <div class='file-icon-wrapper'>
                    <img src='images/16x16/MacOSXAqua_012.png'
                        class='file-list-img'
                        alt='folder' />
                </div>
                <div class='file-list-caption file-caption-wrapper'>
                    <span class='file-name'>media</span>
                </div>
            </div>
        </div>
        <div id='dir-3667'
            class='file-list file-directory'
            title='network'>
            <div>
                <div class='file-icon-wrapper'>
                    <img src='images/16x16/MacOSXAqua_012.png'
                        class='file-list-img'
                        alt='folder' />
                </div>
                <div class='file-list-caption file-caption-wrapper'>
                    <span class='file-name'>network</span>
                </div>
            </div>
        </div>
        <div id='dir-3735'
            class='file-list file-directory'
            title='products'>
            <div>
                <div class='file-icon-wrapper'>
                    <img src='images/16x16/MacOSXAqua_012.png'
                        class='file-list-img'
                        alt='folder' />
                </div>
                <div class='file-list-caption file-caption-wrapper'>
                    <span class='file-name'>products</span>
                </div>
```

```
        </div>
    </div>
    <div id='dir-28'
        class='file-list file-directory'
        title='register'>
        <div>
            <div class='file-icon-wrapper'>
                <img src='images/16x16/MacOSXAqua_012.png'
                    class='file-list-img'
                    alt='folder' />
            </div>
            <div class='file-list-caption file-caption-wrapper'>
                <span class='file-name'>register</span>
            </div>
        </div>
    </div>
    <div id='dir-3784'
        class='file-list file-directory'
        title='search'>
        <div>
            <div class='file-icon-wrapper'>
                <img src='images/16x16/MacOSXAqua_012.png'
                    class='file-list-img'
                    alt='search' />
            </div>
            <div class='file-list-caption file-caption-wrapper'>
                <span class='file-name'>search</span>
            </div>
        </div>
    </div>
    <div id='reg-112'
        class='file-list file-registry-doc'
        title='File Not Found'>
        <div>
            <div class='file-icon-wrapper'>
                <img src='images/16x16/21.png'
                    title='text/html'
                    alt='text/html'
                    class='file-list-img' />
            </div>
            <div class='file-list-caption file-caption-wrapper'>
                <span class='file-name' id='freg-112'>404.html</span>
            </div>
        </div>
    </div>
    <div id='reg-1'
        class='file-list file-registry-doc'
        title='Welcome'>
        <div>
            <div class='file-icon-wrapper'>
                <img src='images/16x16/21.png'
                    alt='text/html'
                    title='text/html'
                    class='file-list-img' />
            </div>
            <div class='file-list-caption file-caption-wrapper'>
```

```
                              <span class='file-name' id='freg-1'>index.html</span>
                        </div>
                  </div>
            </div>
      </div>
      <div id='hfinder-dialog-controls'>
            <form action='javascript:void(0);' method='post'>
                  <table>
                        <colgroup>
                              <col />
                              <col style='width: 5%;' />
                              <col style='width: 5%;' />
                        </colgroup>
                        <tbody>
                              <tr>
                                    <td><input type='text'
                                          name='fname' value='' id='file-name' /></td>
                                    <td><input type='submit'
                                          name='save' value='Save' /></td>
                                    <td><input type='submit'
                                          name='cancel' value='Cancel' /></td>
                              </tr>
                        </tbody>
                  </table>
            </form>
      </div>
      <div id='hfinder-contextmenu'>
            <ul>
                  <li id='context-open' class='sep'>
                        <span style='font-weight: bold;'>Open</span>
                  </li>
                  <li id='context-control-panel'>
                        <span>Control Panel</span>
                  </li>
                  <li id='context-title-description' class='sep'>
                        <span>Modify Title and Description</span>
                  </li>
                  <li id='context-delete'>
                        <span>Delete</span>
                  </li>
                  <li id='context-rename' class='sep'>
                        <span>Rename</span>
                  </li>
                  <li id='context-properties'>
                        <span>Properties</span>
                  </li>
                  <li id='context-permissions'>
                        <span>Permissions</span>
                  </li>
            </ul>
      </div>
```

2. Save the preceding modifications as `hFinder.saveas.html`.

3. Make the following modifications to `hFinder.css`:

```css
div#hfinder-tree {
    position: absolute;
    top: 0;
    bottom: 0;
    left: 0;
    margin: 73px 0 10px 10px;
    width: 190px;
    background: white;
    overflow: auto;
    border: 1px solid rgb(128, 128, 128);
    z-index: 1;
}
div#hfinder-files {
    margin: 73px 10px 10px 210px;
    position: absolute;
    top: 0;
    bottom: 0;
    left: 0;
    right: 0;
    border: 1px solid rgb(128, 128, 128);
    background: white url('../images/stripes.png');
    z-index: 1;
    overflow: auto;
}
body#hfinder-dialog div#hfinder-toolbar {
    margin: 10px 10px 0 10px;
}
body#hfinder-dialog div#hfinder-files {
    margin: 53px 10px 53px 10px;
}
div#hfinder-dialog-controls {
    position: absolute;
    bottom: 0;
    left: 0;
    right: 0;
    margin: 0 7px 0 7px;
}
div#hfinder-dialog-controls input#file-name {
    background: white url('../images/stripes.png');
    width: 98%;
}
div#hfinder-dialog-controls table {
    width: 100%;
}
div#file-location {
    height: 30px;
    position: relative;
    z-index: 2;
}
div#file-location-inner {
    background: white url('../images/stripes.png');
    height: 30px;
```

```
    overflow: hidden;
    border: 1px solid rgb(128, 128, 128);
    font: 12px sans-serif;
    position: absolute;
    top: 0;
    left: 0;
    right: 0;
}
div#file-location ul {
    list-style: none;
    margin: 0;
    padding: 0;
    position: absolute;
    bottom: 0;
    left: 0;
}
div#file-location ul li {
    height: 30px;
    white-space: nowrap;
    overflow: hidden;
    background: url('../images/24x24/MacOSXAqua_012.png') no-repeat 10px center;
    padding-left: 40px;
}
div#file-location ul li span {
    line-height: 30px;
    vertical-align: middle;
}
div#file-location ul li:first-child {
    background: url('../images/24x24/MacOSXAqua_037.png') no-repeat 10px center;
}
img#file-location-arrow {
    position: absolute;
    top: 5px;
    right: 5px;
}
```

4. Save hFinder.css.

The result of the modifications is shown in Figure 9-14.

This series of modifications was quite a bit more complicated than implementing Windows-style Details view. In the Save As dialog you've removed the menus and the tree view, where the file location input was. A <div> and <ul> were added, which are intended to be the drop-down menu functionality that you find in a Save As dialog. This can be seen in Figure 9-15.

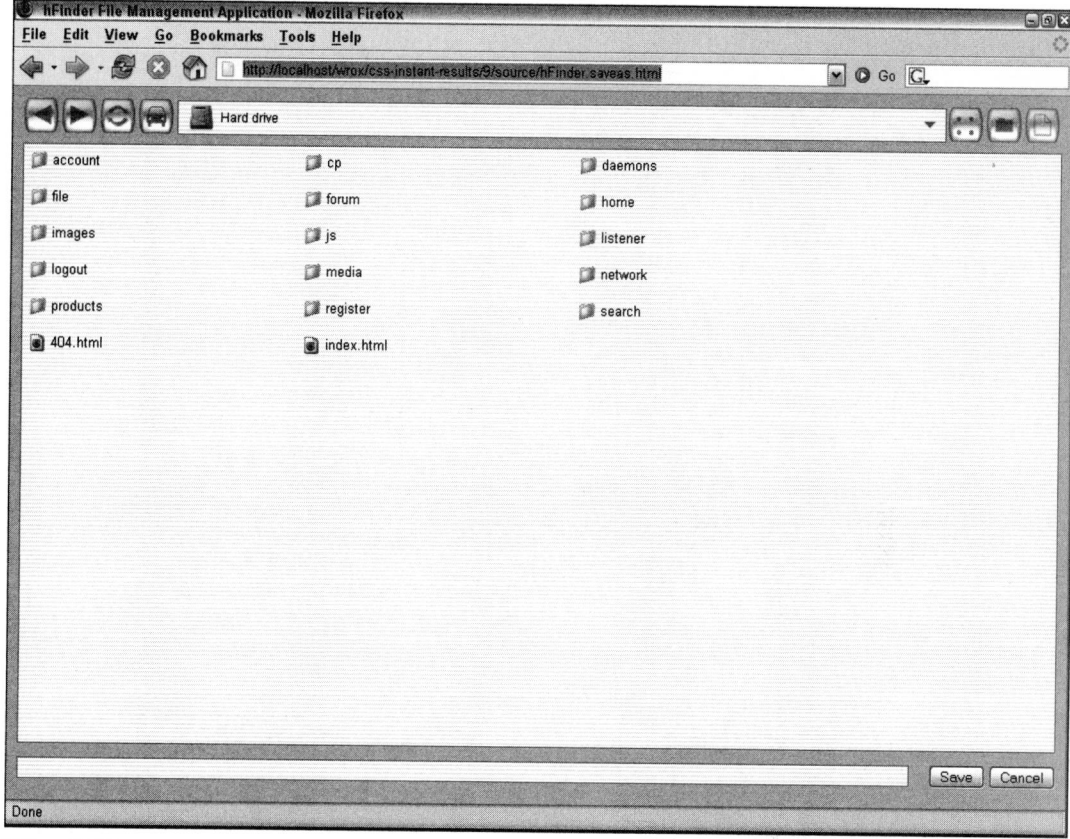

Figure 9-14

Figure 9-16 shows the same dialog with the drop-down dialog closed.

The drop-down navigation in hFinder is more simplified than that used by Windows. Because for this application there are not multiple drives to display, the drop-down navigation in hFinder is intended to show only the file path to the directory the user is currently viewing, and provide an easy method to jump to the other directories in that hierarchy.

When the user is browsing the file system, this box can be populated with the current file path. To the right of the drop-down navigation, a new icon for changing file views is added, and the Go icon was removed. Beneath the `<div>` element containing files and directories is a new form, which would be used to enter the new file name for the file you're saving.

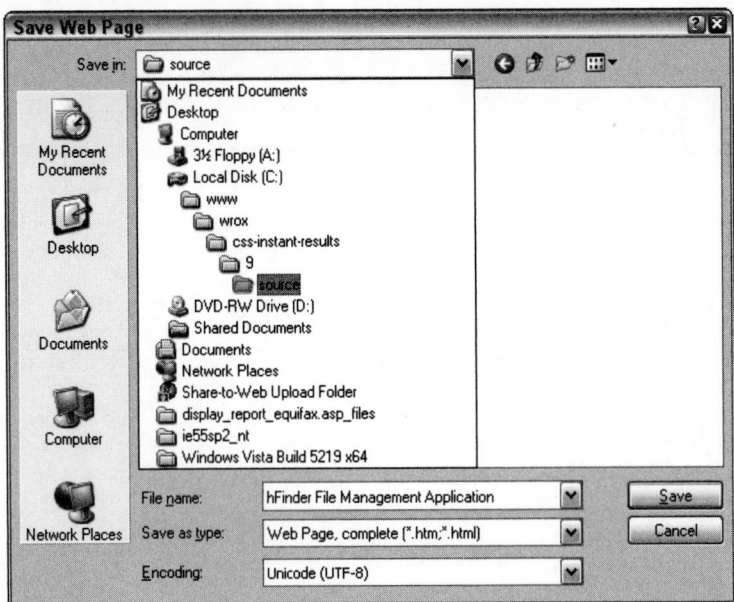

Figure 9-15

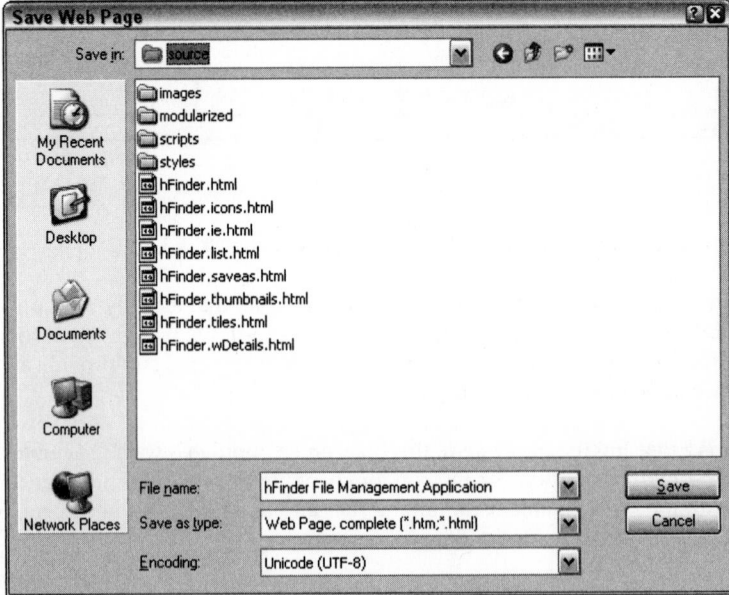

Figure 9-16

In `hFinder.css`, you made some modifications to accommodate the Save As dialog. The first rule you applied takes advantage of the id name you applied to the `<body>` element. The addition of the id name to the `<body>` element allows you to override other style sheet rules via the cascade. In that first rule, you override the margin applied to the `<div>` with an `hfinder-toolbar` id name; its margin is reduced in response to removing the top menus File, View, Admin, and Help:

```
body#hfinder-dialog div#hfinder-toolbar {
    margin: 10px 10px 0 10px;
}
```

As was the case in the previous rule, the margin for the `<div>` with an `hfinder-files` id name also needed a margin adjustment to facilitate the removal of the tree view and the menus from the top. The bottom margin also needed to be larger to make room for the new form at the bottom of the document:

```
body#hfinder-dialog div#hfinder-files {
    margin: 53px 10px 53px 10px;
}
```

Because the `<div>` containing the files and directories is positioned absolutely, any element inserted after it must be positioned absolutely as well. The `<div>` housing the form at the bottom of the hFinder document (which provides controls for a user to enter a new file name to save a document) is positioned absolutely to the bottom of the viewport, and stretched from the left to the right border of the viewport. Then left and right margins are adjusted to line up the form with the `<div>` housing directories and files above it:

```
div#hfinder-dialog-controls {
    position: absolute;
    bottom: 0;
    left: 0;
    right: 0;
    margin: 0 7px 0 7px;
}
```

The `<input />` element for new file names is given a width of 98% and a pinstripe background:

```
div#hfinder-dialog-controls input#file-name {
    background: white url('../images/stripes.png');
    width: 98%;
}
```

The `<table>` housing the `<input />` for a new file name and the Save and Cancel buttons is then given a width of 100%:

```
div#hfinder-dialog-controls table {
    width: 100%;
}
```

The `<div>` at the top of the document that houses the new drop-down navigation control is next to be styled. It receives an explicit height of 30 pixels; a relative position so that descendant elements positioned absolutely will position relative to it, and a position along the z-axis:

```
div#file-location {
    height: 30px;
    position: relative;
    z-index: 2;
}
```

The following rule is for the `<div>` nested within the "file-location" `<div>` element. It has a `file-location-inner` id name. A nested `<div>` is required for purposes of layering. Because a `position: relative;` declaration has no effect when applied to a `<td>` element, a nested `<div>` element allows you to circumvent the need to apply `position: relative;` to the `<td>` element. Now armed with an element to position relative to, the nested `file-location-inner` `<div>` element is positioned absolutely, relative to its parent. It receives a pinstripe background and a height of 30 pixels. The `overflow: hidden;` declaration prevents descendant content that is larger than the boundaries of the `file-location-inner` `<div>` element from being seen, and plays a large role in developing a drop-down menu that displays only the last directory in the current file path. More on that when you get to the next rule. A 12-pixel, generic sans-serif font is specified. Finally, the `<div>` is stretched for the entire width of the element it is positioned relative to, its parent. Stretching the element lets it resize with the width of the window:

```
div#file-location-inner {
    background: white url('../images/stripes.png');
    height: 30px;
    overflow: hidden;
    border: 1px solid rgb(128, 128, 128);
    font: 12px sans-serif;
    position: absolute;
    top: 0;
    left: 0;
    right: 0;
}
```

Within the drop-down navigation `<div>`, the current file path is housed in a `<ul>` element, which would be changed by a JavaScript to reflect the file path for whatever directory the user is currently viewing. As would be the case in a Windows Save As dialog, only the very last directory in the path is visible when the drop-down navigation is inactive. To make this work with CSS, the parent `file-location-inner` `<div>` element is given an explicit height of 30 pixels, and the `overflow: hidden;` declaration. When those properties are applied with those of the `<ul>` element and its children, the result is a drop-down navigation system in which only the last directory in the file path is visible. Ancestor directories in the current file path that exist in the markup are invisible to the user until the user accesses the drop-down navigation, which would be done by attaching a JavaScript `onclick` event to the `file-location-inner` `<div>`. On clicking the `file-location-inner` `<div>`, the `<div>`'s height is adjusted so that all of the directories in the path are visible, thereby giving the user a method to easily navigate to directories in the current file path:

```
div#file-location ul {
    list-style: none;
    margin: 0;
    padding: 0;
    position: absolute;
    bottom: 0;
    left: 0;
}
```

To hide the ancestor directories that exist in the markup but must be invisible until the drop-down navigation is accessed, the `<ul>` element is positioned absolutely to the left and bottom of the `file-location-inner` `<div>`. Then its children `<li>` elements are each given a height of 30 pixels, and some properties to ensure that height is always honored. Though most browsers honor an explicit height, Explorer does not always honor an explicit height if an element has more content than the height allows. The height is forced to be honored by the `white-space: nowrap;` and `overflow: hidden;` declarations. Now if a directory's name is too long to fit, it will be clipped at the width of the `<li>` element. Then each directory needs an icon; `MacOSXAqua_012.png` is the folder icon. It is positioned 10 pixels offset from the left of the `<li>` element and centered vertically. The `padding-left: 40px;` declaration prevents the text of the directory name from overlapping the icon. One essential element of a Save As dialog drop-down navigation is not accomplished with the CSS as it is written here, and that is indenting the directories in the path to show their relationship with one another. This is another aspect of the application that must be done with the JavaScript. In the completed application, the offset of the background image and the `padding-left` property would be adjusted in the JavaScript to indent each descendant directory a little further to the right:

```
div#file-location ul li {
    height: 30px;
    white-space: nowrap;
    overflow: hidden;
    background: url('../images/24x24/MacOSXAqua_012.png') no-repeat 10px center;
    padding-left: 40px;
}
```

Next the text of the directory name must be adjusted so that it is centered vertically just as the icon was in the preceding rule. The text is centered vertically by adjusting the line-height of the `<span>` element to 30 pixels (same height as the parent `<li>` element), and then applying the `vertical-align: middle;` declaration. A nested `<span>` element is required here because the `vertical-align` property only applies to inline or `<tr>`, `<th>`, or `<td>` elements. Because the purpose of the `vertical-align` property is to align text vertically relative to a line's baseline (as applied to inline elements), the line-height must be first adjusted to match the height of the parent `<li>` element for the `vertical-align` property to provide the desired results:

```
div#file-location ul li span {
    line-height: 30px;
    vertical-align: middle;
}
```

The topmost directory is always the first in the list. This directory is special because it is the root directory. It receives a different icon than the other directories, and this is done via the `:first-child` pseudo-class. The image, `MacOSXAqua_037.png`, is a Mac hard drive icon:

```
div#file-location ul li:first-child {
    background: url('../images/24x24/MacOSXAqua_037.png') no-repeat 10px center;
}
```

The last rule positions the arrow for the drop-down navigation. It places the arrow 5 pixels from the top and right of the `file-location` `<div>` element:

```
img#file-location-arrow {
    position: absolute;
```

```
        top: 5px;
        right: 5px;
    }
```

The last alternative implementation of hFinder is how to make a Choose a Directory dialog.

Choose a Directory Dialog

As you've seen throughout this project, hFinder is a complex application that can serve many different functions relating to file management. In fact, I could have spent the entire book on just hFinder alone. Although hFinder is by no means a complete application, you see what's required to handle the presentational aspects of such an application, and what's required to alter such an application to fit different purposes.

In the final alternative implementation of hFinder, you see what goes into creating a Choose a Directory dialog. This time you use the tree view, not the directory view. A Choose a Directory dialog, also known as a Browse for Folder dialog, looks like the one in Figure 9-17, which happens to be from the Windows version of iTunes.

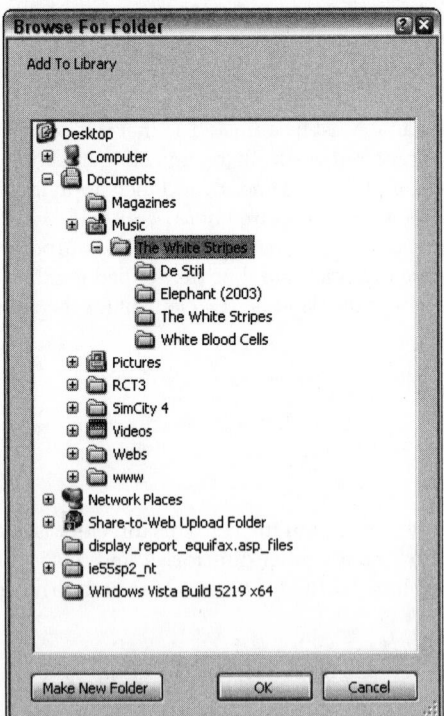

Figure 9-17

To make a Choose a Directory dialog, follow these steps:

1. Make the following alterations to `hFinder.html`:

```
<!DOCTYPE html PUBLIC "-//W3C//DTD XHTML 1.0 Transitional//EN"
"http://www.w3.org/TR/2002/REC-xhtml1-20020801/DTD/xhtml1-transitional.dtd">
<html xmlns='http://www.w3.org/1999/xhtml' xml:lang='en'
      id='hfinder-directory-dialog'>
    <head>
        <meta http-equiv='content-type' content='text/html; charset=utf-8' />
        <meta http-equiv='content-language' content='en-us' />
        <title>hFinder File Management Application</title>
        <link rel='stylesheet' type='text/css' href='styles/hFinder.css' />
    </head>
    <body>
        <h4>Choose a Directory...</h4>
        <div id='hfinder-tree'>
            <ul class='file-tree'>
                <li>
                    <div class='file-tree-directory file-tree-root'
                        id='tree-dir-1'>
                        <span>Hard drive</span>
                    </div>
                    <ul id='directory-1' class='file-tree-dir-list'>
                        <li>
                            <div class='file-tree-directory'
                                id='tree-dir-3645'>
                                <span>account</span>
                            </div>
                            <img src='images/right.png'
                                class='file-has-children'
                                id='tree-3645'
                                alt='+'
                                title='Click to expand.' />
                        </li>
                        <li>
                            <div class='file-tree-directory'
                                id='tree-dir-31'>
                                <span>cp</span>
                            </div>
                        </li>
                        <li>
                            <div class='file-tree-directory'
                                id='tree-dir-3785'>
                                <span>daemon</span>
                            </div>
                        </li>
                        <li>
                            <div class='file-tree-directory'
                                id='tree-dir-3677'>
                                <span>file</span>
                            </div>
                        </li>
                        <li>
                            <div class='file-tree-directory'
                                id='tree-dir-26'>
                                <span>forum</span>
                            </div>
```

```
        </li>
        <li>
            <div class='file-tree-directory'
                id='tree-dir-3651'>
                <span>home</span>
            </div>
            <img src='images/right.png'
                class='file-has-children'
                id='tree-3651'
                alt='+'
                title='Click to expand.' />
        </li>
        <li>
            <div class='file-tree-directory'
                id='tree-dir-3681'>
                <span>images</span>
            </div>
            <img src='images/right.png'
                class='file-has-children'
                id='tree-3681'
                alt='+'
                title='Click to expand.' />
        </li>
        <li>
            <div class='file-tree-directory'
                id='tree-dir-3690'>
                <span>js</span>
            </div>
            <img src='images/right.png'
                class='file-has-children'
                id='tree-3690'
                alt='+'
                title='Click to expand.' />
        </li>
        <li>
            <div class='file-tree-directory'
                id='tree-dir-30'>
                <span>listener</span>
            </div>
        </li>
        <li>
            <div class='file-tree-directory'
                id='tree-dir-29'>
                <span>logout</span>
            </div>
        </li>
        <li>
            <div class='file-tree-directory'
                id='tree-dir-3682'>
                <span>media</span>
            </div>
            <img src='images/right.png'
                class='file-has-children'
                id='tree-3682'
                alt='+'
                title='Click to expand.' />
```

```
            </li>
            <li>
                <div class='file-tree-directory'
                    id='tree-dir-3667'>
                    <span>network</span>
                </div>
            </li>
            <li>
                <div class='file-tree-directory'
                    id='tree-dir-3735'>
                    <span>products</span>
                </div>
                <img src='images/right.png'
                    class='file-has-children'
                    id='tree-3735'
                    alt='+'
                    title='Click to expand.' />
            </li>
            <li>
                <div class='file-tree-directory'
                    id='tree-dir-28'>
                    <span>register</span>
                </div>
            </li>
            <li>
                <div class='file-tree-directory'
                    id='tree-dir-3784'>
                    <span>search</span>
                </div>
            </li>
        </ul>
    </li>
</ul>
</div>
<div id='hfinder-dialog-controls'>
    <form action='javascript:void(0);' method='post'>
        <table>
            <colgroup>
                <col />
                <col style='width: 5%;' />
                <col style='width: 5%;' />
            </colgroup>
            <tbody>
                <tr>
                    <td><input type='submit'
                                name='new_directory'
                                value='New Directory' /></td>
                    <td><input type='submit' name='ok' value='Ok' /></td>
                    <td><input type='submit'
                                name='cancel' value='Cancel' /></td>
                </tr>
            </tbody>
        </table>
    </form>
</div>
</body>
</html>
```

2. Save the altered file as `hFinder.chooseDirectory.html`.

3. Using the version of `hFinder.css` you created to make a Save As dialog in the previous section, make the following modifications:

```css
@import 'menus.css';
@import 'views.css';
@import 'tree.css';
@import 'popup.css';

body,
html {
    width: 100%;
    height: 100%;
    min-width: 500px;
    min-height: 300px;
}
body {
    padding: 0;
    margin: 0;
    background: url('../images/brushed_metal.png');
    -moz-user-select: none;
}
html#hfinder-directory-dialog,
html#hfinder-directory-dialog body {
    min-width: 200px;
}
div#hfinder-toolbar {
    position: absolute;
    top: 0;
    left: 0;
    right: 0;
    margin: 28px 10px 0 10px;
}
html#hfinder-directory-dialog h4 {
    font: normal 12px sans-serif;
    position: absolute;
    margin: 0;
    top: 15px;
    left: 10px;
}
html#hfinder-directory-dialog div#hfinder-tree {
    margin: 43px 10px 53px 10px;
    right: 0;
    width: auto;
}
div#hfinder-tree {
    position: absolute;
    top: 0;
    bottom: 0;
    left: 0;
    margin: 73px 0 10px 10px;
    width: 190px;
    background: white;
```

```
        overflow: auto;
        border: 1px solid rgb(128, 128, 128);
        z-index: 1;
    }
```

4. Save hFinder.css.

The result of the modifications is shown in Figure 9-18.

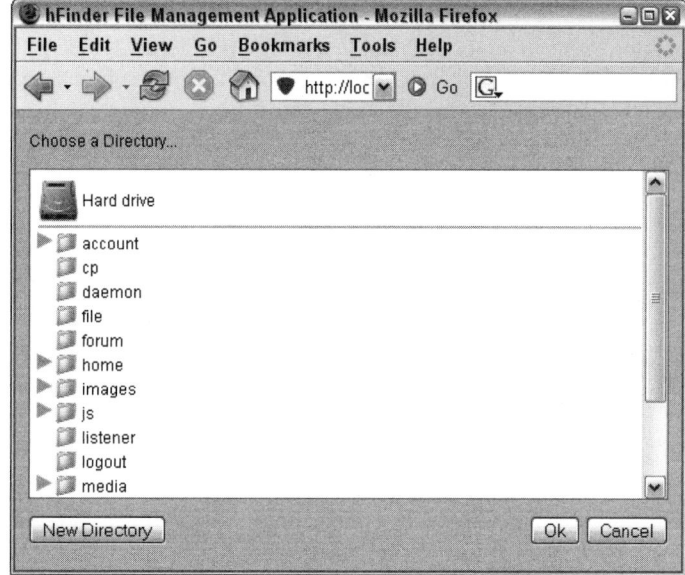

Figure 9-18

The modifications required to create a Choose a Directory dialog are few. In hFinder.html, you removed the menus, toolbar, popups, and directory view window, then added a button for the creation of a new directory, and OK and Cancel buttons. These controls are housed in a <div> named hfinder-dialog-controls, which was the same name used for the <div> element housing controls in the Save As dialog of the last section. The relevant CSS you applied for the Save As dialog for the hfinder-dialog-controls <div> is reused for the Choose a Directory dialog.

The CSS you applied to create the Choose a Directory dialog was only a few lines, and most of it was used to override, via the cascade, the default rules used for the original hFinder application. To facilitate this you added an id name to the <html> element, hfinder-directory-dialog. The first rule you added in hFinder.css overrides the default minimum width. The default minimum width was too large for a Choose a Directory dialog, which need not be very wide to be usable:

```
html#hfinder-directory-dialog,
html#hfinder-directory-dialog body {
    min-width: 200px;
}
```

Then, in the markup you added a new <h4> element with the text "Choose a Directory...". This element is styled in hFinder.css with the following rule:

```
html#hfinder-directory-dialog h4 {
    font: normal 12px sans-serif;
    position: absolute;
    margin: 0;
    top: 15px;
    left: 10px;
}
```

The <h4> element's font is set to remove the bold face, with the normal keyword, and then set to 12-pixel, generic sans-serif. The default margin is removed, and then the element is positioned absolutely 15 pixels from the top and 10 pixels from the left of the viewport.

The last rule added to hFinder.css overrides the margin and width for the hfinder-tree <div> and sets the right offset property to zero so that the hfinder-tree <div> is stretched for the whole width of the window:

```
html#hfinder-directory-dialog div#hfinder-tree {
    margin: 43px 10px 53px 10px;
    right: 0;
    width: auto;
}
```

With the presentation of the hFinder set in place, it can now go on to become a much more complex application with the help of JavaScript, and a server-side language such as PHP, Java, Perl, and so on.

Calendar

In this chapter you see how to mark up and style a calendar. This is based on a personal project that lets a user assign events to dates by clicking dates on a calendar. You can use the techniques in this chapter to create a static calendar, which you must create manually, or to create your own more sophisticated calendar that is generated by a server-side language such as PHP, Perl, Java, and so on, or even client-side JavaScript.

The following are the goals of the calendar project:

❏ The user must be able to quickly and easily navigate to any calendar date, so controls must exist for going to the next and previous months, in addition to a feature that allows a user to go directly to any date.

❏ The application must facilitate the retrieval of dates in Unix timestamps, a format that measures time as the number of seconds elapsed since the Unix Epoch (January, 1, 1970 00:00:00 GMT). Because Unix timestamps are a requirement, and some platforms have difficulty retrieving Unix timestamp values before the Unix Epoch and after January 19, 2038, the application will only support years in that range (at least for this implementation). This application doesn't actually generate these timestamps, but must include them somewhere in the id or class name naming conventions.

❏ The application must show events the user has entered by coloring days on the calendar. If users move their mouse cursor over a date, the details of the event are revealed.

The next section describes some of the details of the project design that must be considered.

Design

The calendar application in this project features three calendars. One, which contains events, is the main focus of the document. The other two are rendered much smaller. One is for the previous month and the other is for the following month. These smaller calendars offer users an intuitive method to navigate to the previous and following months. The application also features a form containing three `<select>` controls, which allow the user to select a date to navigate to, and allows the user to quickly navigate to any date that is in the supported range of years.

Calendars aren't that complex. For this project the markup does most of the heavy lifting. Each calendar is formatted using HTML tables. The names of the days of the week and the name of the month and year are formatted in `<th>` elements within `<thead>` elements. The days of the calendar each appear in `<td>` elements, within the `<tbody>` portion of a `<table>`.

In fact the most complex part of this project is the naming conventions. Different days on the calendar must be identified differently. One day may represent today, a set of days may represent the days of last month leading up to the current month that appear on the calendar, so a complete seven-day week can be represented. And finally, some days are also events. To facilitate the plethora of styling a day may require, each `<td>` representing a calendar day receives one or more class names.

To accommodate the Unix timestamp requirement, each `<td>` element within a calendar receives an id name that contains the Unix timestamp. This gives you the ability to write a JavaScript that can retrieve that timestamp for whatever purpose it is required for.

To show the users events when they mouseover a day, you use simple CSS-enabled popups that function like the pure CSS drop-down menus you saw in Chapter 3.

The next section presents the source code for the calendar.

Code and Code Explanation

To create a calendar, follow these steps:

1.   Enter the following markup:

```
<!DOCTYPE html PUBLIC "-//W3C//DTD XHTML 1.0 Transitional//EN"
"http://www.w3.org/TR/2002/REC-xhtml1-20020801/DTD/xhtml1-transitional.dtd">
<html xmlns='http://www.w3.org/1999/xhtml' xml:lang='en'>
    <head>
        <meta http-equiv='content-type' content='text/html; charset=utf-8' />
        <meta http-equiv='content-language' content='en-us' />
        <title>Events</title>
        <link rel='stylesheet' href='styles/calendar.css' type='text/css' />
    </head>
    <body>
<div class='calendar'>
    <div id='calendar-last-month' title='Navigate to Last Month'>
        <table class='calendar last' id='calendar-1130821200'>
            <thead>
                <tr>
                    <th class='month' colspan='7'>November 2005</th>
                </tr>
                <tr>
                    <th class='weekday'>Sun</th>
                    <th class='weekday'>Mon</th>
                    <th class='weekday'>Tue</th>
                    <th class='weekday'>Wed</th>
                    <th class='weekday'>Thu</th>
                    <th class='weekday'>Fri</th>
                    <th class='weekday'>Sat</th>
                </tr>
```

```
            </thead>
            <tbody>
                <tr>
                    <td class='last-month' id='day-1130648400'>30</td>
                    <td class='last-month' id='day-1130734800'>31</td>
                    <td class='this-month today first' id='day-1130821200'>1</td>
                    <td class='this-month' id='day-1130907600'>2</td>
                    <td class='this-month' id='day-1130994000'>3</td>
                    <td class='this-month' id='day-1131080400'>4</td>
                    <td class='this-month' id='day-1131166800'>5</td>

                </tr>
                <tr>
                    <td class='this-month' id='day-1131253200'>6</td>
                    <td class='this-month' id='day-1131339600'>7</td>
                    <td class='this-month' id='day-1131426000'>8</td>
                    <td class='this-month' id='day-1131512400'>9</td>
                    <td class='this-month' id='day-1131598800'>10</td>
                    <td class='this-month' id='day-1131685200'>11</td>
                    <td class='this-month' id='day-1131771600'>12</td>
                </tr>
                <tr>
                    <td class='this-month' id='day-1131858000'>13</td>
                    <td class='this-month' id='day-1131944400'>14</td>
                    <td class='this-month' id='day-1132030800'>15</td>
                    <td class='this-month' id='day-1132117200'>16</td>
                    <td class='this-month' id='day-1132203600'>17</td>
                    <td class='this-month' id='day-1132290000'>18</td>
                    <td class='this-month' id='day-1132376400'>19</td>
                </tr>
                <tr>
                    <td class='this-month' id='day-1132462800'>20</td>
                    <td class='this-month' id='day-1132549200'>21</td>
                    <td class='this-month' id='day-1132635600'>22</td>
                    <td class='this-month' id='day-1132722000'>23</td>
                    <td class='this-month' id='day-1132808400'>24</td>
                    <td class='this-month' id='day-1132894800'>25</td>
                    <td class='this-month' id='day-1132981200'>26</td>
                </tr>
                <tr>
                    <td class='this-month' id='day-1133067600'>27</td>
                    <td class='this-month' id='day-1133154000'>28</td>
                    <td class='this-month' id='day-1133240400'>29</td>
                    <td class='this-month last' id='day-1133326800'>30</td>
                    <td class='last-month' id='day-1133413200'>1</td>
                    <td class='last-month' id='day-1133499600'>2</td>
                    <td class='last-month' id='day-1133586000'>3</td>
                </tr>
            </tbody>
        </table>
    </div>
<div id='calendar-next-month' title='Navigate to Next Month'>
    <table class='calendar next' id='calendar-1136091600'>
        <thead>
            <tr>
                <th class='month' colspan='7'>January 2006</th>
```

```
        </tr>
        <tr>
            <th class='weekday'>Sun</th>
            <th class='weekday'>Mon</th>
            <th class='weekday'>Tue</th>
            <th class='weekday'>Wed</th>
            <th class='weekday'>Thu</th>
            <th class='weekday'>Fri</th>
            <th class='weekday'>Sat</th>
        </tr>
    </thead>
    <tbody>
        <tr>
            <td class='this-month today first' id='day-1136091600'>1</td>
            <td class='this-month' id='day-1136178000'>2</td>
            <td class='this-month' id='day-1136264400'>3</td>
            <td class='this-month' id='day-1136350800'>4</td>
            <td class='this-month' id='day-1136437200'>5</td>
            <td class='this-month' id='day-1136523600'>6</td>
            <td class='this-month' id='day-1136610000'>7</td>
        </tr>
        <tr>
            <td class='this-month' id='day-1136696400'>8</td>
            <td class='this-month' id='day-1136782800'>9</td>
            <td class='this-month' id='day-1136869200'>10</td>
            <td class='this-month' id='day-1136955600'>11</td>
            <td class='this-month' id='day-1137042000'>12</td>
            <td class='this-month' id='day-1137128400'>13</td>
            <td class='this-month' id='day-1137214800'>14</td>
        </tr>
        <tr>
            <td class='this-month' id='day-1137301200'>15</td>
            <td class='this-month' id='day-1137387600'>16</td>
            <td class='this-month' id='day-1137474000'>17</td>
            <td class='this-month' id='day-1137560400'>18</td>
            <td class='this-month' id='day-1137646800'>19</td>
            <td class='this-month' id='day-1137733200'>20</td>
            <td class='this-month' id='day-1137819600'>21</td>
        </tr>
        <tr>
            <td class='this-month' id='day-1137906000'>22</td>
            <td class='this-month' id='day-1137992400'>23</td>
            <td class='this-month' id='day-1138078800'>24</td>
            <td class='this-month' id='day-1138165200'>25</td>
            <td class='this-month' id='day-1138251600'>26</td>
            <td class='this-month' id='day-1138338000'>27</td>
            <td class='this-month' id='day-1138424400'>28</td>
        </tr>
        <tr>
            <td class='this-month' id='day-1138510800'>29</td>
            <td class='this-month' id='day-1138597200'>30</td>
            <td class='this-month last' id='day-1138683600'>31</td>
            <td class='last-month' id='day-1138770000'>1</td>
            <td class='last-month' id='day-1138856400'>2</td>
            <td class='last-month' id='day-1138942800'>3</td>
            <td class='last-month' id='day-1139029200'>4</td>
```

```
                </tr>
            </tbody>
        </table>
</div>
<div id='calendar-this-month'>
    <table class='calendar current' id='calendar-1133413200'>
        <thead>
            <tr>
                <th class='month' colspan='7'>December 2005</th>
            </tr>
            <tr>
                <th class='weekday'>Sun</th>
                <th class='weekday'>Mon</th>
                <th class='weekday'>Tue</th>
                <th class='weekday'>Wed</th>
                <th class='weekday'>Thu</th>
                <th class='weekday'>Fri</th>
                <th class='weekday'>Sat</th>
            </tr>
        </thead>
        <tbody>
            <tr>
                <td class='last-month' id='day-1133067600'>27</td>
                <td class='last-month' id='day-1133154000'>28</td>
                <td class='last-month' id='day-1133240400'>29</td>
                <td class='last-month' id='day-1133326800'>30</td>
                <td class='this-month today first event' id='day-1133413200'>
                    1
                    <div class='event'>
                        <span class='event-date'>December 1, 2005</span>
                        Finish writing Chapter 6.
                    </div>
                </td>
                <td class='this-month' id='day-1133499600'>2</td>
                <td class='this-month' id='day-1133586000'>3</td>
            </tr>
            <tr>
                <td class='this-month' id='day-1133672400'>4</td>
                <td class='this-month' id='day-1133758800'>5</td>
                <td class='this-month' id='day-1133845200'>6</td>
                <td class='this-month' id='day-1133931600'>7</td>
                <td class='this-month' id='day-1134018000'>8</td>
                <td class='this-month event' id='day-1134104400'>
                    9
                    <div class='event'>
                        <span class='event-date'>December 9, 2005</span>
                        CSS Instant Results deadline.
                    </div>
                </td>
                <td class='this-month' id='day-1134190800'>10</td>
            </tr>
            <tr>
                <td class='this-month' id='day-1134277200'>11</td>
                <td class='this-month' id='day-1134363600'>12</td>
                <td class='this-month' id='day-1134450000'>13</td>
                <td class='this-month' id='day-1134536400'>14</td>
```

```
                    <td class='this-month' id='day-1134622800'>15</td>
                    <td class='this-month event' id='day-1134709200'>
                        16
                        <div class='event'>
                            <span class='event-date'>December 16, 2005</span>
                            Company Christmas party.
                        </div>
                    </td>
                    <td class='this-month' id='day-1134795600'>17</td>
                </tr>
                <tr>
                    <td class='this-month' id='day-1134882000'>18</td>
                    <td class='this-month' id='day-1134968400'>19</td>
                    <td class='this-month' id='day-1135054800'>20</td>
                    <td class='this-month' id='day-1135141200'>21</td>
                    <td class='this-month' id='day-1135227600'>22</td>
                    <td class='this-month event' id='day-1135314000'>
                        23
                        <div class='event'>
                            <span class='event-date'>December 23, 2005</span>
                            Party at Richard's place, BYOB!
                        </div>
                    </td>
                    <td class='this-month event' id='day-1135400400'>
                        24
                        <div class='event'>
                            <span class='event-date'>December 24, 2005</span>
                            Christmas Eve
                        </div>
                    </td>
                </tr>
                <tr>
                    <td class='this-month event' id='day-1135486800'>
                        25
                        <div class='event'>
                            <span class='event-date'>December 25, 2005</span>
                            Christmas Day
                        </div>
                    </td>
                    <td class='this-month' id='day-1135573200'>26</td>
                    <td class='this-month' id='day-1135659600'>27</td>
                    <td class='this-month' id='day-1135746000'>28</td>
                    <td class='this-month' id='day-1135832400'>29</td>
                    <td class='this-month' id='day-1135918800'>30</td>
                    <td class='this-month last event' id='day-1136005200'>
                        31
                        <div class='event'>
                            <span class='event-date'>December 31, 2005</span>
                            New Year's Eve
                        </div>
                    </td>
                </tr>
            </tbody>
    </table>
    <div class='event-info'>
        Roll over colored dates on the calendar to see event information.
```

```
                    </div>
            </div>
    </div>
    <form method='get' action='javascript:void(0);'>
        <fieldset>
            <legend><span>Jump to Date</span></legend>
            <table>
                <tbody>
                    <tr>
                        <td class='form-input'>
                            <select id='calendar-month' name='month'>
                                <option value='1'>January</option>
                                <option value='2'>February</option>
                                <option value='3'>March</option>
                                <option value='4'>April</option>
                                <option value='5'>May</option>
                                <option value='6'>June</option>
                                <option value='7'>July</option>
                                <option value='8'>August</option>
                                <option value='9'>September</option>
                                <option value='10'>October</option>
                                <option value='11'>November</option>
                                <option value='12'
selected='selected'>December</option>
                            </select>
                        </td>
                        <td class='form-input'>
                            <select id='calendar-day' name='day'>
                                <option value='1' selected='selected'>1</option>
                                <option value='2'>2</option>
                                <option value='3'>3</option>
                                <option value='4'>4</option>
                                <option value='5'>5</option>
                                <option value='6'>6</option>
                                <option value='7'>7</option>
                                <option value='8'>8</option>
                                <option value='9'>9</option>
                                <option value='10'>10</option>
                                <option value='11'>11</option>
                                <option value='12'>12</option>
                                <option value='13'>13</option>
                                <option value='14'>14</option>
                                <option value='15'>15</option>
                                <option value='16'>16</option>
                                <option value='17'>17</option>
                                <option value='18'>18</option>
                                <option value='19'>19</option>
                                <option value='20'>20</option>
                                <option value='21'>21</option>
                                <option value='22'>22</option>
                                <option value='23'>23</option>
                                <option value='24'>24</option>
                                <option value='25'>25</option>
                                <option value='26'>26</option>
                                <option value='27'>27</option>
                                <option value='28'>28</option>
```

```
                    <option value='29'>29</option>
                    <option value='30'>30</option>
                    <option value='31'>31</option>
                </select>
            </td>
            <td class='form-input'>
                <select id='calendar-year' name='year'>
                    <option value='1970'>1970</option>
                    <option value='1971'>1971</option>
                    <option value='1972'>1972</option>
                    <option value='1973'>1973</option>
                    <option value='1974'>1974</option>
                    <option value='1975'>1975</option>
                    <option value='1976'>1976</option>
                    <option value='1977'>1977</option>
                    <option value='1978'>1978</option>
                    <option value='1979'>1979</option>
                    <option value='1980'>1980</option>
                    <option value='1981'>1981</option>
                    <option value='1982'>1982</option>
                    <option value='1983'>1983</option>
                    <option value='1984'>1984</option>
                    <option value='1985'>1985</option>
                    <option value='1986'>1986</option>
                    <option value='1987'>1987</option>
                    <option value='1988'>1988</option>
                    <option value='1989'>1989</option>
                    <option value='1990'>1990</option>
                    <option value='1991'>1991</option>
                    <option value='1992'>1992</option>
                    <option value='1993'>1993</option>
                    <option value='1994'>1994</option>
                    <option value='1995'>1995</option>
                    <option value='1996'>1996</option>
                    <option value='1997'>1997</option>
                    <option value='1998'>1998</option>
                    <option value='1999'>1999</option>
                    <option value='2000'>2000</option>
                    <option value='2001'>2001</option>
                    <option value='2002'>2002</option>
                    <option value='2003'>2003</option>
                    <option value='2004'>2004</option>
                    <option value='2005' selected='selected'>2005</option>
                    <option value='2006'>2006</option>
                    <option value='2007'>2007</option>
                    <option value='2008'>2008</option>
                    <option value='2009'>2009</option>
                    <option value='2010'>2010</option>
                    <option value='2011'>2011</option>
                    <option value='2012'>2012</option>
                    <option value='2013'>2013</option>
                    <option value='2014'>2014</option>
                    <option value='2015'>2015</option>
                    <option value='2016'>2016</option>
                    <option value='2017'>2017</option>
```

```
                                    <option value='2018'>2018</option>
                                    <option value='2019'>2019</option>
                                    <option value='2020'>2020</option>
                                    <option value='2021'>2021</option>
                                    <option value='2022'>2022</option>
                                    <option value='2023'>2023</option>
                                    <option value='2024'>2024</option>
                                    <option value='2025'>2025</option>
                                    <option value='2026'>2026</option>
                                    <option value='2027'>2027</option>
                                    <option value='2028'>2028</option>
                                    <option value='2029'>2029</option>
                                    <option value='2030'>2030</option>
                                    <option value='2031'>2031</option>
                                    <option value='2032'>2032</option>
                                    <option value='2033'>2033</option>
                                    <option value='2034'>2034</option>
                                    <option value='2035'>2035</option>
                                    <option value='2036'>2036</option>
                                    <option value='2037'>2037</option>
                                </select>
                            </td>
                            <td class='form-button'>
                                <input type='submit' id='calendar-jump-to-date' value='Go'
/>
                            </td>
                        </tr>
                    </tbody>
                </table>
            </fieldset>
    </form>
        </body>
    </html>
```

2. Save the preceding as `calendar.html`.

3. Enter the following style sheet:

```
body {
    font: 12px sans-serif;
    background: #fff;
}
div.calendar {
    position: relative;
    height: 390px;
    min-width: 760px;
    max-width: 1000px;
    margin: auto;
}
div#calendar-this-month {
    position: absolute;
    left: 50%;
    top: 20px;
    margin-left: -185px;
}
table.calendar {
```

```
        border-collapse: collapse;
        table-layout: fixed;
        border: 1px solid rgb(200, 200, 200);
}
table.calendar td {
        width: 50px;
        height: 50px;
        background: #fff;
        border: 1px solid rgb(200, 200, 200);
        vertical-align: top;
}
td.this-month.today.event {
        background: gold;
}
td.this-month.event {
        background: yellow;
}
div.event,
div.event-info {
        position: absolute;
        bottom: -62px;
        left: -1px;
        right: 0;
        border-bottom: 1px solid rgb(200, 200, 200);
        border-left: 1px solid rgb(200, 200, 200);
        border-right: 1px solid rgb(200, 200, 200);
        background: white;
        display: none;
        height: 51px;
        padding: 5px;
        z-index: 2;
}
div.event-info {
        display: block;
        z-index: 1;
}
span.event-date {
        font-weight: bold;
}
td.this-month.event:hover > div.event {
        display: block;
}
table.calendar th {
        text-align: center;
        background: #fff;
}
table.calendar td.last-month,
table.calendar td.next-month {
        background: rgb(222, 222, 222);
}
table.calendar td.today {
        background: rgb(242, 242, 242);
}
```

```
table.calendar th.month {
    text-align: center;
    font-size: 24px;
    font-weight: normal;
    border-bottom: 1px solid rgb(200, 200, 200);
    background: rgb(242, 242, 242);
}
table.calendar.last,
table.calendar.next {
    font-size: 10px;
    margin: 100px 20px 20px 20px;
    cursor: pointer;
}
table.calendar.last th.month,
table.calendar.next th.month {
    font-size: 10px;
}
table.calendar.last td,
table.calendar.next td {
    width: 20px;
    height: 20px;
}
div#calendar-last-month {
    position: absolute;
    left: 0;
    top: 0;
}
div#calendar-next-month {
    position: absolute;
    right: 0;
    top: 0;
}
fieldset {
    margin: 0 auto;
    border: none;
    border-top: 1px solid rgb(200, 200, 200);
    max-width: 998px;
}
```

4.   Save the preceding as `calendar.css`.

The preceding bit of source code results in the output in Figure 10-1.

The first rule in `calendar.css` is very straightforward: set the font to 12-pixel sans-serif, and specify a white background:

```
body {
    font: 12px sans-serif;
    background: #fff;
}
```

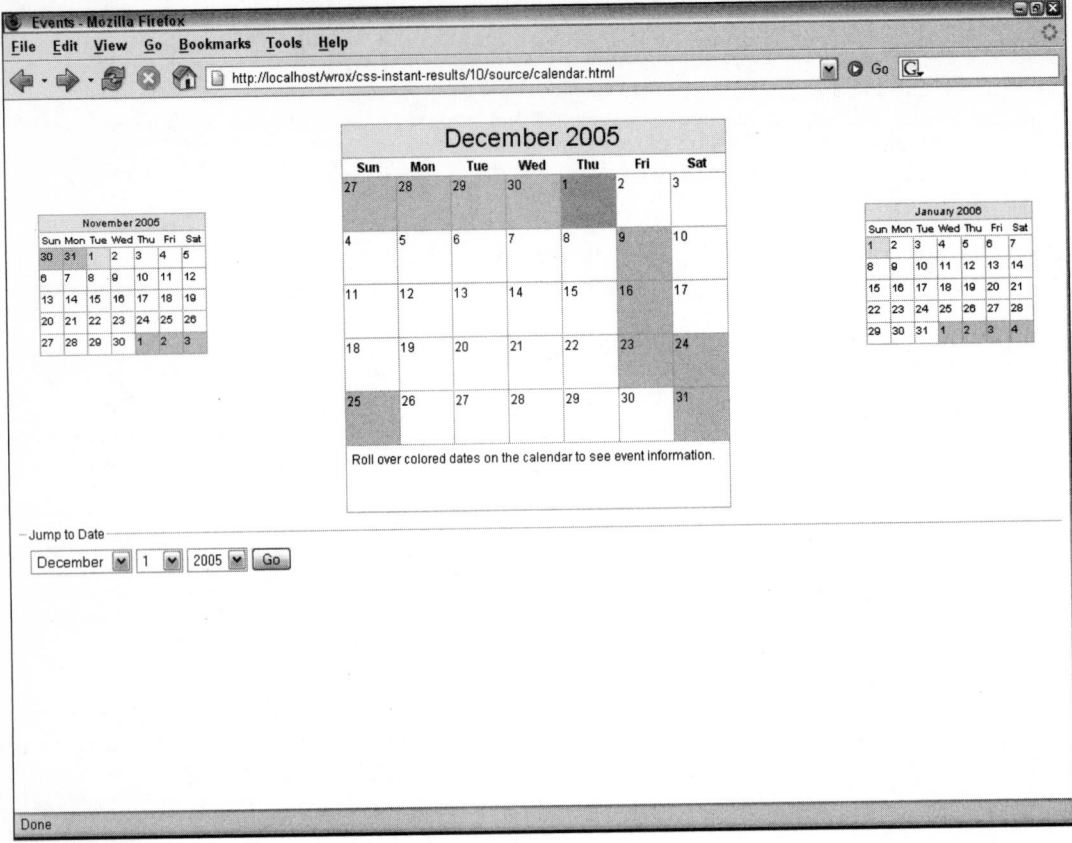

Figure 10-1

In order to position the main calendar in the middle and the smaller calendars to the left and right of the main calendar, each calendar must be absolutely positioned. Each calendar is positioned relative to the `<div>` element with a `calendar` class name. The calendar `<div>` element is given a height of 390 pixels because each of the calendars is absolutely positioned — they have no effect on the height of the calendar `<div>` element. Then to prevent calendars from overlapping when the browser window is small, a minimum width is provided. Conversely, if the browser window is too big, a maximum width prevents the calendars from being spaced too far apart. When the maximum width is reached, the `margin: auto;` declaration centers the `calendar` `<div>` element:

```
div.calendar {
    position: relative;
    height: 390px;
    min-width: 760px;
    max-width: 1000px;
    margin: auto;
}
```

In the following rule, the calendar for the month being viewed is positioned absolutely. It is centered by setting the left offset property to 50%, then subtracting 185 pixels from the left margin (roughly half of its width). Then to provide some space between the top of the calendar and the top border of the viewport, the calendar is offset from the top by 20 pixels:

```
div#calendar-this-month {
    position: absolute;
    left: 50%;
    top: 20px;
    margin-left: -185px;
}
```

In the next rule, styles common to all three calendars are applied. The border-collapse: collapse; declaration removes the space between table cells. The table-layout: fixed; declaration forces explicit width applied to columns or table cells to be honored, whereas in the traditional table sizing algorithm width is taken more as a minimum constraint, and cells still expand to accommodate content as necessary. In the last declaration of the following rule, a 1-pixel, solid gray border is applied around the perimeter of each calendar <table>:

```
table.calendar {
    border-collapse: collapse;
    table-layout: fixed;
    border: 1px solid rgb(200, 200, 200);
}
```

The next rule to follow applies to each <td> element within a calendar, which all happen to be calendar days. A width and height of 50 pixels makes each <td> element perfectly square. A white background is also specified; if the background for the <body> element is changed, the background of each <td> element will still be white. A 1-pixel, solid gray border is applied to each <td> element. In the last declaration, the vertical-align property is set to top, which causes each day to be aligned to the top and left of each cell:

```
table.calendar td {
    width: 50px;
    height: 50px;
    background: #fff;
    border: 1px solid rgb(200, 200, 200);
    vertical-align: top;
}
```

Next you make use of some of the extra class names applied to certain days. The cell for today has four class names: this-month, today, first, and event. So depending on what you want, this day could have quite a few different stylings:

```
td.this-month.today.event {
    background: gold;
}
```

Events that are not "today" receive a yellow background:

```
td.this-month.event {
    background: yellow;
}
```

In the following rule the <div> elements that house event information receive styling. These elements appear in Figure 10-1, where you see the text "Roll over colored dates on the calendar to see event information." The <div> elements are positioned absolutely, relative to the <div> element with a calendar-this-month id name. Each event <div> is offset from the bottom of the calendar-this-month <div> by the height of the event <div>—62 pixels (5 pixels of bottom padding + 5 pixels of top padding + 1 pixel bottom border + height of 51 pixels). The left is offset minus 1 pixel to make the border of the event and event-info <div> elements line up with the table. Then right: 0; stretches the event and event-info <div> elements for the width of the calendar-this-month <div> element. Next, the bottom, left, and right borders are set 1-pixel, solid, and gray. A white background is then applied. The display property is set to none to hide the events from being displayed, because they will be displayed only when the user's mouse hovers over an event:

```
div.event,
div.event-info {
    position: absolute;
    bottom: -62px;
    left: -1px;
    right: 0;
    border-bottom: 1px solid rgb(200, 200, 200);
    border-left: 1px solid rgb(200, 200, 200);
    border-right: 1px solid rgb(200, 200, 200);
    background: white;
    display: none;
    height: 51px;
    padding: 5px;
    z-index: 2;
}
```

In the next rule, the event-info <div> element is given the display: block; declaration, because this <div> element instructs the users how to view the other events. It is then given a lower z-index value than that of the preceding rule, so that event <div> elements appear on top of the event-info <div> element:

```
div.event-info {
    display: block;
    z-index: 1;
}
```

Then in the next rule, the date for the event that appears in each event <div> element is given bold-faced text:

```
span.event-date {
    font-weight: bold;
}
```

The following rule makes the event <div> elements visible when users hover their mouse cursor over a <td> element with both a this-month and event class name:

```
td.this-month.event:hover > div.event {
    display: block;
}
```

Next, the `<th>` elements at the top of the calendar are each center-aligned and given white backgrounds:

```
table.calendar th {
    text-align: center;
    background: #fff;
}
```

In each calendar the `<td>` elements that represent the days of the previous month and the `<td>` elements representing the days of the next month are given gray backgrounds:

```
table.calendar td.last-month,
table.calendar td.next-month {
    background: rgb(222, 222, 222);
}
```

The following rule sets a background color for "today." When no events are present, the background color is a lighter shade of gray than the background color used to represent the days of last month and the days of next month:

```
table.calendar td.today {
    background: rgb(242, 242, 242);
}
```

The next rule styles the name of the month within each calendar. It aligns the text to the center, and makes the text a large, 24-pixel font size. The default bold-face is removed with the `font-weight: normal;` declaration. Then, a 1-pixel, solid gray bottom border is applied, and the background is made a lighter gray:

```
table.calendar th.month {
    text-align: center;
    font-size: 24px;
    font-weight: normal;
    border-bottom: 1px solid rgb(200, 200, 200);
    background: rgb(242, 242, 242);
}
```

Next the calendars for the previous month and following month are styled differently than that of the current month. The font-size is made 10 pixels, and the margin is adjusted so there are 100 pixels of margin between the top of both calendars and the top of the viewport, and 20 pixels on every other side. The cursor is set to the `pointer` keyword, which makes each calendar appear as though it is a link. In a fully functioning, JavaScript-enabled application, these calendars can then be made into links by attaching the appropriate events, and the user has a visual cue to believe that they are links because the cursor changes to a pointer while mousing over them:

```
table.calendar.last,
table.calendar.next {
    font-size: 10px;
    margin: 100px 20px 20px 20px;
    cursor: pointer;
}
```

The next rule forces the 10-pixel font height on the <th> elements containing the month name, which is needed because the preceding rule did not have great enough precedence to make the month name a 10-pixel font size as well. With greater specificity, the following rule succeeds in overriding the 24-pixel font size originally specified for the month name:

```
table.calendar.last th.month,
table.calendar.next th.month {
    font-size: 10px;
}
```

Days of the calendars for the previous and following months are made smaller in the following rule. The <td> elements are made 20 pixels by 20 pixels, so that they take up less space than the calendar for the current month:

```
table.calendar.last td,
table.calendar.next td {
    width: 20px;
    height: 20px;
}
```

The calendars for the previous and following months are both positioned absolutely — the previous month on the left side of the current month, and the following month on the right side of the current month. This is done in the following two rules:

```
div#calendar-last-month {
    position: absolute;
    left: 0;
    top: 0;
}
div#calendar-next-month {
    position: absolute;
    right: 0;
    top: 0;
}
```

The last rule appearing in calendar.css applies styles to the <fieldset> element that encompasses the form controls for jumping to a specific date. First, default margin is removed from the top and bottom, and the <fieldset> is centered horizontally by applying the auto keyword to the left and right margins. The border for the <fieldset> is removed with the border: none; declaration, followed by setting the top border to 1 pixel, solid, and gray. The last declaration sets the maximum width to 998 pixels:

```
fieldset {
    margin: 0 auto;
    border: none;
    border-top: 1px solid rgb(200, 200, 200);
    max-width: 998px;
}
```

The next section describes what to do to make the calendar.html document work just as well in Internet Explorer as it does in the other browsers.

Testing and Caveats

In this section you take the completed project of the previous section and test it in Internet Explorer.

As has been the case with every project in this book, the source code doesn't work out-of-the-box in Internet Explorer 6.0. But with some hacks, patience, and diligence, this too can work in Internet Explorer.

Figure 10-2 shows what `calendar.html` looks like with no additional hacks applied in Internet Explorer 6.0.

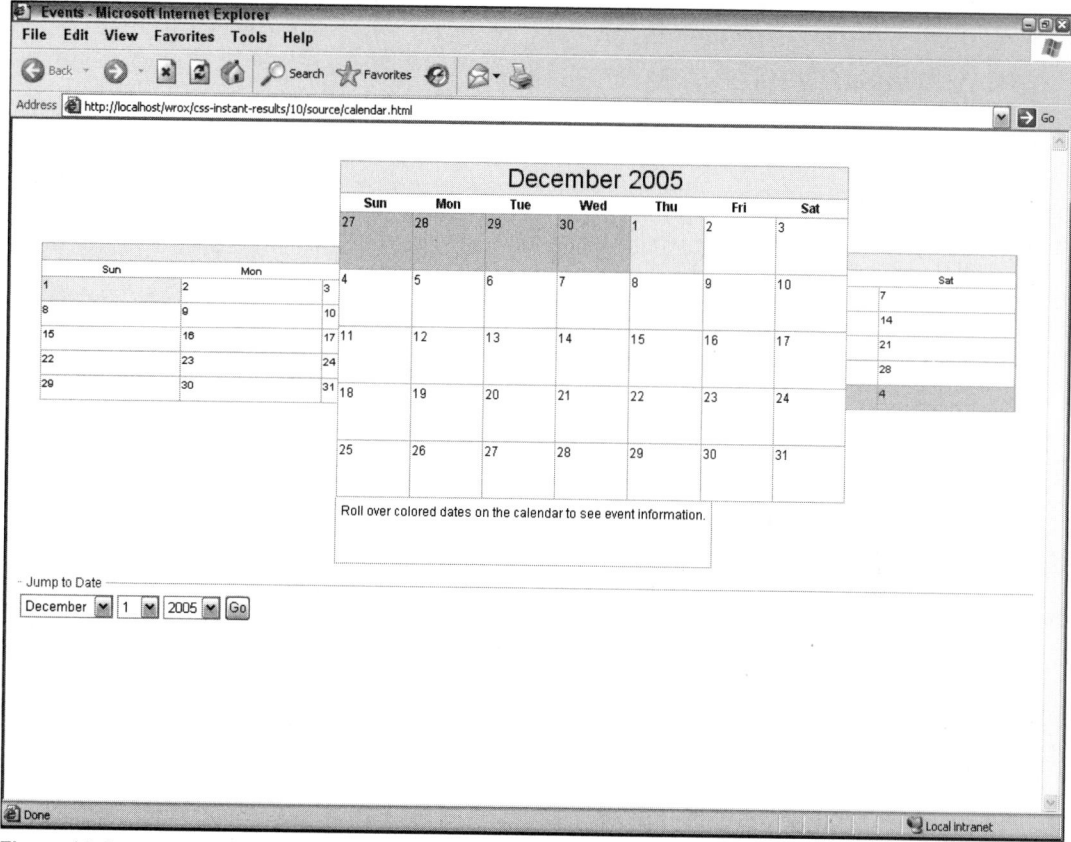

Figure 10-2

Figure 10-3 shows what `calendar.html` looks like with Dean Edwards' IE7 JavaScript applied.

Comparing Figure 10-2 to Figure 10-3 you see that it doesn't appear that anything has changed. The screenshot doesn't show it, but in Figure 10-3 the rollovers are working!

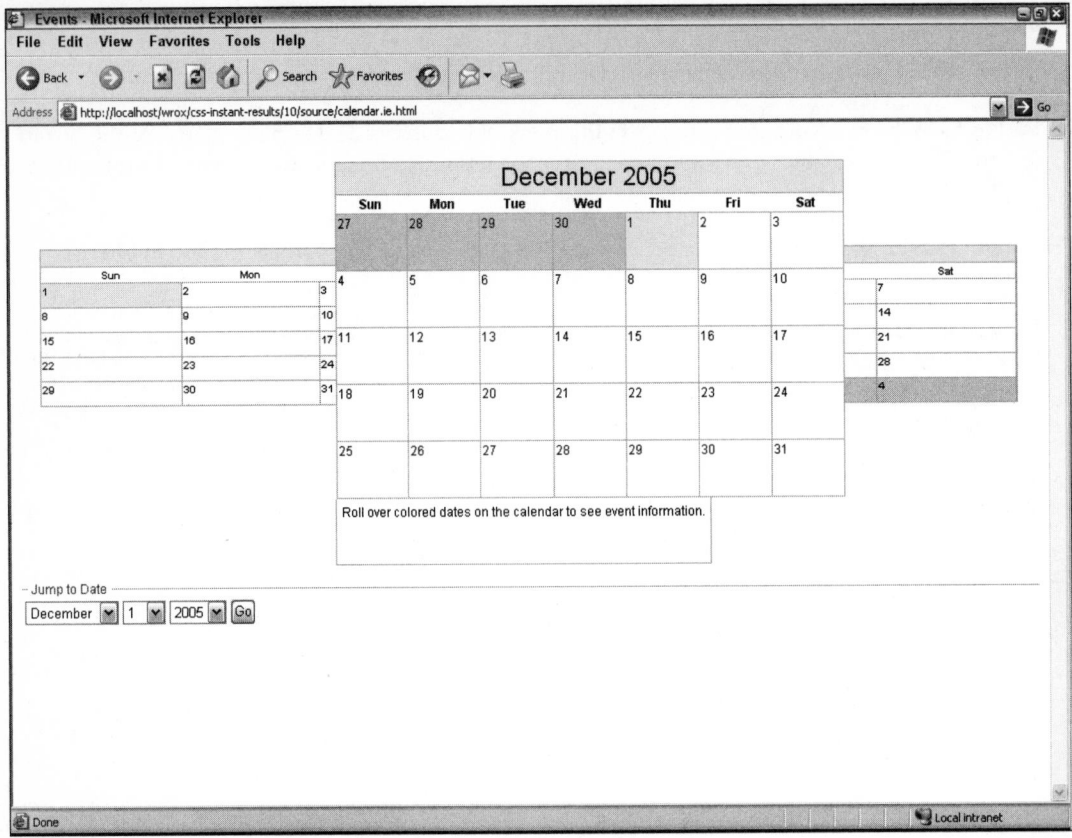

Figure 10-3

It turns out the tables are out-of-whack in Internet Explorer because of the presence of a single declaration, the `table-layout: fixed;` declaration.

Figure 10-4 shows the output in Internet Explorer after removing this declaration.

Now, it's much closer to Firefox's rendering. The `table-layout: fixed;` declaration turned out to be problematic because Internet Explorer automatically stretches `<table>` elements with this declaration applied to 100% of the width of their parent element. With the `table-layout: fixed;` declaration removed, the design is fixed.

Some things are still off, though:

❑   The events do not show up as colored days on the calendar.

❑   The width of the `event` and `event-info` elements are off.

❑   Although you cannot see it in the screenshot in Figure 10-4, the `<legend>` for the `<fieldset>` element has blue text instead of black.

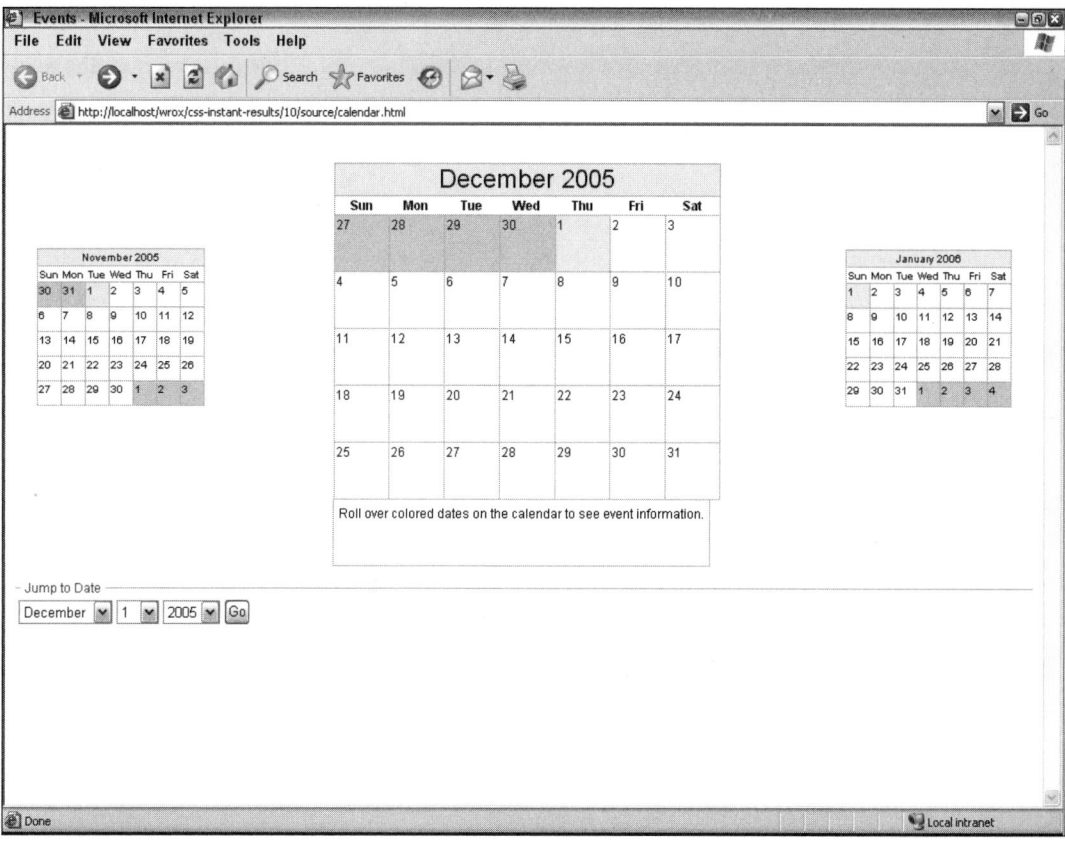

Figure 10-4

To correct Internet Explorer's off-rendering, follow these steps:

1. Open `calendar.html` and make the following modifications:

```
<!DOCTYPE html PUBLIC "-//W3C//DTD XHTML 1.0 Transitional//EN"
"http://www.w3.org/TR/2002/REC-xhtml1-20020801/DTD/xhtml1-transitional.dtd">
<html xmlns='http://www.w3.org/1999/xhtml' xml:lang='en'>
    <head>
        <meta http-equiv='content-type' content='text/html; charset=utf-8' />
        <meta http-equiv='content-language' content='en-us' />
        <title>Events</title>
        <link rel='stylesheet' href='styles/calendar-2.css' type='text/css' />
        <!-- compliance patch for microsoft browsers -->
        <!--[if lt IE 7]>
            <script src="/ie7/ie7-standard-p.js" type="text/javascript"></script>
            <link rel='stylesheet' href='styles/calendar.ie.css' type='text/css' />
        <![endif]-->
    </head>
    <body>
<div class='calendar'>
```

2. Save `calendar.html` as `calendar.ie.html`.

3. Open `calendar.css` and remove the `table-layout: fixed;` declaration from the following rule:

```
div#calendar-this-month {
    position: absolute;
    left: 50%;
    top: 20px;
    margin-left: -185px;
}
table.calendar {
    border-collapse: collapse;
    table-layout: fixed;
    border: 1px solid rgb(200, 200, 200);
}
table.calendar td {
    width: 50px;
    height: 50px;
    background: #fff;
    border: 1px solid rgb(200, 200, 200);
    vertical-align: top;
}
```

4. Save `calendar.css` as `calendar-2.css`.

5. Still working with `calendar-2.css`, reorder the rules for events so that they appear as follows:

```
div.event,
div.event-info {
    position: absolute;
    bottom: -62px;
    left: -1px;
    right: 0;
    border-bottom: 1px solid rgb(200, 200, 200);
    border-left: 1px solid rgb(200, 200, 200);
    border-right: 1px solid rgb(200, 200, 200);
    background: white;
    display: none;
    height: 51px;
    padding: 5px;
    z-index: 2;
}
div.event-info {
    display: block;
    z-index: 1;
}
span.event-date {
    font-weight: bold;
}
td.this-month.event:hover > div.event {
    display: block;
}
```

```css
table.calendar th {
    text-align: center;
    background: #fff;
}
table.calendar td {
    width: 50px;
    height: 50px;
    background: #fff;
    border: 1px solid rgb(200, 200, 200);
    vertical-align: top;
}
table.calendar td.last-month,
table.calendar td.next-month {
    background: rgb(222, 222, 222);
}
table.calendar td.today {
    background: rgb(242, 242, 242);
}
table.calendar td.this-month.event {
    background: yellow;
}
table.calendar td.this-month.today.event {
    background: gold;
}
table.calendar th.month {
    text-align: center;
    font-size: 24px;
    font-weight: normal;
    border-bottom: 1px solid rgb(200, 200, 200);
    background: rgb(242, 242, 242);
}
```

6. Save `calendar-2.css`.

7. Create the following style sheet:

```css
div.event,
div.event-info {
    width: expression(
            document.getElementById('calendar-this-month').offsetWidth - 12
        );
    left: 0;
}
legend {
    color: black;
}
```

8. Save the preceding style sheet as `calendar.ie.css`.

The preceding modifications result in the screenshot in Figure 10-5.

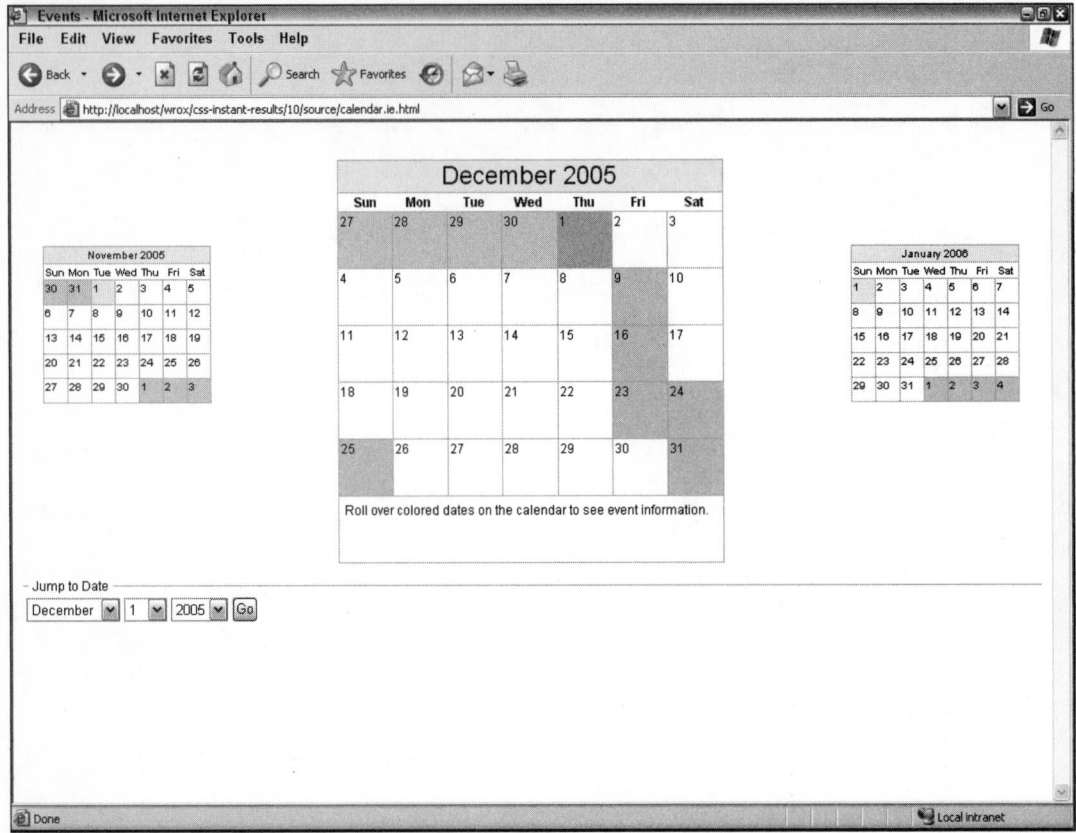

Figure 10-5

Fixing up Internet Explorer required some analysis of how Dean Edwards' IE7 JavaScript fixes buggy multiple class name support in Internet Explorer. Internet Explorer supports multiple class names by default; it, however, doesn't support chaining class name selectors in a style sheet, which is what Dean's JavaScript fixes behind the scene. The problem is that Dean's IE7 doesn't take precedence into account when applying fixes. In the original `calendar.css`, the rules that applied backgrounds to `<td>` elements containing events appeared before other `<td>` elements that apply backgrounds for generic days.

The style sheet works in Firefox because the selector `table.calendar td.this-month.event` has greater specificity than `table.calendar td`. Dean's IE7 doesn't take precedence into account by default, because doing so could have a great impact on performance. The specificity is broken because of the way IE7 applies fixes. Dean's IE7 takes selectors Internet Explorer doesn't understand and turns them into selectors that it does understand — class names. So `td.this-month.event` (as it appeared in the original `calendar.css`) becomes something like `td.ie7_22`, which has less specificity than `table.calendar td`, and results in the `<td>` event elements having white backgrounds rather than the yellow backgrounds they were supposed to have.

To correct this you reordered the flow in which the rules appear in the style sheet like so:

```
table.calendar td {
    width: 50px;
    height: 50px;
    background: #fff;
    border: 1px solid rgb(200, 200, 200);
    vertical-align: top;
}
table.calendar td.last-month,
table.calendar td.next-month {
    background: rgb(222, 222, 222);
}
table.calendar td.today {
    background: rgb(242, 242, 242);
}
table.calendar td.this-month.event {
    background: yellow;
}
table.calendar td.this-month.today.event {
    background: gold;
}
```

Now the rules appear in order of greater specificity, and when the rules have the same specificity, the last rule wins over the previous. So when IE7 turns the selector `table.calendar td.this-month.event` into `table.calendar td.ie7_22`, and `table.calendar td.this-month.today.event` into `table.calendar td.ie7_23`, the selectors end up having the same specificity, but the latter one wins out because it appears after the former.

The specificity problem could also have been fixed by including another IE7 module, `ie7-css-strict.js`, which would be done as follows:

```
<!-- compliance patch for microsoft browsers -->
<!--[if lt IE 7]>
    <script src="/ie7/ie7-standard-p.js" type="text/javascript"></script>
    <script src="/ie7/ie7-css-strict.js" type="text/javascript"></script>
    <link rel='stylesheet' href='styles/calendar.ie.css' type='text/css' />
<![endif]-->
```

I recommend adding this module only if it isn't feasible to reorder the rules in the way that I have, because taking precedence into account can cause IE7 to perform more slowly, depending on the number of style sheets and rules there are to process.

To correct the other bits, you included two rules in a new style sheet that only Internet Explorer version 6 and earlier can see. In the first rule within that style sheet, you corrected the width problem with the event and event-info <div> elements. The dynamic `expression()` feature sets the width of the event and event-info <div> elements based on the `offsetWidth` of the `calendar-this-month` <div> element, then 12 pixels are subtracted to accommodate padding and borders. The second declaration sets the left offset property to zero to correct the event and event-info <div> elements from being 1 pixel too far to the left:

```
div.event,
div.event-info {
    width: expression(
```

```
                        document.getElementById('calendar-this-month').offsetWidth - 12
                );
        left: 0;
}
```

Finally, in the last rule you correct the color of the `<legend>` element's text being blue by simply setting the color to black:

```
legend {
        color: black;
}
```

The next section shows you how to modify the project so that the calendar is bigger, and the events are included in each day, instead of being visible only by rollover.

Using and Modifying the Project

To modify the project so that the calendar is much bigger, follow these steps:

1. Open `calendar.ie.html` and restructure the document like the following:

```
<!DOCTYPE html PUBLIC "-//W3C//DTD XHTML 1.0 Transitional//EN"
"http://www.w3.org/TR/2002/REC-xhtml1-20020801/DTD/xhtml1-transitional.dtd">
<html xmlns='http://www.w3.org/1999/xhtml' xml:lang='en'>
    <head>
        <meta http-equiv='content-type' content='text/html; charset=utf-8' />
        <meta http-equiv='content-language' content='en-us' />
        <title>Events</title>
        <link rel='stylesheet' href='styles/calendar.fullPage.css'
            type='text/css' />
        <!-- compliance patch for microsoft browsers -->
        <!--[if lt IE 7]>
            <script src="/ie7/ie7-standard-p.js" type="text/javascript"></script>
        <![endif]-->
    </head>
    <body>
<div class='calendar'>
        <div id='calendar-this-month'>
            <table class='calendar current' id='calendar-1133413200'>
                <thead>
                    <tr>
                        <th class='month' colspan='7'>
        <div id='calendar-last-month' title='Navigate to Last Month'>
            <table class='calendar last' id='calendar-1130821200'>
                <thead>
                    <tr>
                        <th class='month' colspan='7'>November 2005</th>
                    </tr>
                    <tr>
                        <th class='weekday'>Sun</th>
                        <th class='weekday'>Mon</th>
                        <th class='weekday'>Tue</th>
```

```
                    <th class='weekday'>Wed</th>
                    <th class='weekday'>Thu</th>
                    <th class='weekday'>Fri</th>
                    <th class='weekday'>Sat</th>
            </tr>
        </thead>
        <tbody>
            <tr>
                    <td class='last-month' id='day-1130648400'>30</td>
                    <td class='last-month' id='day-1130734800'>31</td>
                    <td class='this-month today first' id='day-1130821200'>1</td>
                    <td class='this-month' id='day-1130907600'>2</td>
                    <td class='this-month' id='day-1130994000'>3</td>
                    <td class='this-month' id='day-1131080400'>4</td>
                    <td class='this-month' id='day-1131166800'>5</td>

            </tr>
            <tr>
                    <td class='this-month' id='day-1131253200'>6</td>
                    <td class='this-month' id='day-1131339600'>7</td>
                    <td class='this-month' id='day-1131426000'>8</td>
                    <td class='this-month' id='day-1131512400'>9</td>
                    <td class='this-month' id='day-1131598800'>10</td>
                    <td class='this-month' id='day-1131685200'>11</td>
                    <td class='this-month' id='day-1131771600'>12</td>
            </tr>
            <tr>
                    <td class='this-month' id='day-1131858000'>13</td>
                    <td class='this-month' id='day-1131944400'>14</td>
                    <td class='this-month' id='day-1132030800'>15</td>
                    <td class='this-month' id='day-1132117200'>16</td>
                    <td class='this-month' id='day-1132203600'>17</td>
                    <td class='this-month' id='day-1132290000'>18</td>
                    <td class='this-month' id='day-1132376400'>19</td>
            </tr>
            <tr>
                    <td class='this-month' id='day-1132462800'>20</td>
                    <td class='this-month' id='day-1132549200'>21</td>
                    <td class='this-month' id='day-1132635600'>22</td>
                    <td class='this-month' id='day-1132722000'>23</td>
                    <td class='this-month' id='day-1132808400'>24</td>
                    <td class='this-month' id='day-1132894800'>25</td>
                    <td class='this-month' id='day-1132981200'>26</td>
            </tr>
            <tr>
                    <td class='this-month' id='day-1133067600'>27</td>
                    <td class='this-month' id='day-1133154000'>28</td>
                    <td class='this-month' id='day-1133240400'>29</td>
                    <td class='this-month last' id='day-1133326800'>30</td>
                    <td class='last-month' id='day-1133413200'>1</td>
                    <td class='last-month' id='day-1133499600'>2</td>
                    <td class='last-month' id='day-1133586000'>3</td>
            </tr>
        </tbody>
    </table>
```

```
        </div>
        <div id='calendar-next-month' title='Navigate to Next Month'>
            <table class='calendar next' id='calendar-1136091600'>
                <thead>
                    <tr>
                        <th class='month' colspan='7'>January 2006</th>
                    </tr>
                    <tr>
                        <th class='weekday'>Sun</th>
                        <th class='weekday'>Mon</th>
                        <th class='weekday'>Tue</th>
                        <th class='weekday'>Wed</th>
                        <th class='weekday'>Thu</th>
                        <th class='weekday'>Fri</th>
                        <th class='weekday'>Sat</th>
                    </tr>
                </thead>
                <tbody>
                    <tr>
                        <td class='this-month today first' id='day-1136091600'>1</td>
                        <td class='this-month' id='day-1136178000'>2</td>
                        <td class='this-month' id='day-1136264400'>3</td>
                        <td class='this-month' id='day-1136350800'>4</td>
                        <td class='this-month' id='day-1136437200'>5</td>
                        <td class='this-month' id='day-1136523600'>6</td>
                        <td class='this-month' id='day-1136610000'>7</td>
                    </tr>
                    <tr>
                        <td class='this-month' id='day-1136696400'>8</td>
                        <td class='this-month' id='day-1136782800'>9</td>
                        <td class='this-month' id='day-1136869200'>10</td>
                        <td class='this-month' id='day-1136955600'>11</td>
                        <td class='this-month' id='day-1137042000'>12</td>
                        <td class='this-month' id='day-1137128400'>13</td>
                        <td class='this-month' id='day-1137214800'>14</td>
                    </tr>
                    <tr>
                        <td class='this-month' id='day-1137301200'>15</td>
                        <td class='this-month' id='day-1137387600'>16</td>
                        <td class='this-month' id='day-1137474000'>17</td>
                        <td class='this-month' id='day-1137560400'>18</td>
                        <td class='this-month' id='day-1137646800'>19</td>
                        <td class='this-month' id='day-1137733200'>20</td>
                        <td class='this-month' id='day-1137819600'>21</td>
                    </tr>
                    <tr>
                        <td class='this-month' id='day-1137906000'>22</td>
                        <td class='this-month' id='day-1137992400'>23</td>
                        <td class='this-month' id='day-1138078800'>24</td>
                        <td class='this-month' id='day-1138165200'>25</td>
                        <td class='this-month' id='day-1138251600'>26</td>
                        <td class='this-month' id='day-1138338000'>27</td>
                        <td class='this-month' id='day-1138424400'>28</td>
                    </tr>
                    <tr>
```

```
                <td class='this-month' id='day-1138510800'>29</td>
                <td class='this-month' id='day-1138597200'>30</td>
                <td class='this-month last' id='day-1138683600'>31</td>
                <td class='last-month' id='day-1138770000'>1</td>
                <td class='last-month' id='day-1138856400'>2</td>
                <td class='last-month' id='day-1138942800'>3</td>
                <td class='last-month' id='day-1139029200'>4</td>
            </tr>
        </tbody>
    </table>
</div>
<span class='this-month'>December 2005</span>

                </th>
            </tr>
            <tr>
                <th class='weekday'>Sun</th>
                <th class='weekday'>Mon</th>
                <th class='weekday'>Tue</th>
                <th class='weekday'>Wed</th>
                <th class='weekday'>Thu</th>
                <th class='weekday'>Fri</th>
                <th class='weekday'>Sat</th>
            </tr>
        </thead>
        <tbody>
            <tr>
                <td class='last-month' id='day-1133067600'>27</td>
                <td class='last-month' id='day-1133154000'>28</td>
                <td class='last-month' id='day-1133240400'>29</td>
                <td class='last-month' id='day-1133326800'>30</td>
                <td class='this-month today first event' id='day-1133413200'>
                    1
                    <div class='event'>
                        <span class='event-date'>December 1, 2005</span>
                        Finish writing Chapter 6.
                    </div>
                </td>
                <td class='this-month' id='day-1133499600'>2</td>
                <td class='this-month' id='day-1133586000'>3</td>
            </tr>
            <tr>
                <td class='this-month' id='day-1133672400'>4</td>
                <td class='this-month' id='day-1133758800'>5</td>
                <td class='this-month' id='day-1133845200'>6</td>
                <td class='this-month' id='day-1133931600'>7</td>
                <td class='this-month' id='day-1134018000'>8</td>
                <td class='this-month event' id='day-1134104400'>
                    9
                    <div class='event'>
                        <span class='event-date'>December 9, 2005</span>
                        CSS Instant Results deadline.
                    </div>
                </td>
                <td class='this-month' id='day-1134190800'>10</td>
            </tr>
```

```
<tr>
    <td class='this-month' id='day-1134277200'>11</td>
    <td class='this-month' id='day-1134363600'>12</td>
    <td class='this-month' id='day-1134450000'>13</td>
    <td class='this-month' id='day-1134536400'>14</td>
    <td class='this-month' id='day-1134622800'>15</td>
    <td class='this-month event' id='day-1134709200'>
        16
        <div class='event'>
            <span class='event-date'>December 16, 2005</span>
            Company Christmas party.
        </div>
    </td>
    <td class='this-month' id='day-1134795600'>17</td>
</tr>
<tr>
    <td class='this-month' id='day-1134882000'>18</td>
    <td class='this-month' id='day-1134968400'>19</td>
    <td class='this-month' id='day-1135054800'>20</td>
    <td class='this-month' id='day-1135141200'>21</td>
    <td class='this-month' id='day-1135227600'>22</td>
    <td class='this-month event' id='day-1135314000'>
        23
        <div class='event'>
            <span class='event-date'>December 23, 2005</span>
            Party at Richard's place, BYOB!
        </div>
    </td>
    <td class='this-month event' id='day-1135400400'>
        24
        <div class='event'>
            <span class='event-date'>December 24, 2005</span>
            Christmas Eve
        </div>
    </td>
</tr>
<tr>
    <td class='this-month event' id='day-1135486800'>
        25
        <div class='event'>
            <span class='event-date'>December 25, 2005</span>
            Christmas Day
        </div>
    </td>
    <td class='this-month' id='day-1135573200'>26</td>
    <td class='this-month' id='day-1135659600'>27</td>
    <td class='this-month' id='day-1135746000'>28</td>
    <td class='this-month' id='day-1135832400'>29</td>
    <td class='this-month' id='day-1135918800'>30</td>
    <td class='this-month last event' id='day-1136005200'>
        31
        <div class='event'>
            <span class='event-date'>December 31, 2005</span>
            New Year's Eve
        </div>
```

```
                            </td>
                        </tr>
                    </tbody>
                </table>
            </div>
        </div>
<form method='get' action='javascript:void(0);'>
    <fieldset>
        <legend><span>Jump to Date</span></legend>
        <table>
            <tbody>
                <tr>
                    <td class='form-input'>
                        <select id='calendar-month' name='month'>
                            <option value='1'>January</option>
                            <option value='2'>February</option>
                            <option value='3'>March</option>
                            <option value='4'>April</option>
                            <option value='5'>May</option>
                            <option value='6'>June</option>
                            <option value='7'>July</option>
                            <option value='8'>August</option>
                            <option value='9'>September</option>
                            <option value='10'>October</option>
                            <option value='11'>November</option>
                            <option value='12' selected='selected'>
                                December
                            </option>
                        </select>
                    </td>
                    <td class='form-input'>
                        <select id='calendar-day' name='day'>
                            <option value='1' selected='selected'>1</option>
                            <option value='2'>2</option>
                            <option value='3'>3</option>
                            <option value='4'>4</option>
                            <option value='5'>5</option>
                            <option value='6'>6</option>
                            <option value='7'>7</option>
                            <option value='8'>8</option>
                            <option value='9'>9</option>
                            <option value='10'>10</option>
                            <option value='11'>11</option>
                            <option value='12'>12</option>
                            <option value='13'>13</option>
                            <option value='14'>14</option>
                            <option value='15'>15</option>
                            <option value='16'>16</option>
                            <option value='17'>17</option>
                            <option value='18'>18</option>
                            <option value='19'>19</option>
                            <option value='20'>20</option>
                            <option value='21'>21</option>
                            <option value='22'>22</option>
                            <option value='23'>23</option>
```

```
                                <option value='24'>24</option>
                                <option value='25'>25</option>
                                <option value='26'>26</option>
                                <option value='27'>27</option>
                                <option value='28'>28</option>
                                <option value='29'>29</option>
                                <option value='30'>30</option>
                                <option value='31'>31</option>
                        </select>
                </td>
                <td class='form-input'>
                        <select id='calendar-year' name='year'>
                                <option value='1970'>1970</option>
                                <option value='1971'>1971</option>
                                <option value='1972'>1972</option>
                                <option value='1973'>1973</option>
                                <option value='1974'>1974</option>
                                <option value='1975'>1975</option>
                                <option value='1976'>1976</option>
                                <option value='1977'>1977</option>
                                <option value='1978'>1978</option>
                                <option value='1979'>1979</option>
                                <option value='1980'>1980</option>
                                <option value='1981'>1981</option>
                                <option value='1982'>1982</option>
                                <option value='1983'>1983</option>
                                <option value='1984'>1984</option>
                                <option value='1985'>1985</option>
                                <option value='1986'>1986</option>
                                <option value='1987'>1987</option>
                                <option value='1988'>1988</option>
                                <option value='1989'>1989</option>
                                <option value='1990'>1990</option>
                                <option value='1991'>1991</option>
                                <option value='1992'>1992</option>
                                <option value='1993'>1993</option>
                                <option value='1994'>1994</option>
                                <option value='1995'>1995</option>
                                <option value='1996'>1996</option>
                                <option value='1997'>1997</option>
                                <option value='1998'>1998</option>
                                <option value='1999'>1999</option>
                                <option value='2000'>2000</option>
                                <option value='2001'>2001</option>
                                <option value='2002'>2002</option>
                                <option value='2003'>2003</option>
                                <option value='2004'>2004</option>
                                <option value='2005' selected='selected'>2005</option>
                                <option value='2006'>2006</option>
                                <option value='2007'>2007</option>
                                <option value='2008'>2008</option>
                                <option value='2009'>2009</option>
                                <option value='2010'>2010</option>
                                <option value='2011'>2011</option>
                                <option value='2012'>2012</option>
                                <option value='2013'>2013</option>
```

```
                                <option value='2014'>2014</option>
                                <option value='2015'>2015</option>
                                <option value='2016'>2016</option>
                                <option value='2017'>2017</option>
                                <option value='2018'>2018</option>
                                <option value='2019'>2019</option>
                                <option value='2020'>2020</option>
                                <option value='2021'>2021</option>
                                <option value='2022'>2022</option>
                                <option value='2023'>2023</option>
                                <option value='2024'>2024</option>
                                <option value='2025'>2025</option>
                                <option value='2026'>2026</option>
                                <option value='2027'>2027</option>
                                <option value='2028'>2028</option>
                                <option value='2029'>2029</option>
                                <option value='2030'>2030</option>
                                <option value='2031'>2031</option>
                                <option value='2032'>2032</option>
                                <option value='2033'>2033</option>
                                <option value='2034'>2034</option>
                                <option value='2035'>2035</option>
                                <option value='2036'>2036</option>
                                <option value='2037'>2037</option>
                            </select>
                        </td>
                        <td class='form-button'>
                            <input type='submit'
                                    id='calendar-jump-to-date'
                                    value='Go' />
                        </td>
                    </tr>
                </tbody>
            </table>
        </fieldset>
    </form>
        </body>
    </html>
```

2. Save the preceding as `calendar.fullPage.html`.

3. Open `calendar-2.css` and make the following modifications. For this project many declarations were removed as well as added. The resulting style sheet follows:

```
body {
    font: 12px sans-serif;
}
div.calendar {
    position: relative;
    min-width: 760px;
    max-width: 1000px;
    margin: auto;
}
table.calendar {
    border-collapse: collapse;
    border: 1px solid rgb(200, 200, 200);
}
```

```css
table.calendar.current {
    width: 100%;
    table-layout: fixed;
}
span.this-month {
    font-size: 50px;
}
div.event {
    padding: 5px;
}
span.event-date {
    font-weight: bold;
}
table.calendar th {
    text-align: center;
    background: #fff;
}
table.calendar td {
    background: #fff;
    border: 1px solid rgb(200, 200, 200);
    vertical-align: top;
}
table.calendar td.last-month,
table.calendar td.next-month {
    background: rgb(222, 222, 222);
}
table.calendar td.today {
    background: rgb(242, 242, 242);
}
table.calendar td.this-month.event {
    background: yellow;
}
table.calendar td.this-month.today.event {
    background: gold;
}
table.calendar th.month {
    text-align: center;
    font-size: 24px;
    font-weight: normal;
    border-bottom: 1px solid rgb(200, 200, 200);
    background: rgb(242, 242, 242);
}
table.calendar.last,
table.calendar.next {
    font-size: 10px;
    cursor: pointer;
}
table.calendar.last th.month,
table.calendar.next th.month {
    font-size: 10px;
}
table.calendar.last td,
table.calendar.next td {
    width: 20px;
    height: 20px;
}
```

```
div#calendar-last-month {
    float: left;
}
div#calendar-next-month {
    float: right;
}
fieldset {
    margin: 0 auto;
    border: none;
    border-top: 1px solid rgb(200, 200, 200);
    max-width: 998px;
}
legend {
    color: black;
}
```

4. Save the preceding document as `calendar.fullPage.css`.

The modifications result in the output you see in Figure 10-6.

Figure 10-6

Making the calendar take up more screen space required a restructuring of the markup. First, you updated the file referenced for the style sheet to reflect the style sheet being renamed `calendar .fullPage.css`. Next, the IE-specific style sheet then was no longer needed, so you removed it. Dean's IE7 is still needed to interpret the minimum and maximum width properties, although as you have seen throughout this book, this can also be done with the proprietary dynamic `expression()` feature of Internet Explorer. In the body of the markup, the calendars for the previous and following months were moved to appear in the `<th>` element containing the month name for the current month, and the `event-info` `<div>` element was removed.

In the style sheet you removed several rules that were no longer used and modified existing rules to make the calendar much larger.

In the following rule you removed the `height: 390px;` declaration so the calendar would be free to expand vertically as necessary:

```
div.calendar {
    position: relative;
    min-width: 760px;
    max-width: 1000px;
    margin: auto;
}
```

The next rule was added so that the calendar for the current month would take up all the space available horizontally with the `width: 100%;` declaration. Then the `table-layout: fixed;` declaration forces explicit width and height as applied to table cells or columns to be honored. This time the layout of the table element calls for it to take up all the space available to it, so the table still renders properly in Internet Explorer:

```
table.calendar.current {
    width: 100%;
    table-layout: fixed;
}
```

You added a `<span>` element with a `this-month` class name around the name and year of the current month. In the next rule you enlarged the text contained in that `<span>` element to 50 pixels:

```
span.this-month {
    font-size: 50px;
}
```

In the next rule you removed several declarations that were previously applied for positioning the event beneath the table. Eleven declarations were removed, and only the single declaration of `padding: 5px;` remains, which is used to space the text within the event `<div>` element from the borders of the `<td>` element that contains it:

```
div.event {
    padding: 5px;
}
```

In the next rule, you removed the width and height constraints on the `<td>` elements of the calendar for the current month:

```
table.calendar td {
    background: #fff;
    border: 1px solid rgb(200, 200, 200);
    vertical-align: top;
}
```

Then, in the following rule, you removed the `font-size: 24px;` declaration because it is no longer needed. You added the `font-size: 50px;` declaration to the `this-month` `<span>` earlier in the style sheet to replace it:

```
table.calendar th.month {
    text-align: center;
    font-size: 24px;
    font-weight: normal;
    border-bottom: 1px solid rgb(200, 200, 200);
    background: rgb(242, 242, 242);
}
```

In the preceding rule, you removed the margin declaration, because the calendars for the following and previous months are now positioned to the left and right of the name and year of the current month:

```
table.calendar.last,
table.calendar.next {
    font-size: 10px;
    cursor: pointer;
}
```

Next, you position the calendars to the left and right of the name and year of the current month with the following two rules:

```
div#calendar-last-month {
    float: left;
}
div#calendar-next-month {
    float: right;
}
```

Because you deleted the Internet Explorer–specific style sheet, the fix for the text of the `<legend>` element being blue was lost, which is why you added the following rule to `calendar.fullPage.css`:

```
legend {
    color: black;
}
```

And there you have it. You now have a calendar application that takes up as much of the browser window as is practical and feasible.

Index

SYMBOLS AND NUMERICS

+ (adjacent sibling selector)
IE7 JavaScript providing, 13
input forms using, 229

> (direct child selector)
drop-down menus using, 64
IE7 JavaScript providing, 13

- (indirect adjacent sibling selector), 13

456bereastreet.com web site, 138

A

`<a>` **element**
drop-down menus using, 71, 100
input forms using, 225
slide show using, 133
tabs using, 11, 12

`:active` **pseudo-class**
drop-down menus using, 100
IE7 JavaScript providing, 13

adjacent sibling selector (+)
IE7 JavaScript providing, 13
input forms using, 229

`::after` **pseudo-element**
IE7 JavaScript providing, 13
webmail application using, 174

alpha transparency, PNG images
borders and corners using, 146
definition of, 76
drop-down menus using, 91–92
file viewer using, 300, 305–307
webmail application using, 179

`amazon.html` **file, 3–4, 25–26**

anchors, HTML (URL fragments), 100

Aqua
input fields rendered by, 200
user interface for, 243

attribute selectors, 13

B

`background` **declaration**
calendar using, 345, 347
drop-down menus using, 92
file viewer using, 268, 325
input forms using, 233
tabs using, 19, 22
webmail application using, 170, 184–185

background images for tabs
with text, 19–23
without text, 16–19

`::before` **pseudo-element**
IE7 JavaScript providing, 13
input forms using, 229
webmail application using, 174

Beginning CSS: Cascading Style Sheets for Web Design
(York), 13, 49

Beginning JavaScript, 2nd Edition (Wilton), 78

Bergevin, Holly (Holly Hack), 240–241

`<body>` **element**
borders and corners using, 141, 149
drop-down menus using, 69
file viewer using, 267, 303–304, 325
input forms using, 220
margin in, removing, 9
multi-column layout using, 36, 59
slide show using, 132
tabs using, 2, 9, 11
webmail application using, 169

books. *See* **publications**
`border` **declaration**
  calendar using, 350
  file viewer using, 278
borders
  `<body>` element for, 141, 149
  browser incompatibilities with, 145–147
  challenges implementing, 137
  code for
    `borders.css` file, 140–141
    `borders.html` file, 138–140
  CSS 3 features for, 137
  designing, 138
  `<div>` element for, 138, 142–144, 146
  for drop-down menus, 85–93
  images for, 141
  for input forms project, 230
  results of, 142, 145–147
  `<span>` element for, 143, 152
  transparent PNG images in, 146
`borders.css` **file, 140–141**
`borders.html` **file, 138–140**
`borders.kalsey.css` **file, 149–150**
`borders.kalsey.html` **file, 148–149**
`borders.kalsey.ie.css` **file, 150–151**
`bottom` **property**
  `expression()` feature and, 56, 58, 60
  IE7 JavaScript providing, 15, 39
  when to use, 32
bread crumbs, input forms, 227–230, 241
browsers. *See also* **Internet Explorer (IE)**
  Firefox browser
    fixed width for `<ul>` element, 10
    `:hover` pseudo-class support, 15
    input forms used by, 200
    margins in `<body>` element, 9
    `:target` pseudo-class support, 101
  Gecko browser, 268
  incompatibilities between
    with borders, 145–147
    with calendar, 351–353, 356–358
    with drop-down menus, 71, 77
    with file viewer, web-based, 299–307
    with input forms, 200, 236, 238, 240–241
    with multi-column layout, 31, 39, 40, 60
    with rounded corners, 145–147
    with slide shows, 123–124
    with tabs, 1, 13
    with webmail application, 175–180
  Konqueror browser, 31

Mozilla Firefox browser
  fixed width for `<ul>` element, 10
  `:hover` pseudo-class support, 15
  input forms used by, 200
  margins in `<body>` element, 9
  `:target` pseudo-class support, 101
Opera browser
  fixed width for `<ul>` element, 10
  forms, look and feel of, 200
  `:hover` pseudo-class support, 15
  input forms used by, 200
  `:last-child` pseudo-class support, 145–146
  margins in `<body>` element, 9
  `opacity` property support, 123–124
  `:target` pseudo-class support, 101, 123–124
Safari browser
  forms, look and feel of, 200
  `:hover` pseudo-class support, 15
  input forms used by, 200
  styling of input fields, support for, 200
  `:target` pseudo-class support, 101

C

calendar
  `background` declaration for, 345, 347
  `border` declaration for, 350
  browser incompatibilities with, 351–353, 356–358
  code for
    `calendar.css` file, 343–345
    `calendar.fullPage.css` file, 365–367
    `calendar.fullPage.html` file, 358–365
    `calendar.html` file, 336–343
    `calendar.ie.css` file, 354–355
    `calendar.ie.html` file, 353–354
    `calendar-2.css` file, 354
  designing, 335–336
  `<div>` element for, 346–347, 348, 368–369
  events in
    designing, 335–336
    in Internet Explorer, 352, 354–358
    styling of, 347–348, 349
  `expression()` feature for, 368
  `<fieldset>` element for, 350, 352
  IE7 JavaScript used for, 351–352, 356–357
  increasing size of, 358–369
  `<legend>` element for, 352, 358, 369
  links used in, 349
  positioning of calendars, 346–347
  results of, 346, 356, 367

`<select>` element for, 335
`<span>` element for, 368, 369
styling of calendars, 347–350
tables for
  designing, 336
  implementing, 347–350
  for Internet Explorer, 352, 356–357
  large-sized calendar, 368–369
`vertical-align` declaration for, 347
`calendar.css` **file, 343–345**
`calendar.fullPage.css` **file, 365–367**
`calendar.fullPage.html` **file, 358–365**
`calendar.html` **file, 336–343**
`calendar.ie.css` **file, 354–355**
`calendar.ie.html` **file, 353–354**
`calendar-2.css` **file, 354**
Cascading Style Sheets (CSS)
  event-driven functionality in, 111
  role in application development, 157
Choose a Directory dialog, file viewer, 328–334
`color` **declaration**
  file viewer using, 268
  tabs using, 11, 12
column layout, multiple
  `<body>` element for, 36, 59
  browser incompatibilities with, 31, 39
  code for
    `float-columns.css` file, 50–51
    `float-columns.html` file, 50
    `float-columns-ie.css` file, 51–52
    `liquid-columns.css` file, 46–47
    `liquid-columns.html` file, 45
    `liquid-columns-ie.css` file, 47
    `multi-column.css` file, 34–35
    `multi-column.html` file, 33–34
    `multi-column-ie.css` file, 35, 40
    `two-column.css` file, 42–43
    `two-column.html` file, 42
    `two-column-ie.css` file, 43
  content column, fluid, 33, 38
  designing, 31–33, 41
  `<div>` element for
    browser incompatibilities with, 40, 60
    for float method, 52–55
    for liquid secondary columns, 44–45, 48–49
    for three-column layout, 32, 37–39
  `expression()` feature for, 56–59
  float method for, 49–55
  footer for, 33, 36, 38–39
  header for, 36, 38–39
  IE7 JavaScript used for, 39–41
  Internet Explorer hacks for, 56–61
  JavaScript for, 55–56, 59
  margins for
    float method, 54–55, 60
    Internet Explorer solution, 40
    liquid columns, 44, 48–49
    three-column layout, 32, 36–39
    two-column layout, 42
  markup for, guidelines regarding, 32
  results of
    float method, 52
    for Internet Explorer, 58
    liquid columns, 47–48
    three-column layout, 41
    two-column layout, 44
  secondary columns, liquid, 44–49
  tables for, when to use, 45
  three-column layout, 32, 37–39
  two-column layout, 42–44
`content` **property**
  IE7 JavaScript providing, 13
  webmail application using, 174
corners, rounded
  `<body>` element for, 141, 149
  browser incompatibilities with, 145–147
  challenges implementing, 137
  code for
    `borders.css` file, 140–141
    `borders.html` file, 138–140
    `borders.kalsey.css` file, 149–150
    `borders.kalsey.html` file, 148–149
    `borders.kalsey.ie.css` file, 150–151
  CSS 3 features for, 137
  designing, 138
  `<div>` element for, 138, 142–144, 146, 151–154
  images for, 141, 152–154
  for input forms project, 230
  Kalsey's technique for, 147–155
  results of, 142, 145–147, 151, 153, 155
  `<span>` element for, 143, 152
  transparent PNG images in, 146
CSS (Cascading Style Sheets)
  event-driven functionality in, 111
  role in application development, 157
***CSS the Definitive Guide* (Meyer), 111**
cssQuery JavaScript, 78, 306–307

D

dates as Unix timestamps, 335, 336
Details view, file viewer, 288–289, 290–293
direct child selector (>)
　drop-down menus using, 64
　IE7 JavaScript providing, 13
directories, viewing. See file viewer, web-based
`<div>` **element**
　borders using, 138, 142–144, 146
　calendar using, 346–347, 348, 368–369
　directory window using, 284
　drop-down menus using, 90, 92, 94, 96–97
　input forms using
　　bread crumbs, 227–229
　　content, 220, 230, 231–232
　　footer, 231
　　form controls, 222–223, 224–225, 235
　　header, 219–221, 240–241
　　left column, 225–227
　multi-column layout using
　　browser incompatibilities with, 40, 60
　　for float method, 52–55
　　for liquid secondary columns, 44–45, 48–49
　　for three-column layout, 32, 37–39
　rounded corners using, 138, 142–144, 146, 151–154
　for Save As dialog, 325–328
　slide show using, 112, 122–123, 132, 134
　tabs using, 12, 28
　webmail application using
　　browser incompatibilities with, 176
　　for buttons, 169
　　for mailboxes, 170
　　for message preview, 184–185
　　for message window, 171–173, 179–180, 183, 195–196
drop-down menus
　`<a>` element for, 71, 100
　`:active` pseudo-class for, 100
　`background` declaration for, 92
　background for, 85–93
　`<body>` element for, 69
　borders for, 85–93
　browser incompatibilities with, 71, 77
　clicking to open menus, enabling, 100–109
　code for
　　`drop_down_menus.css` file, 67–68, 82–83, 89–90, 94–95, 106–107
　　`drop_down_menus.html` file, 64–67, 71–75, 79–82, 85–88, 94, 101–106
　　`drop_down_menus.js` file, 83–84, 90

　CSS-only solution for, 64–71
　designing, 63–64
　direct child selector (>) for, 64
　`<div>` element for, 90, 92, 94, 96–97
　dropping down instead of sideways, 94–97
　in file viewer application, 269–274, 304
　`:first-child` pseudo-class for, 91, 327
　`:focus` pseudo-class for, 109
　`:hover` pseudo-class for, 64, 71, 77, 84
　IE7 JavaScript used for, 71–77
　JavaScript-enhanced solution for, 78–84, 90, 91
　`:last-child` pseudo-class for, 91
　links used in
　　custom backgrounds and borders solution, 91, 93
　　JavaScript-enabled solution, 83, 84
　　pure-CSS solution, 63, 69
　　`:target` pseudo-class solution, 109
　`list-style` declaration for, 70
　`position` declaration for, 93
　results of
　　custom backgrounds and borders solution, 90
　　drop down (not sideways) solution, 96
　　Internet Explorer solution, 76
　　JavaScript-enabled solution, 83
　　pure-CSS solution, 68
　　`:target` pseudo-class solution, 108
　`<span>` element for, 77, 93
　`:target` pseudo-class for, 100–109
　transparent PNG images in, 91–92
　unordered lists for
　　for drop down (not sideways) solution, 97
　　in file viewer application, 269–274, 304
　　for Internet Explorer solution, 77
　　for JavaScript-enabled solution, 84
　　for pure-CSS solution, 68–71
　`visibility` property for, 70
`drop_down_menus.css` **file**
　for custom backgrounds and borders, 89–90
　for drop-down solution, 94–95
　for JavaScript-enabled solution, 82–83
　for pure-CSS solution, 67–68
　for `:target`-enabled solution, 106–107
`drop_down_menus.html` **file**
　for custom backgrounds and borders, 85–88
　for drop-down solution, 94
　for Internet Explorer solution, 71–75
　for JavaScript-enabled solution, 79–82
　for pure-CSS solution, 64–67
　for `:target`-enabled solution, 101–106
`drop_down_menus.js` **file, 83–84, 90**
dynamic drop-down menus. See drop-down menus

E

ECMAScript, 56

Edwards, Dean
cssQuery JavaScript, 78
IE7 JavaScript, 13
`ie7-recalc.js` module, 91

Eric Meyer on CSS **(Meyer), 111**

events
in calendar
designing, 335–336
in Internet Explorer, 352, 354–358
styling of, 347–348, 349
capturing fragment links as, 100
CSS functionality for, 111

`expression()` **feature, Internet Explorer**
calendar using, 368
file viewer application using, 303–304
multi-column layout using, 56–59
slide show using, 131–132
webmail application using, 185

F

`<fieldset>` **element**
calendar using, 350, 352
input forms using, 232–233, 241

file viewer, web-based
`background` declaration for, 268, 325
`<body>` element for, 267, 303–304, 325
`border` declaration for, 350
browser incompatibilities with, 299–307
Choose a Directory dialog, 328–334
code for
`hFinder.chooseDirectory.html` file, 329–332
`hFinder.css` file, 258–259, 321–322, 332–333
`hFinder.html` file, 246–258
`hFinder.ie.css` file, 301
`hFinder.ie.html` file, 300–301
`hFinder.saveas.html` file, 313–320
`hFinder.wDetails.html` file, 309–312
`menus.css` file, 259–261
`png.js` file, 302
`popup.css` file, 263–264
`tree.css` file, 261
`tree.ie.css` file, 301–302
`views.css` file, 261–263, 312
`color` declaration for, 268
cssQuery JavaScript used by, 306–307
designing, 243–245
Details view, 288–289, 290–293

directory tree, 268–269, 274–279, 304–305
directory window, 269, 279–293
drop-down menus, 269–274, 304
`expression()` feature for, 303–304
`filter` property for, 300, 306
Hierophant framework for, 243, 246
`<iframe>` element for, 298
`left` property for, 268
List view, 287–288, 289–290, 293
`list-style` declaration for, 273, 277
`list-style-type` declaration for, 271
`moz-user-select` declaration for, 268
`opacity` property for, 273
overall layout for, 266–269
popup windows, 293–298
`position` declaration for, 277, 288, 326
results of, 265–266, 285–288, 290, 313
`right` property for, 268
Save As dialog
code for, 313–322
implementing, 322–323, 325–328
results of, 323–324
`<span>` element for
directory tree, 278
drop-down menus, 274
images, 306
Save As dialog, 327
Thumbnails view, 291
tables for, 308
`:target` pseudo-class for, 272
Thumbnails view, 284–285, 289, 291
Tiles and Icons view, 284–287, 291, 293
toolbar, 268, 300
transparent PNG images in, 300, 305–307
unordered lists for, 269–274, 304
`vertical-align` declaration for, 327
`visibility` property for, 272, 273
`white-space` declaration for, 277
Windows Details view, 308–313

`filter` **property**
as alternative to `opacity` property, 124
slide show using, 132–133, 134
transparent PNG images supported using
drop-down menus, 76, 77, 91
file viewer, 300, 306

Firefox browser
fixed width for `<ul>` element, 10
`:hover` pseudo-class support, 15
input forms used by, 200
margins in `<body>` element, 9
`:target` pseudo-class support, 101

`:first-child` **pseudo-class**
  drop-down menus using, 91, 327
  file viewer using, 327
  IE7 JavaScript providing, 13
  Internet Explorer support, 145
`float-columns.css` **file, 50–51**
`float-columns.html` **file, 50**
`float-columns-ie.css` **file, 51–52**
`:focus` **pseudo-class**
  drop-down menus using, 109
  IE7 JavaScript providing, 13
forms, input
  `<a>` element for, 225
  adjacent sibling selector (+) used in, 229
  `background` declaration for, 233
  `::before` pseudo-element for, 229
  `<body>` element for, 220
  borders for, 230
  bread crumbs for, 227–230, 241
  browser incompatibilities with, 200, 236, 238,
      240–241
  code for
    `p2p-body.css` file, 215–216
    `p2p-form.css` file, 216–218
    `p2p-header.css` file, 213–214
    `p2p-ie.css` file, 239
    `register.html` file, 202–212
    `register-ie-hacks.html` file, 238–239
    `register-ie.html` file, 236–237
  designing, 199–202
  `<div>` element for
    bread crumbs, 227–229
    content, 220, 230, 231–232
    footer, 231
    form controls, 222–223, 224–225, 235
    header, 219–221, 240–241
    left column, 225–227
  `<fieldset>` element for, 232–233, 241
  footer for, 231
  header for, 219–221
  Holly Hack used by, 240–241
  IE7 JavaScript used for, 236–237
  left column for, 225–226, 227
  `<legend>` element for, 199, 232–233, 238, 241
  links used in, 219, 220–221, 226–228
  `position` declaration for, 220, 230, 233, 241
  registration form in, 231–235
  results of, 218–219, 237, 240
  rounded corners for, 230
  search box for, 222–225
  `<select>` element for, 235

  `<span>` element for, 230, 232
  tables for, 202, 232–233
  tabs in, 221–222
  two-column layout for, 220
  unordered lists for, 221–222
  validating markup for, 223–224
  `vertical-align` declaration for, 225
456bereastreet.com web site, 138
fragment links, capturing as an event, 100
frames, for webmail application, 160–161, 169

G
Gecko browser, 268
`google.html` **file, 4, 25–26**
greater than sign (>), direct child selector
  drop-down menus using, 64
  IE7 JavaScript providing, 13

H
`hasLayout` **feature, Internet Explorer, 241**
hFinder application. See file viewer, web-based
`hFinder.chooseDirectory.html` **file, 329–332**
`hFinder.css` **file, 258–259, 321–322, 332–333**
`hFinder.html` **file, 246–258**
`hFinder.ie.css` **file, 301**
`hFinder.ie.html` **file, 300–301**
`hFinder.saveas.html` **file, 313–320**
`hFinder.wDetails.html` **file, 309–312**
Hierophant framework, 243, 246
Holly Hack, input forms using, 240–241
`:hover` **pseudo-class**
  drop-down menus using, 64, 71, 77, 84
  IE7 JavaScript providing, 13
  tabs using, 2, 10–11, 15
HTML anchors (URL fragments), 100
Hyatt, Dave (Safari developer), 200
hyperlinks
  calendar using, 349
  drop-down menus using
    custom backgrounds and borders solution, 91, 93
    JavaScript-enabled solution, 83, 84
    pure-CSS solution, 63, 69
    `:target` pseudo-class solution, 109
  fragment links, capturing as an event, 100
  input forms using, 219, 220–221, 226–228
  slide show using, 123, 133
  tabs using, 2, 11, 12
  webmail application using, 169, 172, 196
hyphen (-), indirect adjacent sibling selector, 13

I

IE. *See* Internet Explorer

IE7 JavaScript
alpha transparency feature enabled by, 76
benefits of, 55
calendar using, 351–352, 356–357
downloading, 14
drop-down menus using, 71–77
features of, 13–14
input forms using, 236–237
installing, 14
multi-column layout using, 39–41
tabs using, 14–15
`:target` pseudo-class enabled by, 109–110
webmail application using, 176
`IE7_PNG_SUFFIX` **variable, 91**
`ie7-recalc.js` **module, 91**
`<iframe>` **element**
file viewer using, 298
tabs using, 15
webmail application using, 183–184, 185, 196–197

images
background images for tabs
with text, 19–23
without text, 16–19
borders using, 141
rounded corners using, 141, 152–154
transparent PNG images
borders and corners using, 146
definition of, 76
drop-down menus using, 91–92
file viewer using, 300, 305–307
webmail application using, 179

indirect adjacent sibling selector (-), 13

input forms
`<a>` element for, 225
adjacent sibling selector (+) used in, 229
`background` declaration for, 233
`::before` pseudo-element for, 229
`<body>` element for, 220
borders for, 230
bread crumbs for, 227–230, 241
browser incompatibilities with, 200, 236, 238, 240–241
code for
`p2p-body.css` file, 215–216
`p2p-form.css` file, 216–218
`p2p-header.css` file, 213–214
`p2p-ie.css` file, 239
`register.html` file, 202–212
`register-ie-hacks.html` file, 238–239
`register-ie.html` file, 236–237
designing, 199–202
`<div>` element for
bread crumbs, 227–229
content, 220, 230, 231–232
footer, 231
form controls, 222–223, 224–225, 235
header, 219–221, 240–241
left column, 225–227
`<fieldset>` element for, 232–233, 241
footer for, 231
header for, 219–221
Holly Hack used by, 240–241
IE7 JavaScript used for, 236–237
left column for, 225–226, 227
`<legend>` element for, 199, 232–233, 238, 241
links used in, 219, 220–221, 226–228
`position` declaration for, 220, 230, 233, 241
registration form in, 231–235
results of, 218–219, 237, 240
rounded corners for, 230
search box for, 222–225
`<select>` element for, 235
`<span>` element for, 230, 232
tables for, 202, 232–233
tabs in, 221–222
two-column layout for, 220
unordered lists for, 221–222
validating markup for, 223–224
`vertical-align` declaration for, 225

Internet Explorer (IE). *See also* **IE7 JavaScript**
`bottom` property support, 15, 39
chaining class name selectors and, 300, 356–357
`display:block`, bugs in, 93
`expression()` feature, 56–59
`:first-child` pseudo-class support, 145
float method, bugs in, 49, 52–55
forms, look and feel of, 200
hacks for multi-column layout, 56–61
`hasLayout` feature, 241
`height` property support, 60
Holly Hack for, 240
`:hover` pseudo-class support, 15, 77
`:last-child` pseudo-class support, 145
`left` property support, 15
margins in `<body>` element, 9
`max-width` property support, 39
`min-height` property support, 39
`min-width` property support, 39

Internet Explorer (IE) (continued)
`opacity` property support, 123–124
`right` property support, 15
`table-layout:` declaration support, 352
`:target` pseudo-class support, 101, 123–124
`top` property support, 15, 39
transparent PNG images and, 76, 91, 146, 300

J

JavaScript
cssQuery JavaScript, 78, 306–307
drop-down menus using, 78–84, 90, 91
456bereastreet.com using, 138
IE7 JavaScript
alpha transparency feature enabled by, 76
benefits of, 55
calendar using, 351–352, 356–357
downloading, 14
features of, 13–14
input forms using, 236–237
installing, 14
multi-column layout using, 39–41
tabs using, 14–15
`:target` pseudo-class enabled by, 109–110
webmail application using, 176
`ie7-recalc.js` module, 91
multi-column layout using, 39–41, 55–56, 59
slide show using, 129–130, 133–136
Johansson, Roger (456bereastreet.com web site), 138

K

Kalsey, Adam (custom corner technique), 147–155
Konqueror browser, 31

L

`<label>` **element**
input forms using, 199
popup windows using, 297
`:last-child` **pseudo-class**
drop-down menus using, 91
IE7 JavaScript providing, 13
Internet Explorer support, 145
Opera browser support, 145–146
`left` **property**
file viewer using, 268
Internet Explorer support, 15
`<legend>` **element**
calendar using, 352, 358, 369

input forms using, 199, 232–233, 238, 241
`<li>` **element, in unordered lists. See unordered lists**
links
calendar using, 349
drop-down menus using
custom backgrounds and borders solution, 91, 93
JavaScript-enabled solution, 83, 84
pure-CSS solution, 63, 69
`:target` pseudo-class solution, 109
fragment links, capturing as an event, 100
input forms using, 219, 220–221, 226–228
slide show using, 123, 133
tabs using, 2, 11, 12
webmail application using, 169, 172, 196
liquid tabs, 23–30
`liquid-columns.css` **file, 46–47**
`liquid-columns.html` **file, 45**
`liquid-columns-ie.css` **file, 47**
List view, file viewer, 287–288, 289–290, 293
lists, unordered
directory tree using, 277–279
drop-down menus using
for drop-down solution, 97
in file viewer application, 269–274, 304
for Internet Explorer solution, 77
for JavaScript-enabled solution, 84
for pure-CSS solution, 68–71
for Save As dialog, 322, 327–328
slide show using, 123
tabs in input forms using, 221–222
tabs using
background images in, 18–19
background images with text in, 22–23
layout for, 9–12
liquid tabs, 26–30
markup for, guidelines regarding, 2
`list-style` **declaration**
drop-down menus using, 70
file viewer using, 273, 277
slide show using, 123
tabs using, 2, 9
webmail application using, 172
`list-style-type` **declaration, file viewer using, 271**

M

mail application, web-based. See webmail application
`mail.css` **file, 165–168**
`mail.html` **file, 161–165**
`mail.ie.css` **file, 178**

`mail.ie.html` **file, 177–178**
`mail.ie.messagePreview.css` **file, 182–183**
`mail.ie.outlook2k3.css` **file, 193–194**
`mail.messagePreview.css` **file, 181–182**
`mail.messagePreview.html` **file, 180–181**
`mail.outlook2k3.css` **file, 190–193**
`mail.outlook2k3.html` **file, 186–190**
margins
  borders and corners using
    footer, 153
    header, 143–144, 152, 154
    images, 146
  calendar using, 346–347, 349, 350, 369
  drop-down menus using, 69–70, 97
  file viewer using
    Choose a Directory dialog, 334
    Details view, 291, 292–293
    directory tree, 277, 278
    directory window, 268–269
    drop-down menus, 271–272, 273, 274
    List view, 288
    popup windows, 296–297
    Save As dialog, 325
  input forms using
    bread crumbs, 228–230, 241
    left column, 227
    navigational links, 220
    right column, 233
    search box, 224, 225
    tabs, 222
  multi-column layout using
    float method, 54–55, 60
    Internet Explorer solution, 40
    liquid columns, 44, 48–49
    three-column layout, 32, 36–39
    two-column layout, 42
  removing, 36
  slide show using, 122–123, 132
  tabs using, 2, 9–10, 19, 28
  webmail application using
    Internet Explorer solution, 176, 179
    mailbox folders, 170, 172
    message preview pane, 184–185
    messages window, 195–196
    overall layout, 169
`max-width` **property, 13, 39, 58**
menus, drop-down. See drop-down menus
`menus.css` **file, 259–261**
Meyer, Eric
  CSS the Definitive Guide, 111
  CSS-based drop-down navigation, 63

  Eric Meyer on CSS, 111
  "Pure CSS Menus" demo, 63
  S5 (Simple Standards-based Slide Show System), 111
`min-height` **property, 13, 39, 58**
minus sign (-), indirect adjacent sibling selector, 13
`min-width` **property, 13, 39, 58**
mouseover effect
  calendar using, 336
  slideshow using, 111, 134
  for tabs
    background images and, 19
    designing, 2
    implementing, 10–11, 12
    liquid tabs, 29
Mozilla Firefox browser
  fixed width for `<ul>` element, 10
  `:hover` pseudo-class support, 15
  input forms used by, 200
  margins in `<body>` element, 9
  `:target` pseudo-class support, 101
`-moz-outline` **property, 298**
`::-moz-selection` **pseudo-element, 268**
`moz-user-select` **declaration, file viewer using, 268**
multi-column layout
  `<body>` element for, 36, 59
  browser incompatibilities with, 31, 39
  code for
    `float-columns.css` file, 50–51
    `float-columns.html` file, 50
    `float-columns-ie.css` file, 51–52
    `liquid-columns.css` file, 46–47
    `liquid-columns.html` file, 45
    `liquid-columns-ie.css` file, 47
    `multi-column.css` file, 34–35
    `multi-column.html` file, 33–34
    `multi-column-ie.css` file, 35, 40
    `two-column.css` file, 42–43
    `two-column.html` file, 42
    `two-column-ie.css` file, 43
  content column, fluid, 33, 38
  designing, 31–33, 41
  `<div>` element for
    browser incompatibilities with, 40, 60
    for float method, 52–55
    for liquid secondary columns, 44–45, 48–49
    for three-column layout, 32, 37–39
  `expression()` feature for, 56–59
  float method for, 49–55
  footer for, 33, 36, 38–39
  header for, 36, 38–39
  IE7 JavaScript used for, 39–41

multi-column layout (continued)

Internet Explorer hacks for, 56–61

JavaScript for, 55–56, 59

margins for

float method, 54–55, 60

Internet Explorer solution, 40

liquid columns, 44, 48–49

three-column layout, 32, 36–39

two-column layout, 42

markup for, guidelines regarding, 32

results of

float method, 52

for Internet Explorer, 58

liquid columns, 47–48

three-column layout, 41

two-column layout, 44

secondary columns, liquid, 44–49

tables for, when to use, 45

three-column layout, 32, 37–39

two-column layout, 42–44

`multi-column.css` **file, 34–35**

`multi-column.html` **file, 33–34**

`multi-column-ie.css` **file, 35, 40**

N

`<noscript>` **element, 84**

O

`opacity` **property**

browsers not supporting, 123

file viewer using, 273

slide show using, 123–124, 134

Opera browser

fixed width for `<ul>` element, 10

forms, look and feel of, 200

`:hover` pseudo-class support, 15

input forms used by, 200

`:last-child` pseudo-class support, 145–146

margins in `<body>` element, 9

`opacity` property support, 123–124

`:target` pseudo-class support, 101, 123–124

`outline` **property, 298**

`overflow` **property, 268, 269, 272, 326**

P

`p2p-body.css` **file, 215–216**

`p2p-form.css` **file, 216–218**

`p2p-header.css` **file, 213–214**

`p2p-ie.css` **file, 239**

plus sign (+), adjacent sibling selector

IE7 JavaScript providing, 13

input forms using, 229

PNG images, alpha transparency feature of

borders and corners using, 146

definition of, 76

drop-down menus using, 91–92

file viewer using, 300, 305–307

webmail application using, 179

`png.js` **file, 302**

popup windows, file viewer, 293–298

`popup.css` **file, 263–264**

`position` **declaration**

drop-down menus using, 93

file viewer using, 277, 288, 326

input forms using, 220, 230, 233, 241

tabs using, 2, 10, 26, 27

webmail application using, 161, 170, 174

"Position is Everything" web site, 240–241

publications

Beginning CSS: Cascading Style Sheets for Web Design (York), 13, 49

Beginning JavaScript, 2nd Edition (Wilton), 78

CSS the Definitive Guide (Meyer), 111

Eric Meyer on CSS (Meyer), 111

"Pure CSS Menus" demo (Meyer), 63

R

`register.html` **file, 202–212**

`register-ie-hacks.html` **file, 238–239**

`register-ie.html` **file, 236–237**

registration form. See input forms

resources

publications

Beginning CSS: Cascading Style Sheets for Web Design (York), 13, 49

Beginning JavaScript, 2nd Edition (Wilton), 78

CSS the Definitive Guide (Meyer), 111

Eric Meyer on CSS (Meyer), 111

"Pure CSS Menus" demo (Meyer), 63

web sites

cssQuery JavaScript, 78

456bereastreet.com, 138

Hierophant framework, 246

IE7 JavaScript, 14

Kalsey's technique for custom corners, 147

"Position is Everything", 240–241

Safari Team weblog, 200

W3 validation service, 223

Wrox Programmer to Programmer forum, 199

right angle bracket (>), direct child selector
drop-down menus using, 64
IE7 JavaScript providing, 13
`right` **property**
file viewer using, 268
Internet Explorer support, 15
`:root` **pseudo-class, 13**
rounded corners
`<body>` element for, 141, 149
browser incompatibilities with, 145–147
challenges implementing, 137
code for
`borders.css` file, 140–141
`borders.html` file, 138–140
`borders.kalsey.css` file, 149–150
`borders.kalsey.html` file, 148–149
`borders.kalsey.ie.css` file, 150–151
CSS 3 features for, 137
designing, 138
`<div>` element for, 138, 142–144, 146, 151–154
images for, 141, 152–154
for input forms project, 230
Kalsey's technique for, 147–155
results of, 142, 145–147, 151, 153, 155
`<span>` element for, 143, 152
transparent PNG images in, 146

S

S5 (Simple Standards-based Slide Show System), 111
Safari browser
forms, look and feel of, 200
`:hover` pseudo-class support, 15
input forms used by, 200
styling of input fields, support for, 200
`:target` pseudo-class support, 101
Save As dialog, file viewer
code for, 313–322
implementing, 322–323, 325–328
results of, 323–324
`<select>` **element**
calendar using, 335
input forms using, 235
selectors
adjacent sibling selector (+)
IE7 JavaScript providing, 13
input forms using, 229
attribute selectors, IE7 JavaScript providing, 13
direct child selector (>)
drop-down menus using, 64
IE7 JavaScript providing, 13

indirect adjacent sibling selector (-), IE7 JavaScript providing, 13
Simple Standards-based Slide Show System (S5), 111
`slashdot.html` **file, 4–5, 25–26**
slide shows
`<a>` element for, 133
`<body>` element for, 132
browser incompatibilities with, 123–124
code for
`slideshow.css` file, 114–115, 128–129
`slideshow.html` file, 112–114, 125–127
`slideshow.js` file, 129–130
designing, 111–112
`<div>` element for, 112, 122–123, 132, 134
`expression()` feature for, 131–132
`filter` property for, 132–133, 134
Internet Explorer version of, 123–124, 130–136
JavaScript-enhanced solution for, 129–130, 133–136
links used in, 123, 133
`list-style` declaration for, 123
`opacity` property for, 123–124, 134
Opera version of, 123–124, 130–136
results of, 116–121, 130–131
S5 (Simple Standards-based Slide Show System) for, 111
`:target` pseudo-class for, 111–112
unordered lists for, 123
`slideshow.css` **file, 114–115, 128–129**
`slideshow.html` **file, 112–114, 125–127**
`slideshow.js` **file, 129–130**
`<span>` **element**
borders and corners using, 143, 152
calendar using, 368, 369
drop-down menus using, 77, 93
file viewer using
directory tree, 278
drop-down menus, 274
for Internet Explorer, 306
Save As dialog, 327
Thumbnails view, 291
input forms using, 230, 232
tabs using, 12, 19, 22
webmail application using, 174

T

`table-layout`: **declaration, 352**
tables
calendar using
designing, 336
implementing, 347–350
for Internet Explorer, 352, 356–357
large-sized calendar, 368–369

tables (continued)
file viewer using, 308
input forms using, 202, 232–233
multi-column layout using, 45
reasons not to use, 32
webmail application using, 161, 169, 171
when to use, 45, 138
tabs
`<a>` element for, 11, 12
`background` declaration for, 19, 22
background images for
with text, 19–23
without text, 16–19
`<body>` element for, 2, 9, 11
browser incompatibilities with, 1, 13
code for
`amazon.html` file, 3–4, 25–26
`google.html` file, 4, 25–26
`slashdot.html` file, 4–5, 25–26
`tabs.css` file, 6–7, 16–17, 20–21, 23–25
`tabs-ie.css` file, 26
`twit.html` file, 5, 25–26
`wrox.html` file, 3, 25
`color` declaration for, 11, 12
designing, 2, 16
`<div>` element for, 12, 28
highlighting current tab, 2, 8
`:hover` pseudo-class for, 2, 10–11, 15
IE7 JavaScript used for, 14–15
`<iframe>` element for, 15
for input forms project, 221–222
links used in, 2, 11, 12
liquid tabs for, 23–30
`list-style` declaration for, 2, 9
markup for, guidelines regarding, 2
mouseover effect for
background images and, 19
designing, 2
implementing, 10–11, 12
liquid tabs, 29
`position` declaration for, 2, 10, 26, 27
results of
background images and, 18
background images with text and, 22
Internet Explorer solution, 15
liquid tabs, 27
pure-CSS solution, 7, 8
`<span>` element for, 12, 19, 22
unordered lists for
background images in, 18–19
background images with text in, 22–23

layout for, 9–12
liquid tabs, 26–30
markup for, guidelines regarding, 2
`vertical-align` declaration for, 10
`tabs.css` **file, 6–7, 16–17, 20–21, 23–25**
`tabs-ie.css` **file, 26**
`:target` **pseudo-class**
browsers not supporting, 101, 123
drop-down menus using, 100–109
features of, 100
file viewer using, 272
limitations of, 111
slide show using, 111–112
three-column layout
for multi-column layouts, 32, 37–39
for webmail application, 185–186, 194–197
Thumbnails view, file viewer, 284–285, 289, 291
Tiles and Icons view, file viewer, 284–287, 291, 293
timestamps, Unix, 335, 336
`top` **property**
`expression()` feature and, 56, 58, 60
IE7 JavaScript providing, 15, 39
when to use, 32
transparent PNG images
borders and corners using, 146
definition of, 76
drop-down menus using, 91–92
file viewer using, 300, 305–307
webmail application using, 179
`tree.css` **file, 261**
`tree.ie.css` **file, 301–302**
`twit.html` **file, 5, 25–26**
two-column layout
for input forms, 220
with multi-column layout, 42–44
`two-column.css` **file, 42–43**
`two-column.html` **file, 42**
`two-column-ie.css` **file, 43**

U

`<ul>` **element. See unordered lists**
Unix timestamps, 335, 336
unordered lists
directory tree using, 277–279
drop-down menus using
for drop-down solution, 97
in file viewer application, 269–274, 304
for Internet Explorer solution, 77
for JavaScript-enabled solution, 84
for pure-CSS solution, 68–71

for Save As dialog, 322, 327–328
slide show using, 123
tabs in input forms using, 221–222
tabs using
    background images in, 18–19
    background images with text in, 22–23
    layout for, 9–12
    liquid tabs, 26–30
    markup for, guidelines regarding, 2
URL fragments (HTML anchors), 100

V

`vertical-align` **declaration**
    calendar using, 347
    file viewer using, 327
    input forms using, 225
    tabs using, 10
`views.css` **file, 261–263, 312**
`visibility` **property**
    drop-down menus using, 70
    file viewer using, 272, 273

W

W3 validation service, 223–224
web site resources
    cssQuery JavaScript, 78
    456bereastreet.com, 138
    Hierophant framework, 246
    IE7 JavaScript, 14
    Kalsey's technique for custom corners, 147
    "Position is Everything", 240–241
    Safari Team weblog, 200
    W3 validation service, 223
    Wrox Programmer to Programmer forum, 199
web-based file viewer. *See* **file viewer, web-based**
webmail application
    `background` declaration for, 170, 184–185
    `::before` pseudo-element for, 174
    `<body>` element for, 169
    browser incompatibilities with, 175–180
    buttons for, 169–170
    code for
        `mail.css` file, 165–168
        `mail.html` file, 161–165
        `mail.ie.css` file, 178
        `mail.ie.html` file, 177–178
        `mail.ie.messagePreview.css` file, 182–183
        `mail.ie.outlook2k3.css` file, 193–194

        `mail.messagePreview.css` file, 181–182
        `mail.messagePreview.html` file, 180–181
        `mail.outlook2k3.css` file, 190–193
        `mail.outlook2k3.html` file, 186–190
    `content` property for, 174
    designing, 158–161
    `<div>` element for
        browser incompatibilities with, 176
        for buttons, 169
        for mailboxes, 170
        for message preview, 184–185
        for message window, 171–173, 179–180, 183,
            195–196
    `expression()` feature used for, 185
    frames for, 160–161, 169
    `hasLayout` feature, Internet Explorer, 241
    IE7 JavaScript used for, 176
    `<iframe>` element for, 183–184, 185, 196–197
    link style for, 169
    links used in, 169, 172, 196
    `list-style` declaration for, 172
    mailbox folders for, 170–171, 172–174, 197
    message summary for, 171–172, 179–180, 195–196
    `position` declaration for, 161, 170, 174
    preview pane for, 180–185, 197
    results of, 168, 178, 194
    `<span>` element for, 174
    tables for, 161, 169, 171
    three-column layout for, 185–186, 194–197
    transparent PNG images in, 179
    `white-space` declaration for, 172, 179
`white-space` **declaration**
    file viewer using, 277
    webmail application using, 172, 179
Wilton, Paul (*Beginning JavaScript, 2nd Edition*), 78
Windows Details view, file viewer, 308–313
Windows Internet Explorer. *See* **Internet Explorer (IE)**
Wrox P2P registration page. *See* **input forms**
Wrox Programmer to Programmer forum, 199
`wrox.html` **file, 3, 25–26**

Y

**York, Richard (*Beginning CSS: Cascading Style Sheets
    for Web Design*), 13, 49**

Wiley Publishing, Inc.
End-User License Agreement

READ THIS. You should carefully read these terms and conditions before opening the software packet(s) included with this book "Book". This is a license agreement "Agreement" between you and Wiley Publishing, Inc. "WPI". By opening the accompanying software packet(s), you acknowledge that you have read and accept the following terms and conditions. If you do not agree and do not want to be bound by such terms and conditions, promptly return the Book and the unopened software packet(s) to the place you obtained them for a full refund.

1. **License Grant.** WPI grants to you (either an individual or entity) a nonexclusive license to use one copy of the enclosed software program(s) (collectively, the "Software") solely for your own personal or business purposes on a single computer (whether a standard computer or a workstation component of a multi-user network). The Software is in use on a computer when it is loaded into temporary memory (RAM) or installed into permanent memory (hard disk, CD-ROM, or other storage device). WPI reserves all rights not expressly granted herein.

2. **Ownership.** WPI is the owner of all right, title, and interest, including copyright, in and to the compilation of the Software recorded on the disk(s) or CD-ROM "Software Media". Copyright to the individual programs recorded on the Software Media is owned by the author or other authorized copyright owner of each program. Ownership of the Software and all proprietary rights relating thereto remain with WPI and its licensers.

3. **Restrictions on Use and Transfer.**

   (a) You may only (i) make one copy of the Software for backup or archival purposes, or (ii) transfer the Software to a single hard disk, provided that you keep the original for backup or archival purposes. You may not (i) rent or lease the Software, (ii) copy or reproduce the Software through a LAN or other network system or through any computer subscriber system or bulletin-board system, or (iii) modify, adapt, or create derivative works based on the Software.

   (b) You may not reverse engineer, decompile, or disassemble the Software. You may transfer the Software and user documentation on a permanent basis, provided that the transferee agrees to accept the terms and conditions of this Agreement and you retain no copies. If the Software is an update or has been updated, any transfer must include the most recent update and all prior versions.

4. **Restrictions on Use of Individual Programs.** You must follow the individual requirements and restrictions detailed for each individual program in the About the CD-ROM appendix of this Book. These limitations are also contained in the individual license agreements recorded on the Software Media. These limitations may include a requirement that after using the program for a specified period of time, the user must pay a registration fee or discontinue use. By opening the Software packet(s), you will be agreeing to abide by the licenses and restrictions for these individual programs that are detailed in the About the CD-ROM appendix and on the Software Media. None of the material on this Software Media or listed in this Book may ever be redistributed, in original or modified form, for commercial purposes.

5. Limited Warranty.

(a) WPI warrants that the Software and Software Media are free from defects in materials and workmanship under normal use for a period of sixty (60) days from the date of purchase of this Book. If WPI receives notification within the warranty period of defects in materials or workmanship, WPI will replace the defective Software Media.

(b) WPI AND THE AUTHOR(S) OF THE BOOK DISCLAIM ALL OTHER WARRANTIES, EXPRESS OR IMPLIED, INCLUDING WITHOUT LIMITATION IMPLIED WARRANTIES OF MERCHANTABILITY AND FITNESS FOR A PARTICULAR PURPOSE, WITH RESPECT TO THE SOFTWARE, THE PROGRAMS, THE SOURCE CODE CONTAINED THEREIN, AND/OR THE TECHNIQUES DESCRIBED IN THIS BOOK. WPI DOES NOT WARRANT THAT THE FUNCTIONS CONTAINED IN THE SOFTWARE WILL MEET YOUR REQUIREMENTS OR THAT THE OPERATION OF THE SOFTWARE WILL BE ERROR FREE.

(c) This limited warranty gives you specific legal rights, and you may have other rights that vary from jurisdiction to jurisdiction.

6. Remedies.

(a) WPI's entire liability and your exclusive remedy for defects in materials and workmanship shall be limited to replacement of the Software Media, which may be returned to WPI with a copy of your receipt at the following address: Software Media Fulfillment Department, Attn.: CSS Instant Results, Wiley Publishing, Inc., 10475 Crosspoint Blvd., Indianapolis, IN 46256, or call 1-800-762-2974. Please allow four to six weeks for delivery. This Limited Warranty is void if failure of the Software Media has resulted from accident, abuse, or misapplication. Any replacement Software Media will be warranted for the remainder of the original warranty period or thirty (30) days, whichever is longer.

(b) In no event shall WPI or the author be liable for any damages whatsoever (including without limitation damages for loss of business profits, business interruption, loss of business information, or any other pecuniary loss) arising from the use of or inability to use the Book or the Software, even if WPI has been advised of the possibility of such damages.

(c) Because some jurisdictions do not allow the exclusion or limitation of liability for consequential or incidental damages, the above limitation or exclusion may not apply to you.

7. U.S. Government Restricted Rights.
Use, duplication, or disclosure of the Software for or on behalf of the United States of America, its agencies and/or instrumentalities "U.S. Government" is subject to restrictions as stated in paragraph (c)(1)(ii) of the Rights in Technical Data and Computer Software clause of DFARS 252.227-7013, or subparagraphs (c) (1) and (2) of the Commercial Computer Software - Restricted Rights clause at FAR 52.227-19, and in similar clauses in the NASA FAR supplement, as applicable.

8. General.
This Agreement constitutes the entire understanding of the parties and revokes and supersedes all prior agreements, oral or written, between them and may not be modified or amended except in a writing signed by both parties hereto that specifically refers to this Agreement. This Agreement shall take precedence over any other documents that may be in conflict herewith. If any one or more provisions contained in this Agreement are held by any court or tribunal to be invalid, illegal, or otherwise unenforceable, each and every other provision shall remain in full force and effect.